The School and the University

The School
and the University

An International Perspective

Edited by
Burton R. Clark

UNIVERSITY OF CALIFORNIA PRESS
Berkeley • Los Angeles • London

University of California Press
Berkeley and Los Angeles, California

University of California Press, Ltd.
London, England

Copyright © 1985 by The Regents of the University of California

Library of Congress Cataloging in Publication Data

Main entry under title:

The School and the university.

Includes index.
1. Education, Higher—Congresses.   2. Comparative
education—Congresses.   I. Clark, Burton R.
LB2301.S36   1985   378   85-1158
ISBN 0-520-5423-7

1 2 3 4 5 6 7 8 9

Contents

Acknowledgments

As EDITOR OF THIS VOLUME I am particularly indebted to the ten colleagues who prepared the basic papers and, after critical review, revised them for publication. Chosen for their expertise on education in nine countries and continents, and representing a half-dozen nationalities, the authors faced a difficult task in responding to my request for parallel categories and comparative statements. I believe their efforts deserve an integrated presentation to a larger audience.

The authors of the papers and I are indebted to the other seventeen participants in a four-day seminar held at the University of California, Los Angeles, in July 1983, who prepared critiques of the papers and discussed their strengths and weaknesses. Their criticisms deepened our working knowledge and broadened our comparative capacity on a perplexing and troubling topic. The participants in the conference are listed at the end of this volume.

The Exxon Education Foundation generously provided the funds that supported the 1983 conference and made possible this volume. I want particularly to thank Robert Payton, President, and Arnold Shore, Program Officer, for their continued faith in the effort of the UCLA Comparative Higher Education Research Group to improve the state of the art in the comparative study of higher education. Their support has helped build an international community of scholars whose critical comments and published work help inform the wider public about the growing complexities of modern educational systems.

This volume is the third in a series of efforts to devise useful comparative statements about higher education. The first volume, *The Higher Education System: Academic Organization in Cross-National Perspective*, was published by the University of California Press in 1983. It drew upon the working knowledge I had developed during the 1970s, particularly from the many empirical investigations of the Yale Higher Education

Research Group I chaired between 1974 and 1980. The second volume, *Perspectives on Higher Education: Eight Disciplinary and Comparative Views*, drawn from a 1982 UCLA conference, was published by the University of California Press in 1984. A fourth effort will follow on the subject of the academic profession.

In the selection of topics and experts for this collective effort, I was joined particularly by Gary Rhoades (United States), Maurice Kogan (United Kingdom), and Ladislav Cerych (France). Patricia Carlson served superbly as conference organizer for our summer meeting. Adele Halitsky Clark ably provided the general editing that helped shape the papers of the volume for a wider audience. It is a pleasure to thank all the above for their contribution.

Burton R. Clark

Santa Monica, California
February 1984

Contributors

BURTON R. CLARK is Allan M. Cartter professor of higher education and sociology and chairman of the Comparative Higher Education Research Group, University of California, Los Angeles. He taught previously at Stanford University, Harvard University, University of California, Berkeley, and Yale University in departments of sociology and schools of education, serving as chairman of the sociology department at Yale between 1969 and 1972 and as chairman of the Yale Higher Education Research Group, 1974–1980. His publications include: *The Open Door College*, 1960; *The Distinctive College*, 1970; *Academic Power in Italy*, 1977; *The Higher Education System*, 1983; and (editor) *Perspectives on Higher Education*, 1984.

WILLIAM K. CUMMINGS is centerwide fellow in international education, East-West Center, Hawaii. Since taking his Ph.D. in sociology at Harvard University in 1972, he has taught at Tsuda College in Tokyo, the University of Chicago, and the National University of Singapore. He has served as a Ford Foundation project specialist in educational research and planning with the Indonesian Ministry of Education and Culture. His publications include: *Nihon no Daigaku Kyoiyu* (The Japanese University Professor), 1972; *The Changing Japanese University*, edited with Ikuo Amano and Kazuyuki Kitamura, 1979; and *Education and Equality in Japan*, 1980.

LARS EKHOLM is director of higher education and head of department in the Ministry of Education and Cultural Affairs, Stockholm, Sweden. Since completing his doctoral thesis in history at the University of Uppsala in 1974, he has served in various posts in the Office of the Chancellor of the Swedish Universities and in the Higher Education Department he now heads. He has been chairman or member of a number of commissions and working groups in the fields of higher education and health care in Sweden and has served as a representative of the Swedish government in various European conferences on higher education.

PHILIP FOSTER is professor of education and sociology, State University of New York, Albany. English by birth, he completed his first degree in economics at the London School of Economics; he took his Ph.D. in comparative education at the University of Chicago in 1962. He has taught at the University of Chicago, where he has also served as director of the Comparative Education Center, and at Macquarie University in Australia. His principal publications include: *Education and Social Change in Ghana*, 1965; *The Fortunate Few*, with Remi Clignet, 1967; and *Ghana and the Ivory Coast*, edited with Aristide Zolberg, 1971.

MARGARET MADEN is director of the Islington Sixth Form Centre, London. After taking her postgraduate certificate in education at the University of London in 1963, she has been a teacher and an administrator in four different schools in London and Oxfordshire as well as serving as lecturer in education at the University of London. Since 1967 she has been a senior officer in the British National Union of Teachers, chaired the Programme for Reform in Secondary Education (1975–78), contributed chapters on the teaching profession to a number of volumes on British education, and contributed regularly to the *Times Educational Supplement*, the *Guardian*, the *Times*, and BBC television and radio programs.

GUY NEAVE has served since 1976 as director of research for the Institute of Education and Social Policy of the European Cultural Foundation, Paris and Brussels. After completing his Ph.D. in French political history at University College, London, in 1967, he taught modern European history for several years and then converted to a career as a researcher in the sociology of education. He has served in numerous consultancies on education in Europe. His publications include: *How They Fared*, 1975; *Patterns of Equality*, 1976; and *Education and the European Community 1963–1982* (in preparation).

STANLEY ROSEN is assistant professor of political science, University of Southern California. Before and after taking his Ph.D. in political science at the University of California, Los Angeles, in 1979, he traveled frequently to Hong Kong and the People's Republic of China, where he also spent four years on research for his dissertation between 1972 and 1976. An active participant in conferences on contemporary China, his early publications include: *The Role of Sent-Down Youth in the Chinese*

Cultural Revolution, 1981; *Red Guard Factionalism and the Cultural Revolution in Guangzhou*, 1982; and *Policy Conflicts in Contemporary China*, edited with John P. Burn, forthcoming.

ERNESTO SCHIEFELBEIN is a senior researcher in the Centro de Investigacion y Desarrollo de la Educacion (CIDE) and coordinator of the educational research exchange network (REDUC), both located in Santiago, Chile. He took his first degree in economics at the University of Chile in 1959 and his Ph.D. in educational planning at Harvard University ten years later. A former head of the Chilean Educational Planning Office during 1965–1970, he has taught in Latin American universities and has been Visiting Professor of Educational Planning in Developing Countries at Harvard. He has held a number of research posts in education and economic development and has served as a consultant to the World Bank and UNESCO. His publications include over twenty essays and articles in English on education in Latin America, and he is coauthor of *Development of Educational Planning Models*.

CAROL STOCKING is study director in the Center for the Study of Social Policy, Chicago. Before taking her Ph.D. in sociology at the University of Chicago in 1978, she served for fourteen years as a survey research director in the National Opinion Research Center. Since 1978 she has worked, with James S. Coleman, on major national longitudinal studies of "high school and beyond" students. Her recent research papers on education include reports on the characteristics of good schools and the comparison of Japanese and American high school students.

GARY SYKES is a graduate student in the Graduate School of Education, Stanford University. Early in his career he taught mathematics and English in two New Jersey secondary schools. Interrupting his work toward a Ph.D., he served for seven years (1976–83) as research associate and then team leader in planning research on teaching in the National Institute of Education. In addition to many conference reports and articles, his publications include: *Value Conflicts and Curriculum Issues*, with J. Schaffarzick (1979); *Handbook of Teaching and Policy*, with Lee Shulman (1983); and *The Condition of Teaching*, forthcoming.

ULRICH TEICHLER is director of the Center for Research on Higher Education and Work (Wissenschaftliches Zentrum für Berufs—und Hochschulforschung), Kassel, and professor in the Department for Applied Social Science, Comprehensive University of Kassel (Gesamthochschule Kassel), Federal Republic of Germany. He took his Ph.D. in 1975 after completing a doctoral dissertation on education and social status in Japan and has been research fellow in the Max Planck Institute for Educational Research in Berlin from 1968 to 1978. Since joining the Comprehensive University of Kassel, he served two years as university vice-president. His many publications in English include: *Admission to Higher Education in the United States*, 1978; *Higher Education and the Needs of Society*, with Dirk Hartung and Reinhard Nuthmann, 1980; and *Higher Education and the Labour Market in the Federal Republic of Germany*, with Bikas C. Sanyal, 1982.

Introduction

BURTON R. CLARK

We may conceive of the relation between secondary and higher education at the outset as a two-way street along which the nature of traffic in one direction is quite different from the flow of people and activities in the other. Up the street, from the "school" to the "university," we encounter primarily a flow of students. The school selects them, trains them, orients them, certifies their competence, and sends them on. The student traffic may be heavy or light: in access to higher education, the question of quantity is always present. Those allowed into the flow may be only the most able or virtually all who wish to try: issues of quality and equality are inherent. Whatever the quantity and the quality, and the degree of opportunity, the school clearly shapes the human resources made available to the university. In education, generally, an impelling principle of sequence gives lower units this particular role in determining the nature of higher levels.[1]

Down the street, from the university to the school, the traffic is different, consisting always of two major vehicles of influence. One is personnel: in one form or another the institutions of higher education select, train, orient, and help certify the teachers and administrators who staff the schools. In a primitive sense the school can be no better in quality of personnel than what the university will allow it to be. A second vehicle is curricular in nature: the university sets course requirements for its own students, and often itself sets entry requirements that influence what teachers will teach and what students will study in the school. Students who want to go on must master those materials and pass those examinations that permit them to be a part of the upward flow.

These streams of influence are inescapable, always a part of educational systems. But they vary in their nature and efficacy from one society to another, and, in each nation, from one time to another. They can be

1

cast in forms and procedures that are relatively stable and widely accepted, even firmly institutionalized over long periods of time. But they
can also be in flux and in doubt. Since about 1960 the highly industrialized nations, and many developing societies, have moved into a problematic stage. In a context of expansion and growing complexity at each
level, officials, scholars, teachers, and citizens alike have become uncertain about how to distribute students from secondary to tertiary education. Some countries are sorely troubled by the problems of preparing
and distributing teachers and of defining school curricula that articulate
with the requirements of postsecondary institutions. Practitioners and
observers become aware that the upward and downward flows of influence may interact in ways that generate a vicious rather than a virtuous circle of effects, especially in the quality of student and teacher
performance. Where the vicious circle is currently strongest, the benefits
of expansion and variety have clearly brought in their wake some major
educational and social costs that are as undesired as they were
unanticipated.

The huge American system of education has cut the problems of the
school-university relationship on a grand scale, managing periodically
to excite public attention to the level of grave concern, even a sense of
crisis. That sense centers on a perception that something is fundamentally wrong with the American secondary school. It includes more than
a faint suspicion that higher education has contributed to the steering
of secondary education into a major weakness of the American system.
And the sense of crisis has its most sensitive nerve in invidious international comparisons. In the years immediately after Sputnik, it was a
concern about the apparent success of the Russians in the preparation
of scientists and engineers. In the early 1980s it has centered on "a nation
at risk"[2] in economic competition with other countries, Japan in particular. In search of the basic defects of the American school, numerous
studies have been initiated, with over a half-dozen major commission
reports and research volumes issued in 1983 and early 1984.[3] Dozens of
recommendations have been floated, many reminiscent of those offered
twenty-five years ago that led to little or no lasting beneficial reform.
Major universities and colleges have established new programs and new
institutional linkages with the intent of helping at least some secondary
schools improve themselves, toward ensuring a flow of better-prepared
students in the transition from school to university.

Thus, in the United States in particular, but also in other countries
more generally, the question of how these two major levels of education
interact and shape each other is a practical as well as a theoretical issue.
On both grounds the question is one to which answers should be sought
steadily and systematically. Public concern is volatile, affected by a

crowded agenda of national and international issues, and when that concern in a particular country dies down, as it has before and will again, the question still remains important. At home and abroad the linkages between these two levels of education will never be simple again. The connections, we may safely assert, become more numerous, often more indirect, and always more ambiguous: they will continue to be problematic, recalcitrant to the touch of the easy answer and the quick reform. Thus, when the momentary headlines have vanished, steady inquiry should remain. There is much to be done in contemporary research beyond the national reports that multiply in times of perceived crisis.

The purpose of this volume is to look broadly at the relation between secondary and higher education in a way that can enlarge practical and theoretical perspectives and thereby possibly lead to greater insight. Basic to our approach is cross-national comparison: to ensure breadth that reaches beyond one's own system, the chapters that follow range far afield, across continents as well as specific countries. We thereby first learn quite simply how things are done elsewhere and then gain genuine points of comparison that allow us to observe some fundamental similarities and differences among national modes of education. We learn about our own system by standing outside it and perceiving it in a larger frame. The larger picture, at first seemingly more remote, usefully turns the mind toward empirical detail. If we study only our own educational system, our statements about its strengths and weaknesses, its basic nature and distinctive features, commonly contain, often implicitly, comparisons to either an ideal system of affairs or to imagined features of other countries. Even simple descriptions of actual practices elsewhere then become a definite improvement, particularly when the practices are shown to be interconnected and embedded in tradition and deeply rooted structure.

We have also sought breadth by seeking to identify a number of significant aspects of the two-way stream of influence. By what means other than the flow of students does the school shape the university? And beyond teacher training and some curricular determination, what else does higher education do directly or indirectly that significantly molds the secondary system? Articulation between the two levels is almost everywhere seen as an issue largely of curricular continuity and smooth flow of students. Yet other connections may be of equal or greater importance. If they exist in latent or manifest form, an international search is an appropriate way to ferret them out.

Our international coverage extends over seven highly industrialized countries, all of Latin America, and much of Africa. Among the advanced democracies, we selected three major European powers, the United

Kingdom, France, and the Federal Republic of Germany, each significant internationally as a center of learning. We also included Sweden as a small country that has been at the cutting edge of educational change in recent decades, a laboratory of educational reform in which research and public policy have been closely connected. Experts in these four countries have at hand vital information about the school-university relationship, together offering an account that is at once varied and integrated, marked with sharp differences among four traditions but, in a worldwide frame, sharing features of advanced systems that have a European heritage. In these chapters, for example, we have the chance to study closely the special role selective tracks in upper secondary education play in Europe in defining the nature and quality of the secondary level, including the prestige of schoolteaching and teacher preparation. Even after major reforms during the last twenty years, these European systems, each in its own way, continue to have structures and procedures that stand in marked contrast to American ones, particularly to the comprehensive school that has come to dominate the American secondary level.

Moving away from Europe, Japan is an imposing world power that is increasingly central in international comparisons. In the late 1970s and early 1980s, it seems as though half the world has been trying to figure out how to catch up with the Japanese in education and industry. We, too, want to know more about how schools and universities in that country operate and relate to one another, particularly in coupling secondary schools that are apparently both universal and academically effective with a system of higher education that is large, differentiated, and virtually as open to age-group participation as the American. The Japanese way, as we shall see, is rooted in a combination of tough examinations for entry to the secondary level *and* competition and prestige hierarchy among secondary schools, as well as severe examinations for entry into the best universities. Schooling in Japan is a stubborn institutional phenomenon in its own right, driving the motivations of parents and students as much as it is in turn driven by the often-noted educational ambitions of the Japanese family.

Another three chapters plunge into the Third World. Research on education in the People's Republic of China has blossomed in the early 1980s, and there is much to be learned from the dramatic story of vast swings in educational policy in the world's largest country. We also learn what it is like for young people to attempt to make their way through the secondary level and on to higher education in a huge country where the rate of college entrance approximates 1 percent. The concept of the keypoint secondary school is a striking one that we are able to apply to the phenomenon of sharply selective academic schools in other countries. Latin America remains a fascinating laboratory of educational experiments and developments among the more advanced of the "developing societies," with the relation between secondary and higher education often centrally in question. There, expansion has been enormous, moving at a rate far in excess of the doubling, tripling, and quadrupling of enrollments in higher education which occurred in Europe and America in the last two decades. Nonetheless, the universities dominate the schools more than ever, laying claim to an unusually large share of the money made available for education. Anglophonic Africa is yet another story, one of educational tragedy, in which high expectations for educational development, stimulated from the outside as well as from within, have been dashed on the hard rocks of population explosion, insufficient economic resources, and political repression and mismanagement. To think cross-nationally from the vantage point of China, or of nations in Latin America or in Africa, is to open new vistas in comprehending the range of possible relations between the school and university. The wider comparisons serve to highlight the special features of advanced industrial societies.

The coverage of countries and continents concludes with two chapters on the United States. This complex, ambiguous, and confusing case first requires a chapter that describes the enormous variety of structures and practices as they appear among fifty highly decentralized states. This chapter (chapter nine) also maps the links connecting schools to universities and the many ways students can negotiate this transition. Amidst the confusing details, some general patterns may be discerned. Chapter ten is devoted to a central aspect of the American system which becomes more troublesome with each passing decade: the nature of the teaching profession and the state of teacher education. Here we observe a vicious circle of effects difficult to arrest and reverse, a major point to which we return in the concluding chapter.

The chapters that follow are for the most part formed around some parallel subjects that facilitate cross-national comparisons. Each describes in some detail the systems of secondary and higher education as a necessary background for all who are not experts on education in the country or continent at hand. Each speaks to the question of how the school shapes the university, mainly analyzing the flow of students and problems of access to higher education, but also sometimes branching off into such topics as how unions and associations of secondary school teachers influence public policy on higher education. And each chapter turns to the issue of how the university shapes the school, in particular taking up the nature of teacher selection and training and the effects of university requirements and examinations on school curricula. But each author also varies his or her approach and selects issues within these broad categories according to what is important in the country in question. Each author's imagination and insight operate freely within the general framework.

A significant analytical category that emerges in the volume is the growth of a third element, a set of practices, agencies, and professional groups that mediate between schools and universities, particularly those public agencies in some countries and private associations in others which write and administer examinations. The case can readily be made, as in Ulrich Teichler's interpretation of the German system, that the state examination apparatus is indeed an imposing mediating element, one that is not directly within the control of the school or the university; or, as in Lars Ekholm's account of Swedish education, that there is a marking and grading system that takes on virtually a life of its own as part of the political determination of public policy; or, as in Carol Stocking's grasp of the American system, that a congeries of mediating bodies have emerged to bridge the gap between increasingly separate secondary and postsecondary systems.

The most important analytical problem that emerged in constructing the volume was how to remain centered on the relationship between the two levels of education while taking into account the important external forces and trends that shape the development of one or the other level, or both. Our solution is three-sided. First, we have retained the initial focus, since it allows for systematic comparisons that might lead to insight and some minimal generalizing. We have set our faces against doing yet another book on "education and society" which would loosely roam across the many connections of education to the economy, the polity, the social class system, the church, the family, demographic shifts, the cultures of adolescence, and so on. Second, we have sought to weave some of the more significant external relations and influences around the primary focus. If the school is heavily shaped by a vigorous adolescent culture, then analysis should center on its impact on the school-university relationship. Finally, we have attempted to view those who staff schools and institutions of higher education as active agents rather than as merely passive recipients of irresistible demands; that is, as actors who perceive and react to some outside groups but not to others and who translate outside demands into actions within the school or the university which affect the relationship of the one to the other. The relation between education and society, or more precisely between parts of one and parts of the other, may thus be seen as itself a two-way street, with the school-university relationship inducing or otherwise shaping a so-called external demand. For example, a higher education system that formally admits only 1 percent—or 10 percent—of the age group will cause the great mass of students at the elementary and secondary levels not to expect ready access, thereby shaping the expectations of families and young people in the most basic way possible.

Throughout this volume we sometimes use the metaphor *school* to indicate the entire secondary school system of a nation and the metaphor *university* for the higher education system. These terms clear the mind, simplify our prose, and thereby aid communication. But they carry the twin dangers of confusing the individual institution with an entire system and particularly of giving an impression of simplicity in what are ever more complex sets of institutions and practices. All educational systems of any magnitude and any significant degree of modernity contain different types of secondary schools, even in the United States, where the effort to group the young in public, comprehensive high schools has been under way for a half-century or more. And higher education has normally consisted not of universities alone but also of various nonuniversity sectors and enterprises, sometimes for purposes of elite recruitment and training, as in the leading *grandes écoles* of France, or, more widely, to handle technological fields and teacher training. Such differentiation is considerable in Japan, which has junior colleges and a wide range of private colleges, and great in the United States, where only several hundred institutions among some three thousand do research and give the Ph.D. and otherwise fully qualify as modern universities. Such internal variation will normally be made clear and appropriate terms used; but the limitations of our occasional use of *school* and *university* should be kept in mind.

The concluding chapter has three goals. One is to make some general observations, rooted in what we have learned across nations, about how schools and universities are connected and thereby shape one another. For example, we note that clear, direct connections between the two levels follow from intensive tracking at the secondary level. To reduce tracking is, for good or bad, to blur the linkages. Similarly, the reduction of tracking tends to reduce the prestige of schoolteaching, another outcome that apparently has not been much anticipated in reforms that favor the elimination of streaming in the upper secondary years. A second goal is to clarify a particular vulnerability of the American system against the backdrop of the experiences of other countries. As reflected in the conditions of schoolteaching and the recruitment problems of the teaching profession, the secondary school has been a distinctive American problem for some decades. Why is it so problematic? There is a confluence of conditions in the school *and* in the university *and* in the rest of postsecondary education which show up sharply in international relief, ones that together spell a circle of effects that reduces quality. These conditions need not be fully repeated in other countries, nor will they be. But other national systems edge toward the American problem as they make first the school and then the university more accessible and load each with more expectations, responsibilities, and tasks. What was "elite" work becomes "mass" work, and things are never the same again, particularly the status of schoolteaching and the conditions under which teachers work.

The third goal of chapter eleven is to identify one or more basic trends that deeply affect all educational systems and thereby alter the school-university relationship. The key trend is complexity. The tasks of education multiply in number and, individually and collectively, become more complex. The scale of operations expands significantly. It follows that the agendas of the school and the university diverge, rendering the relation of the two more ambiguous and more problematic. It is not only the United States that is, and will be, troubled. Everywhere there is an erosion of certainty. In the face of growing complexity, the structures of schooling are pushed and pulled in contradictory directions. Are the young to be educated in common secondary schools or in different types of schools, even ones that compete for prestige? Should students in higher education be grouped as much as possible in comprehensive universities that attempt to embrace the universe or ought they be divided by rule or personal choice among many kinds of postsecondary education? More than ever, nations face the integration and differentiation of secondary and higher education, and the linkages between them, as central problems. The growing complexity of educational tasks will not allow it to be otherwise.

Notes

1. For a general statement of this principle, see Green, *Predicting the Behavior of the Education System*, pp. 8–9.

2. National Commission on Excellence in Education, *A Nation At Risk*.

3. National Commission on Excellence in Education, *A Nation At Risk*; Task Force on Education for Economic Growth, *Action for Excellence*; Goodlad, *A Place Called School*; Boyer, *High School*; College Entrance Examination Board, *Academic Preparation for College*; The Twentieth Century Fund, *Making the Grade*; Ravitch, *The Troubled Crusade*; Sizer, *Horace's Compromise*.

Bibliography

BOYER, ERNEST, L. *High School: A Report on Secondary Education in America*. New York: Harper and Row, 1983.

College Entrance Examination Board. *Academic Preparation for College: What Students Need to Know and Be Able to Do*. New York: CEEB, 1983.

GOODLAD, JOHN I. *A Place Called School*. New York: McGraw-Hill, 1983.

GREEN, THOMAS F. *Predicting the Behavior of the Education System*. Syracuse, N.Y.: Syracuse University Press, 1980.

National Commission on Excellence in Education. *A Nation at Risk: The Imperative for Educational Reform*. Washington, D.C.: U.S. Government Printing Office, 1983.

RAVITCH, DIANE. *The Troubled Crusade: American Education, 1945–1980*. New York: Basic Books, 1983.

SIZER, THEODORE R. *Horace's Compromise: The Dilemma of the American High School*. Boston: Houghton Mifflin, 1984.

Task Force on Education for Economic Growth. *Action for Excellence: A Comprehensive Plan to Improve our Nation's Schools*. Denver: Education Commission of the States, 1983.

Twentieth Century Fund. *Making the Grade: Report of the Twentieth Century Fund Task Force on Federal Elementary and Secondary Education Policy*. New York, 1983.

1

France

GUY NEAVE

FRANCE, OVER THE PAST TWO decades or more, and in common with most Western European countries, has been faced with the twin imperatives of meeting growing individual demand for education while having to remold its education system in the light of economic, industrial, and social change. The reforms that emerged from these considerations were comprehensive and wide ranging. Secondary education underwent root and branch reorganization. So, too, did higher education. If the drive for reform in higher education began well before the uproar of May 1968, the events of that date ushered in what may be seen as one of the most sustained efforts by a Western European government to deal with the pressures and contradictions arising out of the transition from an elite to a mass based system of higher education.

During the past twenty-five years or so, scarcely any minister of education has passed up the opportunity to associate his name with educational reforms that have had equally varying degrees of radicalism and success. Berthoin (1959), Fouchet (1963), Fontanet (1974), Haby (1975), and Beullac (1978)—such is the litany of secondary education. To this war memorial of past reforms one might add the names of Edgar Faure (1968), father of the Higher Education Guideline Law of that year (current revisions of which have given rise to much parading and shouting between the Bastille and the Gare d'Austerlitz), Mme Alice Saunier Seité (1976), and finally, the present incumbent, M. Alain Savary. The unhappy M. Savary faces a coincidence of reforms at all levels of the education system: the internal structures of lower secondary education (the Legrand Commission Report); changes in the relationship between the private—more accurately termed, the "nonstate"—sector of both primary and secondary schooling;[1] the redefinition of the structures and objectives of undergraduate study; and last but not least, changes to the balance of power in the internal governance of universities.

Comprehensive though these reforms have been, their strategy tends to differ from the more usual one found in other countries, notably in the Federal Republic of Germany and in Sweden. The difference resides in one outstanding feature. In no way did any of these transformations ever pose a threat to those parts of French education which are intimately associated with the raising and eventual training of the country's administrative, economic, and political elites. Without exception, both in secondary and higher education, reform applied to nonelite institutions. In secondary education, for example, the key institution, the *classes préparatoires des grandes écoles*, have remained untouched. To be sure, the numbers of students entering them have increased. But their prestige and their highly selective nature (one being closely related to the other) are untarnished. Their position across that golden road to posts of high preferment is as commanding as ever it was. The same may be said for the *grandes écoles*, that truly elite sector of French higher education, to which the classes préparatoires are linked both by their curriculum and by their structural relationships. The uproar and protestation that accompanied the overhaul of French higher education left them an oasis of tranquility, unmentioned in the Higher Education Guideline Law of 1968. The past ten years have, if anything, seen the prestige and attractiveness of the grandes écoles increase by leaps and bounds. In part this is owing to the rigorous selection they continue to impose on candidates, in part to the widely held conviction that the training they give is more relevant to the needs of high-level technocracy, administration, and management in both the public and the private sectors of the nation's economy.

Thus, the particular strategy that successive French governments have endorsed may have enabled the country to meet the apparently irreconcilable demands of preserving excellence, on the one hand, while responding to the tidal wave of individual demand for higher education on the other. But the consequences of such a policy are particularly marked. The already highly segmented nature of French higher education has been increased still further. Viewed from a long-range perspective, such a strategy has effectively transferred upward toward higher education the high level of institutional and curricular stratification which traditionally characterized French secondary schooling.

The French Education System: Today and Yesterday

As in the United Kingdom, Sweden, Denmark, and Norway, the thrust of reform in French secondary education has involved a gradual move toward a pattern of "all in" schooling, based on catchment areas (*carte scolaire).* Pupils of a given age range attend the same school, at least through the end of the compulsory education period. Beginning at age eleven plus, secondary education is grounded on a middle and upper school pattern. The age range eleven to fifteen constitutes the first cycle of secondary schooling and takes place in so-called colleges. Upper secondary schooling, known as the second cycle, is split between two separate types of schools. The first, the *lycée*, covers the age range fifteen plus to nineteen. It leads to the *baccalauréat* (the academic, school-leaving certificate), which is general in nature, to the technician's *baccalauréat*, or to the technician's certificate *(brevêt de technicien)*. Official terminology calls this long-cycle secondary education, and although legally there is held to be no disparity of esteem between long- and short-cycle upper secondary schooling, it is nevertheless true that the overwhelming majority of students in higher education pass through the long-cycle lycée. Its companion establishment, the two-year *lycée d'enseignement professionnel*, for ages fifteen to seventeen, provides a course that has, principally, a vocational or practical bent. There is, however, a high degree of segmentation within the vocational area between the *brevêt d'études professionnelles* and the *certificat d'aptitude professionnelle* (the vocational skills certificate). The former qualifies a pupil to exercise a series of occupations linked to a particular sector of the economy—industrial, commercial, administrative, or social. The industrial sector contains at present some thirty-eight different qualifications, and the services sector a further eight.[2] The latter certificate is less a generic than a specialist qualification and is intended to attest to a pupil's capacity to perform a particular job. In 1981 there were 260 different specialties, 233 corresponding to the industrial and 27 to the service sector of the labor force. In both cases these qualifications lead on to blue-collar jobs of a skilled or semiskilled nature.

Thus, a clear stratification exists between the type of skills fostered in the lycée d'enseignement professionnel and those imparted in the lycée. Recent reforms have sought to soften this distinction by providing certain facilities for particularly able pupils to switch tracks in the lycée d'enseignement professionnel. Students presenting the certificat d'aptitude professionnelle are permitted the possibility of moving into a special transfer class *(seconde spéciale)* in the long-cycle lycée. Here, after three years, they may qualify to sit for the technician's baccalauréat or diploma. There are similar openings for the more successful candidates of the brevêt;[3] their preparation time for the technician's baccalauréat is one year shorter.

The current structures of French secondary education were put in place by the law of 11 July 1975, the last in a long line of reforms that had the effect of moving up, to a later academic stage in the life of the student, the historic pattern of secondary education usually found in Western European countries, namely, a system of vertically differentiated types of schools—academic, technical, and vocational—which admit pupils starting at age eleven. Although French secondary school reforms did not reach the degree of curricular and structural integration found in either Sweden or Norway, for example,[4] the move toward the comprehensive model in France was certainly more wide-ranging than its British counterpart. External structural change went hand in hand with the inner organizational reform of the school. Both the creation of more flexible student groupings and the remolding of the curriculum were integral parts of the French strategy of innovation and were not treated separately as they had been in Britain.[5]

The intellectual origins of the integrated secondary school in France go back to the end of the First World War, when the idea of creating one school for all (*école unique*) was first mooted by a body calling itself *Les Compagnons de l'Université Nouvelle*.[6] The idea received further backing toward the end of the Second World War with the setting up of the Langevin-Wallon Commission in 1944 by the provisional government.[7] This commission laid down two guiding principles that have influenced French thinking to the present day. The first was the notion of democratization, the second the notion of guidance and orientation. The Langevin-Wallon proposals revolved around an eleven-to-fifteen and a fifteen-to-nineteen middle and upper school model, where the upper school was to be integrated rather than split between two different types. The eleven-to-fifteen middle school was seen as providing a period of orientation and offering a common core of subjects and flexible transfers between various options. The upper school, though physically integrated, was to retain a pattern of traditional tripartite tracking between practical, commercial, and academic learning.[8] It is clear from the nature of these proposals that, even then, considerable difficulty was posed by the need, on the one hand, to open secondary education to all and, on the other, to maintain that traditional concern of French education, namely, the formation of intellectual elites.

If today such ideas appear perfectly acceptable to most people in the world of education, it is important to underline how far they were in advance of their time, at least in the French context. Until 1959, French education was grounded on a system of rigorous selection that decided who went on to the lycée, occurring at the end of primary education. The majority of pupils continued in primary schools until age fourteen, when they left; others, however, found some accommodation in a species of postprimary establishment, the *cours complémentaire*. In effect, the notion of secondary education for all, launched in Britain by the 1944 Education Act (1945 in Scotland), was a matter of debate rather than practice.[9] Elite education and thus access to higher education began officially at age eleven. Two factors altered this situation: the so-called *explosion scolaire*, in which enrollments in state education almost doubled between 1950 and 1967; and the irresistible demand for universal access to secondary education.

Although the Berthoin reforms of 1959 did not challenge the established links between secondary and higher education, they did impart a greater degree of flexibility by setting up a two-year observation period for the years eleven to thirteen. This innovation did not essentially alter the nature of the linkage between secondary and higher education, which still remained largely determined by the weeding-out process at the end of primary school.[10] The first moves in this direction came with the Fouchet reforms, introduced in August 1963. These provided for a multilateral (or tracked) eleven-to-fifteen comprehensive school divided into four sections: a lycée-type section, subdivided into a classical or a modern, mathematics based grouping; a short, "practical" section not dissimilar to the type of secondary modern schooling found in the United Kingdom; a transitional section designed as a remedial grouping; and, finally, a terminal section for those leaving school immediately at fifteen.[11]

The main thrust of subsequent reforms has been to attenuate the tracking system, often in the face of ferocious resistance from teachers. Among the various steps taken along the way were the suggestions outlined by Joseph Fontanet in 1974 in favor of grouping by ability, subject by subject. Finally, in 1975, along with the introduction by René Haby of the eleven-to-fifteen integrated comprehensive school, came the decision to allow teachers the discretion of whether or not to destream.

Higher Education

In France the baccalauréat, the school-leaving certificate taken at age eighteen, is defined as the first university degree. Higher education is defined as all those courses taking place after the baccalauréat. The structure of French higher education is exceptional in several ways from the usual pattern found elsewhere in Western Europe. In the first place, the university sector is not, as it often tends to be elsewhere, the elite part of higher education. Elite higher education in France is rather to be found in the state-sector grandes écoles, the best known of which are the Ecole Polytechnique, which trains top-notch engineering administrators, the Ecole Nationale d'Administration, which trains administrators, inter alia, for the Cour des Comptes (Court of Public Audit), or at a slightly less exalted level, SupAero, which specializes in aeronautical engineering. There is also an important private sector within the grandes écoles which specializes mainly in business management and administration. One example of this is the Ecole des Hautes Etudes Commerciales. It provides top-level management trainees for many of the leading French firms. In all there are some 226 of these specialist schools, enrolling around 100,000 students.[12] Their principal feature is their highly selective admissions policy based on a competitive examination that takes place some two years after candidates have sat the baccalauréat.

The training required for preparation to sit the grandes écoles examination is so rigorous that it determines the second feature unique to French higher education: the presence of institutions that, though physically located in secondary schools, in fact cross the boundary line between secondary and higher education. The most important of these are the classes préparatoires des grandes écoles, where candidates for entry to the elite sector of higher education are polished and groomed for the various competitive entry examinations to the grandes écoles. There are some two hundred of these "forcing houses" across the country, attached to the most reputable lycées and characterized by a highly specific curriculum not found elsewhere in the education system. They are not, however, evenly distributed but show a high concentration in the Paris region. In 1981–1982, 40,845 students were enrolled in the classes préparatoires,[13] an expansion of 30 percent over the past ten years. A further example of these supraordinate institutions are the higher technicians sections (*sections de techniciens supérieurs*), which currently number 623 and, like the classes préparatoires, are outgrowths of certain secondary schools specializing in technical education. The feature they share with the classes préparatoires is their selective and competitive entry system, although they are officially designated as part of the short-cycle, closed, or highly selective, sector of higher education, as distinct from the classes préparatoires, which are regarded as part of the long-cycle closed sector. In 1981–1982 the higher technicians sections enrolled 74,999 students, a massive leap of 10 percent in student numbers over the previous year.[14]

Taken together, the grandes écoles and the classes préparatoires represent what has sometimes been termed the closed, long cycle of higher education in France.[15] Strictly speaking, to this should be added certain sectors in the university. Medical and dental studies are undergraduate courses in France, for example, unlike the American pattern where they are part of graduate training. In 1974 the government decided to cut back, mainly on demographic grounds, the numbers of medical and dental students. The effect has been to increase the competitive nature of admissions to these two fields.[16]

Against the elite sector stands what one exquisitely qualified denizen of the grandes écoles once termed "the university swamp."[17] Grouped around the faculties (officially, units of training and research) of letters, arts, sciences, law, and economics, its principal feature is its nonselective admissions policy. Unofficially, however, law and economics faculties do operate a system of selection to which past governments have turned a blind eye. Studies are organized into three cycles of two years each, the first leading to the *diplôme d'études universitaires générales* two years after passing the baccalauréat. In turn, this may lead on through the *licence* (three years after the baccalauréat) to the *maîtrise* (the master's degree passed four years after the baccalauréat), to the so-called short-cycle doctorate (*doctorat de troisième cycle*), or even to the monumental *doctorat d'état,* which painstaking and scrupulous historians have been known to take upwards of ten years to complete.

Finally, there is the short-cycle closed sector. This consists of two types of institutions: first are the two-year university institutes of technology, founded in 1966 and today numbering sixty-six establishments;[18] second are the higher technicians sections, which the university institutes of technology were intended to replace. The former are officially part of the university, though under slightly different legal status. Both university institutes and higher technicians sections are selective, post-baccalauréat institutions. The first offer two-year courses in applied subjects such as civil engineering, applied biology, and information careers and admit on the basis of results obtained during the last two years and interviews with a selection panel. Their original remit was to increase the numbers of intermediary personnel in industry in positions halfway between higher technician and full-fledged engineer. Indications are that their admissions policy over the past few years has become even more selective, for if the demand has increased by 20 to 30 percent, the number of successful candidates has not grown at the same pace. There were 54,814 students in the university institutes of technology in 1981–1982, compared with 50,283 in 1978–1979.[19]

THE IDEOLOGICAL CONTEXT

The linkage between secondary and higher education can, of course, be regarded as a technical exercise involving student flows as a function of the staying-on rate after the end of compulsory schooling, of the proportion of a given age cohort reaching those qualifications that afford access to higher education, and of the proportion of those who, duly qualified, in fact take up a place in the varying institutes of that sector of the nation's educational provision. Such an approach voluntarily eschews the nature of the value system that surrounds higher education, its place in a particular society, and the historical role that has befallen it. Yet these elements are highly significant. They influence, although not always favorably, the way governments formulate their policy vis-à-vis the higher education system. They also influence the perceptions of and thus the choice of, institutions, quite apart from the course of study, of able school-leavers. Before examining the way the school influences the higher education system in France, it is useful to see how French higher education differs in its value context from its counterpart in the United States.

From its earliest days, the European university has been closely associated with the institutions of government, the church, the law, and the gathering of taxes. The emergence of the modern, as opposed to the medieval, university appeared with the modern central state and the establishment of formal rules and conditions governing examinations for admission to a central civil service.[20] This latter process can be observed throughout the eighteenth century, when monarchs—Spanish, Austrian, Prussian, Swedish—of varying degrees of enlightenment sought to harness the university to the training of the state bureaucracy. The linkage was established either by endowing universities with a monopoly over the examinations leading to posts in the administration or by manipulating the university curriculum or both.[21] In France a series of decrees by Napoleon I in 1811, establishing the Imperial University, came as a somewhat belated form of this long, drawn-out process. Such a relationship between higher education and the services of the state is not merely different from the factors that determined the rise of higher education in the United States; it would have profound effects on the transition from the elite to a mass system of higher education in Europe and, a fortiori, in France. Although the problems thus created may be essentially similar, they are closely bound up with both the political and the value context of which higher education is a part and which it also generates. These are very different in France than, say, in the United States.

It is a matter of some dispute how close or, for that matter, how enduring has been the relationship between higher education and the services of the French central state. It may be argued that from a quantitative standpoint it was not always close. After all, large numbers of graduates did make their careers outside government service. But this point of view deemphasizes values as a matter of perception. In this regard, state service—which also numbers primary and secondary school teachers among its ranks—has not inconsiderable advantages, namely, a guaranteed lifetime income, job security, and a pension at the end. These advantages, important today, were no less so in the days before the advent of the welfare state. Thus, if large numbers of university graduates did not find places as functionaries, this invalidates neither

that such a status was closely linked with higher education nor that
many had this as their primary ambition. Failure to attain one's ambition
does not mean that it is any the less a powerful force. And the apparent
quantitatively weak links between higher education and central government in the earlier part of the century certainly do not undermine the
powerful career linkage between both institutions today.

The rise of mass higher education in France during the sixties did not
dissolve this nexus. Quite the contrary, it may have served to reinforce
it. For the rise of mass higher education also coincided with the growth
of state administration in education, social welfare, and the services
associated with the redistribution of wealth. Twenty percent of higher
education's output was, during those splendid times, reabsorbed by
higher education itself. The question that began to tax those in charge
of this sector after 1968—although it had also sorely tried those in national planning before—was whether higher education should continue
to be viewed primarily in terms of state employment. Thus, one of the
foremost external influences brought to bear on higher education was
the question of whether the administration, let alone the economy, could
absorb the numbers emerging from mass higher education into the same
type of occupation that history, ambition, and parental aspirations saw
as the rightful reward of graduates. Put another way, the dilemma facing
both politicians and planners was, first, how to break the perceived
historical nexus between state employment and higher education; second, how to create those qualifications thought necessary by the Com-
missariat Général du Plan, France's national planning agency, to maintain
the nation's competitiveness; third, how to make students and professors
aware of the need to adapt courses and expectations to these twin imperatives; and finally, how to increase the interplay of market forces in
that sector of higher education, namely the university, whose history
and ethics had served to attenuate them. Together, these four elements
constitute one of the most important external influences affecting government policy during the past eighteen years and thus one of the major
forces underlying not only curricular and institutional development but
also changes in the articulation between secondary and higher education.

Along with linkages to government, the second distinction between
higher education in France and the United States is that of a *national*
education system. This concept has particular overtones in France; it
yields further insight into difficulties that elsewhere, and in other circumstances, might appear as banalities or as simply incomprehensible.

Despite many and continuing attempts to give greater initiative to its
basic units, whether schools or individual universities, education in France
remains a highly centralized enterprise. The contents of the school curriculum, the number of hours to be taught in each subject, and the

structure of school options and tracks are defined by the central Ministry of Education. The certificates awarded, and most particularly the baccalauréat, are national examinations. That is to say, the state delegates its authority to award this qualification to selected teachers in schools and universities. Over the past decade various measures have been introduced to make the examination system more responsive to specific local demands. The right to sit papers in the so-called minority languages, Breton, Corsican, and Languedocien, is one illustration of this development. The situation is not dissimilar in higher education. Course structures require national validation at all levels. And, no less important, such validation can be withdrawn if student numbers fall below a stipulated level or if the courses are no longer believed to correspond to perceived national needs. In the summer of 1980, for example, some five hundred second-cycle courses found their validation withdrawn overnight. Although many were subsequently reinstated in an untypical act of contrition by Mme Alice Saunier Seité, then minister of higher education, such repentance merely underlines the power of central authority, further reinforced by the budgetary reforms of 1977. The introduction of the GARACES system (after the unit that put it into operation, the Groupe d'Analyses et de Recherches sur l'Activité et le Coût des Enseignements Supérieurs) was seen as a means of decoupling university finance from student numbers. Its effect, however, has been to lend new strength to the traditional centralizing forces that both permeate and hold together the French higher education system.[22] No less significant, since it also contributes to the centralized nature of French higher education, is the dual system of national degrees, on the one hand, and those awarded by the individual university, on the other.

National degrees are underwritten by the state; that is, the state guarantees their standards, which are held to be nationally consistent. Such underwriting is not afforded to degrees awarded by individual universities. The difference between the two is not just prestige. National degrees are held to be far more valuable than those of a particular university. It is also a matter, once again, of access to state employment. This cannot be obtained by holders of individual university degrees. Furthermore, private-sector employers appear to attach more weight to a state diploma than to that of an individual university whose reputation may not be the best.

Such centralizing tendencies in French education may impart a high degree of formal uniformity in public structures or programs, in courses, curriculum, and diplomas, but they have the not inconsiderable drawback of making reform extremely difficult since, if reforms are to have any standing at all, they have to be introduced at a system level rather than at the individual establishment.

The third distinction between higher education in France and the United States is rather more value-laden. It revolves around the notion of the state's role in education. To many involved in French education, one highly vexatious characteristic is its bureaucratic nature, reliant on formal procedures and with initiatives springing more from the central administration than from the grass roots. Why this should be so is a matter both of history and of political ideas. Between the Anglo-Saxon world and France lies a vast gulf of misunderstanding and deep disagreement over the legitimate role the central state should play in general and its role in education in particular. In Britain and the United States the concept of the state is heavily influenced by a combination of eighteenth-century Whig constitutional theory and nineteenth-century liberalism. The Anglo-Saxon ideology identifies the state as a barely tolerable evil that must be reduced to a minimum if individual enterprise is to flourish and the common good to benefit from initiative and inventiveness. This ethic has permeated the development of higher education in the United States. It is not, however, seen with the same gladsome eye in France. The establishment of the Republic, one and indivisible, by the Revolution of 1789 did not in itself alter the accumulated power that one and one-half centuries of monarchical centralization laid upon the services of the state. It did, however, bring about a profound transmutation in the state's moral purpose. Henceforth, its role was that of an arbiter, a check against the arbitrary power of sectional interests, an instrument to hold down the rapacity of local elites.

Such an interpretation is a highly interventionist one. It is the legitimate purpose of the state to place all on a footing of equality, defined either legally or by administrative frameworks that ensure similarity of provision and treatment. It follows from this that the right of the individual to operate outside the state's oversight is not necessarily regarded as desirable. It is instead seen as a rather suspect privilege not always conducive to the public good but more likely to be in the interests of private gain or particular advantage. This does not exclude the possibility that bodies other than the state may set up educational establishments. But they are regarded with a high degree of suspicion. Private education, then, where it exists at all in France, does not have the same ideological and positive overtones as it does in the context of higher education in the United States.

Diametrically opposed views exist, then, on the role of the state in education, between the United States, on the one hand, and France, on the other. The former sees the state as a negative imposition; the latter regards it as a benefit. From this difference springs a host of variations that have affected the institutional development of education in the two countries and the way education is allowed to respond to pressures resulting from economic and social change. If an outsider were asked to characterize the two systems, he would be tempted to see in the United States a confederal enterprise regulated predominantly by market forces and in France a national service regulated by the state's interpretation and perception of present and future economic needs.

The School Influences the Higher Education System

In any country the linkage between secondary and higher education is determined by the availability and subject structure of public examinations leading to higher education, the manner in which the educational process either positively selects (sometimes called the "sponsorship mode of social mobility") or, alternatively, "cools out" those it deems unsuitable, and the way students self-select for particular tracks or options. The precise point at which such factors begin to operate decisively in any education system is subject to wide variation. It is also affected by practices generic to specific educational systems. In the French context one of the most important of these is the practice of grade repeating or lock-step advancement by year. Students failing to reach a stipulated level of performance are obliged to stay back a year and repeat the class over again. The importance of this obstacle is considerable both for its extent and also for the repercussions it has on the track for which a student may opt later. In short, grade repeating is the first hurdle in the educational assault course that links school to higher education. Follow-up studies of students born in 1962 have shown that by the time they reached upper secondary education (*classe de seconde*), 3.4 percent were ahead of their class, 21.9 percent had not repeated at all, and 32.6 percent of the age group had repeated at least once (the residual 42.1 percent having left at that point).[23]

Before describing the finer details of the effect of the school on the articulation between secondary and higher education, it is useful to place current French developments in a broader perspective. Table 1.1 sets out the staying-on rate for the age groups sixteen, seventeen, and eighteen by gender of student, over the decade 1970–1981, for certain selected member states of the European community. From this it may be seen that France is well ahead of the community average for staying beyond compulsory schooling both at the start and at the end of this period. Furthermore, although the chances of girls and boys remaining in school improved by 79 percent, by the end of the decade far more girls remained in formal secondary education than boys.[24]

By contrast, the United Kingdom presents a very different picture. With the exception of eighteen-year-olds, the British staying-on rate for

TABLE 1.1

Staying-on Rate for 16- 17- and 18-Year-olds in Selected Member States of the European Community, by Sex of Student 1970/71–1980/81.
(Percent of relevant age group)

| | 16-Year-olds | | | | 17-Year-olds | | | | 18-Year-olds | | | |
| | Boys | | Girls | | Boys | | Girls | | Boys | | Girls | |
	1970/71	1980/81	1970/71	1980/81	1970/71	1980/81	1970/71	1980/81	1970/71	1980/81	1970/71	1980/81
All member states of the European Community	49.8	60.5	47.5	64.9	36.1	44.5	33.8	48.6	28.1	35.8	23.4	36.1
France	59.5	74.4	67.1	84.2	41.6	55.4	48.4	70.4	29.6	37.4	33.0	47.5
Federal Republic of Germany	34.7	59.8	31.8	66.9	24.2	38.3	23.1	44.9	19.3	39.8	17.4	42.1
Netherlands	68.3	91.5	52.3	89.3	49.3	71.8	32.9	67.3	36.5	51.8	19.3	41.1
Belgium	69.3	82.3	63.4	83.6	51.4	67.4	49.6	72.5	42.5	46.7	37.5	50.0
United Kingdom	41.5	38.3	41.0	46.6	26.5	24.2	25.3	28.5	18.3	17.0	16.0	14.9
Denmark	46.1	82.6	41.3	90.2	35.0	66.4	25.5	69.2	27.8	63.7	15.5	58.1

Source: *Statistiques de l'Enseignement*, EUROSTAT 2/82, Luxembourg, Office Statistique des Communautes Européennes.

girls has continued to increase. But, uniformly, that of boys has fallen over the eleven years from 1970–1981.

Although France is moving toward the universalization of upper secondary education, structural differentiation at the level of upper secondary schooling—the split between the lycée on the one hand and the lycée d'enseignement professionnel on the other—still plays an important part. At this point, around 40 percent of the age cohort find themselves in vocational tracks, in special schools, or, following short-cycle upper secondary education, with very few, if any, chances of access to higher education.[25]

If we are to trace the flow of students from school to higher education, we must make certain assumptions about the size of the age cohort and about the nature of candidates sitting the baccalauréat. We assume that the age cohort of eighteen-year-olds in 1982 was approximately 844,100. The second assumption, more dubious by far, is that all sitting the baccalauréat in June 1982 were uniformly of this age cohort. Evidently this is not the case, but national statistics, as they have been released, do not give an age breakdown of candidates. In June 1982, 371,013 students sat this examination, in all 43.9 percent of the age cohort, bearing in mind the caveats mentioned previously. Of those sitting, 64.9 percent passed, a slight increase of 1.3 percent over the previous year and a 4 percent growth rate in the number of candidates. Hence, the total pool from which entrants to higher education was drawn amounted to 28.6 percent of the age cohort.[26] Given the nature of our assumptions, this is somewhat of an overestimate, since time-series statistics covering the period from 1964–1965 to 1981 show that the percentage of the relevant age group qualified to enter higher education doubled during that period, jumping from 12.6 to 25 percent.[27] France, however, in contrast to Britain, where the proportion of students qualified to enter higher education has virtually stagnated since 1974, continues to see growth in the numbers passing from school to university, with the result that total enrollments in all sectors of higher education have expanded from 524,000 students in 1965 to 1,071,000 in 1981–1982.[28]

SUBJECT OPTIONS IN THE UPPER SECONDARY SCHOOL

Crucial to the way the school influences higher education is the type of track or subject options into which students are channeled prior to the baccalauréat. In this regard the last two years of upper secondary education act as major determinants. During this period students must opt for a particular series of subjects, and these, in turn, set the pattern of the type of course in higher education upon which an individual is likely to embark. Just as upper secondary education is split between two types of schools, so the baccalauréat itself is divided between the general baccalauréat and the technician baccalauréat. The general baccalauréat is composed of five subject-option tracks. All of them have common elements, grouped around seven subjects, with the major difference between them being less the type of subject as the emphasis and the number of hours set aside for each subject per week.[29] The option tracks are as follows:

Option A: literature
Option B: economics and social studies
Option C: mathematics and physical sciences
Option D: mathematics with biological sciences
          mathematics with technical studies
          mathematics with agronomic studies
Option E: mathematics with technology
In the technician baccalauréat, there are three option tracks:
Option F: industrial studies, social and medical sciences, music and
          dance
Option G: secretariat and accountancy studies
Option H: computer science

Subject choice among students is not, of course, stable. Between 1970–1971 and 1982 considerable shifts have taken place. Most marked has been the rapid decline in the proportion of candidates for the field of literature, which fell from 46 percent to 26.2 percent over this eleven-year period. A similar decline is observable in the area of mathematics and physical sciences (22.4 percent in 1977, 16.9 percent in 1982). Option D has remained by and large stable with around 30 percent of all presentations. The main growth areas have been economics and social studies, which accounted for 22.3 percent of candidates in 1982,[30] and also the technician baccalauréat. When first introduced in 1968–1969, 10.5 percent of all candidates opted for this field. By 1982 it had attracted 31.2 percent of all examinees.

On the surface, this latter development would seem to be particularly heartening since it has been part of the long-term policy of successive French governments to increase the technical/technological element in the culture of the upper secondary school. Within the confines of the technician baccalauréat, the majority of students took option G (58 percent of last year's candidates). A further 41 percent took option F, a slight fall over the year 1980.[31]

A further factor affecting the quantitative nature of the links between secondary and higher education in France is that the success rate between the various options is by no means uniform. The highest chances of success are associated with option C, mathematics and physical sciences (a 77.4 percent pass rate) and the lowest with option G, secretariat and accountancy studies (a 58.3 percent pass rate). Nor is the prestige enjoyed by the various options the same. In the French secondary school, high ability is associated with mathematical competence. And this in turn means that not only are the best pupils encouraged to take option C, but, for this reason, the pass rate tends to be higher. The standing of mathematics as a star subject derives in large part because it is the first step along the road leading to the glittering prize of a place in a grande école, via the classes préparatoires.

The academic significance of option C, its standing as the latter-day replacement of the classical languages requirements in elite education, can be readily perceived by examining the qualification background of those entering the classes préparatoires des grandes écoles. During the academic year 1982–1983, 22,335 students entered these antechambers of the elite. Six out of ten had sat option C in the baccalauréat.[32] Or, put another way, 40 percent of students who passed option C took up places in the classes préparatoires. Compare this with 6.3 percent for those unfortunates who chose option A, literature. In truth, the paths to France's educational Jerusalem are narrow indeed. And yet, to him who hath, it shall be given. For there is another advantage for those who opt, or rather, are allowed to opt, for this track. The range of subjects a student may subsequently take at the university are far less restricted. Option C, in effect, permits those fortunate enough to be admitted to it to keep their choice of university subject relatively open. Follow-up studies of such students have shown their eventual choice of subject to be far wider than that of their fellows who took other tracks. Clearly then, option C enjoys a rare standing, both as regards the type of openings to which it later leads in the higher education system and, from there, into the highest levels of public service.

But the value, both real and symbolic, of mathematics as an indicator of excellence in the French secondary school is not without its negative effects. Selection between tracks tends, in consequence, to be closely associated with the individual's ability in this subject. Furthermore, it appears to reinforce a very special form of coping strategy that increases the amount of grade repeating during the last two years of secondary schooling. Many students, often urged on by frantic and ambitious parents, repeat a year in the fond hope of placing themselves on the magic roundabout of option C, having failed in the first attempt.[33]

Selection into a particular track is not always the result of teachers' reports nor of the formal opinion of the class council (conseil de classe).[34] It is equally affected by family aspirations, cultural capital, and a rough estimate by the student of how far he is likely to succeed. In the past few years some evidence has accumulated regarding the effect of external factors, principally the deteriorating economic climate, upon student choice of subject during the last two years in upper secondary education. Among farming families whose children opted for track A (literature), the tendency is increasingly to eschew higher education and go straight out into the labor market. They do not, as they would have done previously, take up places in teacher training programs, an interesting example of the way the collapse of this particular field of employment affects student behavior in secondary school. Added to this, and doubtless amplified by it, is a second phenomenon. This is the strategy of "cooling out." It is especially marked among students choosing baccalauréat options A, B, F, and G. Many students decide deliberately to avoid taking those options where their chances of success are small. And, in this respect, it is notable that this mechanism operates most clearly in those subject combinations leading to the classes préparatoires. In short, the segmented nature of French higher education creates a species of aspirational segmentation among students at the secondary school level.

Higher Education Influences the School

How far such a phenomenon is a sustained response to the various reforms introduced into the structures of higher education after 1966 is difficult to determine precisely, but it is unlikely that they are independent of them. At a high level of generalization, the main thrust of higher education policy—from the establishment of the university institutes of technology in 1966, to the creation of the diplôme d'études universitaires générales in 1972, to the vocationalization of the second cycle in higher education (years three and four after the baccalauréat) in 1976—came in response to two enduring concerns. The first was to introduce a greater degree of professionalism in university studies; the second was to impart a greater degree of flexibility in student choice in higher education. Both of these may be seen as components of a single overriding problem: how to link higher education more closely with the realities of working life.

The university institutes of technology, as short-cycle establishments, were drawn up in direct response to the forecast of manpower needs in the fourth 4-year plan (1962–65). Their justification was very similar to the considerations that had given rise to the English polytechnics. They were conceived to channel additional student demand into economically relevant fields of study; and they were seen as providing a type of education that would correspond more closely to the perceived interests of the growing number of working-class students coming through secondary education. Their purpose was to fill a particular slot in the nation's manpower requirements at the level of middle management.

The second deliberate and planned reform, rather than the panic measures taken in the aftermath of May 1968, was the further extension of short-cycle higher education to the university itself. Moves in this direction antedated the student uprising with the introduction in 1967 of the *diplôme d'études universitaires scientifiques* and its humanities equivalent the *diplôme d'études universitaires literaires*. In an effort to give further flexibility in the type of job for which students might apply after graduation, these two diplomas were merged to form the diplôme d'études universitaires générales five years later. The motives behind such moves were varied. In part, the foreshortening of the usual university course by one year was seen as a means to improve student motivation and thus to increase the abysmally low pass rate, often as low as 40 percent. Another consideration linked to this was the need to increase the efficiency of French higher education by tightening costs. Finally, there was a more strategic consideration: the need to develop palliative measures in anticipation of the reduction of the major sector supplied by higher education, the education system itself. By the early seventies, if not before, France, like many other Western countries, stood on the threshold of a major drop in pupil numbers. The demographic crisis, and its subsequent moratorium on teacher recruitment, posed severe problems. In short, new career outlets had to be found for students outside the educational service.[35]

These pressures were made more acute with the onset of the economic crisis in 1974. The combination of the planned and the unexpected led the government to extend deeper into the university sector the principle that already underpinned the rise of the university institutes of technology. The policy of vocationalizing second-cycle studies was unveiled by a ministerial circular in January 1976. The overall goal of this new initiative was set forth unambiguously. It was "to give a high level academic [*scientifique*] training [*formation*] that will prepare students for working life and for the undertaking of professional responsibilities."[36] In an effort to stem the rising tide of eternal students flitting from one degree course to another, the government attempted to make the *licence* a terminal degree. And, to bring doctoral work closer in line with a "professional orientation," a new advanced diploma, the *diplôme d'études supérieures specialisées,* to be taken five years after the baccalauréat, was created.

Whatever the intentions of the reform, the reality was very different. The attempt to guide students away from careers in the educational system and to reknit the links between the university and the private sector through a policy of vocationalization had certain perverse results. Prime among them was that, for the first time, university graduates were forced to compete in that sector of the labor market where the commanding heights rested firmly in the grasp of the grandes écoles; more particularly, it rested with those who specialized in business management (*gestion*), on the one hand, and—with the introduction of engineering courses in the university—the state-sector grandes écoles, on the other. Not only did this increase competition between the elite and the nonelite sectors of higher education, it also resulted in the development by certain universities, especially those specializing in economics and business management, of a specific form of institutional coping strategy. This took the form of increased, though unofficial, selection of students at entry. Thus, competition between the elite and the nonelite subsystems of higher education led the latter into aping the characteristic features of the former. Nor was this emulation an entirely one-way process. For just as the management and economics faculties sought to preserve the value of their diplomas by becoming a pale reflection of certain grandes écoles, so the grandes écoles, for their part, began to assume characteristics hitherto the *image de marque* of the universities. This they did by expanding their research capacity. Traditionally, the task of the grandes écoles tended to be high-level technical training of a specific nature. Research was not previously seen as part of their prime remit.

It is perhaps too early to state definitively that the policy of vocationalization has failed, although the considerable effort by the present administration in this area suggests that the earlier version of this strategy was not as successful as had been hoped. Nevertheless, it is now evident that its relative lack of success sprang from a major oversight in higher education policy. Despite all the reforming zeal that successive governments lavished on higher education, in no instance, either in the sixties or the seventies, was such reform brought to bear on the real centers of excellence in French higher education. The turbulence of 1968 bypassed the grandes écoles. Although the university might roar its disapproval, the caravan of French elite higher education continued on its tranquil way.

What has been the overall effect of such a dual strategy of reform? And what have been the consequences for the linkage between secondary and higher education? Generally speaking, the development of French higher education over the past two decades has carried it increasingly in the direction of further stratification and selection. The one outstanding feature of higher education, its institutional segmentation, has grown. The introduction of the university institutes of technology stands as a specific illustration of this general trend. In this France is not alone. In

Britain the polytechnics, in Norway the regional colleges, and in the Irish Republic the national institutes of higher education are all examples of progressive segmentation of higher education along institutional lines.[37]

The question remains, of course, how the nature of this institutional segmentation affects both the type of qualifications demanded of students and the character of the obstacles that lie in wait for the unwary along the road to higher education. Of those successful in the baccalauréat, between 75 and 77 percent continue. In 1978–1979, 22.6 percent went directly to the labor market. Recalling that two types of institutions attached to particular lycées, the classes préparatoires des grandes écoles and the higher technicians sections, also dispense a form of postsecondary education, student flows to higher education were as follows in 1978–1979: 9.5 percent of all baccalauréat graduates entered the classes préparatoires, 11.7 percent entered the higher technicians sections; 44.7 percent entered the university, properly speaking; 9.4 percent entered the university institutes of technology; and a further 2.1 percent entered various, miscellaneous, residual establishments designated as having higher education status.[38]

These statistics, however, give no indication of the barriers the student must still confront. These are of two types: first, further instruments of selection associated with specific institutions or areas of study; second, the exceedingly high attrition rate among the hopeful at the end of the first year at the university. The classes préparatoires are an example of the former. Here the barriers set around elite education are ferocious. Baccalauréat results are not enough. Additional evidence is required from the individual's school record sheet (livret scolaire). Furthermore, the proportion of baccalauréat holders eligible for a place in the higher mathematics section is limited to 37 percent of all those sitting options C and D in any one year. Finally, lycées endowed with classes préparatoires are in no way obliged to fill all their places. Thus are absolute standards maintained and the fortunes of the few built on the frustrations of the many. And though the number of places in the antechambers of the elite have grown considerably in the course of the past decade,[39] there is still a heavy bias against females. They account for 31 percent of classes préparatoires students, by far the greater majority of whom are following a literary program. In the scientific programs, girls constitute 24 percent.[40]

The higher technicians sections, along with the university institutes of technology, also operate a policy of selection based on school performance in addition to successfully passing the baccalauréat. There is, however, an important difference between these two closed, short-cycle, postsecondary institutions. Whereas the dropout rate in the university institutes of technology is around 30 percent at the end of the first year, the corresponding figure for the higher technicians sections is around 10 percent.[41] This second type of selection, the very high dropout rate at the end of the first year, is one of the more remarkable aspects of university education in France. A follow-up study of the 1975 cohort of baccalauréat holders showed that by the end of the first year at the university, 35 percent of those traceable had not continued;[42] a further 12 percent had changed disciplines; and 20 percent were still in the first year in their original field of study. This leaves a mere 33 percent still on course. These figures hide a rather complex situation subject to variation between the different disciplines. High mortality rates are to be found in sciences (39 percent disappear at the end of the first year), social sciences (*sciences humaines*, 38 percent), and in economic and administrative sciences (38 percent). In fact, one student in five alone completes the diplôme d'études universitaires within the stipulated two-year time limit and goes forward to the licence without changing discipline.

Though many students of French higher education have had good cause to remark on its relative inefficiency in transforming qualified entrants from school into qualified university graduates, there are other factors at play beneath the bald statistics.[43] The first of these is the role first-year university studies fulfill from the student's point of view. For a substantial group, the first year involves little commitment to a particular diploma. Rather, it serves as a period of orientation and feeling the ground. For some, obviously, orientation means elimination, self-imposed or otherwise. For others, it is a period for chopping, changing, and testing the water. A third group may use this year to reach that age when they may sit the competitive entry examination for nursing studies, in the case of women, or for the *instituts d'études politiques*, in the case of men. The instituts d'études politiques provide an alternative route to the top posts in central government administration via the Civil Service Staff College (Ecole Nationale d'Administration). Another group may eventually opt to transfer to the university institutes of technology, whose diploma is often held to be more valuable in the marketplace. This shifting pattern of student flows at the lower level of university life is one of the major characteristics of French higher education. It is all the more remarkable since it takes place spontaneously, without the assistance of any comprehensive service of guidance and counseling.

Along with the phenomenon of self-selection, there are two disciplinary fields where selection is positive and institutionally based: medicine and pharmacy. Two factors have intervened in recent times to make selection more drastic than it ever was. The first results from demographic change and the belief by the national medical service that sufficient doctors are already available to meet the country's needs. The second is the well-known tendency of the medical profession to indulge in restrictive practices. Government restrictions on the number of students admitted to medical studies have been on the order of 15 percent over the last decade. An analysis of the 1975 cohort entering the university showed that 55 percent of all first-year enrollments in premedical courses were eliminated after one or two attempts at the competitive examination to enter full-fledged medical studies. This examination takes place at the end of the first year. Some of those failing subsequently move over to the two-year science course. In pharmacy, where similar institutional restrictions operate, the death rate is about 46 percent.

This Brownian movement between courses and across subject areas during the first year in the open sector of French higher education (such displacement activities are far less marked in the closed sector, whether short or long) may seem quintessential of the internal inefficiency of that institution.[44] There is, for all that, another way of viewing this phenomenon. Inefficient though it may appear, the structure of undergraduate studies does accommodate an extraordinary variety of student adjustment strategies, revisions in hopes, and changes in career plans. The practice that approximately one-third of the first year entrants can repeat a year or opt for another track without apparent penalty, a situation unthinkable in Britain, for instance, should not stand condemned outright. On the contrary, it may be the first time students are able to make a conscious, self-directed choice, free from the pressures of parents and teachers and free also from the built-in rigidities of a highly structured curriculum that hitherto determined their passage through the education system. The system, then, for good or for evil, does possess a margin of maneuverability for the bold, the desperate, or the incompetent. To this extent, it may effectively offset the considerable degree of predictability entailed in the type of higher education diploma course that results from the necessity to opt for one track in the baccalauréat as opposed to another.

But how predictable are the various option tracks in the baccalauréat? What weight or advantage does the university accord to them? In the case of the highly prestigious option C (mathematics and physical sciences) and option D, this is very clear. Three-quarters of the baccalauréat graduates holding these two combinations go forward to take science based courses at the university. Among those taking option A (literature) or B (economics and social studies) who go on to long-course higher education, 96 percent find themselves in law, economics, or the humanities. Twenty-seven percent of all first-time entrants in humanities followed the literature option in school. Among this student group, law is a good second choice.[45]

But this situation is further complicated by the massive reshuffling, sorting out, and readjustment at the end of the first year. From this, two other features emerge, both of them interesting. One involves movement patterns of students between courses, and the other, largely a consequence of the first, is a species of domino effect. Students holding highly valued options in the baccalauréat begin to force out those whose options are deemed less meritorious. They, in turn, are obliged to seek their fortunes in other fields of study.

Let us look at this more closely. Of those students leaving law at the end of their first year, 32 percent shift to the humanities, a further 21 percent move over to the social sciences, and 12 percent hie themselves to the university institutes of technology. Among those leaving administrative and social economics, there is a massive migration into economics—some 44 percent who are busy reorienting themselves. There is also a minor subflow into law (18 percent). In sciences, the predominant migratory pattern is toward the university institutes of technology (33 percent) or to first-year premedical courses (22 percent). This latter is particularly interesting since it suggests that for some students, at least, the first year of the science diplôme d'études universitaires générales (DEUG) serves as a temporary "parking lot," a place to mark time before trying their luck in the assault course leading to medicine.[46]

As for the domino effect, this is especially noticeable in the case of students who, holding option C, failed to get a place in medicine. Their port of refuge lies in economics, with the result that they tend to squeeze out those who opted for this track (option B) in school. Having thus been thrown out of their nest, option B students, in turn, move increasingly toward the humanities and law. Given the value stratification between the different options in the baccalauréat, it is obvious that as higher education itself becomes more marked by institutional segmentation, so a greater premium is conferred on those in possession of elite options in school. And this continues to operate in higher education. However, the same cascade effect in which holders of highly esteemed options drive out those with lesser ones also reinforces what was earlier termed aspirational segmentation. Such a phenomenon is especially marked in the case of school-leavers with option B, economics and social studies. They are far less inclined to compete in those areas where selection is both notoriously ruthless and feral, for instance in medicine and in the university institutes of technology.[47]

The Training of Teachers

Since the structure of French secondary education was, and higher education is, highly stratified and segmented, it is hardly surprising to find that the teaching profession itself shares many of these characteristics. Like many of its Continental counterparts, the French teaching body is an official service of the state. In times past its purpose was not merely to provide educational enlightenment. It was also to create, through uniformity of provision and practices, an intellectual unity and a cultural homogeneity that was seen by many as the essence of the Republic one and indivisible. Until well into the present century, the teaching body performed a particularly important political and ideological role: that of purveying a cultural model based on Cartesian rationalism, on the one hand, and secularism, on the other. In the end, it formed the shock troops of republicanism, fighting the good fight in support of the democratic revolutionary tradition of 1789 against the forces of Midian represented by the church, inherited wealth, vested privilege, and those vestiges of the French Right symbolic of the ancien régime. The teaching body was then the vanguard of the meritocracy against authoritarianism, and of radical republicanism against the forces of legitimism, Bonapartism, and French conservatism. This historic role, together with the services it rendered to the cause of political progressivism, the fact that it was seen as a bulwark for the French republican cause, has conferred upon the teaching body a considerable standing in the political life of the country. Thus, in France, education is far more closely linked with the national political process than it appears to be in Britain.

Even so, the French teaching profession is highly stratified, both regarding its patterns of training and the institutions where this takes place. Consequently, it is equally stratified in its status hierarchy. Between the humble *instituteur*, the primary school teacher trained in departmental *écoles normales* (local teacher training colleges), and that symbol of intellectual brilliance and erudition, the *professeur agrégé*, the finely honed product of the *école normale supérieure* who teaches in a classe préparatoire des grandes écoles or, alternatively, in the classe terminale of a lycée, a world of difference exists which is not merely financial. If the former is a workaday member of the teaching fraternity, the latter is seen as the very quintessence of the French intelligentsia whose activities overlap into all fields of intellectual activity and into national politics as well. Edouard Herriot, president during the 1920s, was an agrégé and a former teacher. So, too, was Georges Pompidou, president of the French republic during the early seventies. Prior to entering politics on de Gaulle's shirttails after 1944, M. Pompidou had been a lycée teacher and an agrégé.

The training structures for teachers in France tend not to have evolved as rapidly as elsewhere. The practical artisan tradition of teacher training in teacher training institutions outside the university (the écoles normales) is only today undergoing change. Teacher training for primary school teachers is only gradually and with reluctance being coordinated with courses given in the university. Thus, there is a basic rift both in institution and in status between primary school teachers trained in teacher training establishments and secondary school teachers, more theoretically inclined and disciplinary based, who receive their education at universities. The training of secondary school teachers is not primarily professional; nor is it based on the precepts of didactics or pedagogy. Prospective secondary school teachers follow the same courses as other students in the particular subject areas at the university. Their pedagogic training does not take place there. It takes place after they have sat and passed a highly competitive series of examinations, the most important of which is the *certificat d'aptitude pédagogique de l'enseignement secondaire* (CAPES), or the *agrégation* itself.[48]

Within secondary education, there are four broad bands of teacher qualification, represented by the agrégation, the *professeurs certifiés*, lower secondary school teachers, and teachers in the lycée d'enseignement professionnel. The agrégés, the elite of the teaching profession in France, are interesting not merely on account of their training but also because the agrégation is a dual qualification. Those holding it may teach in upper secondary schools and also in universities. Not only does this provide a firm intellectual and structural linkage between the two sectors, it also corresponds to those institutions, especially the classes préparatoires, which lie athwart both secondary and higher education.

The professeur agrégé usually holds a master's degree, involving at least four years of study at the university. He has also successfully surmounted the obstacles of the agrégation examination. Some idea of the severity of this examination may be garnered from these statistics: in 1980, 12,800 candidates sat it and 960 were successful, a rejection rate of 92.5 percent.[49]

Professeurs certifiés, holders of the CAPES, usually possess a licence as well. The latter involves three years of study at the university. They have passed the CAPES examination in one of fifteen areas. In 1980, of the 20,200 candidates 94.1 percent were rejected. Candidates for these two examinations are drawn either from university students (around 25 percent in each case) or from personnel already teaching or in school administration at the secondary level. Lower secondary school teachers, by contrast, are recruited mainly from primary school teachers, are at least thirty years old, have at the minimum three years of teaching experience, and hold a first-cycle university diploma, for example, the diplôme d'études universitaires générales. They are usually required to teach two subjects (*professeurs bivalents*).

Finally, there is the group of teachers in the lycée d'enseignement professionnel. They are trained in one of the six national apprenticeship training colleges (écoles normales nationales d'enseignement professionnel), a course that lasts about two years. Admission to these establishments is, once again, highly competitive and limited to those holding a two-year university diploma and who, in addition, have practical experience in their particular field.[50]

If this is the general structure of the French teaching profession, there are a number of characteristics that set it apart from its equivalents elsewhere. First, it is not the qualification alone that gives an individual teacher status. This requires, in addition, that the individual be nominated into a permanent post. Such a nomination depends on having succeeded in one of the above examinations and is undertaken by the central Ministry of Education or its regional educational officer, the *recteur*. The significance of this is considerable since it determines both the nature of the recruitment and also the status of teachers. Recruitment, as we have seen, is national through competitive examination. And the number of successful candidates is directly related to the number of posts the central administration has assigned across the country. Once nominated into a post, the individual is officially termed a teacher and also a civil servant, with a lifetime income and guaranteed job security. Less of an advantage, he or she is subject to periodic inspection by the national corps of inspectors.

If such a highly competitive system upholds high formal competence for the teaching profession, it also makes for a relatively unadventurous body, to whom innovation is not necessarily rewarding. The long preparation required to sit the national competitive examinations, and its formal rigor, tends to make for a body that, though politically radical, is extremely conservative in professional matters.

The second feature of the French teaching profession is that formal training in matters didactic and pedagogic takes place after success in one of the national competitive examinations. This is not in the hands of the university and is still less influenced by professors of education, who, in France, tend to be rather few and relatively powerless. Rather, the main source of influence and the main value-allocating body is the National Inspectorate, which is in charge of various courses of induction and pedagogical training in various specialized training centers linked to the National Ministry of Education. In other words, the training of teachers, in contrast to the development of a disciplinary competence, is contained in a separate subsystem of higher education located not in the university so much as in the inspectorate and the ministry.

This separation of powers explains a great deal of the reluctance of those in charge of teacher induction to relinquish responsibility to the university. Such a move would reduce the influence of the ministry and its servants in this area; it is also held that the university is not capable of upholding standards similar to those imposed by central authority.

Then, too, it is believed that if both disciplinary education and practical training were united within the university, it would lead to further ideological destabilization in the teaching profession. Considerations such as these have been instrumental in the reluctance of the National Inspectorate to yield responsibility for initial teacher training to the universities. It also explains why the historic structures of separate teacher training colleges, weakly associated with the university in the form of the écoles normales, have persisted for so long in France.

Mediating Bodies

The high degree of stratification within the teaching body, coupled with the responsibility for professional training resting in hands other than those of the university, means that the mediating bodies in France tend to be located elsewhere in the system. In this, it is different from Britain, for instance. Though the teaching body itself is both numerous and relatively highly unionized, it is characterized by a high degree of cleavage, both professional and political. Teachers in France, as elsewhere, are organized along two lines: level in the educational system—for example, primary school teachers grouped in the Syndicat National des Instituteurs—and subject groups. Moreover, there is a political split between Right and Left among French teacher organizations which makes them far more fragmented than their fellows in Britain, Sweden, or Denmark. Though all teacher organizations come together in an umbrella organization, the Federation de l'Education Nationale, this body is, in fact, composed of fifty-four different organizations, subunions, and associations, whose interests are highly divergent. Hence it is by no means an easy matter to push forward with reform since this entails a large degree of consensus among all interests, and consensus is often more easily obtained in resistance to reform than in its advancement. However, it is not without significance that the main backing for creating expanded secondary education came from the primary school teachers, the instituteurs, who saw in this reorganization the opening of promotions and an accrued status.

Within the teaching body, however, one crucial association stands out. This is the Societé des Agrégés, which brings together, irrespective of subject and disciplinary allegiance, that select band of elite teachers in upper secondary school, the classes préparatoires, and the university. Though it may be somewhat exaggerated to attribute to this one body the responsibility for maintaining intact the elite tradition in French education at a time when popular demand was toward democratization, yet it is nevertheless a fact that this association is extremely powerful.

Its power derives from its permeation and penetration across key institutions in the educational system, in political life, and in other fields of central administration. As a stalwart of the French intellectual tradition, with members and sympathizers in all the crucial policy and value-allocating bodies in society, it is one of the most influential elements in maintaining intact and untouched such national institutions as the baccalauréat and the classes préparatoires, of which its members are often the most brilliant products and where they tend to be the most concentrated. Furthermore, the Societé des Agrégés links with that other mediating body, the National Inspectorate, which recruits members from its ranks.

The National Inspectorate, unlike its British counterpart, has wide-ranging powers. Not only is it the secular arm of the minister, translating political directives into educational practice; it also plays an essential role in determining promotion and advancement of individual teachers. In short, the French National Inspectorate still retains that inquisitorial puissance that its British counterpart let fall twenty years ago. Promotion and advancement for individual teachers depends on the inspector's formal assessment of teaching ability and competence. On the average, such an assessment is carried out every two years and the result duly noted in the teacher's dossier. Such a form of administrative accountability is a device by which nationally determined norms are upheld and maintained. We have already noted the role played by the inspectorate in initial teacher training once candidates have been successful in the various national competitive examinations. From this it is readily apparent that the role of the inspectorate is to lay down the value framework, the norms and concepts of what is held to be good practice. Given that it is also charged with the upkeep of these norms, the power of this institutionalized mediating body cannot be overestimated. Not only is the inspector judge and jury in his own case, he is the national norm incarnate. Finally, the inspectorate has a no less crucial activity in the elite sector of French education. Appointments of teachers to the classes préparatoires des grandes écoles are made by a joint committee composed of five university teachers and five national inspectors.[51]

We have touched upon only three mediating bodies, but they are the most significant. If we put these together, we can arrive at an explanation for the maintenance of the elite subsystem in both secondary and higher education in France. The stratification and divergent interests of the French teaching profession, plus its civil servant status (which makes it subject to the rigors of administrative accountability), means that it is relatively weak in determining overall, positive national education policy. This does not mean that it is possible to make national policy in education without the agreement of teachers. But in determining national norms, in the maintenance and upkeep of those elements and institutions that play a vital part in shaping the elite subsector of the French education system, the decisive influence lies neither in the hands of the university nor in those of teachers overall. Rather, the determinant value-allocating bodies are a series of interlocking subgroups that occupy portal positions in the central administration of education and hold posts in the key institutions that, within the confines of a certain limited number of upper secondary schools, are also part of higher education.

Certainly, the university exercises considerable influence on the tracks pupils choose. But the university, strictly speaking, is neither the most important nor the most crucial influence on the upper secondary school. The prime element is rather the grandes écoles and their preparatory classes. It is a delicate matter to assess the impact one type of institution may exercise compared to another. But as far as direct influence is concerned, it is remarkable that the one feature setting off the elite classes préparatoires/grandes écoles nexus from the subelite classe terminale (thirteenth grade)/university linkage is the relatively direct flow, in the case of the former, and the degree of subsequent adjustment at the end of first-year university study, in the case of the latter. Once selected at age eighteen, the prospective entrant to the classes préparatoires is marked off from his or her fellows not merely by a separate curriculum but also because he or she is now subject to a sponsorship mode of social mobility in education. The dropout rate is low and the degree of self-adjustment and reorientation is limited. By contrast, the university entrant, while still subject to a competitive mode of educational mobility, is also forced into a position whereby he or she must readjust to the new type of courses available. Such a strategy of adjustment means that the influence of the university upon the career paths of school-leavers is, relatively speaking, more diffuse and less direct, save in those elite sectors of the subelite system, such as medicine.

Conclusion

On paper, at least, the number of reforms that have taken place in French education, secondary as well as higher, are legion. Since 1959 the sheer volume and scope of the reforming impulse in France is equalled only by Sweden. The outcome of these changes, symbolically represented by the creation of the comprehensive middle school and the dual-track, upper secondary lycées, has been to bring forward a very high proportion of the school population to those areas of the education system hitherto the preserve of the elite. But this development has not been accompanied by the complaint often heard elsewhere that the "comprehensivization" of secondary education means a decline in intellectual standards.[52] The proportion of the age group qualified to enter higher education has more than doubled over the past sixteen years, a situation which, if not directly comparable to that of the United States, is rather more heartening than the dismal position of the United Kingdom, where the proportion of the age group attaining that level formally required to enter higher education has stagnated for the past ten years.[53]

This achievement is perhaps all the more remarkable when one remembers that, in 1959, French secondary education—as opposed to postprimary schooling—was still fixed in what can only be described as its elite phase of development. Nevertheless, one should not be deceived by the rainbow image that paper reforms often tend to convey. Though outward appearances may change, it is often far more difficult to change the essential reality. And in France many problems remain. Premature tracking is still considerable. The linkage between secondary and higher education is still characterized by a high degree of selection via subject options and the public examination for which one presents. The outcome of this is that for the future higher education student the process of selection, in earlier times relatively protracted throughout the eleven-to-nineteen period, has become compressed into that crucial stage represented by the last two years of upper secondary schooling.

All indications are that such selection, ferocious by tradition, is becoming more so. There are a number of reasons for this, some linked with the particular nature of French reform strategies, others associated with more short-term external influences. With regard to the former, French reform strategy may be represented as dualistic: on the one hand, it sought to open up certain nonelite sectors of upper secondary and higher education to the imperatives of democratization; on the other, it adhered to an approach that in no way comprised its long-term and historic commitment to excellence. The influence of the elite subsystem has remained intact. In this respect we have seen that insofar as higher education influences the subject choice and career strategies of school students, such influence is far more potent in the elite sector than it is in the university. Regarding the consequences of short-term external factors, these, too, have worked toward reinforcing selection at entry to higher education, as well as institutional segmentation inside it. The economic crisis of 1974, by bringing the nonelite university sector into competition for a share of the labor market that had been the stomping ground of the elite grandes écoles, has forced the former to seek to improve its position by assuming some features and practices previously identified with the latter. Further selection is one such feature.

This internal self-adjustment of the nonelite university subsystem to short-term factors may be seen as an autonomous response of fine tuning within the overall context of major reform in both the institutional structure and the structure of courses in this sector. The purpose of the macroreform was primarily to bring the type of qualification dispensed by the university into line with the demands of economic change and working life. However, the fact that the present minister of education is engaged in working up a second version of this early 1980s reform suggests that the previous version was not overly successful. Nor, seen with the advantage of hindsight, did the restructuring of undergraduate courses serve to reduce the considerable dropout rate. It is one of the paradoxes of French higher education that as it moved toward becoming a mass system, so too did it move with equal rapidity toward yet further institutional segmentation, not only between elite and subelite establishments but also between those various institutions contained within the subelite university system.

To those in search of the ways and means of preserving excellence and at the same time throwing open higher education to broader sections of the school-age and adult population, France provides an interesting case study. It has managed to reconcile the apparently irreconcilable only because certain value-allocating and mediating bodies, for which the traditional notion of excellence was a paramount vested interest, managed to hold reform at arm's length. The French administrative, political, and educational elite carried out a strategy in which change was never extended to those institutions that still constitute its intellectual heartland, whether in secondary or in higher education.

Notes

1. Neave, "The Non-State Sector in the Educational Provision of Members States of the European Community," pp. 1–2.

2. Ministère de l'Education Nationale, *L'Enseignement Primaire et Secondaire en France*.

3. Ibid.

4. Neave, "Some Lessons from Western Europe" and "New Influences on Educational Policies in Western Europe During the Seventies," pp. 71–86; Marklund and Bergendal, *Trends in Swedish Education Policy*.

5. Bellaby, *Sociology of the Comprehensive School*.

6. Prost, *L'Enseignement en France 1800–1967*.

7. Ponteil, *L'Histoire de l'Enseignement en France*.

8. Société Française de Pédagogie. *Le Plan Langevin-Wallon de l'Enseignement en France*.

9. Organisation for Economic Co-operation and Development (OECD). *Reviews of National Policies for Education*, pp. 36ff.

10. OECD. *The Development of Secondary Education;* Neave, *How They Fared.*

11. OECD. *Reviews of National Policies for Education,* p. 37.

12. Lasibille et al., *De l'Inéfficacité du Système Français de l'Enseignement Superiéure.*

13. Ministère de l'Education Nationale, "Situation des Effectifs d'Elèves en 1981–82 dans les Classes Préparatoires des Grandes Ecoles."

14. Ministère de l'Education Nationale, "Situation d'Ensemble des Effectifs dans les Instituts Universitaires de Technologie en 1981–82."

15. Pautler, "Links between Secondary and Higher Education in France," p. 189.

16. Ibid.

17. Kosciusko-Morizet, *La Mafia Polytechnicienne.*

18. Lamoure, *Les Instituts Universitaires de Technologie en France.*

19. Ministère de l'Education Nationale, "Situation d'Ensemble des Effectifs dans les Instituts Universitaires."

20. This matter is explored for a number of Western European countries in the *European Journal of Education* 17, no. 3 (1982), whose contents are devoted to higher education and the state; Svensson, *Från Bildning Till Utbildning. Del II. Universitetensomandling Från 1100 Talet Till 1870 Talet;* Hammarstein, "University Development from the 16th to the 18th Centuries."

21. Neave, "On Wolves and Crises," pp. 20–21.

22. Gruson and Markiewicz-Lagneau, *L'Enseignement Supérieur et Son Efficacité,* p. 33.

23. Ministère de l'Education Nationale, *Scolarité des Elèves Nés en 1962.*

24. Office Statistique des Communautes Européennes, "Statistiques de l'Enseignement."

25. Ministère de l'Education Nationale, *Scolarité des Elèves Nés en 1962.*

26. Ministère de l'Education Nationale, "Les Resultats Provisoires du Baccalauréat et du Baccalauréat de Technicien."

27. Cerych and Colton, "Summarising Recent Student Flows," *European Journal of Education,* table I, pp. 17–19.

28. Ibid., table V, p. 29.

29. Bert, "Les Clés de l'Orientation," pp. 10–23.

30. Pautler, "Links Between Secondary and Higher Education in France," p. 186; Ministère de l'Education Nationale, "Les Resultats Provisoires du Baccalauréat et du Baccalauréat de Technicien."

31. Pautler, "Links Between Secondary and Higher Education in France," p. 186.

32. Ministère de l'Education Nationale, "Situation des Effectifs d'Elèves en 1982–1983 dans les Classes Préparatoires des Grandes Ecoles."

33. Pautler, "Links Between Secondary and Higher Education in France," p. 192.

34. Bert, "Les Clés de l'Orientation," pp. 10–23.

35. EURYDICE, *Impact of Demographic Change Upon the Education Systems of the Member States of the European Communities.*

36. Fragniere, "Changes in the Structure and Content of Courses," p. 109.

37. Quermonne, "The Place and Role of the University Institutes of Technology in the New French University," pp. 218–228; Boursin, *Les Instituts Universitaires de Technologie;* Neave, "Academic Drift," pp. 219, 225.

38. Gruson and Markiewicz-Lagneau, *L'Enseignement Supérieur et Son Éfficacité,* p. 39.

39. Pautler, "Links Between Secondary and Higher Education in France," p. 192; Ministère de l'Education Nationale, "Situation des Effectifs d'Élèves en 1982–83 dans les Classes Préparatoires."

40. Ibid.

41. "Quarante Diplômes Performants," pp. 22–25.

42. Ministère de l'Education Nationale, "Le Déroulement des Etudes Universitaires des Bacheliers Français de l'Année 1975 Inscrit à l'Université en 1975–6."

43. Ibid.

44. Gruson and Markiewicz-Lagneau, *L'Enseignement Supérieur et Son Efficacité.*

45. Pautler, "Links Between Secondary and Higher Education in France," p. 187.

46. Ministère de l'Education Nationale, "Le Déroulement des Etudes Universitaires," p. 4.

47. Pautler, "Links Between Secondary and Higher Education in France," pp. 185–195.

48. Leon, "Vers l'Integration de la Théorie et de la Pratique," pp. 2–5.

49. Neave, "The Status of the Teaching Body in the Member States of the European Community," pp. 5–6.

50. Leon, "Vers l'Integration de la Théorie et de la Pratique," p. 20.

51. "Reforme de l'Inspection Générale."

52. Benn and Simon, *Halfway There.*

53. Shattock, "Demography and Social Class," table 2, p. 384.

Bibliography

BELLABY, DAVID. *The Sociology of the Comprehensive School.* London: Methuen Books, 1979.

BENN, CAROLINE, and BRIAN SIMON. *Halfway There.* Maidenhead, England: McGraw-Hill, 1970.

BERT, CLAUDIE. "Les Clés de l'Orientation: Derrière les Mots, les Faits." *Le Monde de l'Education,* no. 91 (Feb. 1983): 10–23.

BOURSIN, JEAN-LOUIS. *Les Instituts Universitaires de Technologie.* Paris: Bordas, 1970.

CERYCH, LADISLAV, and SARAH COLTON. "Summarising Recent Student Flows." *European Journal of Education* 15, no. 1 (1980): 15–33.

EURYDICE. *Impact of Demographic Change Upon the Education Systems of Member States of the European Communities.* Brussels, September 1981.

FRAGNIERE, GABRIEL. "Changes in the Structure and Content of Courses." *Paedagogica Europaea* 13, no. 1 (1978): 107–119.

GRUSON, PASCAL, and JANINA MARKIEWICZ-LAGNEAU. *L'Enseignement Supérieur et Son Efficacité: France, Etats Unis, URSS, Pologne.* Paris: La Documentation Française, 1983.

HAMMARSTEIN, NOTKER. "University Development from the 16th to the 18th Centuries: A Comparative Perspective." *CRE Information* 62, no. 2 (1983): 81–88.

KOSCIUSKO-MORIZET, E. *La Mafia Polytechnicienne.* Paris: Seuil, 1974.

LAMOURE, JEAN. *Les Instituts Universitaires de Technologie en France.* Paris: Institut d'Education de la Fondation Européenne de la Culture, 1981.

LASIBILLE, G. L. LEVY-GARBOUA, L. NAVARRO-GOMES, and F. ORIVEL. *De l'Inéfficacité du Système Française de l'Enseignement Supérieure.* Paris: CREDOC/IREDU, 1980.

LEON, ANTOINE. "Vers l'Integration de la Théorie et de la Pratique dans la Formation Initiale et Continue des Enseignants du Second Degré." Communication à la Conference Européenne sur la Formation des Enseignants. Kolymbari, Crete, 1983. Mimeo.

MARKLUND, SIXTEN, and GUNNAR BERGENDAL. *Trends in Swedish Education Policy.* Stockholm: Swedish Institute, 1979.

Ministère de l'Education Nationale. "Situation d'Ensemble des Effectifs dans les Instituts Universitaires de Technologie en 1981–82." *Note d'Information 82–21.* Paris, June 1982.

———. *L'Enseignement Primaire et Secondaire en France.* Paris, 1982.

———. "Le Deroulement des Etudes Universitaires des Bacheliers Français de l'Année 1975 Inscrits à l'Université en 1975–6." *Note d'Information 82–13.* Paris, May 3, 1982.

———. "Les Resultats Provisoires du Baccalauréat et du Baccalauréat de Technicien: Session Normale de Juin 1982." *Note d'Information 82–27.* Paris, August 1982.

———. "Situation des Effectifs d'Elèves en 1981–82 dans les Classes Préparatoires des Grandes Ecoles." *Note d'Information 82–34.* Paris, September 27, 1982.

———. *Scolarité des Elèves Nés en 1962: Taux de Scolarisation par Age et par Niveau (Publique et Privée).* Paris, December 1982.

———. "Situation des Effectifs d'Elèves en 1982–3 dans les Classes Préparatoires des Grandes Ecoles." *Note d'information 83–08.* Paris, February 1983.

NEAVE, GUY R. *How They Fared: The Impact of the Comprehensive School Upon the University.* London: Routledge and Kegan Paul, 1975.

———. "On Wolves and Crises." *Paedagogica Europaea* 13, no. 1 (1978): 20–21.

———. "Academic Drift: Some Views From Europe." *Studies in Higher Education* 6, no. 2 (1979): 106–118.

———. "Some Lessons From Western Europe." In *Education and Equality,* ed. David Rubenstein. Harmondsworth, Middlesex, England: Penguin, 1979. Pp. 94–103.

———. "New Influences on Educational Policies in Western Europe in the

Seventies." In *Politics and Educational Change*, ed. Patricia Broadfoot, Witold Tulasiewicz, and Colin Brock. London: Croom Helm, 1981. Pp. 71–86.

————. "The Non-State Sector in the Educational Provision of Member States of the European Community." Memorandum to the Educational Services of the Commission of the European Community. Brussels, August 1983. Photocopy.

————. "The Status of the Teaching Body in the Member States of the European Community." Memorandum to the Educational Services of the Commission of the European Community. Brussels, August 1983. Xerox.

Office Statistique des Communautes Européennes. "Statistiques de l'Enseignement." *EUROSTAT 2/81*. Luxembourg, 1982.

Organisation for Economic Co-operation and Development. *Development of Secondary Education*. Paris, 1969.

————. *Reviews of National Policies for Education*. Paris, 1971.

PAUTLER, EMANNUELLE. "The Links Between Secondary and Higher Education in France." *European Journal of Education* 16, no. 2 (1981): 185–195.

PONTEIL, FELIX. *L'Histoire de l'Enseignement en France: Les Grandes Etapes 1789–1944*. Paris: Presses Universitaires de France, 1960.

PROST, ANTOINE. *L'Enseignement en France 1800–1967*. Paris: Presses Universitaires de France, 1968.

"Quarante Diplômes Performants." *Le Monde de l'Education* 90 (January 1983): 22–25.

QUERMONNE, JEAN-LOUIS. "The Place and Role of the University Institutes of Technology in the New French University." In *Short Cycle Higher Education: A Search for Identity*, ed. Dorotea Furth. Paris: OECD, 1973. Pp. 218–228.

"Reforme de l'Inspection Générale." *Le Republicain Lorrain*, January 19, 1983: 1.

SHATTOCK, MIKE. "Demography and Social Class: The Fluctuating Demand for Higher Education in Britain." *European Journal of Education* 16, no. 3–4 (1981): 381–392.

Société Française de Pédagogie. *Le Plan Langevin-Wallon de l'Enseignement en France*. Paris, 1964.

SVENSSON, LENNART G. *Från Bildning Till Utbildning. Del II. Universitetensomandling Från 1100 Talet Till 1870 Talet*. Goteborg: Lindomme, 1978.

2

The Federal Republic of Germany

ULRICH TEICHLER

IN THE COMPARATIVE ANALYSIS OF the relation between secondary and higher education, the Federal Republic of Germany is an instructive case. Here students who pass the final examination of the academic secondary school traditionally have had the automatic right to enroll in institutions of higher education, making the Federal Republic in this respect an extreme case of close linkage and tight coordination between the two levels. We can examine the preconditions as well as the strengths and weaknesses of this form of close relationship and thereby perhaps identify modes of connection that are useful analytically in other settings. Then, too, the nature of this German pattern causes the observer to conceive the organization of education somewhat differently than in countries where the two levels of education are more autonomous, and ideas about an active mutual shaping seem more appropriate. Two centuries of debate in Germany about a close correspondence between the tasks of academic secondary schools and those of universities, and about the need for an appropriate tuning of those tasks, have encouraged an awareness of a unitary inner logic in the educational system.

The traditional notion of a close coordination has been questioned to some extent in the changes that have taken place in the school and the university in the last twenty years. This questioning raises the issue of whether the Federal Republic and other industrialized countries follow a common trend in educational change or whether they preserve unique national patterns. Will the German system converge with others upon a common pattern of mass secondary and mass higher education or will the traditional concept of the *Abitur*—the final certification offered by the academic secondary stream—prevail, with only modest modification, as central to the understanding that these two major levels of education closely correspond to, and intimately complement, each other in a fashion fundamentally different from that found in most other countries.

Close examination of the German system should measurably broaden the comparative understanding of the relation between secondary and higher education. It is particularly useful to emphasize the peculiar features of the German relationship that challenge internationally prevalent notions drawn from experience elsewhere.

The Educational System

Three characteristics of the educational system in the Federal Republic of Germany are particularly indicative of the formal relationship between its schools and universities. First, the basic structure of secondary education is a tracking system. After four years of primary education for all (a requirement introduced after World War I), at the *Grundschule* (primary school), pupils must choose between three options: the *Hauptschule* (main school), where after finishing nine years of full-time schooling pupils typically attend part-time vocational schools, often combined with apprenticeship training, up to the age of eighteen; the *Realschule*, the intermediate track of secondary schools comprising the fifth to tenth year of education, normally leading to higher vocational schools that in turn lead to intermediate positions in the occupational hierarchy; or the *Gymnasium*, the academic track of the secondary schools that typically prepares the students for university education.

A second significant characteristic of the German educational system is that the student who reaches the thirteenth grade and passes the Abitur, the final examination of academic secondary education, is entitled to enroll in any field of study at any university. The Abitur is thus a certificate of successful completion of academic secondary education and signifies readiness ("maturity") to study at institutions of higher learning. In principle, it defines the point of transfer from academic secondary education to the university as merely a stage of self-allocation to specialized study, not as a stage of selection. The third characteristic is that German universities have more or less the same standards, including those of admission. Even though differences of prestige exist, students may, in principle, transfer freely from one institution to another at any time during the course of their studies.

These characteristics imply an extremely simple model. There are hundreds of ways of reaching the maturity needed for admittance to institutions of higher education. There are also areas of restricted admissions and selection procedures, and there are different types of institutions of higher education. Nevertheless, the tracking system, the Abitur, and the principle of equivalent university standards are the most important factors shaping the relation between secondary and higher education in the Federal Republic of Germany.

ACADEMIC SECONDARY EDUCATION AND THE *ABITUR*

In historical perspective, the Abitur may be seen as the major linking element.[1] Efforts to state formal prerequisites for university entrance can be observed in Prussia since the beginning of the eighteenth century. Most historians agree that the Abitur, as a final examination based on certain guidelines regarding school curricula and examination standards, and as the entitlement to enroll at institutions of higher education, was first introduced in 1788. It finally took its long-lasting shape in the so-called Humboldt-Süversche Reform of 1812.

The introduction of the Abitur has been closely linked to the interest of the absolutist state in having a highly qualified civil service. This final examination helped to set standards as well as to provide an *éntre billet* for capable persons from the lower social strata. At the same time, it helped raise the reputation of the universities and of the academic secondary schools. The universities were relieved of the task of offering preparatory courses; and, since all students had previously passed a demanding examination guaranteeing their maturity, a certain standard of excellence for all universities was ensured. The secondary schools were entrusted with the task of selecting among the most capable youth. They were charged with preparing them to be mature, that is, to be broadly educated; training them to work independently; ensuring they were capable of pursuing academic studies that require the understanding of fields of knowledge; and making certain that students select appropriate teachers and make use of the freedom of knowledge wisely. These tasks and responsibilities raised the status of the teachers in the academic schools and the status of the schools themselves. The teachers always considered themselves specialists in a select number of fields, not educational specialists like teachers in other types of schools.

Tracking systems and examination oriented education systems have been criticized frequently in recent decades as being outmoded with respect to reducing the gap between academic and vocational education, promoting equality of opportunity, and coping with the increasing social demand for education. Nevertheless, the historical tasks of such systems were to guarantee a certain minimum standard of achievement at all schools; to establish a meritocratic setting that would open schools, in principle, to all social strata and open careers to talented graduates; to weed out those who could not cope with school standards and thus with job requirements in the more demanding careers; and to establish a well-organized and clearly structured educational system.

These elements were also true for the *baccalauréat* in France and the entrance examination system of prewar Japan. But two additional elements of the Abitur were different. First, the student passing the final exam had the right to enroll at institutions of higher education. Thus, the student's transfer from secondary to higher education entailed only an allocation to a field of study, not selection. At first glance this may seem very surprising, for neither were the controls of a common *niveau* of the final examination as rigid as those in France, nor did the universities have any direct influence on the level of their intake, as in Japan. This may be explained by a considerable confidence that the interplay of administrative supervision by state ministries of education combined with the leeway given to individual school teachers guaranteed high standards. In a university system that has avoided a clear-cut hierarchy of institutions, the individual universities could also afford a relatively relaxed attitude toward entering students, knowing that the intake was uniformly high.

The second specific element of the Abitur refers to content. Transferring from secondary to higher education did not mean simply advancing a level; it was also a turning point from an educational setting to an arena where intellectual maturity was expected. It was a transition from relatively passive exposure to teaching and learning processes to one of open transmission and sharing of knowledge, as well as a transition from generalized to specialized learning. The 1812 reform of secondary education shaped the philosophical foundation of the Abitur. Maturity meant that the student had acquired sufficient broad knowledge as he was being taught by others to enable him to learn by himself. Also, during the same period, the neoclassical ideal became prevalent. According to the course requirements in the Humanistisches Gymnasium in Prussia in 1816, students in the last three years were required to take the following hours of instruction each week: twenty-four in Latin, twenty-one in Greek, eighteen in mathematics, twelve in German, nine in history/geography, and six in the sciences.[2]

Although the principle of the final examination of academic secondary education both as a prerequisite of, and as guaranteeing the right to, enrollment at universities was upheld for two centuries, access to higher education did, over time, undergo some significant changes. Curricula, institutions, and the final examinations were the subjects of many reform efforts, and changes took place that challenged a clear-cut tracking system of secondary education and access to higher education.

Debates on academic secondary education, the concept of maturity, and the pattern of the final examinations tended to focus on the underlying educational and philosophical priorities, as well as on the issue of breadth and depth of knowledge. Four types of changes took place:

1. The range of subjects was broadened. As neoclassical ideals in education were gradually challenged, traditional academic secondary education began to incorporate the study of modern foreign languages and reduce emphasis on ancient ones.

2. A variety of types of academic secondary schools were established. In the mid-nineteenth century a so-called *Real-Gymnasium* already existed, which added courses in English, French, and Latin while deleting ancient Greek. In the first decade of the twentieth century, graduation from *Ober-Realschulen* (no courses in Latin), as well as from schools for women, might have led to some institutions of higher education. In the twentieth century a variety of types of Gymnasien that emphasized ancient languages, mathematics and sciences, social sciences, economics, or fine arts developed; some of them, however, led to so-called *Fakultätsreife* or *fachgebundene Hochschulreife*, the right only to enroll in those fields of university study corresponding in focus to the specialized secondary school curricula.[3]

3. The number of subjects in which students were examined in the Abitur was reduced. As part of its first major decision regarding upper secondary education, in 1960, the Permanent Conference of the Ministers of Education, the highest postwar authority for the coordination of the educational system, made a significant reduction. The traditional concept of maturity was confirmed, but various types of institutions were recognized as formally equivalent, or as at least leading to the right to enroll in fields of study corresponding to prior specialization in secondary education.

4. Individualized specialization in upper secondary education was established. A second major agreement by the ministers conference in 1972 substituted a course system for the old school-class system. Instead of having to take more than ten subjects, eleventh-to-thirteenth-grade students were able to individualize their program and focus on a select number of subjects in three different fields (languages-literature-fine arts, social sciences, or mathematics-sciences-technical fields). The Abitur examination was limited to four subjects selected by the students. In recent years, however, this system of individualized specialization has been frequently criticized and steps have been taken to broaden course requirements to some extent.

These four changes offset the curricular uniformity of academic secondary education. But they did not challenge the basic characteristics of the relationship between secondary and higher education: the tracking system, early selection, and the right of those passing the final examination to enroll at universities.

After World War II, in place of tracking systems many countries postponed the process of selection and established a more open system of education. In the Federal Republic of Germany, however, the basic structure of a tracking system was upheld, but various elements were added which led toward an increased openness. Some states, especially in the 1950s, established schools designed to promote upward mobility within the system (downward mobility existed to a large extent as a dropout phenomenon). Talented pupils of the main school were able to transfer to the intermediate track of a specific type of school, and from there promising pupils could transfer to special types of academic secondary schools, thus correcting their early decision after a few years. Also, various part-time and full-time schools were established to offer employed persons a chance to acquire the Abitur. This "second route of education" (*Zweiter Bildungsweg*) was designed as a mechanism to increase equality of opportunity, but in effect it frequently helped dropouts from higher social backgrounds to correct their earlier failures.

Further, some comprehensive secondary schools were established in the 1960s and the 1970s. These schools have made it easier for students to transfer from one curricular program to another, but the requirements for the Abitur are as demanding as they are at academic secondary schools. Thus, tracking is blurred but not eliminated. Programs formally equivalent to general and vocational ones found elsewhere are not found in comprehensive schools at the upper secondary educational level. Finally, some schools established in the seventies lead to the Abitur and also incorporate full-fledged vocational training. These schools are still in a stage of experimentation.

CHANGES IN HIGHER EDUCATION

The relation between secondary and higher education has been affected by changes in the formal structure of the latter. Up to the late sixties, the Abitur was a prerequisite for admittance to all institutions of higher education except art academies, and as late as the 1950s only those institutions that offered a broad range of faculties, especially those of theology, philosophy, social sciences, and medicine, were considered universities. During the fifties and sixties, technical colleges, teacher-training colleges, and theological seminaries raised their status in order to become formally equal to the traditional university: the right to grant the *Habilitation,* the *venia legendi,* was the most obvious symbol of being equivalent. The development of higher education up to the late sixties can therefore be considered a process both of increasing homogeneity through upgrading and of raising the standards of those institutions that had formerly not been recognized as belonging to the university level (*wissenschaftliche Hochschulen*). Art academies (music, fine arts), which traditionally had special admissions regulations and enrolled talented persons who had not passed the Abitur, were exceptions.

In 1968 the state governments agreed to establish nonuniversity-level institutions of higher education. Former engineering colleges and higher vocational schools were upgraded to *Fachhochschulen*. These institutions, established in 1971, offer three-and-one-half-year courses, especially in engineering, business administration, and social work. The process of upgrading was accompanied by new regulations regarding access. Previously, individuals who had completed the main school as well as apprenticeship training could, after some years of occupational experience, register for selective admission examinations. Now, for admittance to the Fachhochschule students either have to successfully complete the twelfth grade of the academic secondary school or the two-year vocational high school (*Fachoberschule*) that follows successful completion of the Realschule. Thus, the Abitur lost its status as the only gate to higher education.

Students in the Fachhochschule are entitled to transfer to corresponding fields at universities after a certain period of study or to any field at the university after graduation.[4] According to recent estimates, about 10 percent of the graduates at these institutions transfer to universities. Further, around 1970 it was popular to combine all institutions of higher education into *Gesamthochschulen* (comprehensive universities) and thus integrate, or at least ease transfer between, nonuniversity-level and university-level programs. Only six institutions offering partially or fully integrated programs were established, however.[5]

EXPANSION AND CHANGES IN ACCESS

The variety of types of secondary education and of routes to higher education grew under conditions of rapid expansion and, in turn, contributed to increased enrollment. As table 2.1 shows, the percentage of secondary school graduates of the corresponding age group entitled to enroll at institutions of higher education grew from 5.6 percent in 1960 to 10.9 percent in 1970. Partially owing to the introduction of new routes leading to short-cycle higher education, the number of graduates reached 20.2 percent in 1975 and moderately increased to 22.4 percent in 1980. A further substantial increase can be expected in the future: projections for 1990 go as high as 38.4 percent.[6]

Calculated on the basis of today's definition of institutions of higher education, 8.7 percent of the corresponding age group enrolled at institutions of higher education in 1960. The corresponding figures in 1970 and 1980 were, as table 2.1 shows, 14.8 and 19.5 percent. Among all beginning students at institutions of higher education in the Federal Republic of Germany in 1980, 68 percent had passed the final examination of an academic secondary school; 5.5 percent came from specialized academic secondary schools; 1.8 percent had previously attended

TABLE 2.1

SECONDARY SCHOOL GRADUATES, ACCESS TO HIGHER EDUCATION, AND HIGHER EDUCATION GRADUATES IN THE FEDERAL REPUBLIC OF GERMANY, 1960–1980

	1960	1965	1970	1975	1980
Secondary school graduates (in 1,000)					
Academic track	55.4	51.7	89.2	125.2	168.0
Higher vocational track				46.7	50.6
Total	55.4	51.7	89.2	172.7	218.6
Secondary school graduates as percent of corresponding age group*					
Academic track	5.6	7.2	10.9	14.7	17.2
Higher vocational track				5.5	5.2
Total	5.6	7.2	10.9	20.2	22.4
Beginning students in higher education (in 1,000)					
At universities	65.4	63.2	92.2	120.7	138.2
At short-cycle institutions	20.6	26.5	29.2	42.8	51.7
Total	86.0	89.7	121.4	163.4	189.9
Beginning students as percent of corresponding age group*					
At universities	6.6	8.8	11.2	14.2	14.2
At short-cycle institutions	2.1	3.7	3.6	5.0	5.3
Total	8.7	12.5	14.8	19.2	19.5
Higher education graduates (in 1,000)**					
From universities	27.9	40.5	47.3	70.7	70.9
From short-cycle institutions	11.3	15.3	22.0	30.6	33.3
Total	39.2	55.8	69.3	101.3	104.2
Graduates as percent of corresponding age group†					
From universities	3.4	4.3	7.2	9.6	8.9
From short-cycle institutions	1.4	1.6	3.3	4.1	4.2
Total	4.8	5.9	10.5	13.7	13.1

SOURCE: Based on Wissenschaftsrat, *Zur Lage der Hochschulen Anfang der 80er Jahre*, 2 vols., Köln 1983.
* 18–21 years old.
** Final exams except for those doctoral promotions based on previous degrees.
† 23–27 years old.

comprehensive schools; 2.6 percent had taken a "second route" to higher education; 16 percent had successfully finished vocational high school; 0.5 percent had passed special examinations for the gifted; and 5.6 percent had acquired the right to enroll at institutions of higher education by other means.[7] Taking into account variations existing among the states, one could easily list several hundred routes to higher education.[8]

Traditionally, almost all qualified graduates of secondary education could, and did, enroll at institutions of higher education. But the possibility of enrolling at any institution in any field has been gradually restricted since the mid-1960s, in medical fields at first and later in others. In 1981, 34 percent of all beginning students at universities in the Federal Republic of Germany were enrolled in studies administered by the Central Admissions Agency, equally divided between highly selective fields and moderately selective fields for which a mechanism of regional distribution had been established.[9]

Regulations regarding access to *numerus clausus* fields have been changed several times, but all regulations have been aimed at establishing a compromise between selective admissions and the right of the qualified school graduates to enroll at the next level. Priority has always been given to the better qualified student. In contrast to individuals who passed an Abitur, those who successfully completed vocational high school have not had the right to enroll at short-cycle higher education institutions; however, most fields of study at these institutions tend to be open for all applicants. Students themselves do not necessarily intend to enroll at institutions of higher education any longer. According to recent estimates, about 80 percent of qualified secondary school graduates enroll at these institutions, some of these only after a few years of military service, vocational training, or other intermissions.[10]

Thus, both restricted admissions as well as declining intentions to continue have changed the traditional picture of the more or less automatic transfer from secondary to higher education. This does not mean, however, that the modal relation between the two levels in Germany has completely eroded; the transfer from primary to secondary education continues to be, by far, the more important selection point. Neither has the track structure been abolished; only the openness and variety in secondary education has grown. The right of the qualified school graduate to enroll at any institution in any field has been neither completely upheld nor completely eroded. The principle of more or less equal standards maintained by all universities has not been fundamentally shaken. Considering the basic understanding of the Abitur, the changes have been substantial, but considering the rapid expansion of education and widespread ideas about the need for structural change in the process of expansion, the changes have been moderate.

The Impact of Secondary on Higher Education

Assuming the analogy to a traffic or delivery system, secondary education shapes higher education through its output, or at least through the share of its output transferred to higher education. From such a perspective Germany could be considered an extreme case in which higher education is strongly shaped by secondary education, since the higher education system, in general, and the individual institutions, in particular, have been obligated to admit all qualified secondary school graduates intending to enroll.

But, paradoxically, in a system in which higher education has to accept delivery from the lower level, the notion of secondary education as shaping higher education does not prevail; instead the logic of the educational system shapes the relationship between various stages or areas. The Abitur, both in terms of the implicit right to enroll at institutions of higher education and as a concept of educational division of labor between secondary and higher education, is not so much a part of secondary education as an element of linkage.

This leads us to a general contention not at all specific to the German setting: that is, secondary education does not automatically deliver upward; instead, the system of access and admissions determines the selection and allocation of students as well as the role institutions of higher education themselves play. Educational concepts, curricula, and achievement standards in higher education are not set by the outcomes of secondary education; rather, general concepts regarding the educational system determine the tasks of secondary and higher education. The focus of this analysis will therefore be the impact of the "intake" and its modes on higher education, regardless of whether they can be attributed primarily to secondary education, to the conditions of access and admissions, or to overall concepts about the educational system.

THE QUANTITATIVE DEVELOPMENT OF HIGHER EDUCATION

According to the traditional understanding of the Abitur entitling a person to enroll at any university in any field of study, the higher education system had to adjust to the supply provided by academic secondary education. This holds true not only for the system in general but also for the individual institution. The adjustment requires a high short-term flexibility, for the number of freshmen in any field of study in a given institution may vary substantially from one semester to another. The universities must also cope with long-term changes in the supply of qualified secondary school graduates.

The impact on higher education of the increasing number of graduates from secondary schools can be summarized according to the following parameters: (1) the overall quantitative development of higher education; (2) changes in the access and admissions system; (3) the structure of the higher education system, that is, types of institutions and courses; (4) the quantitative development of individual institutions of higher education. The third parameter will be discussed in a later section.

As documented in table 2.1, the number of secondary school graduates entitled to enroll at universities almost tripled from 1960 to 1980. In addition, many youths became eligible to enroll at short-cycle institutions. The 1960 proposals of the Science Council[11] represented the first major planning document to indicate that substantial efforts were needed to expand higher education in accordance with the expected growth in student numbers. The Sputnik shock, as well as arguments by the Organisation for Economic Co-operation and Development (OECD) regarding the need to expand higher education in order to insure economic growth, affected the thinking of educational planners. Efforts to reduce inequality of educational opportunity also grew. As a result of efforts to expand higher education, the university student-teacher ratio was successfully reduced during the period from 1960 to 1970, although the number of students almost doubled.[12]

This does not imply that quantitative policies interpreted the traditional right of qualified graduates to enroll at universities to mean a strict social demand policy of higher education. In the early sixties, social demand and manpower requirements did not seem to be in conflict. But in the latter half of the 1960s both the quantitative stagnation of medical fields and efforts to introduce short-cycle higher education indicated that social demand was not to be the major criterion for higher education planning, at least as far as the pattern of fields, courses, and institutions was concerned.

There are conflicting interpretations regarding the historical moment at which the intent to expand higher education was considerably shaken. According to some views, expansionist policies dominated until the early seventies. Then, financial constraints as well as growing economic problems led, beginning in 1972–1973, to a more cautious policy. The view I consider more accurate is that reservations regarding the expansion of higher education had been very strong in the 1960s.[13] Most university representatives did not conceive of the universities as beneficiaries, but rather as victims, of the growing demand for higher education. In spite of the reduced student-teacher ratio and the rapid growth of expenditures in higher education, there seemed to be a definite concern about lowering of standards and overcrowding of the universities. Also, the first systematic forecast made on the basis of the manpower requirement approach, in 1967, concluded that the number of university graduates in the early 1980s might be twice as high as the number of appropriate job offerings. Many employer representatives warned about the danger of an "academic proletariat."

According to both views, higher education policies since 1972 assumed that expansion should continue but at a lower pace than the increasing demand. The policy to keep the expansion of higher education within bounds was reinforced by deliberations of the Science Council in 1975 regarding demographic development: since a reduction of student numbers was predicted for the late eighties, owing to declining births after 1964, the targets for the expansion of facilities, especially for the construction of buildings, were lowered. Views regarding job prospects of graduates were also very pessimistic at that time, contributing to a widespread sentiment that further expansion ought to be avoided.

In 1976–1977, however, higher education policy in the Federal Republic of Germany took a surprising turn toward what was called the "opening of higher education." This political compromise was made by all major parties, governments, and major interest groups and was primarily based on two considerations. First, concern had grown about the detrimental educational effects of the numerus clausus on secondary schools. Second, the argument had gained wide support that for some years all institutions of higher education were obliged to accept larger numbers of pupils without a corresponding enlargement of staff and facilities. This was proposed to avoid intolerable educational disadvantages for those age groups belonging to the demographic bulge.

In the early eighties, debate about the continuance of such a policy was revived, given the projected 25 percent increase of students within five years and the prognosis of even further substantial increases, without a corresponding enlargement of staff and facilities.[14] Efforts to discourage secondary school graduates from turning to higher education have become stronger, and probably the number of numerus clausus fields has increased, but the right of qualified graduates to enter institutions of higher education is no longer challenged as it was in the debates of the early seventies. This prevailing higher education policy in the Federal Republic of Germany is based neither on a firm belief in social demand as a proper guideline nor, by any means, on the belief that expansion of higher education is needed to guarantee a required manpower supply. Rather, it is a carryover of the traditional understanding of the Abitur, which survived even though many modifications occurred.

These higher education policies were only in part the outcome of an open political process. Court decisions regarding the access and admissions system also played an important role. From about the mid-1960s medical fields, and subsequently others, introduced selective admissions. It only seemed a matter of time until open access to higher education for the qualified student would be completely eroded. In 1972, while the Federal Constitutional Court in an important decision principally upheld the right of the *Abiturient* to enroll at universities as an integral part of the constitutional right to freely select an occupation, it also provided a legal basis for restricted admissions. Numerus clausus was justified if the capacity of the university was exhaustively utilized. Clearly, the government could not increase expenses for higher education without endangering other responsibilities and if enrollment growth obviously contradicted manpower requirements.[15] In 1977 the Federal Constitutional Court underscored the right of qualified graduates more strongly. It also ruled that admission tests could only be introduced if they measured capabilities different from those measured by final exams in the secondary schools.[16]

The admissions regulations for numerus clausus fields subsequently attempted to demonstrate a compromise between restricted admissions and some chance for all those qualified to enroll. Simply put, the 1972 regulations introduced selective admissions on the basis of high grade point averages and access for those who did not get selected the first time by a quota based on waiting time. Because the waiting periods surpassed six years in some fields, a new compromise was introduced in the late seventies. The new scheme was a weighted lottery system that gave an edge to students with high grade point averages and high admission test scores but did not exclude opportunities for others.

The ruling of the Federal Constitutional Court and the subsequent establishment of corresponding admissions schemes affected the traffic from secondary education to universities. First, the ruling neither demanded open access for qualified graduates nor permitted systematic quantitative planning of higher education on the basis of manpower or financial rationales; instead it anticipated solutions based on compromise. Second, it neither restored nor abolished the principle that qualified secondary graduates might enroll in any field of study, since the less successful of them had a less than average chance to enroll in numerus clausus fields. Third, it gave some leeway for the development of moderate hierarchies of institutional prestige but counteracted rigid institutional hierarchies by means of centralized admissions systems. Fourth, it also had an ambiguous impact on individual university intake. On the one hand, it did not uphold the tradition of open enrollment, but on the other, it pushed universities to increase intake by stating that they could only refuse incoming students if capacity was exhaustively utilized. The risk of losing court trials led in most cases to increased intake.

The impact of secondary education on the size of institutions of higher education ought to be explained more thoroughly. In many countries the expansion of higher education led only to marginally increased numbers of students at many prestigious universities. In the Federal Republic of Germany, however, all universities grew substantially. Table 2.2 provides an overview of the growth in enrollment at sixteen major universities from 1955 to 1980. In 1980 the number of students at these universities was, on the average, more than four times higher than twenty-five years earlier. Table 2.2 shows that, contrary to public belief, this increase did not primarily affect universities in large cities; it took place at a similar pace at universities located in intermediate-size cities and small towns.

The right of qualified students to enter any institution in any field leads, of course, to increased enrollment if there are larger numbers of qualified students ready to enter those institutions. Higher education planning measures around 1960 aimed primarily at enlarging the size of existing universities. In the mid-1960s, however, the pendulum swung toward establishing new universities. A major reason for this shift was the desire to reduce regional enrollment barriers by providing better regional institutional dispersion. Although many new universities were established, the growing number of students was primarily absorbed by the enlargement of older ones.[17] This was in part the consequence of slower planning and construction at new institutions and of their difficulties in attracting large numbers of students. But to a considerable extent it was also a result of the access and admissions policies of the older institutions, because policies regarding both open and numerus clausus fields required extensive utilization of available resources. Higher education planning from the early sixties emphasized expansion. Thus, individual universities might establish new areas of research and improve the quality of teaching most easily by advocating the enlargement of the institution. It is not surprising then that institutional policies were largely in tune with only moderate restriction of the open enrollment tradition.

THE QUALITATIVE DEVELOPMENT OF HIGHER EDUCATION

The traditional notion of the Abitur certainly influenced the quantitative development of German higher education. But the underlying concept of maturity, accorded to those who passed the final examination of academic secondary education, had a substantial influence on higher education's qualitative development.

A fairly high level of beginning student competence has always been taken for granted. The concept of tertiary education, that is, education

TABLE 2.2

STUDENT ENROLLMENT AT SELECT WEST GERMAN UNIVERSITIES, BY SIZE OF CITY

Large cities (500,000 and more)			
Berlin (free university)	8,772	15,438	42,929
Frankfurt	12,016	22,574	24,683
Hamburg	6,765	15,206	36,499
Köln	9,521	18,711	36,495
München	12,016	22,574	41,997
Average enrollment	8,449	16,613	36,521
Intermediate cities (100,000–500,000)			
Bonn	7,122	13,208	34,399
Freiburg	5,145	10,905	19,127
Heidelberg	5,323	10,944	21,563
Kiel	2,136	6,416	14,039
Mainz	3,598	7,944	22,309
Munster	6,145	14,665	38,662
Nurnberg-Erlangen	3,694	9,143	19,103
Wurzburg	2,262	7,030	13,537
Average enrollment	4,428	10,032	22,842
Small cities (less than 100,000)			
Gottingen	4,905	9,995	28,834
Marburg	4,216	7,929	12,705
Tubingen	5,177	9,643	19,904
Average enrollment	4,766	9,187	19,148

SOURCE: Based on W. Albert and C. Oehler, *Materialien zur Entwicklung der Hochschulen 1950 bis 1967*, Hannover: Hochschul-Informations-System 1969, Bundesminister für Bildung und Wissenschaft, *Grund- und Strukturdaten 1981/82*, Bonn: BMBW, 1981.

for persons eighteen years and older, which is found to some degree or another in the United States, Sweden, and Japan, does not find support in the Federal Republic of Germany. Nor, as in the United States, is there an effort to improve equality of educational opportunity regarding access to higher education to compensate for inequalities at the lower educational levels. For example, it was almost unconceivable to the German members of the German-U.S. Study Group on Access to Higher Education[18] that their American counterparts thought foreign guest workers should be an important issue in German higher education. As long as the children of foreign workers hardly succeed in coming close to the Abitur or passing it, any measures of compensation are considered the task of primary, secondary, or vocational education.

There remains a strict division in course work between secondary and higher education. For those who have not taken the traditional route, programs for completing secondary education are only rarely incorporated in universities as preparatory programs. Rather, they tend to be established as special types of secondary schools. German universities are also very reluctant to establish any kind of remedial work. And it would be inconceivable in Germany to grant university credits for achievements in secondary education. The concept of maturity implies a strict division. Academic secondary schools are in charge of the general foundations of knowledge, and they thereby free the universities from any formal obligation to care for the broader, more universal aspects. According to this division of labor, the universities are able to focus totally on specialized programs.

There is also a strict separation in didactical concepts. Whereas schools are considered educational institutions, and teachers are obliged to look after the personality development of the student as well as teaching and learning, German universities are not conceived to be educational institutions in that sense. No term corresponding to *higher education* exists. Traditionally, universities do not intentionally educate in the sense of employing teaching techniques, setting personality development goals, or trying to socialize students. Their task, rather, is to transmit knowledge and to offer mature persons an opportunity to become involved in scholarship and science.

Qualitatively, individual universities have little influence upon their intake. As the qualified student can choose a university freely, any effort on the part of the university to match the intake of students to specific concepts and programs is bound to be virtually without influence. The free choice of university, as well as the easy transfer from one university to another, induces little attachment of the student to the institution, a fact that does not cause any major concern. What might be criticized in other countries as a lack of institutional identification is perceived in Germany as an integral part of a cosmopolitan approach.

This strict division of labor between academic secondary and higher education has not been considered a burden or a restriction by the universities. Rather, the latter are happy to rely on the delivery of mature persons who expect to receive high-level, specialized, research oriented knowledge. Neither is this division of labor conceived to be an impact of secondary on higher education. This is understandable if we look at the history of academic secondary education as a form of preparation for universities. More important, the Abitur and its implication of maturity is conceived to be an element of the educational system in general, rather than of a certain type of school. The school is noticed only when complaints arise about declining standards, thus endangering the concept of maturity. Nevertheless, it would be misleading to believe that the inertia implied in the concept of maturity proves that there is always a harmonious relationship between academic secondary education and universities. It can easily be shown that controversy has existed all through the two hundred years since this system began, on such issues as standards for school graduates, tasks of general education, and the university's role in personality development. During the 1970s, criticism by the universities regarding the quality of secondary education intensified. Many university representatives complained that beginning students lacked the knowledge traditionally taken for granted. They noted that entering students were much more varied than before in their mastery of basic knowledge in certain fields of study.

Research available on this topic is very limited. A few surveys compared basic physics test scores,[19] or admission achievement tests taken after completion of propaedeutic studies in medicine, with secondary educational background in terms of type of school, courses selected, grades, and so forth.[20] A survey in 1982 asked students, after one year at the university, whether they felt sufficiently prepared for their studies: 19 percent felt sufficiently prepared in terms of working techniques; 44 percent considered the knowledge acquired at school sufficient to follow the content of university courses during their first year without major difficulty; 18 percent felt prepared for their studies as far as having learned the basic research methods of their field at school; 25 percent considered themselves well-prepared for university studies in general.[21] In particular, the survey showed that students who attended academic secondary and comprehensive schools considered themselves better prepared for higher education than those who attended evening or vocational high schools. There was also a positive correlation between grades in school and choice of secondary school courses corresponding to field of study, on the one hand, and ratings regarding sufficient preparation, on the other.

Although such surveys support the view that university intake is quite heterogeneous, there is the danger of overinterpreting such findings. We do not have data to show historical changes; presumed past homogeneity may be overestimated. Further, most of these complaints assume that a high degree of continuity of learning and achievement in secondary and higher education is appropriate. This continuity has neither been confirmed by research in the past, nor has it been the implicit norm of the linkages between the two levels in the Federal Republic of Germany. For example, most studies of the relationship between school grades and university achievement conducted in the sixties interpreted the resulting correlations as quite low.[22] Recent surveys on achievement of students at comprehensive universities—institutions of higher education having an extremely diverse student intake—also concluded that there is a large difference between Abiturienten and graduates from vocational high schools in terms of scores in academic ability tests, but little difference in achievement measured by grades during their studies at the comprehensive universities.[23]

Student heterogeneity in terms of a knowledge base provided by secondary education shapes teaching and learning at universities, but it is difficult to establish in what way. Some critics assume that a lowering of standards occurs at universities; however, no convincing evidence for it exists. Scholars and some professional organizations seem to lean strongly toward not accepting such a decline. That students in the seventies and eighties take more time to get a degree than students in the sixties some consider an indicator of the lack of preparation for university studies. There are, however, other factors that undoubtedly contribute to the prolongation of study, such as increased formal course requirements and more knowledge to be mastered as part of one's general preparation. There are some efforts to strengthen interdisciplinary studies and propaedeutical requirements in some fields, but the dominant mood is in favor of disciplinary approaches and specialization.

Regarding teaching and learning styles, reforms around 1970 stressed teaching skills of university teachers as an important issue, along with instructive elements in course design, and so forth. Efforts of this kind took root to some extent but are now in retreat. With respect to the role of the university in the personality development of students, the Framework Act for Higher Education (Hochschulrahmengesetz), passed in 1976, calls for the universities to assume this responsibility. But when a study reform commission made proposals about how to realize these aims,[24] the West German Rectors Conference rejected them, arguing that any emphasis on the social skills of students and on the responsibilities of graduates as citizens would only downgrade universities to the level of schools and encourage universities to play an indoctrinary role.[25]

Only in terms of the capacity of students to freely choose courses and teachers have universities appeared to change substantially. Belief that students were mature in this respect has declined considerably. Regulations that guide courses of study are not yet as tightly knit as they are in countries in which this concept of maturity never existed, but, nevertheless, they are increasing in number and are influencing the inner life of universities.

It is not easy to summarize how recent changes in secondary education have affected higher education with regard to the concept of maturity. In my view, the desire of the university to uphold the traditional notion of maturity, with its comforting implications for the traditional Idee of the German university, has proved much stronger than pressures exerted by changing enrollment levels.

STRUCTURES OF HIGHER EDUCATION

The traditional system of academic education and of access to higher education has contributed to limiting differences of quality and prestige between universities. It has prevented the long-term reinforcement of once-established prestige hierarchies one can observe in many other countries. Prestige hierarchies already existed during a time when there were no limits placed on secondary school graduates in choosing an institution and a field of study. But these hierarchies were considered marginal because students were able to move freely from one university to another, academic careers were based solely on evaluation through a "call" from another university, and a decentralized society supported a decentralized system of higher education.

The expansion of higher education in recent decades as well as the introduction of numerus clausus could easily have led to a stronger hierarchy of institutions. On the one hand, there is a widespread belief that expansion leads to a student body heterogeneity that is better served by diversity of institutions and that institutional diversity also better serves manpower requirements. On the other hand, restricted admissions makes for more visible prestige differences, which in most countries tend to reinforce institutional hierarchies rather than challenge them.

There have been many efforts to establish variety among institutions of higher education and among programs of study, but the results of these activities cannot be demonstrated in detail. The only far-reaching change has been the upgrading of former engineering colleges and higher vocational schools to short-cycle institutions of higher education. Altogether, one can summarize that more differences of quality and prestige now exist than would be considered appropriate according to the traditional notion of homogeneity of the system, but there are fewer differences than any proponent of a diversified structure would consider desirable.[26]

In this context the question of how changes in secondary education and in the access and admissions system have influenced the structure of higher education arises. The most prominent change, the introduction of the vocational high school as a new track leading to short-cycle higher education, underscores the variety of higher education. But this can hardly be considered an impact of secondary upon higher education because in the decision-making process regarding the establishment of these new institutions of higher education a need was felt to establish a new route of secondary education leading to those institutions. Apart from that, most changes in secondary education or in the access and admissions system have been aimed at keeping institutional variety in bounds. Most obvious are the following examples:

1. Resistance to the introduction of comprehensive schools on a large-scale basis, as well as the decision not to substitute for the Abitur a new *Aditur*—a type of entrance examination proposed by the West German Rectors Conference in the early seventies—augmented the reluctance to open universities to vocationally experienced persons without traditional credentials. All these resistances indicate a widespread desire to maintain a degree of homogeneity among beginning students.

2. A central administration for admission to numerus clausus fields of study gives less scope for institutional hierarchies than admissions administered by individual institutions. In addition, the Central Admissions Agency barely publishes any data regarding institutional preferences; this is a deliberate policy aimed at avoiding increased competition for entrance to certain fields and institutions.

3. Within the framework of admissions regulations regarding numerus clausus fields, there is only one element that adjusts for different standards in the grading of secondary school students. Average grades for all the schools in each state are calculated and compensated for by an interstate weighting system. This means that differences among schools in a given state or among courses chosen by secondary school students are implicitly considered negligible.

4. During the seventies, when most experts concluded that secondary education had become more heterogeneous, attempts were made to keep differences in bounds, including the introduction of norm books for curricula, examinations in academic secondary schools, and the restriction of choice of subjects.

The Impact of Higher on Secondary Education

The foregoing analysis of the impact of secondary on higher education has established that there is a traffic system from lower to higher levels of education; however, in the reverse direction analysis is much more difficult. Apart from the impact of teachers, a direct channel does not exist. In some countries the higher education system has a supervisory function over secondary education, as, for example, by participation in examining commissions; but this is not the case in the Federal Republic of Germany. It is therefore necessary to consider indirect influences of higher on secondary education. Let us consider first the impact on secondary institutional patterns, curricula, teaching and learning styles, selection, and so forth, and following that, the impact through teacher training. Although the impact on curricula and selection may take place through formal regulations or through the behavior of teachers, it seems heuristically important to separate these two areas.

INSTITUTIONAL PATTERNS, SELECTION, AND CONTENT

The educational system in the Federal Republic of Germany is designed so that types of secondary education correspond to types of last-stage, preoccupational education: the main school primarily leads to apprenticeship training and part-time vocational schools, the Realschule to intermediate vocational schooling, and the academic secondary school to higher education. Thus, individual secondary schools can be more closely geared to later stages than comprehensive settings that prepare for several later stages, or than educational settings with lesser vocational components, where secondary education may be preparatory and terminal at the same time.

This structural correspondence of secondary education and vocational and higher education was underscored when the decision was made to introduce Fachhochschulen as a new type of higher education. Most state governments decided concurrently to introduce vocational high schools as a new type of upper secondary school preparing for this new type of higher education. In general, whenever preparations for major reforms of academic secondary education or secondary education have been initiated, higher education associations—for example, councils of the various disciplines (the so-called *Fakultätentage*), the West German Rectors Conference, and various other groups and institutions—have tried to become involved and substantially influence the future of academic secondary education. Representatives of the West German Rectors Conference state that these groups strongly influenced upper secondary education reforms in 1960 and 1972.[27]

Undoubtedly, universities have contributed to the preservation of a tracking system of secondary education. Although complaints are occasionally voiced that the right of Abituren to enroll at a university has put an almost intolerable burden on the universities to accept a growing number of students, the traditional concepts of academic secondary education and maturity tend to be viewed as indispensable. Whereas the views of educators and educational researchers in the sixties and seventies were quite divergent, and many of them favored a comprehensive setting for secondary education, a majority of university representatives clearly favored preservation of the tracking system. Most university representatives expressed concern about the preservation of a minimal high-level requirement for passing the Abitur. For example, when criticism grew in the early seventies emphasizing that the rapid expansion of secondary education and the individualization that occurred by means of course electives might lead to a lowering of standards, the West German Rectors Conference supported the idea of establishing so-called norm books to guarantee the same standards at all academic secondary schools at the upper secondary level.

It is very difficult to establish to what extent universities have shaped both the subjects taught in the Gymnasium and its teaching and learning styles. Did Latin lose its strong role in secondary education because it was gradually abolished as a prerequisite for the final examination in many fields at the university, or did these examination regulations at the university change because the neoclassical concept lost its previously strong influence on secondary education? Did the universities encourage the improvement of modern language and mathematics teaching as preparation for university studies, or did these subjects gain importance in the view held by society in general about the appropriate elements of education for the elite? Did the schools improve their efforts to prepare pupils in techniques of independent study and encourage specialization rather than promoting encyclopedic knowledge because the universities required such changes, or did the universities become aware of such deficiencies only because they themselves became more "educational" due to the schools' influence on the universities? It is impossible to establish clear causal chains.

The universities tended to strongly emphasize the importance of broad knowledge versus specialization at the Gymnasium. Clearly, the universities did not favor upper secondary education specialization that might lead to the need for general education at the higher level. Nevertheless, some specialization was favored in order to increase the entering student's knowledge of some subjects, for example, mathematics for those planning to study science or engineering. The growth of this concern in the sixties certainly contributed to the breakthrough in 1972 of very individualized curricula in the eleventh through thirteenth grades.

In the early seventies it became obvious how strongly the climate of the Gymnasium was shaped by selection mechanisms at the point of access to higher education and within it. Traditionally, pupils at academic secondary schools needed to be concerned about passing the final examination. But many pupils did not reach the required level of achievement each year and were obliged to repeat a class. Many dropped out after failing to be promoted to the next class. Up to the 1960s less than half of all students enrolling at the Gymnasium "survived" all nine classes and finally passed the Abitur.[28] Final examination grades were more or less meaningless because access to all fields of study and to all institutions was open to any person having successfully completed academic secondary education. In 1972, however, when a formal system of numerus clausus was introduced according to which the majority of places in restricted admission subjects were allotted on the basis of grade point average, secondary education was overwhelmed by competition for grades. Educators complained that the negative effects of rivalry, social isolation, instrumental views on education, and so on, far outweighed the positive effect of higher achievement.[29] Efforts to reduce numerus clausus in 1976–1977 by opening up higher education at a time of financial constraints and dim job prospects would have been unthinkable without an almost national consensus that the numerus clausus had led to overcompetition within the high schools.

The introduction of the restricted admissions system coincided with the 1972 reforms of the eleventh through thirteenth grades of the Gymnasium, reforms that gave students a choice among school subjects. When secondary education reforms were designed, no one took into consideration the possible impacts of the numerus clausus regulations. After 1972 it turned out that many students used the new system to choose the easiest subjects in order to acquire a good grade point average. Many tried to find loopholes in the regulations to increase their chances of admittance to numerus clausus fields. This led to a decline of standards and the broad knowledge base of graduates. Later, various measures were taken to limit choices in upper secondary education.

TEACHER TRAINING

Higher education may shape secondary education through teacher training; certainly knowledge, styles of thinking, attitudes and beliefs, as well as teaching and learning modes may be transferred from one to the other.

Up to the 1960s colleges of education provided training for primary school teachers and, in part, for those who taught in Realschulen. These future teachers needed to prepare themselves to teach many subjects, and learning pedagogical technique was a major part of their training. Their course of study, about three years, was not considered equivalent to university courses. Those intending to become teachers of academic secondary education enrolled at universities and specialized in two subjects. In addition they had to take only a few courses in philosophy and pedagogy and were obliged to pass only moderately difficult corresponding exams. They considered themselves experts in certain fields rather than educators. At the end of their studies both types of teachers had to pass state examinations in which some examiners were professors and some representatives of the school system, such as school supervisors. After passing this first exam, both types of teachers underwent a practical training period and then had to pass a second state examination.[30] During the sixties and seventies, there were changes in the training of teachers. On the one hand, in most states, colleges of education were incorporated into universities, and the training of primary and Realschulen teachers stressed more strongly the subjects to be taught. On the other, the pedagogical function of academic secondary teachers was stressed by increasing course requirements in education, psychology, sociology, and so on to about one-quarter of their studies. Thus, to some extent, the gap between different types of teacher training narrowed. Some universities abolished certain types of training according to tracks and substituted training according to stages of schooling (primary, lower secondary, upper secondary education).[31]

Teacher training reforms were based on the assumption that teachers at academic secondary schools should not only have the knowledge to transmit but also be expert in the process and conditions of education. It was assumed and stated by the Education Council in 1970,[32] however, that modern society requires knowledge oriented and research oriented learning and understanding in all types of secondary education. Thus, it was considered appropriate that, to some extent, universities transmit their modes of thinking and learning to secondary education.

In many countries it is assumed that universities ought to train teachers in subjects, but some efforts are made in the preparatory process to desocialize prospective teachers from the world of universities and thus to avoid the direct transmission of thoughts and attitudes from the university to the school. In the Federal Republic of Germany, prospective teachers undergo completely divergent experiences in their studies at institutions of higher education and their second phase of training.

It is generally thought that in the sixties and seventies conflict increased between the attitudes and expectations of students versus the goals of the second teacher training phase and prevailing expectations in the school system. After the first phase of training, prospective teachers are more likely to promote scientific and research oriented thinking and to consider themselves experts in certain subjects rather than educators, to be skeptical about grading as well as promoting achievement through extrinsic measures, to stress emancipatory goals of personality development, to emphasize the freedom of teaching, and to mistrust educational administration. Most graduates perceive the second phase to be a dramatic contrast to the first one, and some surveys have shown that young teachers must adjust to a school environment that does not appreciate their early attitudes and expectations. Nevertheless, there are many indicators that changes in educational thought, changes in new dimensions of knowledge, and the changing values and attitudes of university students are, to some extent, transmitted to secondary schools through the channel of teacher training.

Conclusion

If we observe deliberations on the relationship between secondary and higher education in various countries, we find very similar concerns, such as notorious complaints by university professors about the deficient state of knowledge of beginning students. A closer look reveals substantial cross-national differences, however, in the articulation between secondary and higher education and in the understanding of their respective functions. The traditional educational system in the Federal Republic of Germany emphasizes a very close relationship between secondary and higher education. A secondary tracking system in which each track leads to a further level at the university or to vocational training stresses the close relationship between stages of education and later training. This is most strongly demonstrated in the traditional provision that all persons who successfully complete academic secondary education are entitled to enroll at any university in any field of study.

This close relationship is not necessarily supported by mutual or one-way controls between these sectors of education or by similar educational goals. In the Federal Republic of Germany, universities do not have formal power to shape secondary education. Further, the educational goals of these institutions are not considered similar but complimentary; once a student has acquired the broad, basic knowledge provided by secondary education and has demonstrated maturity by passing the final exam, he transfers to the research oriented and specialized environment of the universities, which do not "educate" but instead transmit knowledge and offer the opportunity to participate in an open process of searching for knowledge. Thus, secondary and higher education are not subsectors of educational systems that shape each other; rather, they are parts of the general logic of the system. One may rightly ask if this is true, to a certain extent, of all educational systems. The notion of subsystems may be somewhat misleading in understanding the relationship between stages of educational systems in general.

The traditional German system of close linkages between academic secondary and higher education has been challenged in the last twenty years or so for many reasons. It has been criticized especially for reinforcing inequality of opportunity, for limiting opportunities to correct early educational choices, and for not serving the diversity of talent and manpower requirements in the process of educational expansion. It also has been criticized for not adequately fulfilling the traditional function of guaranteeing the maturity of entering students in terms of academic achievement and personality development.

The changes that have taken place within secondary and higher education, as well as those between these two sectors, have been significant because they have established new types of secondary schooling leading to the next level, they have encouraged a gradual revision of the open-access pattern for qualified graduates, and they have brought about some variety of institutions and courses in higher education. But these were rather small modifications within the mutually reinforcing traditional structure of a tracking system of secondary education, guaranteeing open access for those passing the Abitur and a homogeneous system of higher education. They were not complete changes identifiable as a movement toward a convergent, international pattern. From a broader, comparative perspective, however, the debates and changes in the relationship between these levels indicate some degree of convergence and the establishment of compromises between conflicting goals. A permeable and somewhat comprehensive structure of secondary education and a hierarchical pattern of higher education may easily provide opportunities for a variety of options, interests, and achievements, and may offer opportunities for easy correction of wrong educational choices, but the price of such a pattern seems to be a lack of articulation, which may lead to inadequate preparation for university studies or to rigorous learning processes intended solely as screening devices. Alternatively, a tracking system in secondary education closely related to a homogeneous system of higher education provides articulation and quality, but the price is inflexible secondary channels, limited equality of opportunity, and restricted provision for a variety of talents and job requirements. Some compromise among such major alternatives appears necessary in all countries.

In the pessimistic educational climates of the late 1970s and early 1980s, compromises developing in each country between conflicting approaches to the shaping of secondary and higher education and the relationship between them are commonly assessed negatively. For example, complaints regarding the lack of quality in secondary education tend to prevail in the United States, whereas in the Federal Republic of Germany the complaints are mainly about too many students enrolling at universities in long courses. One might consider instead the opportunities that inhere in the educational context of a given country. The maintenance of the Abitur in the Federal Republic of Germany, in the context of a fairly homogeneous system of higher education, may well be a fruitful alternative to the tendency to respond to educational expansion by diluting quality for the majority. The traditional close linkage between the school and the university, as modified in recent years, may serve to provide high-quality education at both levels for the many instead of for the few.

Notes

1. See various articles in Blankertz et al., eds., "Sekundarstufe II - Jugendbildung zwischen Schule und Beruf," especially Herrlitz, "Geschichte der Gymnasialen Oberstufe," pp. 89–107.

2. Ibid., p. 99. The corresponding figures at the *Gymnasium* for ancient languages in 1956 were 14 in Greek, 13 in Latin, 12 in German literature, 9 in sciences, 6 in mathematics, and 42 in 9 additional subjects.

3. See Blankertz et al., "Sekundarstufe II - Jugendbildung zwischen Schule und Beruf," pp. 437–438.

4. See Peisert and Framhein, *Systems of Higher Education*, pp. 8–13; Gieseke, "The 'Fachhochschulen' in the Federal Republic of Germany," pp. 42–46.

5. See Cerych et al., *Implementation of Higher Education Reforms*; cf. Hermanns, Teichler, and Wasser, *The Compleat University*.

6. See Teichler, "*Öffnung der Hochschulen*," p. 41.

7. Bundesminister für Bildung und Wissenschaft, *Grund - und Strukturdaten 1982/3*, pp. 42–43.

8. See Becker, *Barriers to Higher Education in the Federal Republic of Germany*.

9. See Wissenschaftsrat, *Zur Lage der Hochschulen Anfang der 80er Jahre*, p. 6.

10. Ibid., pp. 14–15.

11. Wissenschaftsrat, *Empfehlungen des Wissenschaftsrats zum Ausbau der Wissenschaftlichen Hochschulen*, pp. 37–59.

12. It decreased from 15:1 in 1960 to 9:1 in 1970 and rose again to 13:1 in 1980; see Teichler, "Recent Developments in Higher Education in the Federal Republic of Germany," p. 168.

13. See Hüfner and Naumann, *Konjunkturen der Bildungspolitik in der Bundesrepublik Deutschland*; Teichler and Sanyal, *Higher Education and the Labour Market in the Federal Republic of Germany*, pp. 52–78.

14. Teichler, "*Öffnung der Hochschulen*," pp. 31–33.

15. See for example, Burn, "Access to Higher Education in the Federal Republic of Germany and the United States."

16. See Westdeutsche Rektorenkonferenz. *Numerus Clausus Urteile des Bundesverfassungsgerichts vom 18, Juli 1982 und 8, Februar 1977.*

17. See Bundesminister für Bildung und Wissenschaft, *Alte und Neue Universitäten.*

18. See *Access to Higher Education.*

19. Bundesminister für Bildung und Wissenschaft, *Der Bundesweite Studieneingangstest Physik 1978.*

20. See references in Bundesminister für Bildung und Wissenschaft, *Studienerfolg.*

21. Kazemzadeh and Schaeper, "Vorbereitung auf das Studium Durch die Schule," p. 2.

22. See Goldschmidt and Sommerkorn, "Some University Problems Today," pp. 62–63.

23. See Hitpass and Trosien, "The Contribution of the Comprehensive University to Equality of Opportunity."

24. Sekretariat der Ständigen Konferenz der Kultusminister der Länder in der Bundesrepublik Deutschland, *Entwurf: Grundsätze für Studium und Prüfungen.*

25. See Teichler, "Recent Developments in Higher Education in the Federal Republic of Germany," p. 170.

26. See the overview in Teichler, "Quantitative and Structural Development of Higher Education in the Federal Republic of Germany."

27. Kunle, "Was Erwarten die Hochschulen von den Schulen?"

28. See Peisert, *Der Vorzeitige Abgang vom Gymnasium.*

29. See the overview of this debate in Flitner, ed., *Der Numerus Clausus und Seine Folgen.*

30. See Fuehr, "Teacher Training in the Federal Republic of Germany."

31. See Händle, "Lehrerausbildung (Organisation)," and "Lehrerausbildung (Studium)."

32. Deutscher Bildungsrat, *Strukturplan für das Bildungswesen.*

Bibliography

Access to Higher Education: Two Perspectives. A Comparative Study of the Federal Republic of Germany and the United States of America. Final Report of the Germany-U.S. Study Group. New York: International Council for Educational Development, 1978.

ALLESCH, JÜRGEN, and DAGMAR PREISS. *Struktureller Wandel und Wissenschaftliche Weiterbildung an den Hochschulen.* Berlin: Technische Universität Berlin, 1983.

ANWEILER, OSKAR, and ARTHUR G. HEARNDEN, eds., *From Secondary to Higher Education.* Cologne: Böhlau, 1983.

BECKER, WILLI. *Barriers to Higher Education in the Federal Republic of Germany.* New York: International Council for Educational Development, 1977.

BERCHEM, THEODOR, "Studierfähigkeit - Berufsfähigkeit." In *Bildungspolitik Kein Thema Mehr?* Bonn: Westdeutsche Rektorenkonferenz, 1981. Pp. 67–85.

BLANKERTZ, HERWIG, JOSEPH DERBOLAV, ADOLF KELL, and GUNTER KUTSCHA, eds. "Sekundarstufe II - Jugendbildung zwischen Schule und Beruf." In *Enzyklopädie Erziehungswissenschaft*, vol. 9.2. Stuttgart: Klett-Cotta, 1983.

Bundesminister für Bildung und Wissenschaft. *Report of the Federal Government on Education 1970.* Bonn, 1970.

_____ . *Der Bundesweite Studieneingangstest Physik 1978.* Bonn, 1981.

_____ . Framework Act for Higher Education (Hochschulrahmengesetz) Bonn: s.t.

_____ . *Grund - und Strukturdaten 1982/83.* Bonn, 1982.

_____ . *Studienerfolg - Aufwand und Ertrag.* Bonn, 1983.

_____ . *Alte und Neue Universitäten.* Bonn, 1983.

Bund-Länder-Kommission für Bildungsplanung und Forschungsförderung, and Bundesanstalt für Arbeit. *Studien - und Berufswahl 1982/83.* Bad Honnef: Bock, 1982.

BURN, BARBARA B. "Access to Higher Education in the Federal Republic of Germany and the United States." *International Review of Education* 22, (1978): 193–201.

CERYCH, LADISLAV, AYLÂ NEUSEL, ULRICH TEICHLER, and HELMUT WINKLER. *Implementation of Higher Education Reforms: The German Gesamthochschule.* Paris: Institute of Education, European Cultural Foundation, 1981.

DEUTSCHER BILDUNGSRAT. *Strukturplan für das Bildungswesen.* Bonn, 1970.

_____ . *Zur Neugestaltung der Abschlüsse im Sekundarschulwesen.* Bonn: Bundesdruckerei, 1971.

DREWEK, PETER, and DETLEF K. MÜLLER. "Zur Sozialen Funktion der Gymnasialen Oberstufe." In *Enzyklopädie Erziehungswissenschaft,* vol. 9.1. Stuttgart: Klett-Cotta, 1982. Pp. 108–129.

FICHTNER, DIETER. "Es handelt Sich un Keine Wohltat." *Deutsche Universitätszeitung* 9 (1981):298–300.

FINGERLE, KARLHEINZ, and ERHARD WICKE. "Die Neugestaltete Gymnasiale Oberstufe Ohne Bildungstheoretische Legitimation." *Zeitschrift für Pädagogik* 28 (1982): 1, 93–110.

FLITNER, ANDREAS, ed. *Der Numerus Clausus und Seine Folgen.* Stuttgart: Klett, 1976.

FUEHR, CHRISTOPH. "Teacher Training in the Federal Republic of Germany." *Western European Education* 2 (1970): 2–3, 109–125.

FUEHR, CHRISTOPH, and G. ULRICH, eds. *Educational Reform in the Federal Republic of Germany: Initiatives and Trends.* Hamburg: UNESCO Institute for Education, 1970.

GIESE, ERNST. "Die Anziehungskraft Wissenschaftlicher Hochschulen in der Bundesrepublik Deutschland für Studenten." *Die Erde* (1982): 113, 115–132.

GIESEKE, LUDWIG. "The 'Fachhochschulen' in the Federal Republic of Germany." *Higher Education in Europe* 6 (1981): 2, 42–46.

GELLERT, CLAUDIUS. "The Implications of Upper-Secondary School Reform for Universities in the Federal Republic of Germany." *European Journal of Education* 16 (1981): 175–183.

GOLDSCHMIDT, DIETRICH. "West Germany." In *Students, University and Society,* ed. Margaret S. Archer. London: Heinemann, 1972. Pp. 154–167.

GOLDSCHMIDT, DIETRICH, and INGRID N. SOMMERKORN. "Some University Problems Today. Transmission from School to University in the Federal Republic of Germany." In *The University Within the Education System.* Ghent: Comparative Education Society in Europe, 1968. Pp. 59–75.

HÄNDLE, CHRISTA. "Lehrerausbildung (Organisation)." In *Ausbildung und Sozialisation in der Hochschule,* ed. Ludwig Huber. Stuttgart: Klett-Cotta, 1983. Pp. 623–632.

———. "Lehrerausbildung (Studium)." In *Ausbildung und Sozialisation in der Hochschule,* ed. Ludwig Huber. Stuttgart: Klett-Cotta, 1983. Pp. 632–638.

HASEMANN, KLAUS. *Kriterien der Hochschulreife.* Weinheim: Bletz, 1970.

HERMANNS, HARRY, ULRICH TEICHLER, and HENRY WASSER, eds. *The Compleat University.* Cambridge, Mass.: Schenkman, 1983.

HEIDENHEIMER, ARNOLD. "The Politics of Educational Reform: Explaining Different Outcomes of School Comprehensivization Attempts in Sweden and West Germany." *Comparative Education Review* 18 (1974): 388–410.

HERRLITZ, HANS-GEORG. "Geschichte der Gymnasialen Oberstufe: Theorie und Legitimation Seit der Humboldt-Süverschen Reform." In *Enzyklopädie Erziehungswissenschaft,* vol. 9.1. Stuttgart: Klett-Cotta, 1982. Pp. 89–107.

HITPASS, JOSEPH, and JURGEN TROSIEN. "The Contribution of the Comprehensive University to Equality of Opportunity." In *The Compleat University,* ed. Harry Hermanns, Ulrich Teichler, and Henry Wasser. Cambridge, Mass.: Schenkman, 1983. Pp. 205–210.

"Hochschule und Weiterbildung: Stellungnahme des 137. Plenums der WRK vom. 28 Juni 1982." *Mitteilungen der Westdeutschen Rektorenkonferenz Dokumentation* (1982): 26, 55–63.

HOCHSCHULVERBAND. "Soziale Offnung der Universität?" *Forum des Hochschulverbandes* 25 (1981): 1–39.

HÜFNER, KLAUS, and JENS NAUMANN. *Konjunkturen der Bildungspolitik in der Bundesrepublik Deutschland,* vol. I. Stuttgart: Klett, 1977.

KARPEN, ULRICH. *Access to Higher Education and Its Restrictions under the Constitution.* München: Minerva, 1980.

KARPEN, ULRICH, ed. *Constitutional Aspects of Access to Higher Education.* Tübingen: Mohr (Siebeck), 1978. Special issue of *Wissenschaftsrecht, Wissentschaftsverwaltung, Wissenschaftsförderung.*

KAZEMZADEH, FOAD, and HILDEGARD SCHAEPER. "Vorbereitung auf das Studium Durch die Schule." *HIS Kurzinformationen* A6 (1983): 1–12.

KEWENIG, WILLIAM A. "Probleme des Hochschulzugangs -- Ein Alter Hut?" In *Hochschulzugang in den USA und der Bundesrepublik Deutschland,* ed. James A. Perkins and Barbara B. Burn. Göttingen: Vandenhoeck and Ruprecht, 1980. Pp. 9–25.

KLUGE, NORBERT, AYLÂ NEUSEL, and ULRICH TEICHLER. *Beispiele Praxisorientierten Studiums.* Bonn: Bundesminister für Bildung und Wissenschaft, 1981.

KÖHLER, GERD. *Soziale Öffnung der Hochschulen.* Frankfurt: Gewerkschaft Erziehung und Wissenschaft 1982. Mimeo.

KÖHLER, HELMUT. "Probleme der Erfassung von Übergängen Zwischen den Bildungseinrichtungen und Zwischen Bildungs- und Beschäftigungssystem." In *Beruflich-Soziale Lebensperspektiven von Jugendlichen*, ed. Ingrid N. Sommerkorn. Munich: Verlag Deutsches Jugendinstitut, 1981. Pp. 105–144.

KORTE, ELKE. "Der Numerus Clausus als Zulassungsverfahren der Bundesrepublik Deutschland." In *Studienaufnahme und Studienzulassung*, ed. Paul Kellerman. Klagenfurt: Kärtner Verlagsgesellschaft, 1984. Pp. 69–78.

KUNLE, HEINZ. "Was Erwarten die Hochschulen von den Schulen?" In *Qualität und Quantität—Die Hochschule im Schatten des Studentenberges*. Bonn: Westdeutsche Rektorenkonferenz, 1977. Pp. 109–128.

LAURIEN, HANNA-RENATE. "Studierfähigkeit—Berufsfähigkeit." In *Bildungspolitik—Kein Thema Mehr?* Bonn: Westdeutsche Rektorenkonferenz, 1981. Pp. 87–103.

MULLER-SOLGER, HERMANN. *Hochschulzulassung in der Bundesrepublik Deutschland.* Bonn: Bundesminister für Bildung und Wissenschaft, 1976.

NEUSEL, AYLÂ, and ULRICH TEICHLER. "Comprehensive Universities: History, Implementation Process and Prospects." In *The Compleat University*, ed. Harry Hermanns, Ulrich Teichler, and Henry Wasser. Cambridge, Mass.: Schenkman, 1983. Pp. 175–196.

Numerus Clausus Urteile des Bundesverfassungsgerichts vom 18. Juli 1982 und 8. Februar 1977. Bonn: Westdeutsche Rektorenkonferenz, 1977.

Organisation for Economic Co-operation and Development (OECD). *Review of National Policies for Education: Germany.* Paris, 1972.

PEISERT, HANSGERT. *Der Vorzeitige Abgang vom Gymnasium.* Villingen-Schwenningen: Neckar-Verlag, 1968.

PEISERT, HANSGERT, and GERHILD FRAMHEIN. *Systems of Higher Education: Federal Republic of Germany.* New York: International Council for Educational Development, 1978.

"Politisch Vorgegebenes Bildungsziel Abgelehnt," *Deutsche Universitätszeitung* 23 (1978): 718–719.

Sekretariat der Ständigen Konferenz der Kultusminister der Länder in der Bundesrepublik Deutschland. *Entwurf: Grundsätze für Studium und Prüfungen.* Bonn, 1979.

Stifterverband für die Deutsche Wissenschaft. *Ingenierbedarf und Studienmotivation.* Essen, 1983.

TEICHLER, ULRICH. "Problems of West German Universities on the Way to Mass Higher Education." *Western European Education* 8 (1976–77): 1–2, 81–120.

―――. "Recent Developments in Higher Education in the Federal Republic of Germany." *European Journal of Education* 17 (1982): 161–176.

―――. "Hochschulzugang und Hochschulzulassung im Internationalen Vergleich." In *Studienaufnahme und Studienzulassung*, ed. Paul Kellerman. Klagenfurt-Kärtner Verlagsgesellschaft, 1984. Pp. 9–24.

―――. *"Öffnung der Hochschulen"—Auch eine Politik für die 80er Jahre?* Bremen: Senator für Wissenschaft und Kunst, 1983.

————. "Quantitative and Structural Development of Higher Education in the Federal Republic of Germany: Trends, Issues and Policies." Paper presented at the conference "The Making and the Remaking of Modern Europe," Washington, D.C., October 13–15, 1983. Mimeo.

TEICHLER, ULRICH, and BIKAS C. SANYAL. *Higher Education and the Labour Market in the Federal Republic of Germany.* Paris: UNESCO Press, 1982.

WISSENSCHAFTSRAT. *Empfehlungen des Wissenschaftsrats zum Ausbau der Wissenschaftlichen Hochschulen.* Bonn, 1960.

————. *Empfehlungen zu Umfang und Struktur des Tertiären Bereichs.* Bonn, 1976.

————. *Empfehlungen zur Weiterbildung an den Hochschulen.* Köln, 1983.

————. *Zur Lage der Hochschulen Anfang der 80er Jahre: Texteil.* Köln, 1983.

————. *Zur Lage der Hochschulen Anfang der 80er Jahre. Statistischer Anhang.* Köln, 1983.

3
England and Wales

MARGARET MADEN

I N THE UNITED KINGDOM THERE are basic differences in educational structure among the several major regions. The Scottish tradition has been noticeably separate from the English. In order to probe closely the changing nature of the school and the university, and the interaction between them, this chapter will not attempt to cover Scotland and Northern Ireland but instead concentrate entirely on education in England and Wales.

The Basic Structure: Secondary Education

The contemporary structure of secondary education in England and Wales, like that of the greater part of the public education system, derives from the 1944 Education Act.[1] This law was one of a series of major reforms the British parliament enacted in the last years of the Second World War as part of a comprehensive program of reconstruction, and it was the first to be brought to the statute books. To many people in the United Kingdom (UK) today it still seems a monumental achievement. The act recognized, for the first time, the necessity of providing secondary education for all, and it laid down, under a complex and subtle system of distributed powers, the terms under which such education was to be provided. The major providers were to be the local education authorities, locally elected bodies that would draw funds largely from local sources.

The act defined secondary education, with that air of high-sounding tautology common to UK legislation, as "full-time education appropriate to the needs of senior pupils other than full-time education which may be provided for senior pupils in institutions of further education."[2] The education provided should offer pupils "such variety of instruction and training as may be desirable in view of their different ages, abilities and aptitudes."[3] It defined secondary education as beginning at age eleven and the compulsory period of education as ending at age sixteen, though largely for reasons of cost the school-leaving age remained at fifteen until 1972.

There was little resistance at the time to the proposals of contemporary reports[4] that a "varied and comprehensive school" could be best achieved by dividing children into "academic," or "bookish," types and others.[5] Norwood described three kinds of children for whom three kinds of schools were needed: English education had "in practice recognised the pupil who is interested in learning for its own sake, . . . the pupil whose abilities and interests lie markedly in the field of applied science or applied art," and the pupil who "deals more easily with concrete things than with ideas."[6] Hence, the white paper preceding the act in 1943 proposed that the division at eleven be threefold, with a set of special technical schools for those children who were able but "practical" in bent. Perhaps significantly, nothing came of technical schools. Most authorities followed a straightforward binary division, with selective grammar schools and secondary moderns catering for the majority of children. They were assisted in this by developments in intelligence testing in the 1930s. These developments appeared to add some credibility to the selection process, which was only to be eroded during the 1950s.

From the beginning there were doubts about the desirability, on social and educational grounds, of this split at age eleven. Almost immediately after the 1944 act, the old London County Council, forerunner of the Inner London Education Authority, began to consider truly comprehensive schools. Others, such as the West Riding Council, considered that selection at eleven was too early and lobbied to be allowed to set up middle schools, which would enable the selection process to be delayed to twelve or thirteen.

During the 1950s considerable doubt was shed on the validity and social impact of intelligence tests. Hilda Himmelweit, Brian Simon, Jean Floud, A. H. Halsey, P. E. Vernon, and Robin Pedley were among an influential group of academics who analyzed what increasing numbers of parents of "eleven-plus failures" were expressing.

> So insular has the approach been that it has not seemed peculiar to write off 50 percent of British children as virtually ineducable to a secondary standard, capable of following only a strictly modified curriculum, when other advanced countries take all normal children through a complete secondary education.[7]

In 1955 there were sixteen comprehensive schools in England and Wales; this number had increased to 745 by 1968, containing 21 percent of the secondary-age population. The Labor government elected in 1964 announced that it would end selection in secondary education. Circular 10/65 asked local authorities that had not done so to submit plans "for reorganising secondary education in their areas on comprehensive lines."[8] The effect of this circular was to accelerate rather than begin or complete a significant process. Even so, and inevitably, there was opposition. Quintin Hogg (now Lord Hailsham) said in Parliament:

> If Labour members would go and study what was being done in good secondary modern schools they would not find a lot of pupils biting their nails in frustration because they had failed the 11 plus. The pleasant noise of the banging of metal and the sawing of wood would greet their ears. The smell of a cooking meal, produced with expensive equipment, would come out of the front door to greet them. They would find that boys and girls were getting an education tailor-made for their bents and requirements.[9]

By 1981, 89 percent of children in the maintained sector attended comprehensive schools, 15 percent in areas where selective schools also existed. Ten percent of pupils between ages thirteen and eighteen were in independent schools.

There was one further, and highly pertinent, section of the 1944 act. In the bold atmosphere of wholesale reconstruction following the war, it must have seemed as if almost anything was possible. The practicalities were often another matter. It took nearly twenty years for the vision of a school-leaving age of sixteen to be fulfilled. The framers of the act were also concerned about the education of young people between sixteen and eighteen. They made provision for the setting up, in every area, of county colleges, to provide part-time further education, and they made elaborate arrangements for attendance at these colleges to be compulsory following the serving of notices by the local education authority.[10]

Nothing came of the county colleges nor of compulsory attendance beyond sixteen. The main reason for this was the spontaneous growth of conventional further-education colleges in response to demand after the war. Two effects can be discerned: first, further-education provision in the UK is markedly uneven, and the opportunities for young people vary considerably in different parts of the country; second, owing to this factor combined with some others (for example, different traditions of apprenticeship), of all the countries in the European Economic Community, the UK has by far the largest proportion of school-leavers receiving no form of further education or formal training whatsoever.[11]

The existence of these provisions in the 1944 act underlines an important weakness in the overall plan as it was set out. The framers of the act were clear that they wanted the terminal date for compulsory schooling to be sixteen; moreover, they envisaged that in due course some form of education would continue until eighteen for all but a few of the population. Their failure, however, to make serious, planned provisions for the further-education sector, which in turn meant that the plan for county colleges became impractical, left a serious void in the sixteen-to-eighteen age group. It was not that they ignored this sector; they had specific and enlightened plans. It is perhaps more fair to say that they did not see the need for any rethinking of traditional patterns, of provisions with the university at the top and the last two years, the sixth form, of the school providing the preparation for it.

For those who, during the 1950s, increasingly began to believe that selection at eleven was wasteful, unjust, and inefficient, the commitment to the sixth form created a severe problem. The comprehensive ideal as it developed in the UK was fundamentally based on the idea of diversity of choice. Only in this way, it was argued, did the school have a chance of delivering its promise of equal opportunity for all. Severe practical problems derived from this commitment. It meant, in effect, that the schools had to be above a minimum size in order to sustain the variety of choice between thirteen and sixteen and to provide instruction economically at the sixth-form level. This created major problems of resources and reorganization in order to provide sufficiently large groupings.

The problem is well illustrated by the Inner London Education Authority (ILEA), a pioneer of the large comprehensive school. In the 1960s and 1970s, with larger than ordinary costs of land, and with an exceptionally large legacy of nineteenth-century charity in the form of voluntary schools, the creation of a fully comprehensive system with eleven-to-eighteen schools appeared impossible without a massive injection of capital from central government and a more than ordinarily determined set of elected members. The ending of selection in ILEA finally occurred only in 1977, by a combination of administrative dexterity and political determination. But it happened in a way that underlined the fragility of the main premise of eleven-to-eighteen schools. The choice of subjects to cater for pupils of all abilities and to feed the requisite size of the sixth form was only achieved by arrangements that involved two and sometimes more schools cooperating with each other. Few informed observers at the time believed this tenuous way of solving the problem could be regarded as a long-term one. But it ended selection, which was regarded by members and officers alike as the main and first step. Six years after this reorganization, it is now clear that ILEA has to recognize the apparent inevitability of some kind of institutionalized break at sixteen.

For whatever reason, the ILEA has been slower than many areas to recognize the need for such a break. From 14 sixth-form colleges in England and Wales in 1972, there were over 100 such colleges by 1978.[12]

Most were under school regulations, but there was also an increase of so-called tertiary colleges under further-education (FE) regulations, in which a comprehensive range of courses, academic and vocational, was offered. In the same year, half the sixth forms in maintained secondary schools had fewer than 100 students, and with an estimated fall in secondary school rolls from 3.7 million in 1979 to 2.6 million in 1991, it was clear that local authorities would have to accelerate this structural change.[13]

The Basic Structure: Higher Education

Higher education comprises the universities and major institutions of further education, including thirty polytechnics. The latter sector emerged after 1945 from an assortment of technical colleges under local-authority control. Two reports, the 1945 Percy report on higher technological education and the 1946 Barlow report on scientific manpower needs, combined with strongly expressed educational demands from ex-servicemen to produce a new sector of higher education. Priority was given to ex-servicemen to enter universities, and the overflow was directed to larger urban technical colleges where external University of London degree courses were offered as well as higher-level technological courses. In 1952 the Committee on Scientific Manpower warned against too rapid an expansion of the university sector on an American scale "at the cost of so great a decline in entrance standards."[14] Actually, there was no evidence that this was a particular danger, but it was a major factor in later debates concerning the style and purpose of the two sectors. In 1950 there were 32,000 qualified school-leavers; only 13,000 entered the university in that year.[15]

The resistance of the universities to a rapid expansion of student numbers was not straightforward. The University Grants Committee (UGC) confirmed that a "heightened sense of social justice generated by the war has opened the door more widely than ever before."[16] Even though student numbers in universities rose considerably in the immediate postwar period, there was a far greater demand than this sector was able or prepared to study. "The academic principle of excellence and elitism was, however, in tension with the social need for rapid growth."[17]

The major growth of student numbers during the 1950s therefore occurred in local-authority technical colleges. However, many college teachers increasingly felt that the external University of London degree was inappropriate and that it denied them the opportunity to innovate, especially in relation to the assessment and development of practical work. In 1955 the Ministry of Education established the National Council for Technological Awards (NCTA), later to become the Council for National Academic Awards (CNAA). The NCTA was empowered to develop and validate a new degree-equivalent qualification, the dip. tech, a technical diploma. The new body's most important contribution was to require institutions that wished to teach the dip. tech to include liberal education as a course component, to design the course so that at least one-third comprised practical experience in a firm ("sandwich" courses), and to ensure that accommodation facilities were of a standard approved by the council.

The major pressures on both universities and technical colleges during this period were those associated with scientific and technical manpower needs. Employers organizations effectively represented the manufacturing sector, but no similar pressure was exerted by the areas of commerce or design. This was to limit the educational purpose and the role of the public-sector colleges for at least ten years.

In a 1956 government white paper, twenty-four regional colleges were listed as potential major institutions, and in 1957 nine of these were selected as colleges of advanced technology (CATs).[18] What has since been described as "academic drift" began: all part-time enrollments and work below degree level was shed.[19] Meanwhile, the public-sector colleges increased their part-time student enrollment from 250,000 in 1954 to 450,000 in 1962, some 5 percent of the students following degree or degree-equivalent courses.

By the early 1960s it was clear that the number of school-leavers qualified to enter universities had greatly outstripped the available places. The Robbins report on higher education (1963) concerned itself with full-time higher education.[20] Major institutions of further education, especially those listed as regional colleges in the 1956 white paper, and the teacher training colleges pressed for university status or, at least, direct association with the universities. A change of government in 1964 resulted in a new secretary of state for education, Anthony Crosland, who proceeded to consider how the Robbins recommendations should be further implemented. A binary policy emerged. Of this, Crosland said:

> I did not invent it; it had been developing steadily since the turn of the century or earlier. Alongside the universities we had the training colleges under local authority or denominational control; and we had a strong and growing sector of higher education in FE. Indeed Table 3 of the Robbins report showed, perhaps to the surprise of many people, that over 40 percent of students in full-time higher education were outside the universities.[21]

The binary policy remains contentious, giving rise as it does to oversimplified analogies between the "autonomous" university sector and prestigious independent schools, with the public-sector institutions described as "the people's universities" and thus regarded as analogous to comprehensive secondary schools.[22] As Becher and Kogan have noted:

> The case of the polytechnics demonstrates, however, that the basic characteristics of higher education cannot easily be overridden. The polytechnics steadily moved towards the modes and aspirations of the universities. . . . The universities in their turn moved towards adaptations of their course offerings designed to meet identifiable market needs. The distinction between the two types of institution had within a decade become embarrassingly blurred.[23]

Important distinctions remain, however. The Council for National Academic Awards, established after the Robbins report, is the degree-awarding body for the nonuniversity sector. Its 1982–1983 directory states that

> the emphasis of a CNAA-approved course will often differ from that of its university equivalent. Practical competence is highly valued, as is the amount of teaching and guidance given to the student. Project work often forms an important part of the course . . . and will contribute to the final award. Courses are offered on a full-time, part-time, mixed mode or sandwich basis. . . . Efforts are made to ensure that courses lead to satisfying career opportunities.[24]

The references to practical competence and teaching and guidance given to the student apply equally to many university courses, but it is probably in the part-time courses—the subdegree-level work and the special entry systems for mature students without formal qualifications and school-leavers without general certificate of education (GCE) advanced (A)-level qualifications—that more substantial differences occur. Two-thirds of students in advanced FE are currently enrolled in CNAA-approved, first-degree courses; the council now approves courses up to and including M.Phil. and Ph.D. awards in 117 institutions.

A major distinction between the two sectors of higher education remains centered on control and accountability. Following the articulation of the binary policy, the public-sector institutions were encouraged to develop and formalize the machinery of college government, and in 1967 the secretary of state acted upon proposals of both the Robbins committee and the 1966 Weaver committee on the government of colleges of education.[25] Significant increases in staff participation and the powers of governing bodies were recommended, with consequent reduction in the detailed powers that could be reserved by local-authority committees and officers. There was a good deal of resistance to these liberalizing measures from some local authorities, as well as from some principals of colleges, neither being able to recognize the necessary conjunction between academic development and a more sophisticated collegiate decision-making process. Nevertheless, the measures were implemented, and they represented a move toward the universities' mode of internal governance.

The wider context in which transactions between central government and institutions occur remains different in several important respects. The UGC has both a longer tradition and greater powers than the recently established National Advisory Board (NAB) for local-authority higher education. The former advises the Department of Education and Science (DES) on what it believes are appropriate levels of funding, but once these have been established the UGC recommends institutional and departmental allocations across the university system. It concerns itself with teaching and research balances, proportions of undergraduate and graduate numbers, and home and overseas student intakes. The degree to which these details are raised with or by the DES when general funding levels are initially discussed is not made public. More recently the DES restored part of its reduced funding by injecting special grants for courses in information technology, by extending the period over which staff reductions were to be made, and by allowing special allocations for new lecturers in certain institutions and subjects.

The NAB is a more public and, for the present, a less powerful body. It conducts its business with local authorities (the major source of funding), with voluntary bodies, and with the institutions themselves. The different interest groups represented reflect distinct traditions and values. In the recent discussions following central government's requirements for reduced funding, the traditional FE lobby argued for maintenance, and in some cases continued growth, of student numbers, even if this resulted in less resources per student. Most polytechnic directors, however, argued for maintenance of "the unit of resource" and, by implication, reduced student numbers; their concerns were similar to those expressed by the UGC since the immediate postwar period.

A recent white paper on teacher training applies to both the university and public-sector institutions.[26] It is an unusual document in that the formal powers of secretaries of state are extensively deployed. The planned distribution of initial teacher training courses has normally been decided, following due consultation, by the secretary of state; what is uncommon in this instance is the clear statement of criteria for the approval of courses. There are references to the amount of time to be spent on subject studies and practical, school based experience, the involvement of practicing teachers in student selection, and the need for a sufficient proportion of the training institution's staff to have had "re-

TABLE 3.1

PARTICIPATION OF MALE AND FEMALE STUDENTS IN
FULL-TIME HIGHER EDUCATION

	Males per 100	Females per 100
1970–71	15.0	12.5
1980–81	13.9	11.0

cent, substantial and relevant" experience as teachers in schools. Although many of us in the school sector might respond, "and about time,
too," these criteria nevertheless indicate that central government's powers are being used to override important principles of academic autonomy at the institutional level.

Across the two sectors of higher education there are several important
characteristics relating to students that are, finally, worth nothing.

1. *There has been a considerable growth in student numbers.* In universities
the number has more than quadrupled from 50,000 to 210,000 between
1945 and 1971 and now stands at 296,000. In major institutions of further
education, the number rose from 36,000 in 1954 to 212,000 in 1971 and
is now 223,000 plus an additional 193,000 part-time students.[27]

2. *There has been a continuing predominance of students from social classes
I and II (higher professional).* Robbins had noted that 45 percent of the
children of these social classes were in universities compared with
4 percent from the skilled manual class. John H. Farrant states that in
1956, 24.6 percent of students in universities were from skilled manual
backgrounds but that by 1980 this had fallen to 19.4 percent.[28] This trend
is likely to continue as the birthrate has fallen somewhat in lower-middle-
class and working-class categories during 1964–1977, while it has risen
slightly in the higher social classes.[29]

3. *There has been a slightly reduced age participation rate (APR).* This has
fallen from 13.8 percent in 1971 to 12.5 percent in 1981. This has been
accompanied by an increased differential between the APR of male and
female students as shown in table 3.1:[30]

A continued regional disparity is also evident in the APR as shown
in table 3.2:[31]

The School Shapes Higher Education

It is possible to think of the relationship between schools and higher
education as one instance of a more general pattern of relationships
between donor and host institutions. The passing of individuals between

TABLE 3.2
1979 University Entrants per 1,000

North of England	79
East Midlands	82
West Midlands	83
Yorks and Humberside	83
East Anglia	89
Greater London	97
South West	101
North West	104
Wales	106
South East (excluding Greater London)	128

donors and hosts sets up a pattern that is modified by the behavior of the individuals who undertake the passage. The most common pattern can be represented by the following exchange between teacher and pupil:

Teacher: Didn't they teach you that at primary school?
Pupil: (With an air of aggrieved surprise) No, miss!

In this exchange the teacher confronts the pupil with an accusation that offers the pupil a ready scapegoat. Knowing the teacher is ready to hear and believe bad things about primary schools, the pupil need only blame his lack of knowledge on the primary school in the confident knowledge that the explanation will be accepted. The alternative would be to accept the onus himself and admit incompetence, poor memory, or stupidity. It is not surprising that in the transfer from donor to host there should be a marked tendency for the host to lay the blame for many of its difficulties at the door of the donor. (I do not rule out the possibility that the pupil may *not* have been taught whatever it was at primary school.)

We are here concerned with the passage of individuals from schools to higher education, but it is worth noting this general feature of the donor-host relationship, since it applies equally to the transition from schools to employers, and from universities to employers. I know from speaking to university colleagues, for example, that their experiences of employers is very similar to my own. It sometimes passes belief what an employer can be made to believe is not done, or no longer done, in educational institutions.

The general tendency is for donor institutions to feel they are to some degree powerless and misunderstood. The host institution, in the main, controls the nature of the transaction and complains if the donor tries to invade host territory. Further education and employers exert pressure to ensure that their specialized teaching or training is not diluted or corrupted by the donor's improper invasion. Instead, the teaching should be restricted to general education. This pressure has assumed different forms, but the nature of the dialectic is such that the host institution sometimes has to accommodate the changing norms of the donor.

The donor-host metaphor is a variant of the articulation function. The erosion of this in the postwar period in most of the systems described in this volume is also apparent in England and Wales. The dialectic between the school system and the universities—in particular, the pressures from teachers for a more accessible and democratic curriculum and from the university system for a traditionally qualified product—has been a major theme of the postwar period.

In 1951 the school certificate representing normal university matriculation requirements was altered. From its inception in 1917, the school certificate represented a consensus on what constituted a broad general education. All candidates were required to pass in five or more subjects, at least one from each of three main groups: English; a foreign language (usually French); and science and mathematics. From 1951 there were no particular subject-group requirements in the general certificate of education (GCE) ordinary (O)-level, and candidates could be entered for any number and combination, if necessary, over several years.

Universities continued to require, for their purposes, the same three subjects as before. Only recently have they—excepting Oxford and Cambridge—dropped the foreign language requirement. The demise of Latin and Greek and, more recently, foreign languages is an example of how the school system influences higher education. The school regulations of 1902 required the new secondary (grammar) schools to teach two languages, and "if Latin is not one of them, the Board will require to be satisfied that the omission of Latin is for the advantage of the schools."[32] In 1981 there were 146 candidates entered for Latin under the University of London GCE ordinary level compared to 246 candidates for Chinese and 1,724 for French. The comparable figure for French in 1970 was 2,418.[33] While modern language teaching as a whole has declined, falling school rolls and the relatively smaller size of secondary schools have meant that minority languages are increasingly difficult to support. A recent Schools Council study found that at A level, French is taught to fifty times more students than Russian, thirty-five times more than Italian, ten times more than Spanish, and three times more than German.[34] John Farrant notes that between 1960 and 1977 the proportion of candidates being entered for French, German, and Latin A level fell from 12.5 to 7.2 percent.[35]

Another significant trend in A-level teaching in secondary schools has been that of mixed science-art combinations. Between 1968 and 1979 there was a 12 percent increase in the number of candidates offering science, arts, and social science subject combinations.[36] The impact of this on higher education is unclear, and the evidence is contradictory. On one side the CNAA notes that the largest single increase of first-degree enrollments between 1980 and 1981 was in interdisciplinary courses (21 percent).[37] Perhaps, in this case, higher education is accommodating developments in the secondary system. Against this, Oliver Fulton in his introduction to the Leverhulme study, *Access to Higher Education*, comments:

> It is normal for a chemistry department, for example, to insist that its entrants have taken A-level courses not only in chemistry but also in mathematics and another relevant science such as physics. But in doing so it is protecting not so much its standard as the level at which it teaches. The huge increase in recent years in the proportion of A-level candidates who take "mixed" combinations of subjects (i.e. both science and non-science) means that this insistence actually reduced the pool of highly able applicants from which it can draw.[38]

In this case, the host institution is exerting its power; it is unwilling to adjust its teaching strategies to a curricular development in the donor institution.

The effect on the schools begins to take shape much earlier than the sixth form. Thirteen-year-old pupils invariably face an options system that narrows the curriculum in the last two years of compulsory education. Normally, mathematics and English are core subjects, but there is no statutory obligation for this or any other subject (except religious instruction). In recent years local authorities have been asked to report on their policies and practices in curricular matters in an attempt to secure an agreed-upon framework.

Nevertheless, the freedom to be eclectic frequently leads to specialization of a restrictive and often preemptive kind before the pupil reaches the sixth form. In the ILEA only 20 percent of girls in 1981 were studying physics and 39 percent chemistry in the final two years of compulsory secondary education.[39] The survey of secondary education conducted by Her Majesty's Inspectors in 1977 showed that only one-third of all pupils in the fourth year (ages fourteen to fifteen) were studying French, and that "broadly, the system commonly resulted in able pupils having to choose at 14 or earlier between science and languages." In this section of the survey, relating to option choices, the inspectors add, "A disturbing feature however was that in nearly 20 percent of the schools curricular choice was made without the benefit of advice from specialist careers teachers about the possible effects of such choices."[40]

The pool of qualified candidates is reduced, and numbers of pupils, often of considerable intellectual and academic potential, are lost. In particular, girls and members of ethnic minorities suffer unless positive intervention occurs either in the sixth form or in higher education. "Access" courses in polytechnics are now quite common and are designed to attract and support these marginal students. There is little evidence that universities adjust to the vagaries of unbalanced or inappropriate choices exercised at fourteen. However, they recognized that newer sixth forms in many comprehensive schools are at a disadvantage relative to well-established sixth forms in the remaining selective and independent schools. Both Oxford and Cambridge have devised special schemes to assist pupils who are "attending schools with little or no experience of submitting candidates to Oxford."[41] Sussex, York, and City universities have also adopted a special entry scheme for candidates from disadvantaged areas or schools. The effectiveness of these schemes is limited. Oxford and Cambridge continue to require basic matriculation standards, thus ruling out, for example, the able science candidate who (through no fault of his or her own) has no O-level foreign language. An analysis of the special ILEA-Oxford University PPE (philosophy-political science-economics) scheme showed that over the four years of its life, twenty-three candidates have been accepted, of whom six were female, three were from minority ethnic groups, and most were from professional families.[42] One applicant from my own school, the Islington Sixth Form Centre, failed but two months later passed the normal (supposedly overrigorous) Oxford entrance examination.

Recent proposals from the Dover Committee recommend that the Oxford University entrance examination be restricted to sixth-form pupils in their fourth term, thus denying the traditional seventh-term sitting for, in the main, independent-school pupils.[43] The latter are at an advantage because they have had a longer period of preparation, usually intensive and specialized, and their parents can afford this. Sixth-form pupils in maintained schools lack this advantage. In 1980, 48 percent of successful candidates at the University of Oxford were from independent schools,[44] and pupils in these schools represented 4.4 percent of school-leavers (all ages) in England and Wales.[45]

Special entry schemes to universities are largely ineffective and will remain so. The Leverhulme program of study on the future of higher education recognized this. The "gold standard," three-year-honors-degree course is questioned by the study group, particularly in the context of demographic changes:

> There will be substantial excess of capacity by the early 1990s unless universities, polytechnics and colleges can adapt to new tasks and to the needs of new types of students. . . . There is no reason why everything in an undergraduate curriculum should be taught in great depth. Breadth and the ability to integrate different ideas have intellectual as well as practical value. In the probable employment conditions of the 1980s and 1990s, very specialized first degrees are likely to be even less appropriate than they were in the 1960s.[46]

There is a recognition here of new types of students, including those who do not possess conventional A-level qualifications as well as those who continue to be underrepresented in higher education (girls and ethnic minorities).

The Leverhulme study group explicitly carries forward the values of the immediate postwar reconstruction period, placing its priorities in social-democratic objectives as opposed to a clear and narrow curricular assonance between secondary and higher education. The traditional protection of the latter has been eroded through graduate teachers (especially younger, leading teachers in comprehensive schools) no longer being prepared to support a tight articulation function. Graduate teachers are pulled in opposite directions; on the one hand, their membership in subject associations frequently brings them into contact with university teachers, representing, in the main, the preservation of the articulation function. On the other hand, these teachers directly experience the pressures exerted by the majority of secondary pupils, who resist the requirements of university elitist values. The emergence of comprehensive-school pressure groups, concerned primarily with the needs of the majority of pupils, similarly exacerbates these push-pull dynamics.

The call for multiple criteria for policy formation by the Leverhulme study group will go unheeded because of a combination of central government action and the response of those in the education system. Not the least of these factors are the unprecedented financial cuts in the entire education system and a lack of response or sympathy for such multiple criteria within the academic community itself.

The Higher Education System Shapes the School

There is little doubt that a major distinguishing feature of English education is the examination system. To a very large extent it has determined the curriculum of the schools, certainly from age fourteen up, and recent measures requiring the publication of exam results have intensified the degree to which ordinary parents rely on examinations as a primary, perhaps *the* primary, indicator of the quality of schooling.

It is one of the many paradoxes of the English system that examinations were initiated as a democratizing and meritocratic measure. They were intended to eliminate abuses of nepotism and favoritism in the civil service (especially the Indian service) and to provide genuine opportunities for young men of talent but no birth or connections. The present English examination system stems from the second half of the nineteenth century. In the early days the examinations formed part of a system for matriculation, or qualifying for university entrance. As such, they provided the means by which the newer private schools could establish their credentials against the older foundations, such as Eton and Harrow. By the same token, they provided a means by which the grammar schools could gain access to the universities, especially the key, prestigious institutions, Oxford and Cambridge. The two oldest universities were also, predictably, the two first examining boards. They were soon followed by the other universities, either acting in groups or individually.

Concerned about the proliferation of different examining bodies and about possible variations in standards, the Board of Education (as it was called then) proposed in 1912 that the universities be regarded as the responsible bodies and the board itself take on a coordinating role. For this role it set up a Secondary Schools Examinations Council. The underlying principles of the examinations to be taken at age sixteen were set out in a series of circulars. Provision was made for consultation with the teachers in schools: "It is a cardinal principle that the examination should follow the curriculum and not determine it."[47]

The uncoupling of the articulation function so powerfully represented in the examination system was most apparent after the Secondary Schools Examinations Council was reformed in 1964 with the establishment of a broader based Schools Council. The council brought together teacher representatives, all branches of higher education, the inspectorate, and local education authorities. It set out "to secure a happier marriage than in the past between the actual work of the schools . . . and the examinations which . . . can too easily stand in the way of necessary innovation."[48]

The increased participation of teachers in curriculum development and examination reform, coupled with the emergence of a new breed of curriculum-development officers in the Schools Council, reached a new peak in the mid-1970s. The attempt to establish a common examination at sixteen plus (to be more reflective of the comprehensive ideology) was an outcome of this activity. The degree to which the secretary of state can be regarded as a "mediating institution" is questionable; however, the present (1983) incumbent's recent statements approving or disapproving the proposals for syllabi in the proposed common examination at age sixteen plus suggest that he is just this. In new syllabi for the physical sciences, for example, separate requirements for the most able pupils combine with a rejection of applied or social considerations.

The emergence of the Manpower Services Commission (MSC), a quasi-autonomous nongovernmental organization, or QUANGO, linked to the Department of Employment, similarly underlines the current secretary of state's desire to recouple a part of the secondary school system with the university system. The MSC is increasingly promoted as the provider of solutions to the needs of the majority of secondary pupils. The more democratic tendencies of the Schools Council (disbanded in 1983) and the active participation of secondary school teachers are diminishing, and the return of a tighter articulation function between the school and the university is apparent.

The training and supply of teachers is a further component in the articulation process. Two-thirds of secondary school teachers are graduates, mainly of British universities. Except in shortage subjects, such as math or physics, graduates are unable to teach without having pursued a postgraduate training course, usually in a university department of education, although approximately one-third of all graduate teachers are now trained in public-sector institutions, including the former colleges of education, most of which were merged with the polytechnics during the 1970s. In 1982 the secretary of state issued a circular that required a closer link between the first degree subject of the graduate-trainee teachers and their main secondary-school teaching subject. This has had a restricting effect on both the source of graduate teachers and on the broadening of the school curriculum. On the whole, a more traditional and conventional school curriculum will emerge; minority subjects such as anthropology and psychology, as well as most multidisciplinary courses, will disappear as a source of teachers and as components in the secondary-school curriculum.

The status of departments of education within the university community is low, and they also tend to be insular. Most research projects are funded by the Department of Education and Science. This current position contrasts with the early 1970s, when educational research was considered a more glamorous business and attracted major funding from foundations such as Nuffield, Ford, and Gulbenkian. The DES *Teaching Quality* white paper referred to earlier is likely to reduce still further the status and increase the insularity of university departments of education, not least the requirements that the length of the academic year be increased in postgraduate certificate-of-education courses, and that the trainers should be able to demonstrate substantial and recent teaching experiences in school.

Given that the role of the examination system has always been powerful in determining the nature of transactions between the school and the university, in addition, the nature of the sixth form has exerted an equally powerful influence. The sixth form became almost an institution in itself, with its own cultural and political life. Based on grammar- and ultimately public-school values, it was very specifically conceived as a training ground for the university. But it had a dual purpose. Following public-school ideals of leadership and community within the secondary school, it was regarded as important that this separate unit within the school should not be cut off from the eleven-to-sixteen age group. The grounds for this were that this sixth form would provide leadership and set the moral, cultural, and intellectual tone of the whole institution. On all levels, the sixth form was seen as an essential part of the institution. In an Arnoldian way, the community of the school was seen as incomplete or deprived without its elite. In 1944, the criticism that this provided a further age of selection, in addition to that proposed at eleven, would not have seemed valid or relevant. The sixth form was to be the "perfect class" of the secondary school.

The Crowther report of 1959 set out what it thought to be the distinctive features of a sixth form. The key passage reads:

A close link with a university is, in our opinion, one of the essential marks of a Sixth Form. . . . The good and keen sixth former has looked forward to being a science specialist, or a classicist, or a historian: his mind has been set that way by inclination. . . . Whatever hinders specialisation is to him, at first a waste of time. . . . Specialisation is a mark of a Sixth Form, and "subject mindedness" of the Sixth Former. The third mark of the Sixth Form is independent work. . . . Independent work by a pupil, as we understand it, implies a considerable amount of time to devote to a subject, time enough anyhow to make his own discoveries. . . . The fourth mark is the intimate relationship between pupil and teacher which is characteristic of a good Sixth Form. There is no commonly accepted phrase to describe the situation— perhaps "intellectual discipleship" comes as near as any. . . . There is a fifth mark of the Sixth Form, or rather of the Sixth Former, which ought not to be passed over—social responsibility. . . . Two things make it possible. The first is the mere fact of age, and the maturity which comes with it. The second is the thoughtfulness which comes from the intellectual life developed by Sixth Form work.[49]

Reid and Filby's response to this is that "historically and empirically most of the statements just do not stand up. A few leading public schools apart, the relation between sixth forms and universities had never been clear cut. Through the 1920s and 1930s, university entrants had represented only around 50 percent of the grammar school population, and the postwar expansion reduced even this figure."[50] The Crowther report frankly recognized that its description of the sixth form was an ideal, but it is an ideal that remains pervasive.

The recent increase in the number of proposals from local authorities to the secretary of state for a break at sixteen and the establishment of sixth-form or tertiary colleges has provoked reactions based on the ideal sixth form. The current secretary of state, Sir Keith Joseph, rejected a reorganization scheme in Manchester because two of the eleven-to-eighteen schools were "of proven quality which continue to demonstrate their success in the provision they make for *sixth form education*" (emphasis added).[51]

C. B. Cox, professor of English literature at the University of Manchester, at the same time produced a pamphlet, published by the Conservative Political Centre, in which he identified sixth-form colleges as "a particularly dangerous part of a left-wing campaign to control the country's education system." The colleges, he thought, would "downgrade the status of A levels and . . . create an egalitarian ethos instead of an environment of a community of scholars."[52]

Two important issues arise from these statements, and both reinforce the articulation function. First, the concept of the "sponsorship model," creating an elite, is powerfully evident in such reactions. The opposing concept of "association" is more evident in sixth-form or in tertiary colleges, further-education colleges, and increasingly in the universities themselves.[53] The secularization process has moved rapidly. Second, however, the top-down approach is accepted as not too high a price to pay. In the case of Manchester, the secretary of state's rejection of the reorganization scheme resulted in £4 million overspending and the preservation of a secondary education system that was bound to discriminate against those children most in need of help and encouragement. The structural issue has to be recognized as inextricably connected with the top-down examinations, and therefore with the curricular issue. In the recent report of a committee of inquiry into the teaching of mathematics in schools, this problem is clearly stated:

> . . . syllabuses now being followed by a majority of pupils in secondary schools have been constructed by using as starting points syllabuses designed for pupils in the top quarter of the range of attainment in mathematics. Syllabuses for pupils of lower attainment have been developed from these by deleting a few topics and reducing the depth of treatment of others; in other words, they have been constructed "from the top downwards." *We believe that this is a wrong approach and the developments should be "from the bottom*

upwards" by considering the range of work which is appropriate for the lower-attaining pupils and extending this range as the level of attainment of pupils increases. (Original emphasis.)[54]

Irrespective of such statements as this, or those from the Leverhulme study, the influence of universities on secondary schools remains powerful. Indeed, there is evidence that when that influence showed signs of being eroded during the 1970s, the present government intervened to reverse the process. Similarly, academic drift in public-sector institutions is likely to accelerate, partly because dominant cultural values and status are located in the universities, and partly because pressures are being exerted by candidates who five or ten years ago would have been offered places in universities.

Conclusion

It would be overly simple to conclude that current signs of reaction to an uncoupling of the articulation function entirely result from the predilections or idiosyncracies of a particular secretary of state or of the government of which he is a member. The wider social and economic climate has changed, and the government reflects this. The processes that permeate across boundaries such as those of education systems are complex and unclear. It is possible that social and value changes are especially difficult to analyze or locate, or to reverse.

For example, I have referred briefly to an increased secularization of sixth forms and universities. By this I mean that these centers of traditional elitism, in order to continue to be powerful and effective, have assumed some of the more *Gesellschaft* characteristics of public-sector colleges. This is not a direct transaction between the two kinds of educational institution but more, I believe, an extension of wider social mores, probably assisted by the larger sizes of institutions, in which rituals and more arcane expressions of intellectual discipleship are difficult to sustain. Salter and Tapper observe that independent schools have become less concerned with certain expressive values and more concerned with "formally certified academic competence." There is less evidence of compulsory games or church attendance. There is a less strongly hierarchical prefect system, and girls are commonly accepted in the sixth form. "The stress is now upon the attainment of examination success which is seen as the key to future individual promotion."[55] The more instrumental goals represent, in the independent-school sector, the secularization process evident elsewhere in society and in other educational institutions.

A related phenomenon is the spread of a distinct and powerful youth culture. The protective coloring adopted by middle-class pupils in both prestigious independent schools and comprehensive schools represents a social style designed perhaps as an expression of youth solidarity against the adult world. It is difficult to identify a Winchester boy these days; he is as likely as an inner-city, "disadvantaged" boy to be "punk" and to speak in as inarticulate a manner as he can devise. The middle-class boy or girl, however, is likely to enter higher education, and in this sense the fashionable proletarian image is a change of style, not substance. The working-class boy or girl, by contrast, is less likely to enter higher education now than twenty years ago, and it is the choice exercised at sixteen that is crucial. Alan Gordon reports that "a survey of fifth formers undertaken in 1975 found disenchantment with school or with teachers to be a major reason given for the decision to leave at sixteen. Thirty-eight percent of boys questioned and 45 percent of the girls said that they had decided to leave because they were 'fed up' with school."[56]

Paul Willis, in his *Learning to Labour: How Working Class Kids Get Working Class Jobs,* presents an account of the deep-seated cultural hostility to school among working-class pupils.[57] He turns the proposition neatly on its head, however, by suggesting that, paradoxically, schools are actually operating as highly efficient socializers of such pupils into the roles required of them in society at large and developing their ability to cope with the problems this is likely to present to them. This analysis makes schools determinist agents of the socioeconomic system with a directness that would be difficult to sustain, but it does suggest that the grading and selection tasks required of schools continue to override secularization processes and educational reforms already achieved or postulated for the future.

A further influence on the values of the wider society is the employment structure. All major government inquiries into the educational system have included employers and trade union representatives. However, at the level of the individual young person and the school or higher-education institution, there are direct transactions taking place. In the independent schools, Salter and Tapper note that "the curriculum, with its strong applied element in both sciences and social sciences, is attuned to the needs of industry and many, if not most, pupils think in terms of a career in industry."[58]

The point is also made that the continuing success of the independent schools rests on their recognition that the shift toward a stronger academic ethos is a response to the demands of older professions (law, medicine, the army), which now require higher academic standards through the universities. By contrast, the stock exchange and management in industry retain an interest in the more traditional expressive values of the independent schools:

> Public school education is of no significance as a qualification for partnership in a firm of stockbrokers; but the high degree of probity, the capacity for prolonged hard work and personal discipline and the personal connections required to obtain access to business are less frequently found in men who have not attended public schools.[59]

The considerable sums of money donated to the independent schools by members of the Confederation of British Industry for improved science, and more recently design and technology accommodation and facilities bear witness to the continuing articulation function not only between the university and the independent schools but also between industry and that sector.

Substantial numbers of successful A-level students use their qualifications not for access to higher education but for direct entry to employment. This has always been so but has recently increased. In 1966–1967, 17 percent of school-leavers with two or more A-level passes entered permanent employment. By 1978–1979 this had risen to 23 percent.[60] This trend may continue as graduate unemployment becomes more evident. The effect of graduate unemployment could be either a displacement by graduates of middle-level jobs (taking these jobs away from the traditional A-level candidates) or an increased rate of A-level applicants going directly into employment because they prefer not to take undue risks implicit in a further three years of education.

At the point when pupils decide whether or not they ought to stay in full-time education (whether sixth form or further-education college), there is evidence that quite hardheaded calculations are being made concerning career opportunities and earnings:

> There are in fact several ways in which economic considerations might affect demand. The material circumstances of the home is one. A second is the direct and indirect costs of staying on at school or college, the impact of which on any individual is obviously affected by his or her material circumstances. A third is the prospective student's perceptions of the personal economic benefits to be derived from continued education. In addition, there may be more general economic, social and cultural benefits, perhaps related to labour market opportunities.[61]

The impact of policies such as educational maintenance allowances to sixth-form pupils could be significant. At present these allowances are paid at the discretion of local authorities; policies as well as amounts may vary widely. Fulton and Gordon in their 1977 survey of 3,000 sixteen-year-olds calculated that an eight-pound-per-week grant would increase the staying-on rate by 4.8 percent for boys and 5.6 percent for girls.[62] The recent trend by the Department of Health and Social Security to allow unemployed young people to undertake part-time education for less than twenty-one hours a week and still draw unemployment benefits (currently £15.80 a week) will perhaps increase the effective staying-on rate. The different levels and kinds of grants available, as well as the young person's perception of expected returns, will affect the considerations described by Gordon in 1976.

The employment structure has also affected the development and popularity of different degree courses. In the decade 1970–1980, the largest increases of admissions to first-degree courses, in both universities and polytechnics, were in business management, accountancy, land estate management, and town and country planning.[63] The competition factor calculated by the Conference of University Administrators shows that between 1968 and 1970, medicine, dentistry, engineering, and technology significantly increased their competitiveness (demand ranking), while social studies and arts subjects moved down.[64] School-leavers' awareness of the labor market, combined with a rise in required qualifications for entry to professions, explain these trends and underline the important influence of the economic context and, in particular, the employment structure.

Structural unemployment and changing employment needs will increasingly affect higher education. The demand for retraining and non-vocational courses for the adult population is not wholly recognized by universities as part of their mainstream work. A considerable proportion of such demand is likely to be for part-time study, even though mature, full-time students now comprise about a quarter of all home entrants to higher education (compared with 14 percent at the time of the Robbins report). Twenty percent of CNAA first-degree courses are part-time, and the growth of these represents a deliberate policy aimed at increasing the participation rate of adults and is a response to their needs. Such evidence as exists suggests that most mature students are enrolled in vocational courses, but in universities enrollments in humanities and arts courses are also significant.[65]

As the school population continues to decline, with relative increases of young applicants from professional classes, an important social policy consideration will be the attitude of the universities to the balance of places for young as opposed to mature applicants. Central-government and local-authority policies also need to take account of the changing educational needs of adults, not least with regard to maintenance allowances.

The relationship between the secondary and higher education systems, then, is as strongly affected by changes and values in society as a whole, not least by the employment structure, as it is by the particular and connected histories of each system. In the nineteenth century there were dramatic struggles between the state and local authorities, between social classes, between religious groups; these have continued to shape the values and policies of the school and higher education systems. The binary policy, the examination system, and the present debates concerning the fourteen-to-nineteen sector, including the separate powers of the Manpower Services Commission, all reflect dissonances that were thought to have been resolved over a hundred years ago.

Notes

1. Taylor and Saunders, *The Law of Education*, pp. 70–208.

2. *Education Act, 1944*, section 8; Taylor and Saunders, *The Law of Education*, p. 79.

3. Ibid., p. 80.

4. Board of Education, *Secondary Education* (Spens Report). Board of Education, *Curriculum and Examinations in the Secondary Schools* (Norwood Report).

5. Norwood Report.

6. Norwood Report, pp. 23, 139.

7. Benn and Simon, *Half Way There*, p. 17.

8. DES, Circular 10/65.

9. Reported in the *Times Educational Supplement*, 29 January 1965.

10. *Education Act, 1944*, sections 43-6; Taylor and Saunders, *The Law of Education*, pp. 137–141.

11. Manpower Services Commission, *Outlook on Training*.

12. Reid and Filby, *The Sixth: An Essay in Education and Democracy*, pp. 184–185.

13. Briault and Smith, *Falling Rolls in Secondary Schools*, table 1.

14. University Grants Committee, *University Development, 1947–52*, pp. 20–27.

15. Reid and Filby, *The Sixth: An Essay in Education and Democracy*, figure 5.

16. University Grants Committee, *University Development, 1935–47*, p. 6.

17. Becher and Kogan, *Process and Structure in Higher Education*, p. 31.

18. Ministry of Education, *Technical Education*.

19. Burgess and Pratt, *Polytechnics*.

20. DES, *Higher Education* (the Robbins Report).

21. Anthony Crosland, speech at Lancaster University, January 1967, reprinted in Robinson, *The New Polytechnics*, appendix C.

22. *The People's Universities* is the subtitle of Robinson's book, *The New Polytechnics*.

23. Becher and Kogan, *Process and Structure in Higher Education*, p. 37.

24. CNAA, *Directory of First Degree Courses, 1982–3*.

25. DES, *Report of the Study Group on the Government of Colleges of Education*, (the Weaver Report).

26. DES, *Teaching Quality*, 1983.

27. DES, *Future Demand for Higher Education in Great Britain*, table 1.

28. Farrant, "Trends in Admission," table 2.17.

29. DES, *Future Demand for Higher Education in Great Britain*.

30. Farrant, "Trends in Admission," table 2.4.

31. Ibid., table 2.20.

32. Board of Education, School Regulations, 1902, quoted in Reid and Filby, *The Sixth*, p. 93.

33. University of London, *General Certificates of Education Examination Statistics*, January 1970 and January 1982.

34. Schools Council, *Languages Other than French in the Secondary Schools*.

35. Farrant, "Trends in Admission," p. 53.

36. DES, *Provisional Figures of Leavers from English Schools, CSE and GCE Statistics, 1979*, Statistical Bulletin 15/80.

37. CNAA, *Annual Report, 1981*.

38. Fulton, *Access to Higher Education*, p. 25.

39. ILEA, *School Examination Results in the ILEA, 1981*.

40. DES, *Aspects of Secondary Education in England*, 1979.

41. University of Oxford, *Undergraduate Prospectus, 1984–5*, p. 21.

42. A verbal report given to ILEA headteachers by a group of Oxford University teachers, November 1982.

43. Reported in the *Times Educational Supplement*, 10 June 1983.

44. University of Oxford, *Undergraduate Prospectus, 1984–5*, table 1.

45. DES, *English School Leavers, 1979–80*, Statistical Bulletin 12/81, table 6.

46. Society for Research into Higher Education, *Excellence in Diversity* (Leverhulme Report), "Course Content and Structure."

47. House of Commons, *The Secondary Schools Curriculum and Examinations*, Annex III, p. cxvii.

48. Schools Council, *Change and Response*, p. 21.

49. DES, *15–18* (the Crowther Report), pp. 223–225.

50. Reid and Filby, *The Sixth*, p. 146.

51. Reported in the *Times Educational Supplement*, 20 November 1981.

52. Reported in the *Guardian*, 15 November 1981.

53. King, *Schools and Colleges*, p. 151.

54. DES, *Mathematics Counts* (the Cockcroft Report).

55. Salter and Tapper, *Education, Politics and the State,* p. 185.
56. Gordon, "Educational Choices of Young People," p. 133.
57. Willis, *Learning to Labour.*
58. Salter and Tapper, *Education, Politics and the State,* p. 185.
59. Ibid., p. 186.
60. Farrant, "Trends in Admission," table 2.9.
61. Gordon, "Educational Choices of Young People," p. 133.
62. Ibid., p. 135.
63. Farrant, "Trends in Admission," table 2.14.
64. Ibid., p. 53.
65. Ibid., pp. 55–56.

Bibliography

BECHER, TONY, and MAURICE KOGAN. *Process and Structure in Higher Education.* London: Heinemann, 1980.

BENN, CAROLINE, and BRIAN SIMON. *Half Way There.* New York: McGraw-Hill, 1970.

Board of Education. *Report of the Consultative Committee of Secondary Education with Special Reference to the Grammar Schools and Technical High Schools* (the Spens Report). London, 1938.

Board of Education. *Report of the Department Committee on Curriculum and Examinations* (the Norwood Report). London, 1943.

BRIAULT, ERIC W., and FRANCES SMITH. *Falling Rolls in Secondary Schools,* Part 1. Slough: National Foundation for Educational Research, 1980.

BURGESS, TYRELL, and JOHN PRATT. *Polytechnics: A Report.* London: Pitman, 1974.

Central Advisory Council for Education (England). *15–18.* London: HMSO, 1959.

Council for National Academic Awards. *Annual Report, 1981.* London, 1982.

————. *Directory of First Degree Courses, 1982–3.* London, 1982.

Department of Education and Science. *15–18* (the Crowther Report). London: HMSO, 1959.

————. *Higher Education* (the Robbins Report). London: HMSO, 1963.

————. *Report of the Study on the Government of Colleges of Education* (the Weaver Report). London: HMSO, 1966.

————. *Aspects of Secondary Education in England: A Survey by Her Majesty's Inspectors.* London: HMSO, 1979.

————. *Provisional Figures of Leavers from English Schools, CSE and GSE Statistics, 1979.* Statistical Bulletin 15/80. London: HMSO, 1980.

————. *English School Leavers, 1979–80.* Statistical Bulletin 12/81. London: HMSO, 1981.

————. *Mathematics Counts: A Report of the Committee of Enquiry into the Teaching of Mathematics* (the Cockcroft Report). London: HMSO, 1982.

————. *Future Demand for Higher Education in Great Britain.* London: HMSO, 1983.

————. *Teaching Quality.* London: HMSO, 1983.

FARRANT, JOHN H. "Trends in Admission. In *Access to Higher Education,* ed. Oliver Fulton. Guildford: University of Surrey, 1981.

FULTON, OLIVER, ed. *Access to Higher Education.* Leverhulme Programme of Study into the Future of Higher Education, no. 2. Society for Research into Higher Education, University of Surrey. Guildford: University of Surrey, 1981.

GORDON, ALAN. "Educational Choices of Young People." In *Access to Higher Education,* ed. Oliver Fulton. Guildford: University of Surrey, 1981.

House of Commons Select Committee on Education, Science and Arts. *The Secondary Schools Curriculum and Examinations.* Second Report, Session 1981–82. Volume 1. London: HMSO, 1982.

Inner London Educational Authority. *School Examination Results in the ILEA, 1981.* London, 1982.

KING, RONALD. *Schools and Colleges: Studies in Post 16 Education.* London: Routledge and Kegan Paul, 1976.

Manpower Services Commission. *Outlook on Training.* London, 1980.

Ministry of Education. *Technical Education.* London: HMSO, 1956.

REID, WILLIAM, and JANE FILBY. *The Sixth: An Essay in Education and Democracy.* Brighton: Falmer Press, 1982.

ROBINSON, ERIC. *The New Polytechnics: The People's Universities.* Harmondsworth, Middlesex, England: Penguin Education, 1968.

SALTER, BRIAN, and TED TAPPER. *Education, Politics and the State.* London: Grant McIntyre, 1981.

Schools Council. *Languages Other Than French in the Secondary School.* London, 1982.

————. *Change and Response.* Guildford: University of Surrey, 1977.

Society for Research into Higher Education. *Excellence in Diversity.* A Report of the Leverhulme Programme of Study into the Future of Higher Education. Guildford: University of Surrey, 1983.

TAYLOR, GEORGE, and JOHN B. SAUNDERS. *The Law of Education.* 8th ed. London: Butterworth, 1976.

University Grants Committee. *University Development 1935–47.* London: HMSO, 1948.

————. *University Development 1947–52.* London: HMSO, 1953.

University of London. *General Certificate of Education Examination Statistics.* London, January 1970, January 1980.

University of Oxford. *Undergraduate Prospectus, 1984–85.* Oxford, 1984.

WILLIS, PAUL. *Learning to Labour: How Working Class Kids Get Working Class Jobs.* Farnborough: Saxon House, 1977.

4

Sweden

LARS EKHOLM

IN THE NOW DISTANT PAST, the Swedish educational system was much influenced by foreign practices, right down to using the word *gymnasium* for the academic secondary school. Hence, it would not be surprising if we should find some important similarities between Swedish education and the structures of education in Western Europe depicted in the foregoing chapters. Yet, the Swedish system has also long been shaped by the distinctive features of the Swedish context: in particular, it has been greatly altered in the postwar decades by a series of centrally instituted reforms planned and implemented by a Social Democratic government, often with the support of other political parties. Thus, it is at once a traditional European system and a much reformed one upon which a great deal of thought and research have been lavished, and for which more change has already been planned for well into the 1990s.

I shall try to describe this system in some detail, with special attention to the relation between a frequently transformed secondary level and a rapidly changing system of higher education. In the Swedish case it is also compelling to highlight a grading and selection system that receives much public attention and debate. Following the logic of Ulrich Teichler's analysis of the German pattern (chapter 2), we may view this system as a third element, a set of connections so important in its own right and sufficiently separate in thought and practice that we need to isolate it analytically and study its structure and dynamics.

The Basic Structure

The general pattern of Swedish education can be outlined as follows:
Preschool (to age six), is controlled by agencies outside of education.
Comprehensive school (ages seven to sixteen), is a nine-year, compulsory

103

unit divided into junior, middle, and senior levels, each comprising three years; the comprehensive school gives a general education (no vocational training), and elective courses may be chosen at the senior level. Since 1982 all pupils have been given the right to choose any line of study, irrespective of electives, as they proceed to the next level.

Integrated upper secondary school (ages seventeen-eighteen, seventeen-nineteen, seventeen-twenty) consists of twenty-five study lines and a number of special courses. This level is postcompulsory, but provision is made for all of the age groups.

Adult education exists at both the comprehensive and the upper secondary level, offering a second chance for adults to complete courses at these two levels and a chance for students who have already completed the upper secondary school to take courses that will help them qualify for higher education.

Higher education, since 1977, consists of traditional universities and nonuniversity postsecondary institutions. Admission is restricted.

Research training consists of advanced courses in research and a thesis. A full-time research student, entitled to supervision, ought to complete the Ph.D. in four years. Graduates from nonuniversity programs are now encouraged to qualify for such training.

THE INTEGRATED UPPER SECONDARY SCHOOL

The two tasks of the Swedish upper secondary school are reflected in the organization of the curriculum into two major types of programs, after which, in theory, students either enter the labor market or continue their studies in higher education. The vocationally oriented pathways are two years long, and there are also a great number of so-called special courses, lasting from a few weeks to three years, which offer further vocational training. Working-life instruction in upper secondary school is fairly general in character, implying that a pupil leaving upper secondary school must get additional specialized vocational training later, normally offered as on-the-job training in industry and commerce. The other type of program consists of theoretical coursework that takes either two, three, or four years to complete.

The upper secondary school is usually described as an integrated institution, meaning that the overarching goals are the same, irrespective of various objectives for programs or groupings of them. Only to a certain extent is the curriculum actually integrated. Some schools cover the entire range of fields of study—vocational and theoretical. But it is more accurate to describe the upper secondary school as coordinated rather than integrated, since in marked contrast to the lower, comprehensive level of schooling, it is internally highly differentiated. It is the product of a wave of specific reforms that began during the 1960s, efforts that gradually brought together and reshaped several types of schools that originated in different periods.

The academic gymnasium dates to the 1930s, at which time it offered Latin and natural science lines of study; a general line was added in the 1950s. Only university preparatory tasks with a totally academic curriculum was offered. Two more specialized types of gymnasiums, one technical and one commercial, also existed. In a reform effective from 1966, these three types of schools were integrated into a new gymnasium that contained five lines of study. Along with these, a continuation school with three two-year lines of study had been set up in the 1950s. Oriented toward general subjects, it was also based more on practical applications than was the gymnasium. The system also included vocational schools that initially had a large number of highly specialized courses but which were reformed in the direction of providing a basic vocational education followed by in-service training in industry and commerce. Thus, by the 1960s there were three types of education at the upper secondary level: the new gymnasium, the continuation school, and the vocational school.

In 1968 the Swedish parliament decided that these three types of education ought to be integrated. During the following years a new curriculum was prepared, and in 1971 the present upper secondary school was initiated.[1] Its structure is as follows:

- Sixteen vocational study lines, all running for two years. Examples are nursing, building and construction, and distribution and clerical lines. The origin of many of these lines lies in the vocational school.
- Three two-year theoretical lines, social, economic, and technical. Their origins are to be found in the continuation school.
- Four theoretical lines running for three years: liberal arts, social science, economics, and natural science. These programs of study originated in the old academic and commercial gymnasiums.
- One four-year theoretical line, a technical one, with roots in the old technical gymnasium.
- One music line of two years' duration.

Thus, in contrast to the compulsory comprehensive school, the voluntary upper secondary school is heavily streamed. Each line has its own goal, with the contents adjusted accordingly. Teaching is not integrated, save for a few exceptions, such as in the first year across the liberal arts and social science lines. After the second year, many lines are further divided into branches and specializations. As indicated, each line has its own timetable. With regard to subject matter, Swedish, civics or job-world orientation, and gymnastics are given in all the lines. In vocational lines, there are some electives chosen from general subjects in the two-year theoretical lines, but they cover at best only about 10 percent of the timetable. The most common electives are English, mathematics, and drawing; the courses in Swedish and English are important to those wishing to be admitted to higher education. Some of the vocational lines have practical work integrated into the curriculum; for instance, a pupil in nursing also works in a hospital.[2]

Quantitative planning for the upper secondary school is at present programmed for 100 percent of an annual cohort of sixteen-year-olds, about 100,000 places. This does not mean that all sixteen-year-olds attend upper secondary school; current forecasts indicate that about 85 percent will do so. As between the theoretical and vocational lines, the vocational ones have attracted more and more students, with about 45 percent of the total number now found in them.[3]

REFORM PROPOSALS FOR THE UPPER SECONDARY SCHOOL
OF THE 1980s AND 1990s

According to Swedish tradition, much reform planning in education, as in other sectors of society, is carried out by government commissions. In 1976 a Social Democratic government established a commission that had the task of reviewing the basic structure of the upper secondary school. The commission finished its work in 1981 and, again following Swedish tradition, submitted its report to a great number of interested agencies and outside groups, asking for their reactions. Following all this consultation, not yet completed by mid-1983, the government will present a guideline bill to Parliament.

Considering the present line system in the upper secondary school too rigid, the commission has presented a number of major proposals that would further reshape Swedish education. These include ways of easing the transfer of students from the comprehensive school to the upper secondary level and other measures that might insure that all sixteen-year-olds will attend the upper school; major changes in the line system itself; and changes in the linkage between upper secondary and higher education. In principle, the commission has maintained the borderline between comprehensive and upper secondary schools. It has proposed, however, that the last term in the comprehensive school ought to some extent be used deliberately to prepare students for upper secondary schooling. Most important, pupils will choose not among twenty-five study lines as they do today but among three sectors—social, economic, and technical—with the latter divided into four blocks. The current proposals conceive of two kinds of education: three-year, "long" programs that are mainly theoretical, and two-year, "short" programs that are mainly vocational. A better balance between the theoretical and the vocational within each major type of program is sought. The commission has recommended that the long, mostly theoretical programs be supplemented by both applied courses and practical work. At the same time, the programs that are mainly vocational ought to contain more theoretical subjects, in particular, English, Swedish, civics, and cultural knowledge.

A central ambition of this recent commission has been to eliminate dead ends. Students in a short vocational program should be able to choose supplementary theoretical courses that will give them the same qualifications they would have if they had attended a long program. In turn, students in the long theoretical programs, taking some vocationally oriented short courses, should be better prepared to plunge into the labor market if desired.[4]

HIGHER EDUCATION

During the twenty years between 1950 and 1970, the number of university places increased ten times.[5] This is the period when Sweden, like many countries, transformed its universities from institutions of elite education to ones of mass education. Enrollment peaked by the end of the 1960s, then decreased for a short period, only to increase again. At the moment, with large numbers of children born in the 1960s in Sweden, demographic changes pose serious problems for future quantitative planning. The main factor behind rapid expansion was the increased number of educational alternatives at the upper secondary level. Many more students became entitled to enter higher education. In addition to the "push" of the school, there has been the "pull" of the job market. An expanding economy, save for recent stringencies, has increased the demand for highly trained people. It also has measurably increased the resources of government for funding educational expansion, including an improved scheme for student financial aid.

During the 1950s and 1960s a number of reforms were introduced in the Swedish higher education system. In addition to the four existing universities, a fifth was founded in northern Sweden. Just as important was the establishment of four affiliated universities. Thus, university education was dispersed in a way that attracted increased numbers of entrants. Quantitative planning followed two paths. In the faculties of liberal arts, social sciences, natural sciences, theology, and law, admission was "free," that is, unrestricted; a *numerus clausus* applied to the faculties of medicine, dentistry, pharmacy, and technology. These restricted-admissions faculties, however, opened up to more students by increasing their intake capacities. Nevertheless, this policy of division between restricted and unrestricted access led to overcrowded free faculties. Funding was then based on a new, "automatic" system, in which allocations in proportion to the influx of students were granted. Staffing was reorganized; new types of teaching posts were introduced.

An important policy element during this period was the combination of free admission to the above mentioned faculties combined with organizational measures relating to the structure of coursework. Traditionally, the student chose subjects fairly freely in the faculties of liberal arts, social sciences, and natural sciences. However, since government was concerned not only about rising costs but also about meager prospects in the labor market for students with nonvocational programs, it therefore tried to introduce a system with fixed coursework. This system was intended to guarantee a reasonable examination pass-rate; the arrangement, however, was quite unpopular among students and also within academia.

The quantitative problems of the 1960s brought a further issue concerning the overall planning of the educational system to the forefront. There were a number of institutions of postsecondary education outside the university system which provided more professionally and vocationally oriented education. But, with few exceptions, in contrast to the universities, no research was carried on. From a student's point of view, the programs of these postsecondary institutions could be regarded as equal alternatives to university education.

This was the background for reform planning in the late 1960s and the early 1970s, which aimed at creating a comprehensive higher education system in Sweden. It is usually associated with the accomplishments of the 1968 Education Commission known as U68, which began in 1968 and delivered its final report in 1973. The commission's task was to propose major reforms at the postsecondary level. Three subtasks were on the agenda: quantitative planning, localization, and administrative organization. The commission's ideological guidelines, viewing all postsecondary education from a comprehensive perspective, were a major influence on Swedish higher education policy in the 1970s and 1980s.

There were at least four arguments for a comprehensive higher education system. (1) In the face of exploding student numbers, the government thought it necessary to plan to make available an entire spectrum of places for students of school-leaving age. (2) For the sake of equality, it was felt that differences in prestige between various institutions of higher education should be abolished or at least diminished. Closely linked to this was the idea of enhancing the quality of training in the nonuniversity sector by linking it to developments in the research based university sector. (3) In a mass education society, students and employers needed to be informed about the postsecondary system in intelligible terms. (4) Concerning the curriculum, there needed to be a reasonable amount of flexibility and transferability of credits from one type of education to another.

Reforms in higher education were enacted by Parliament in 1975 and 1977 and became effective from 1977. Political compromises were introduced on some points, but the main elements of the original reform proposals were kept. A few years earlier, Parliament had voted on the issue of admission requirements to higher education. An important decision about the linkage between the upper secondary and the higher-education levels, it laid down the basic rules regarding entry to institutions of higher education for graduates from the newly established, integrated upper secondary schools. These rules were incorporated into the parliamentary decision of 1975 on higher education.

In short, the present higher education system can be characterized by such key phrases as broadened recruitment, increased accessibility, regional development, links to working life, connections with research, recurrent education, decentralization of decision-making powers, and participation by various interest groups. The basic principle is that all higher education at one region is brought together in a single administrative unit. With respect to origins, the unified higher education system covers the following types of institutions: the universities and some specialized colleges, such as the Royal Institute of Technology and the Caroline Institute of Medicine, all of which have permanent facilities for research; university colleges without permanent research facilities, whose origins are to be found in the affiliated universities mentioned above; nonuniversity professional colleges, such as schools of social work and schools of journalism; colleges for art education; schools of education (teacher training colleges); schools for health (paramedical) personnel (earlier these schools were affiliated to the upper secondary schools system); and schools for nautical studies.

Most students follow a general study program. There are also local study programs, individual study programs, single courses, and advanced courses. There are about one hundred twenty general study programs ranging in length from one to five and one-half years.

As a direct outcome of some of the reform goals described above, all study programs belong to a so-called occupational sector, and all planning, both quantitative and curricular, takes into account five such sectors: (1) technical professions; (2) administrative, economic, and social-work professions; (3) health (medical and paramedical) professions; (4) teaching professions; and (5) information, communication, and cultural professions.

A completely new type of program has been introduced into Swedish higher education: short-cycle, technical-vocational training. It aims at providing further education to those having less formal schooling but many years of work experience. The curriculum is developed in close cooperation with organizations of employers and employees within industry.

Funds for higher education are allocated according to a number of major principles. Since admission to all higher education is restricted, Parliament makes annual decisions regarding the intake capacity for each general study program or for groups of such programs. Money is given as block grants directly to the various institutions on the basis of the number of entering students, and funds for local and individual study programs and for single courses are allocated through similar channels. Parliament makes these decisions at the proposal of government; government receives annual budget requests from a central government agency; in turn, this agency bases its national planning on requests from each institution of higher education.

The School Shapes Higher Education

All major Swedish educational reforms are reforms of social policy. The expansion of educational possibilities is not only caused by the need to increase the amount of skilled labor in the country; it is also motivated by the goal of giving all citizens, irrespective of their social, economic, cultural, or geographic background, an equal chance to take part in educational activities. Step-by-step, the three levels—lower secondary school, upper secondary school, and higher education—have been reformed to fit a pattern of increased social justice.

The overall pattern of reform has evolved gradually. Secondary schools have been transformed from a binary system into a comprehensive one in which an elective system has played a significant role and in which integration has taken place at the upper secondary level.[6] At the third level of higher education the Swedish drive for comprehensiveness is again easily discerned. Here it seemed logical to create an organization for all postsecondary education, regardless of the degree of vocational orientation, duration of study, or connection with research. These developments can be summed up in the following somewhat simplified way:

1. One of the *goals* in the overall structure has been to avoid dead ends, cul-de-sacs that leave pupils no freedom to choose their future careers. For example, general prerequisites for admission to higher education, defining the lower level of general school ability, have been instituted. In addition, the possibility of taking supplementary courses in adult education enables the student to fulfill the special prerequisites.

2. One of the *means* in the political reform strategy has been to organize the less prestigious parts of the educational system so as to put them on an equal footing with the more prestigious. Two-year study lines are integrated with three-year ones in the upper secondary school; they belong to the same organization as university preparatory lines. Vocationally oriented programs unconnected with research move into the traditional university system.

3. One *result* of these policies is that student career choice has been postponed successively. In the precomprehensive-school system, careers were decided on at age eleven; in the comprehensive system (1969), at age thirteen; and under the present system, at age sixteen.

Noticeably, these policies have included a conscious, or at least half-conscious, sacrifice of skills and knowledge in certain subjects; this has been done in order to promote other, perhaps broader, values. In such cases a price has been paid in curricular content and standards. For example, due to the design of the comprehensive school senior level, the third foreign language was abolished from the curriculum, and less time was given to the second foreign language.

What are the results in terms of how pupils transfer from upper secondary school to higher education? To what extent does school shape higher education in this respect? About three-fourths of all pupils who complete a study line at the upper secondary school meet the general prerequisites, but for a great number of study programs in higher education, special requirements must be fulfilled. In fact, a student meeting only the general prerequisites qualifies for only about 10 percent of the study programs. Whether the student is really qualified depends on which full-degree study line he or she has completed in upper secondary school. As an example, a prospective law student coming from one of the three-year theoretical lines is qualified. If he or she comes from a two-year theoretical line, one subject must be supplemented; from any other two-year line, two or three subjects must be supplemented. Students wishing to become primary school teachers meet the prerequisites if they come from three-year lines or two-year social lines. If a student comes from any other two-year line offering general prerequisites (including Swedish and English), two or three subjects must be supplemented for qualification, or, in some cases, four or more subjects.[7]

From what types of upper secondary education are students admitted

TABLE 4.1

EDUCATIONAL BACKGROUND OF PUPILS IN UPPER SECONDARY SCHOOL
ENROLLING IN HIGHER EDUCATION IN THE ACADEMIC YEAR 1978/79

Occupational sector in higher education	Upper Secondary School (in percent)			
	Three- and four-year lines	Two-year theoretical lines	Two-year vocational lines	Total
Technical	93	6	1	100
Administrative, economic, social work	75	21	4	100
Health	43	17	40	100
Teaching	51	31	18	100
Cultural, communication, and information	84	14	2	100
Total (percent)	67	20	14	101
(number)	(14,000)	(4,200)	(2,900)	(21,100)

SOURCE: Statens Offentliga Utredningar (SOU) 1981:96, *En reformerad gymnasieskola*, p. 68.

to full-degree programs in higher education? Keeping in mind that about one-third of the openings in the upper secondary school are found in three- and four-year theoretical lines, and two-thirds in two-year theoretical and vocational lines, table 4.1 shows the 1978–1979 academic year enrollment, one year after the establishment of the new higher education system.

It is, of course, too early to assess the results, because some first-year students completed upper secondary school before the new entrance rules were introduced, and more important, changes in this pattern, if they are realized, will emerge only gradually. In any case, the figures serve as a reminder that the flow of pupils from upper secondary to higher education is decided by a combination of the organization of school study lines and the admission rules. Given this perspective, let us examine the recommendations made by the government commission on upper secondary schooling. I will confine myself to three points concerning the structural relationships between the two levels.[8]

First, the commission has recommended that practically all pupils who complete secondary school fulfill the general prerequisites for admission to higher education. If realized, this proposal would lead to the abolition of the distinction between various parts of the upper secondary school in terms of general eligibility for studies at the higher-education level.

Second, the commission has proposed that pupils who take a short, vocationally oriented program at school be able to easily supplement their program so that it corresponds to a long, theoretical program; courses for this purpose will be offered as packages. This proposal is in line with the principle of having no dead ends in the educational system; a pupil who changes career plans while at school will have a fair chance of moving on to the next level.

A third proposal relates to postponement of career choice by the student. Some voices in the Swedish debate advocate that all pupils take two-year vocational programs; on completion of such a program a pupil would enter the labor market or continue for a third (theoretical) year of studies. The commission has rejected these proposals on the grounds that such a structure would necessitate a prolongation of studies for many pupils and lead to increased costs; the commission suggests that, in its place, integrated coursework (applied coursework) be taught to students within proposed sectors for about half a year. Thus, career choices will be postponed from the last grade in the comprehensive school to the first grade in the upper secondary school, that is, age sixteen or seventeen.

That brings us to the problem of differentiation. One of the guiding principles in Swedish education reform policies has been to delay differentiation. In the background report for the review done by the Organisation for Economic Co-operation and Development (OECD), this topic was discussed in connection with the comprehensive school:

> To bar most pupils from further theoretical studies and thereby from considerable sections of the more coveted labour market, as was done previously by selecting pupils when they were only 11 years old, was seen as one of the greatest deficiencies of the earlier system and its most "undemocratic" feature.

The examiners suggested that some pupils might benefit from differentiation in length and speed of coursework in the comprehensive school but questioned its degree of tolerability in the upper secondary school. "Should it not be recognised that education encompasses not only the meeting of individual pupil needs but also the practising of several different arts, several different disciplines and several different strengths?"[9]

Taking into account the division of labor in a market economy, combining individual needs with the differentiation necessary at some educational level appears as problematic as squaring the circle. The commission on upper secondary schooling has proposed to bring the two parts of the existing upper secondary school one step closer. At the least, one can say that such measures would be in line with Swedish reform policies during the postwar period.

THE QUANTITATIVE DIMENSION

We have seen how upper secondary school shapes higher education from a structural perspective. Equally important is the influence of the quantitative dimension. Clearly, the very substantial expansion of the upper secondary system which took place during a few decades laid the basis for the ensuing expansion at the next level. Moreover, there is an interdependence between the quantitative policies and certain qualitative effects.

The growth of the gymnasium and its fusion with other kinds of upper secondary education gave rise to the student explosion in higher education. In 1946, 8 percent of the age cohort attended a gymnasium; in 1963 this figure had risen to 23 percent. At present, with the existence of the concept of a broader upper secondary school, in principle 100 percent of sixteen-year-olds are free to continue their studies at this level; about 85 percent of the age cohort makes use of this possibility.[10] At the same time, increasing numbers of pupils in the upper secondary system are admitted to higher education.

Rapidly rising student numbers brought many problems to the universities. For instance, the great influx of students gave rise to a heated debate about the content and general design of university education. This debate centered around the so-called free faculties, those with open-admission policies (humanities, social sciences, natural sciences, theology, and law), which were overcrowded as a result. The government and Parliament tried to solve this problem by not only allocating larger grants but also insuring that students at these faculties carried on their studies more effectively. New regulations sought to safeguard flow through courses and increase examination pass-rates; students in full-degree programs who did not perform well enough were to be excluded from their studies. Another much-debated element in this policy was the government's contention that insufficient vocational orientation was exhibited by the free faculties (law and theology excluded); measures were introduced to promote an increased occupational orientation.

This policy was heavily resisted by the universities during the years around 1968, when it was opposed by a coalition of academics and students. It can be argued that the outcomes of this policy strongly influenced the shaping of the present higher education system, both as to quantitative planning and as to the organization of programs of study.[11]

Deliberations regarding the size of the secondary and tertiary levels have taken place recently because the large numbers of children born in the 1960s constitute an age cohort about 20 percent larger than previously. Having reached upper secondary school in the late 1970s, they are now entering institutions of higher education. Faced with these increases, the government and Parliament could have either held the number of places in secondary schools at the same level as previously or continued efforts to accommodate as many pupils as possible. The first alternative would have prevented increased pressure on institutions of higher education, but for various reasons, among them the risk of rising youth unemployment, it was decided to allow for the larger numbers. This policy has in turn led to the present expansion in the number of applicants for places in higher education.

Comparing the circumstances prevailing during the student explosion of the 1960s with the present situation, it is clear that the increasing numbers are a temporary phenomenon, that the government now has at its disposal the instrument of numerus clausus, and that economic restrictions have been introduced in a manner unknown in the 1960s. The policy suggested by the government and adopted by Parliament was to raise the ceiling for student intake for a number of years. Students today are thus offered the same relative opportunity to be admitted to institutions of higher education as their older schoolmates. Will this policy have any effects on the quality of higher education? Even though it is too soon to answer this question, it should be noted that economic restrictions are now being placed on higher education; institutions are not being given compensation for new tasks to the same extent as before. To what degree academic standards will be negatively affected can only be guessed.

SOCIAL EQUALITY

At the basis of almost all educational reforms in postwar Sweden are efforts to even out social differences. What precisely is meant by social equality (is it equal opportunity or equal realization of opportunity?) is beyond the scope of this chapter. Nevertheless, I shall point to some broad aspects of how the two educational levels relate in terms of social stratification.

Judging by common statistics, social inequalities in upper secondary schools remain. There is a clear distribution of pupils from different social groups among various types of theoretical and vocational education. Children of working-class origin choose two-year vocational study lines; children of academics choose, to a much higher extent, three-year theoretical study lines. In 1976, 80 percent of pupils with academic parents chose a three-year study line, 10 percent a two-year theoretical study line, and less than 10 percent a two-year vocational study line or special course (the figures apply to boys leaving comprehensive school the year before; the corresponding figures for girls are not very different). In contrast, among pupils from families of skilled workers, the corresponding figures are 20, 10, and 45 percent, with 20 percent already employed.[12]

These figures show that social inequalities remain at this level. But the implication that the school reforms in this area are a complete failure is not justified. For instance, recent investigations have shown a very high transition rate from lower secondary school to theoretical studies at the next level among all pupils in the top 10–20 percent in scholastic achievement, including those with a working-class background. One author comments: "I think that the reform-makers' intentions have been met, since they regarded the theoretical study lines as a programme, intended for academically-talented students." These good intentions, however, have been counterbalanced by the tendency for quite mediocre or even relatively weak pupils from higher social strata to take theoretical studies.[13]

Not surprisingly, social inequalities also exist at the higher-education level. The chain effects between the two levels make it impossible to expect improved social recruitment to higher education in comparison to the underlying level (excepting the influx of students admitted by the 25:4 rule). In the second half of the 1970s, 25 percent of the population were in the two highest social groups (out of five) and these two groups represented 60 percent of those enrolled in institutions of higher education. Investigations show that if judged by school performance level, a greater proportion of working-class students would be capable of enrolling in higher education.[14]

Has higher education reform brought any changes in the recruitment pattern? With reference to traditional university education, clearly, there are no signs of improved social recruitment. But because the earlier nonuniversity sector had a more democratic pattern, the overall figures for higher education after 1977 show a trend toward increased democratization. It can be argued that the interpretation of this tendency may be influenced by new terminology. Nevertheless, developmentally the higher education system may be attaining one reform goal, to even out differences in organization and content between its various parts.[15] This change relates to full-degree programs; to these must be added the single courses, in which a substantial number of students are enrolled. However, there are no full-scale investigations about recruitment to single courses. For this reason, at the moment one can only guess that the picture would be somewhat brighter if the single courses were taken into account.

Grading and Selection

The system for grading pupils in upper secondary school and for selecting them to higher education fills the interstices between the two levels in the overall educational structure. It is therefore convenient to deal separately with this question.

Grading and selection play an important role in Swedish educational debate, often to the astonishment of observers from abroad. Essential in policy-making, it is often linked with such important considerations as the curriculum and the work atmosphere of the upper secondary school, social recruitment to higher education, concern for academic standards, and recurrent education. In Sweden it belongs to the eternal category of long-discussed educational topics; so far, although step-by-step a number of changes and reforms have been launched, ultimate solutions have not been found.

In notable contrast to most other European countries, no final examination is given when the pupil leaves upper secondary school. Instead, assessment is continuous and tests are an integral part of schoolwork; nonpromotion occurs only on a voluntary basis. Furthermore, there is no intermediary body between upper secondary school and higher education which has the task of assessing candidates for the higher level; rather, the upper secondary school does the grading, and higher education asks for qualifications and selects. Finally, grading is a very important instrument for selecting students to higher education; however, other instruments do exist.

Marks in upper secondary school are awarded on a five-point scale and are distributed according to the Gaussian curve. The marking system is relative, and there is no pass-fail border in terms of absolute achievement. Measures are taken to safeguard equal standards in different schools, and nationwide standardized tests are given in certain important subjects.[16]

The rules for admission to higher education are complicated and difficult to survey. However, they form a pattern that is intended to promote broadened recruitment and recurrent education, two of the major goals of the higher education reforms effective from 1977.[17] A student must meet two kinds of prerequisites, general and special. The general prerequisites must be fulfilled by all students, regardless of what program they choose. One of the pathways to higher education requires that students must have taken either a full three- or four-year study line or a full two-year study line that includes a two-year course in Swedish and English. The other is through age and gainful employment. This is the so-called 25:4 scheme; with four years of gainful employment, an applicant fulfills the general prerequisite at the age of twenty-five. Applicants must also have a knowledge of English corresponding to a two-year course in upper secondary school.

Special prerequisites are linked to each program of study and are expressed as a rule that a student must have upper-secondary-level knowledge of one or more subjects essential to a particular program. Such special prerequisites also apply to students admitted on the basis of the 25:4 scheme. For candidates applying to short-cycle technical-vocational programs, work experience is a special prerequisite.

Selection takes place along these lines: one-third of the places are set aside for secondary school graduates, a direct-transfer guarantee from upper secondary school to higher education; the remaining applicants are directed to one (in some cases, two) of the following paths: (1) three- and four-year study lines in upper secondary school; (2) two-year study lines in upper secondary school; (3) so-called folk high schools (adult education colleges); and (4) the 25:4 scheme. These four groups are allotted places in proportion to the number of qualified applicants.

Student selection is based on average grades in upper secondary school (5-point maximum), work experience (1.7-point maximum), and an optional aptitude test for those applicants having no upper secondary education (2-point maximum). These credentials can be combined in the following ways: grades, grades and work experience, work experience, and experience and aptitude test results. A lottery is used when no other instrument can differentiate among applicants.

Grading has both defenders and opponents in debates currently taking place in school circles. The argument against grades makes the case that they have negative effects on schoolwork in general and that they are seen as promoting competition and counteracting a spirit of cooperation, one of the ideological goals of the curriculum. The political parties are divided on this issue, the Social Democrats being hesitant about using grades other than pass-fail, and the nonsocialist parties advocating a more elaborate grading scale.

Debate about the grading issue, as seen in the 1981 recommendations by the Commission on Upper Secondary Schooling, reflects the complexity of this issue. The commission was divided in its opinions. All members recommended a transition from the present norm-reference system to a course related one, and a majority, including representatives from nonsocialist parties, advocated a system of pass-fail, plus two or more grades within pass. A minority, including representatives of the Social Democratic party, were in favor of only pass and fail but allowed for modification if the problems of selection to higher education could not be solved in any other way. It was clearly stated that one can arrive at different solutions depending upon the perspective—school or higher education—from which the question is considered; only a balance between them would be permissible as a political solution.[18]

Present academic opinion on this matter is difficult to summarize. The following steps have been proposed: abolishing the present norm-reference marking system; diminishing the relative weight for work experience; and weighting school marks according to how much time a subject requires. According to present rules, credit for work experience may apply to any type of work. Many voices within academia argue that such experience should at least be drawn from a field that borders on the program to which the applicant applies. As to the weighting of marks, this was proposed by a 1981 commission on problems of research and research training, a majority of whose members were from higher education. If it were implemented, greater importance would be attached to subjects such as mathematics and Swedish.[19]

The ultimate solution of the grading question remains undecided. In 1983 the government appointed a commission whose members were drawn from the political parties and whose purpose was to review the rules for admission to higher education. Keeping in mind the overarching goal of broadening recruitment, it was decided that work experience credits will be accepted, while the commission is free to discuss the weighting of marks on the condition that the consequences for instruction in the upper secondary school are properly analyzed.[20]

Does the grading and selection system help the school to shape higher education, or is it the other way around? Most likely it is a two-way street. Obviously, certain elements in the upper secondary school grading system correspond very well with higher education interests. Marks are considered the proper basis for assessing candidates for studies at that level, and admission is, to a large extent, based on them. Further, the rule guaranteeing direct transfer from upper secondary school to higher education (at present 30 percent of the applicants; in reality the figure for direct transfer is much higher) is in line with university interests. But, contrary to these interests, in some school circles and in some political quarters, there is clearly a concern that upper secondary schools ought to have a grading system designed for their own purposes, a policy that would counteract the negative effects of the sharp competition for higher marks. Further, it is clear that school policies affect university admission rules to some extent; this comes about by admitting pupils from two-year study lines in upper secondary school. Certainly this is not in line with traditional university interests.

In short, an equilibrium between school and higher education grading and selection policies has occurred. The transition to course related grading, one demand from higher education, is not disputed, but this probably would have been the case even without pressure from above. The weighting of marks, another demand by higher education, is now being formally discussed, but the basic rule citing work experience as an important credential will be kept.

Higher Education Shapes the School

Since the upper secondary school defines the level from which higher education can start, the concern about academic standards and the quality of education there creates a continuous debate in Sweden. Teacher education (including the education of the specially trained senior subject teacher) and educational research also clearly point to the interdependence between the two levels.

ACADEMIC STANDARDS

Higher education representatives and the media express criticism about low standards among students. But very few, if any, studies give an overall picture of the achievement levels of applicants to higher education. This is not to deny that competence has diminished in some cases; the broadening of enrollment in the upper secondary school must necessarily affect general performance. Further, changes in the curriculum of both the comprehensive and upper secondary school assuredly do have an influence on the level of skills and knowledge in particular subjects. The introduction of a new subject or the increased number of hours allocated to a subject, for example, leads to diminished hours for other subjects, and thus the balance is changed. The cumulative effects of such changes can be considerable, and perhaps were unintended by responsible decision makers.[21] The comprehensive school, specifically the level that provides general knowledge, skills, and attitudes to all citizens, has also had its share of criticism by higher education.

Higher education's concern for academic standards tends to focus on two areas: the level of subject matter knowledge and skills, and the rules for admission required to guarantee appropriate candidates. The general level of competence in various subjects is an important battleground, but perhaps even more energy is devoted to the question of which students ought to be admitted.

With reference to the curriculum, higher education, more or less ex officio, passed judgment in the 1960s on how the school ought to function when a government commission recommended that the technological and commercial gymnasiums be integrated with the traditional gymnasium. The commission requested that a number of investigations be carried out. One of these examined how universities, on the one hand, and the government and the labor market, on the other, looked upon and assessed the students they received. Questions were asked about required knowledge and skills, achievement levels, and possible curricular changes. Although results indicated that university teachers thought students deficient not only in study skills but also in some subjects—such as foreign languages (other than English) and statistics—for some subjects with high requirements such as English, achievement levels were regarded as sufficient. An interesting feature of this investigation were attitudes toward general education. Professors of natural sciences and technology had a high appreciation of humanistic subjects and the social sciences, but no corresponding appreciation was found among professors of humanities and the social sciences. This investigation proved, to some extent, the existence of C. P. Snow's "two cultures." Instead of an absolute gap between the cultures, however, one can characterize the situation as one-sided.[22]

What standards does higher education demand in the 1980s? The proposals made public in 1981 by the commission on upper secondary schooling are illustrative.[23] A starting point for the commission was its recognition that in programs that prepare pupils for higher education, in general, the current level of competence was to be maintained in the new curriculum. Although many subjects were offered in such a way as to satisfy higher education requirements, there were also those in which the level of competence was considered too low, such as in foreign languages other than English. Deficiencies in the integrated course in science for junior- and middle-level teachers were also noted.

We have pointed out that university teachers in the 1960s regarded study skills as an important element in the curriculum, and measures were introduced to satisfy this requirement. Reporting that these measures have not been successful, the commission has encouraged further efforts in this direction: for example, in the senior year students may take electives in some subjects surpassing what is given today as training in independent study. This is, of course, in line with higher education views.

Opinions from higher education are clearly reflected in the commission's proposals regarding foreign languages. Teachers in the traditional areas of the higher education system often complain about the difficulty of using course literature in languages other than English. The commission has thus proposed a revised language curriculum that may well lead to increased competency among students. In addition, it has proposed changing the way the level of knowledge is defined in languages. According to the present system of admission prerequisites, demands for skills and knowledge are expressed in terms of courses at the upper secondary level, for example, a two-year course in English, a three-year course in French. Since investigations have shown that there is a very wide variation among pupils in mastery of subject matter, the commission argued that the fact that a student has followed a three-year course does not provide higher education enough information about real skills.

Instead, requirements in these subjects should be expressed in terms of actual language proficiency.

The 1981 proposals of the government commission on upper secondary schooling reaffirm that this level is responsible for training young people for the labor market and—recognizing that higher education is and will be a major receiver of youth—for providing the basis for further studies at the higher education level. Thus, the influence of the tertiary level upon the secondary one is clear.

Present debate about the linkages between upper secondary school and higher education show that although higher education interests are taken into account on important points, they are not allowed to encroach on the general design of the upper secondary school, a school from which most pupils do not go on to higher education.

TEACHER EDUCATION

Teacher education is a major responsibility for institutions of higher education today. It lies within one of the five major occupational sectors (teaching professions) to which all study programs belong. In the academic year 1982–1983, almost 30 percent of first-year students, and more than 30 percent of program funds (excluding local programs and single courses) were allocated for teacher education.

Teacher education is or should be designed to take into account the school in which the student will eventually work. For this reason, in Sweden it has been changing continuously during the last decades. A major reform in 1967, aimed at adjusting teacher education to the new comprehensive school, as well as the reform of higher education in 1977, brought about the integration of teacher education institutions with other branches of postsecondary education. The task of national planning for teacher education was transferred from the National Board of Education to the National Board of Universities and Colleges.[24]

Students are selected to one of the twenty teacher education programs by the same admissions criteria as apply to any other program. They are selected on the basis of school credits, work experience, and aptitude tests. Courses are quite popular among applicants; in the 1982 fall term, there were 25,000 applicants for 4,500 places; 16,500 listed these places as their first choice. Competition for admission is keen. In some programs a pupil must present top qualifications, but the same holds true for many programs in other occupational sectors as well.[25]

In view of this framework, teacher education is clearly an important instrument by which higher education influences the school. If we wish to understand which forces in higher education use this instrument, however, we need to follow the successive changes teacher education has undergone. Before the reform of 1967, institutions providing teacher education operated separately; they ran the risk of being isolated from one another. The 1967 system promoted a more integrated perspective. But even though subject teachers were taught at the universities and a few professorships in education were established in the major teacher education colleges, the links to other postsecondary education were still weak.

The reform of 1977 finally brought reform goals for these institutions in line with those established for other types of postsecondary education. One of these goals was the decentralizing of decision-making powers. Traditionally, teacher education was controlled rather heavily by the central government and its agencies. Under the new system, the institutions themselves have more freedom and exert a wider influence, on the curriculum, for example. School linkages, which are of decisive importance for the vitality of teacher education, are established in various ways. For each study program or small grouping thereof, there is a program committee that decides on all matters regarding content, course literature, and so forth. (This system applies to all occupational sectors.) The committee is tripartite in nature: one-third teachers, one-third students, and one-third representatives of the occupational sector. This means that individuals from the schools are represented at the "production" level of teacher education.

Another reform goal was to enhance the quality of nontraditional postsecondary education by safeguarding its links to research. This goal is currently being implemented. However, from some quarters in teacher education it is argued that the ideals of a science based university education must not be allowed to pervade teacher education altogether. If so, other important sources of knowledge may be overshadowed. This, it is argued, would be detrimental to the quality of teacher education.[26]

Another channel between higher education and the school is the in-service training of teachers. Under the present system, responsibility for these activities rests with the municipalities (the authorities that run the schools) and with the National Board of Education, but the task of organizing and running the courses has been given to institutions of higher education.[27] It is still too early to assess this new organization for in-service training since it has only been in operation since 1982.

With regard to the present structure of teacher education, a government commission in 1979 presented the report "Teachers for a School in Transition." Its main recommendation was that an integrated program for all prospective teachers in the comprehensive school be substituted for the present system. The current system has three kinds of programs closely linked to the structure of the school system: two and one-half years for junior-level teachers of grades one to three; three years for middle-level teachers of grades four to six; four years for subject teachers of grades seven to nine and upper secondary school. The debate has focused on what range of grades a teacher should cover and what the level of specialization should be. The commission recommended a comprehensive basic education of three and one-half years. After a period of two to eight years of service, a supplementary six-month course ought to be provided. Job experience as a prerequisite for admission to all teacher education was also proposed.[28]

If these proposals were to be implemented, would they increase or decrease the influence of higher education over the school? Academia has reacted on one point, reflecting concern about subject teaching: changing the present system, under which students follow courses at subject departments in the traditional faculties of humanities, social sciences, and natural sciences for three or four years, would mean too little time devoted to core subjects.

SENIOR SUBJECT TEACHERS

Apart from research in education, research in subject fields, a main activity in major institutions of higher education, affects the school in only a general way. This occurs through the vehicle of teacher education and also by means of textbooks. In Sweden, however, a special linkage exists between research and the upper secondary school. A fairly universal type of teaching post has been created, the senior subject teacher. To be qualified, such a teacher must have had research training. Earlier, universities regarded the gymnasium as a normal province of activity for personnel trained in doing research. At a period of university expansion, however, almost all researchers were needed for undergraduate teaching. Thus, many subject-specialist teacher positions were left unoccupied—about 50 percent in the 1960s. School planners tended to devalue this type of position, arguing that subject teachers could just as easily do the job, and in the end either subject teachers or senior subject teachers were permitted to hold these posts. Subject teachers in upper secondary schools numbered 11,200 in 1980. Three percent had training in research. There were 1,700 senior subject teachers; of these 67 percent had research training.[29]

Recently, school reforms have upgraded senior subject teacher posts. The commission on teacher education in 1979 supported this type of position and even recommended it be introduced in other subjects also. Looking toward the future, commission members believed senior subject teachers would also be an asset in the comprehensive school.[30]

Institutions of higher education have not hesitated to express views on this matter; they now want to restore the school as a labor market for people with a doctorate. In a report published in 1981, the commission on problems of research and research training strongly advocated an increased number of posts designated for senior subject teachers. In fact, it proposed extending this kind of position to the two-year study lines in upper secondary school, since pupils from these lines have fulfilled the general prerequisites for admission to higher education.[31]

EDUCATIONAL RESEARCH

Educational research in Sweden is financed either by grants of permanent funds to universities (particularly for professorships), or by allocation from the Council for Research in the Humanities and the Social Sciences to university departments (discipline oriented research), or by allocation from authorities (the National Board of Education and the National Board of Universities and Colleges) and governmental commissions to departments of education (decision and sectorial research). Commission sponsored research has been concerned with differentiation in what later developed into the comprehensive school, curriculum and standards in the gymnasium, and social-selection problems and theories about curriculum development in the upper secondary school. The commission on upper secondary schooling reporting in 1981 has also initiated experimental schemes, with educational researchers called upon to safeguard proper evaluation techniques.[32]

Although educational research and development efforts in Sweden, impressive in themselves, might benefit from more "of a critical stance, or one of counter-analysis," according to an OECD report, it is equally true that "Sweden has always depended upon research and development as one of the known sources of its ideas and mechanisms of reform."[33] Decisions on educational reform policy rest on a number of assumptions about relationships between ends and means, relationships that are researchable. Even though some major issues have been, and will be—and should be—decided upon according to value judgments, on all such occasions educational research has presented factual information that decision makers have taken into account. Clearly, public debate over school issues cannot be carried on without referring to the results of educational research and developmental work.

Conclusion

The Swedish educational system has been thoroughly revised during the postwar period. The comprehensive school has gradually developed into its present shape; the upper secondary school has been subjected to a number of reforms; and higher education has been considerably restructured. In principle, this continuous educational reformation would have permitted the Swedish structure to be rebuilt from the bottom to the top. The first changes were indeed introduced in what is now the comprehensive school. But by and large, reform decisions concerning the three levels have not been taken in strictly chronological order. At present no major changes are to be expected either in the comprehensive school or in higher education. The potential for change lies in the upper secondary school, but the intermediary position of the upper secondary school poses a major difficulty and perhaps reflects a weak point in Swedish reform strategy. At both ends of the upper secondary school, the entrance and the exit, there is very little flexibility. In a way, the upper secondary school seems to be squeezed between the two other levels, and by expectations and demands from the labor market.

This crucial level of education in Sweden is notable for its very diversified curricula and the variety of students who attend the integrated school. Reforms have led toward what Americans call the comprehensive high school, in which an array of academic and vocational alternatives are grouped together. On this feature the current Swedish structure departs considerably from the pattern commonly found in Europe and throughout the world in which different secondary tasks are parceled among different types of secondary schools. However, within the integrated school, streaming has been fine grained, with twenty-five lines of study; recent reform proposals indicate they may be grouped in larger, more comprehensive curricula in the future.

The attempts to open education up to new social strata is central to Swedish policies for all educational levels. Since student input to higher education depends so much on student output from the upper secondary school, one would expect that improved social recruitment at one level would be passed along. Investigations about social recruitment to upper secondary school show that some advancement has been made, although not to the extent hoped for. In higher education, social inequalities remain; expectations have not been fulfilled. The broader concept of higher education introduced in 1977 will perhaps contribute to a more democratic pattern of recruitment. At this point in time, however, one cannot readily state that wider access to the upper secondary school necessarily leads to a similar result in higher education.

When it comes to pure numbers, however, the quantitative growth of the upper secondary school did decisively influence higher education in the days of the student explosion in the 1960s. The upper secondary school expanded so much that higher education had to follow suit to a considerable degree. These developments are easily taken for granted, but what is equally important is that the quantitative growth exerted a great influence on the content and organization of study programs in the liberal arts, social sciences, and natural sciences. Sheer expansion, then, has been an important vehicle of influence of the upper secondary school on higher education. Even in the early 1980s, a period of economic recession, a temporary growth in school enrollments caused a rising intake in the postsecondary realm.

The problem of rising student numbers has run parallel to another question about student recruitment: what should be the proper schooling for a candidate for admission to higher education? The traditional background was a three-year, university preparatory study line in upper secondary school. But in the 1970s decisions were taken that made pupils in a two-year study line eligible for higher education. Institutions of higher education have questioned these admission rules, and as measured by transfer rates from upper secondary school to full-degree, traditional programs in higher education, these policies have had only limited success.

In Sweden, as in so many other countries, academics express concern about declining standards in the schools. Has school achievement declined? The broadening of enrollment in upper secondary school necessarily affects the general level of performance. The overall picture, however, covering all subjects, seems not to be a gloomy one. Clearly, there are subjects in which the level of skill and knowledge has fallen. The interesting thing is that in some subjects this is the result of quite conscious decisions by policymakers. They have sacrificed some values to perhaps achieve other, broader goals.

The question of academic standards is linked to another qualitative issue, that of grading and selection. Two facts are central to an understanding of the Swedish debate on this topic. (1) Pupils are not subject to a final examination; instead, they are assessed continuously, this process being part of ordinary school work. (2) There is no intermediary body, as in some countries, between upper secondary school and higher education which performs tasks in this field. Grading is done within the upper secondary school. There are nationwide rules on admission to higher education, and these rules are applied by higher education. There are elements of the grading and selection system which clearly are in line with higher education interests; but there are strong voices within school circles which advocate measures that markedly serve school purposes.

In sum, what are the relationships between upper secondary school and higher education? In quantitative matters the upper secondary school clearly influences higher education. Qualitatively, higher education has the greater scope for shaping the school. In many matters there is a reasonable state of equilibrium between the two levels. We find no instances in which higher education can be said to encroach seriously on the central values held by the school. Together, these conclusions justify the statement that in Sweden the upper secondary school is a substantial institution in its own right. It responds to wishes and demands from higher education but is definitely not dominated by it. This evolving autonomy and identity perhaps represents what happens when the university preparatory school is transformed into a school for everyone and for all tasks.

Notes

1. Dahllöf, *Svensk Utbildningsplanering Under 25 År*, pp. 66–94; and Dahllöf, "Recent Reforms of Secondary Education in Sweden," pp. 71–92.

2. Organisation for Economic Co-operation and Development (OECD), *Educational Policy and Planning*, pp. 26–30; Swedish Institute, *Primary and Secondary Education in Sweden*, p. 3.

3. Myrberg, *Transition from School to Work*, pp. 4 and 11; Statens Offentliga Utredningar (SOU), *En Reformerad Gymasieskola*, pp. 53, 55. Swedish Institute, *Primary and Secondary Education*, p. 3.

4. SOU, *En Reformerad Gymnasieskola*, chaps. 4, 5, 7, 9, 11, 12, 14.

5. See Bergendal, *Higher Education and Manpower Planning in Sweden*; Dahllöf, *Reforming Higher Education and External Studies in Sweden and Australia*, pp. 5–58; Premfors, *Integrated Higher Education*, pp. 1–32; Premfors and Östergren, *Systems of Higher Education: Sweden*, chaps. 1–2; Swedish Institute, *Higher Education in Sweden*, pp. 1–4.

6. OECD, *Educational Policy*, pp. 51–52 (the comprehensive school).

7. Myrberg, *Studieorganisation och Elevströmmar*, pp. 168, 172–173.

8. See SOU, *En Reformerad Gymnasieskola*, especially chaps. 5, 9, 14, and 15.

9. OECD, *Educational Policy*, p. 52; OECD, *Reviews of National Policies for Education: Educational Reforms in Sweden*, pp. 56–57, 76.

10. Dahllöf, *Svensk Utbildningsplanering*, p. 67; Myrberg, *Transition from School to Work*, p. 9.

11. Dahllöf, *Svensk Utbildningsplanering*, pp. 106–107; Premfors and Östergren, *Systems of Higher Education: Sweden*, pp. 5–8 (student numbers).

12. SOU, *En Reformerad Gymnasieskola*, p. 59.

13. Dahllöf, "Contextual Problems of Educational Reforms: A Swedish Perspective," p. 160; Härnqvist and Svensson, *Den Sociala Selektionen Till Gymnasiestadiet*, pp. 51–53; SOU, *En Reformerad Gymnasieskola*, p. 60.

14. Svensson, *Jämlikhet i Högskolan—Fiktion eller Realitet?* pp. 29–31, 45.

15. Ibid., pp. 46–47.

16. OECD, *Educational Policy*, pp. 28–29; Swedish Institute, *Primary and Secondary Education*, p. 3.

17. See OECD, *Educational Policy*, pp. 31–32; Dahllöf, *Reforming Higher Education*, pp. 10–11.
18. SOU, *En Reformerad Gymnasieskola*, pp. 233–250.
19. SOU, *Forskningens Framtid*, pp. 88–91.
20. Utbildningsdepartementet, *Översyn av Reglerna för Tillträde Till Grundläggande Högskoleutbildning*, pp. 2–8.
21. OECD, *Educational Policy*, pp. 112–114; Dahllöf, *Reforming Higher Education*, pp. 50–54.
22. Dahllöf, "Recent Reforms," pp. 76–78.
23. See SOU, *En Reformerad Gymnasieskola*, chaps. 4–6, 13, 15, appendix 8.
24. SOU, *Lärare för Skola i Utveckling*, pp. 53–54.
25. UHÄ, *Statistik Från Antagningen Till Högskolans Utbildningslinjer Höstterminen 1982*, bilaga p. 26.
26. Bergendal, "Higher Education and Knowledge Policies," pp. 623–627.
27. Proposition 1980/81:97, *Regeringens Proposition om Skolforskning och Personalutveckling*, pp. 47, 57.
28. SOU, *Lärare för Skola i Utveckling*, chaps. 5–6, 9–10, 12.
29. SOU, *Forskarutbildningens Meritvärde*, pp. 57–67.
30. SOU, *Lärare för Skola i Utveckling*, pp. 151–153.
31. SOU, *Forskarutbildningens Meritvärde*, pp. 68–73.
32. Dahllöf, "Recent Reforms," pp. 75–81; SOU, *En Reformerad Gymnasieskola*, pp. 31–33, 351–373.
33. OECD, *Reviews of National Policies*, pp. 57–58.

Bibliography

BERGENDAL, GUNNAR. *Higher Education and Manpower Planning in Sweden*. Stockholm: The National Board of Universities and Colleges, 1977.

———. "Higher Education and Knowledge Policies: A Personal View." *The Journal of Higher Education* 54, no. 6 (1983): 599–628.

DAHLLÖF, URBAN. "Recent Reforms of Secondary Education in Sweden." *Comparative Education* 2 (1966): 71–92.

———. *Svensk Utbildningsplanering Under 25 År*. Lund: Studentlitteratur, 1971.

———. *Reforming Higher Education and External Studies in Sweden and Australia*. Acta Universitatis Upsaliensis. Uppsala Studies in Education 3. Motala: Almqvist & Wiksell International, 1977.

———. "Contextual Problems of Educational Reforms: a Swedish Perspective." In *Educational Research and Policy. How Do They Relate?* ed. Torsten Husén and Maurice Kogan. Oxford: Pergamon Press, 1984. Pp. 143–163.

HÄRNQVIST, KJELL, and ALLAN SVENSSON. *Den Sociala Selektionen Till Gymnasiestadiet*. Stockholm: Sveriges Offentliga Utredningar, 1980. SOU 1980: 30 with English summary.

MYRBERG, MATS. *Studieorganisation och Elevströmmar.* Kungälv: Statens Offentliga Utredningar, 1981. SOU 1981: 98.

———. *Transition from School to Work in the 16–20 Age-Group in Sweden.* Swedish Ministry of Education and Cultural Affairs, 1982. Mimeo.

Organisation for Economic Co-operation and Development (OECD). *Educational Policy and Planning: Goals for Educational Policy in Sweden.* Paris, 1980.

———. *Reviews of National Policies for Education: Educational Reforms in Sweden.* Paris, 1981.

PREMFORS, RUNE. *Integrated Higher Education: The Swedish Experience.* Group for the Study of Higher Education and Research Policy, report no. 14. Stockholm: Department of Political Science, University of Stockholm, 1981. Mimeo.

PREMFORS, RUNE, and BERTIL ÖSTERGREN. *Systems of Higher Education: Sweden.* New York: International Council for Educational Development, 1978.

Proposition 1980/81: 97. *Regeringens Proposition om Skolforskning och Personalutveckling,* Stockholm: Riksdagen, 1981.

Statens Offentliga Utredningar (SOU). *Lärare för Skola i Utveckling.* Stockholm: Bëtankande av 1974 års Lärarutbildningsutredning, 1978. SOU 1978: 86.

———. *Forskningens Framtid. Forskning och Forskarutbildning i Högskolan.* Stockholm: Betänkande av Utredningen om Forskningens och Forskarutbildningens Situation i den Nya Högskolan, 1981. SOU 1981: 29.

———. *Forskarutbildningens Meritvärde.* Stockholm: Betänkande av Utredningen om Forskningens och Forskarutbildningens Situation i den Nya Högskolan, 1981. SOU 1981: 30.

———. *En Reformerad Gymnasieskola.* Stockholm: Betänkande av 1976 ars Gymnasieutredning, 1981. SOU 1981: 96.

SVENSSON, ALLAN. *Jämlikhet i Högskolan—Fiktion eller Realitet? Den Sociala Rekryteringen Till Högre Utbildning Före och Efter Högskole-Reformen.* UHÄ-rapport 1981: 25. Mimeo.

Swedish Institute. *Higher Education in Sweden: Fact Sheets on Sweden.* Stockholm. 1983.

———. *Primary and Secondary Education in Sweden: Fact Sheets on Sweden.* Stockholm, 1982.

UHÄ. *Statistik Från Antagningen Till Högskolans Utbildningslinjer Höstterminen 1982.* Stockholm Universitets—och Högskoleämbetet, 1982. UHÄ-Rapport 1982: 24.

Utbildningsdepartementet. *Översyn av Reglerna för Tillträde till Grundläggande Högskoleutbildning.* Stockholm, 1983. Kommitédirektiv 1983: 58.

5
Japan

WILLIAM K. CUMMINGS

J APAN'S INTELLECTUAL AND CULTURAL HERITAGE can be traced back
through several millennia, but the origins of the modern educational
system are clearly found in various activities surrounding the Meiji Restoration in 1868. After some experimentation with other forms, the educational system, along with some other institutions, took on a Germanic
cast. Modern education was viewed primarily as a means by which
national purposes could be realized. Extensive primary education was
followed by a more selective secondary system, which included several
vocational tracks as well as the academically oriented *kotogakko*, Japan's
analog of the German *Gymnasium*. At the pinnacle of the Japanese system
was the Imperial University, which the state hoped would become a
world-class institution. The university was granted considerable autonomy, not only in intellectual matters but also with respect to
administration.

As in Germany, secondary and higher educational institutions were
supposed to rigorously evaluate students during the course of their
studies, allowing only those who achieved the appropriate standard of
academic maturity to graduate or exit.[1] However, for a variety of reasons,
the exit examinations were soon displaced in importance by entrance
exams, first at the secondary schools and later at the Imperial University.
The simple need to select a few students from many applicants was the
underlying reason for this shift. Yet, perhaps more fundamental was
the Japanese cultural disposition sometimes referred to as "*ie* psychology," that is, the tendency to rigorously evaluate individuals before
permitting them to join a family system or corporate residential group,
but once they are admitted, to accept and adjust to them as full members.[2] The same tendency toward rigorous evaluation prior to acceptance
and accommodation thereafter can be seen in the selection of spouses
for membership in established family groups, as well as of recruits for
"lifetime" membership in Japanese firms.

At the tertiary level, entrance exams were first instituted at the Imperial University's engineering faculty in 1891 and at the law faculty several years later; it was at these two faculties that applicants exceeded places. As the same situation came to prevail in other faculties of leading institutions, they also initiated exams. Thus, the practice of administering an exam became associated with the belief that a faculty or institution was providing a valued educational experience. Eventually, lesser institutions, even when the number of places exceeded applicants, began to administer entrance exams, for not to do so would imply a valueless educational program. Still, in the old system of Japanese education that prevailed through World War II, university entrance exams were not exceptionally stressful and were not believed to be as critical for personal advancement as other selective factors, such as family status and ability.

Due to the major structural reforms that created a new system after World War II, however, university entrance exams became more strategic than virtually any other factor in the Japanese system of social selection. These exams, independently administered by all higher educational institutions, became the focal point for communication between tertiary and secondary education. Thus, it is appropriate to focus on the development and current status of these exams as a way of illustrating the nature of the secondary-tertiary relationship. Although this focus may seem narrow, it in fact leads along many byroads. To understand the examination system, I shall investigate the types of schools in which students prepare for the exams, as well as the types of colleges in which, depending on their performance, they will gain entry. I shall then consider the relation of the exams to two very contrary images of Japanese education current today: on the one hand, the image of academic excellence as noted recently by America's National Commission on Excellence in Education, and on the other, the image of examination hell which so troubles the Japanese public.[3]

The Old System

The Japanese examination system is a creation of the past century. Nearly 1500 years ago, the first wave of Chinese high culture invaded Japan, and with it came the Chinese examination system as a meritocratic mechanism for selecting officials to serve the emperor. Japan briefly experimented with the Chinese examination system only to abandon it in favor of a largely hereditary system of social selection.

Although the exam system was abandoned, education was always valued as a means of preparing people for their ascribed social positions. During the late feudal period of the Tokugawa regime (1600–1868), educational institutions were especially prevalent. Virtually all males of the ruling class attended schools, established by their lords, where they studied standard Confucian texts and practiced the martial arts. Distinct from the schools for samurai were a large number of village schools (*terakoya*), where commoners learned to read, write, and calculate. It has been estimated that 40 percent of the male population attained literacy in this system.[4] The main purpose of the educational system was to transmit the moral dispositions and skills appropriate to the individual's inherited social position. Thus, pupils attended schools appropriate to their status and advanced in these schools primarily according to their age. Social advancement was essentially unrelated to educational performance, and there was little concern with higher education as it is known today. Western learning was in fact officially forbidden, though some adventurous intellectuals clandestinely sought to learn what they could about Western achievements, especially in the areas of anatomy and armaments.

The Tokugawa system experienced a rude shock when, in 1853, Commodore Perry's warships, puffing black smoke, steamed into Edo Bay and fired several warning shots from their cannons. Japan's upper class of samurai, who took great pride in their military prowess, were startled by American military technology, against which Japan seemed defenseless. Immediately, young samurai began to consider how the nation could respond to this challenge. Within a few years these debates led to the toppling of the Tokugawa regime by a coalition of young samurai, who assumed power when the emperor Meiji was crowned and who were determined to modernize their nation. The new leaders, determined to avoid the fate of colonization, exercised firm central leadership and imposed a formula of "Western technology and Eastern spirit" on the Japanese people.

These leaders were deeply conscious of the prime importance of mass education and advanced knowledge in order to achieve modernization. Over the first two decades of the Meiji period (1868–1912), steps were taken to develop what is now called the "old system" of modern education. In the Charter Oath issued soon after their accession to central power, the Meiji leaders announced the need to "seek knowledge widely throughout the world";[5] thus, one concern was to educate a technical elite. At the same time, the government looked to education as a means of forging a closer integration of diverse feudal loyalties. The new curriculum of spiritual training, richly infused with centrist themes of loyalty to the emperor and allegiance to the national purpose, was a principal means toward this goal of national integration.

To insure that local areas received the message, the young government quickly moved to a system whereby the central government ex-

ercised extensive control over local schools: texts were authorized by
the central government, school principals were government appointees,
expenses in the compulsory schools were supported by central government subsidies, and central government inspectors made annual visits
to each local school. In these ways the government directed local schools
to adhere to national policy.

Centralization also affected higher education. In 1886 the government
consolidated several of the stronger higher education institutions into a
single Imperial University located in Tokyo. This institution was asked
to "seek knowledge for the state." Its staff were public officials, and its
chief officers were appointed by the emperor. The state carefully watched
the activities of the university, and although a degree of academic freedom was established, this was always subject to repeal. Enhancing the
importance of the Imperial University were various policies that favored
its graduates in appointments to the higher civil service.

MERITOCRATIC SELECTION OF AN ELITE

The government, determined to make the Imperial University the foremost institution of learning in the nation, bestowed comparatively generous annual grants for its operation. In contrast with lesser educational
institutions, virtually no restrictions were placed on the manner in which
the members of the Imperial University conducted their educational or
research activities. The assumption was that those who joined this institution, whether as professors or students, would already have developed such a strong commitment to national goals that further
indoctrination would be unnecessary.

The university was modeled along the lines of the leading German
universities, but with some important variations. For example, in keeping with the official concern for economic development, from an early
stage faculties were added in the practical disciplines of agriculture and
engineering.

Through the nineteenth century, the Imperial University accepted less
than one person out of every thousand in a given age group who attended primary school. Even as late as the 1930s, when several additional
imperial universities were established, the ratio of primary school entrants to places for new students at all of the imperial universities remained over one hundred to one. The government restricted the scale
of the most prestigious higher educational institutions so that their degrees would confer honor and advantageous career prospects.

Makoto Aso sampled several hundred elites from each of several
editions of the *Jinji koshin roku* (a Japanese *Who's Who*) and investigated

TABLE 5.1

JAPANESE ELITES ATTENDING THE UNIVERSITY OF TOKYO (TODAI), 1903–1964

	Todai graduates as a percent of all elites who attended a higher educational institution					
	1903	1915	1928	1939	1955	1964
National civil service	73	65	76	65	42	41
Business leaders	66	33	28	21	18	14
Landowners	0	0	0	0		
Military	0	20	0	8		
Educators, professors	88	88	52	63	45	36
Doctors		50	100	41	11	17
Lawyers		66		0	17	31
Artists				0	22	25
Religious leaders		0		0	0	50
Opinion leaders				0	0	20
Politicians	0		100	0	18	30
Noblemen	17	100	20	36		
Other	50	0	0	9	8	
Todai graduates as a percent of elites who attended a higher educational institution	55	44	36	46	34	21
Percent of elites who attended a higher educational institution	28	26	37	53	77	94
Todai graduates as a percent of all elites	12	14	17	19	19	17

SOURCE: Makoto Aso, *Erito to Kyoiku (Elites and Education)*, pp. 217–219.

several of their background characteristics (see table 5.1).[6] In the earliest period, a majority of the elites had not attended a university; however, among those who had attended, about half were Imperial University (Todai) graduates. The Todai graduates were especially numerous in the civil service, education, and business. The military, which had its own academy, was the one modern elite sector where Todai graduates failed to gain a significant proportion. Over time, the number of elites who had attended a university increased; up to World War II, nearly half of these continued to be graduates of Todai. The proportion of Todai graduates among the elite civil servants and educators declined only modestly.

After World War II, Todai's proportion of elite civil servants and educators declined somewhat, but not nearly as fast as might be expected given the explosion in the number of university places. Considering all elite fields, the proportion who attended Todai increased from 12 percent in 1903 to 17 percent in 1964. Certainly, the sense that one has to attend Todai or another elite university if one is to succeed has progressively increased, and therein lies the significance of entrance exams.

MULTITRACK SECONDARY EDUCATION

Between the primary schools and the exalted Imperial University there gradually evolved a noncompulsory, multitrack secondary system. In general, once an individual began on one track in this system, he was not permitted to transfer into a different one. A student who finished coursework in a secondary vocational school could not then compete for admission to a college; in order to do so, he was required to go back and complete the middle school course. Similarly, credit in a college was not transferable to the higher school-university track. Three tracks—the higher schools, the colleges (senmongakko), and the higher normal schools—were to be especially influential in later postwar thinking about secondary education.

Higher schools were the first track to take specific form.[7] With the adoption of the German model for the university, the Meiji government sought to create a preparatory institution similar to the Gymnasium. The first attempt was begun in Tokyo in 1886. Parallel curricula of a high academic level in the arts and the sciences were developed, and an able staff was recruited. Over the next few years six additional higher schools were established, but unlike the Tokyo precedent, these later institutions were founded in rural settings to enable the boys to benefit from the natural environment.

In the old system the most severe academic competition was concentrated on entrance to these schools, as they were virtually a prerequisite for entrance to the imperial universities. The first higher school in Tokyo was most sought after because its graduates were the most successful in entering the Imperial University at Tokyo. The third and fourth higher schools, located at Kyoto and Kanazawa, tended to feed Kyoto Imperial University, after it was established in 1897. Similarly, the second higher school, located in Sendai, became associated with Tohoku University, and the fifth, located in Kumamoto, became associated with Kyushu University.

The first tales of "examination hell"—that is, the misery of endless study, repeated attempts to pass the exams, and suicide as a desperate act to escape the pressure of exam preparation—actually date from this period. In 1890 the ratio of middle school to higher school graduates was 8 to 1; from 1905 it was always above 20 to 1.[8] It was at this stage that numerous schools were established to provide special instruction to students attempting to pass examinations. At this point also, the services of university students, and even of teachers, as tutors for those seeking entrance to the higher schools came to be in high demand. Relative to the intense competition to gain admittance to higher schools, graduates of these schools experienced little problem moving on to a university. There were sufficient places for all the qualified graduates at the imperial universities, the only problem being that many had to settle for their second choice of university and field of study. As already noted, university entrance exams were first instituted to solve these allocation problems, which were, at first, relatively minor.

College refers to a great variety of institutions that were created throughout the Meiji period as an expression of both individual and official concern to develop special skills.[9] The colleges tended to receive those students who could not pass the entrance exams for the higher schools or who could not afford the higher-school-to-university course. Each college tended to have a limited academic focus, but this might range from foreign languages to engineering. Standards as well as fees varied immensely. The confusion relating to this diversity led, in 1902, to the promulgation of the College Ordinance, which specified the minimal resources needed by an institution to be recognized as a college. Following the passage of the College Ordinance, the national government instituted a program to establish a number of colleges specializing in engineering skills, which provided much of the technical manpower for late Meiji Japan's shift toward heavy industry. This particular contribution of the colleges tends to be most remembered, although, in fact, their function was much broader.

Normal schools were the third notable group of secondary institutions of this period. Included in this group are both the higher normal schools for training middle school teachers and the regular normal schools for training teachers for future employment in primary schools. During Mori Arinori's tenure as minister of education (1885–1889), he devoted particular attention to the curriculum of the normal schools.[10] Morals texts were designed for these schools, as was a Spartan schedule that included early morning calisthenics conducted by military officers. Mori believed their exemplary presence would help in cultivating the loyal and disciplined character appropriate for teachers. As the state maintained a monopoly of teacher training schools, these provisions were certain to reinforce the official policy of providing systematic training to primary and middle school students. The conspicuous presence of the government in these schools insured the cooperation of teachers in implementing various changes in official educational policy.

The New System

Japanese society, with the aid of the old system, achieved impressive development. By the mid-1930s, national institutions were effectively unified under a strong central regime; the economy was diversified; the military was strong; the people were loyal. Education, despite its many shortcomings, was instrumental in supporting each of these developments. If Japan had managed a more successful conclusion of World War II, the central government might have retained the old system in essentially unaltered form.

In anticipation of Japan's fall, and its unconditional surrender in September 1945, the Allied powers on July 26, 1945, issued the Potsdam Declaration, which declared their intent to remove "all obstacles to the survival and strengthening of democratic tendencies among the Japanese people. Freedom of speech, religion, and of thought, as well as respect for the fundamental rights shall be established." The actual task of implementing the spirit of the Potsdam Declaration was assumed by an occupation government established by the United States and headed by General Douglas MacArthur. The Occupation was instructed to work with the existing Japanese government and emperor but not to support them.

One of the first major goals of the Occupation was to establish the foundation for a more democratic mode of government. A special committee of the Diet was charged with the task of drafting a new constitution, and when it faltered, the Occupation submitted its own proposal. Ultimately, a version identical in most respects to that proposed by the Occupation was ratified in November 1946 by the Diet.

The new constitution, popularly known as the "peace constitution" because it banned a Japanese military force, provided the framework for a parliamentary form of government with members of the two legislative bodies to be elected by universal suffrage. By the middle of the Occupation period, the pattern of popular voting had crystallized around two distinctive political groupings. Parties of the progressive camp sought to advance popular and radical causes in opposition to what they labeled the traditional, conservative establishment of capitalists and militarists. The progressives attracted the support of labor unions and intellectuals, whereas the conservatives obtained theirs from the managerial classes of big business and the traditional sectors of the economy. Over the postwar period the conservative camp has dominated the national elections as well as local elections in all but the highly urbanized areas. The political alignment of conservatives in power and progressives in opposition has had an important bearing on the course of postwar educational reform.

THE STRUCTURE OF THE NEW SYSTEM

Another important feature of the peace constitution concerned education and its relationship to democratic values; specific articles expressed ideas about academic freedom, the accessibility of education, and the separation of church and the schools. Whereas the old system was created through a series of imperial decrees and administrative orders, the new educational system was based in the constitution and in laws that were debated and legislated by the national Diet. The change to a legislative basis, in combination with the emergence of progressive political parties that developed an interest in educational policy, resulted in a lively postwar educational dialogue.

In March 1947 the Occupation invited twenty-seven distinguished educators, the United States Education Mission to Japan, to aid in the development of concrete proposals for educational reforms. Their report provided the clearest statement of the philosophy underlying subsequent reforms, and its opening statement echoed the Occupation's goal of helping Japan to develop a new educational system appropriate to a liberal democratic society. It urged the development of an educational philosophy that recognized "the worth and dignity of the individual" and that would "prepare the individual to become a responsible and cooperating member of society."

The mission also enumerated several weaknesses of the old system:

The Japanese system of education in its organization and curricular provisions would have been due for reform in accordance with modern theories of education even if there had not been injected into it ultranationalism and militarism. The system was based on a nineteenth-century pattern which was highly centralized, providing one type of education for the masses and another for the privileged few. It held that at each level of instruction there is a fixed quantum of knowledge to be absorbed, and tended to disregard differences in the ability and interests of pupils. Through prescription, textbooks, examinations and inspection, the system lessened the opportunities of teachers to exercise professional freedom. The measure of efficiency was the degree to which standardization and uniformity were secured.[11]

The mission then turned to a consideration of reforms that might alleviate these weaknesses. Though many were considered, the changes that were finally adopted by the Education Reform Council of the Japanese government include:

1. The mission recommended the establishment of a six-year, free, compulsory primary school to "prepare children to become healthy, active, thinking citizens eager to develop their innate abilities."

2. In contrast with the old system, in which, after primary school, several different noncompulsory tracks opened up, the mission recommended "that there be established for the next three years beyond the primary school, a 'lower secondary school' for all boys and girls, providing fundamentally the same type of curriculum for all with such adjustments as are necessary to meet individual needs. The main purposes should be similar to those of the primary school, with emphasis upon personal development, citizenship, and community life. Into this school should be introduced certain opportunities of an exploratory nature in the vocational field."[12] Contrasting further with the old system, the mission recommended that the lower secondary (middle) schools be free, compulsory, and coeducational.

3. Beyond the lower secondary school, the report recommended a free, coeducational, three-year high school "open to all who desired to attend" which was modeled, insofar as possible, along the lines of the American comprehensive high school; that is, the school was to include courses that would enable students both to prepare for college and to acquire vocational skills.

4. The report emphasized the potential role of the university in fostering liberal thought, urged that this become "an opportunity for the many, not the few," and suggested that the university, with its liberal atmosphere, provided a more favorable setting for teacher education than the separate normal schools characteristic of the old system.

These recommendations, adopted virtually without modification in the School Education Law of 1947, required a massive reorganization of the existing school facilities. To comply with the new requirements for compulsory, middle school education, many new institutions had to be established—a difficult task that was successfully accomplished by the end of the Occupation despite the damage to existing facilities and the shortage of revenues. A fundamental reorganization was required to realize the mission's proposals for comprehensive three-year high schools; the higher schools, colleges, and normal schools of the old system had no place here. Some of these institutions were consolidated into existing universities; others became components of the new comprehensive high schools.

MAIN THEMES OF EDUCATIONAL CONFLICT

The danger of concentrating too much authority in the hands of the central bureaucracy appeared to be the report's most persistent theme.

With a recommendation that more authority be shifted to local governments, the report encouraged the formation of parent-teacher associations and other popular groups that might serve as checks and as vehicles for generating new viewpoints on education. It also urged the formation of professional teachers associations and even approved the organization of teachers unions, adding that "no democratic principle is more crucial than the right to assemble for the extension of ideas."

The Occupation enthusiastically supported the mission's recommendation for a more decentralized educational system and quickly took several steps to implement the changes: the Ministry of Education was relieved of its power to censor textbooks; special funds were made available to support the formation of parent-teacher associations; teachers unions were allowed to organize at the expense of the progovernment teachers association, which rapidly lost membership.

These reform proposals were welcomed by progressively disposed educators. Teachers especially jumped at the chance to organize independently from governments. Their various organizations soon consolidated in a single union known as Nikkyoso, which became a staunch defender of democratic education; to realize its program, Nikkyoso allied itself with the progressive political camp. Thus, in many respects Nikkyoso strove to reinforce the reforms of the Occupation.[13]

Nevertheless, the traditions of the old system had supporters, especially in the civil service and the top ranks of corporations, and even in the rural areas. These supporters became an important, though not dominant, voice in the conservative camp; they argued that the new system would lead to a lowering of academic standards and would not preserve Japan's traditional morality.

Thus, a basis for conflict over educational issues came to be institutionalized in the two opposing political camps. Throughout the postwar period this conflict was pursued at all levels: in the schools, at local assemblies and the national Diet, and through the media. Its main themes, which we summarize below, have obvious parallels to the Red-versus-expert conflict that has characterized recent Chinese education.

1. *Are teachers workers or professionals?* The conservative camp has contended that teachers should be professionals who implement the curriculum and other educational policies determined by the neutral state. As professionals, teachers should be trained in professional skills under state auspices and promoted according to criteria such as teaching skills as well as their cooperation with authorities. In contrast, the progressive camp has contended that teachers, who are at the bottom of the educational hierarchy, are workers who should seek to advance the interests of their class. As workers, they ought to establish autonomy from the official personnel system and play an independent role in devising and implementing the school curriculum.

2. *Is the primary aim of education to fully develop an individual's personality or simply to develop skills?* The educational ideology of the old system emphasized skill development, and the conservative camp has continued to favor this emphasis. This has become evident in its manpower studies, its tendency to emphasize vocational and technical curricula in the schools and universities, and in its campaign, from the late fifties, to reinstate the old-system technical colleges (finally enacted in 1962). The progressives, insisting that education's primary goal ought to be the development of a rich personality, resisted these technocratic and vocational biases and sought instead to identify the means by which schools become happier and less competitive institutions. They have also sought to use the schools as vehicles for developing a more "democratic" personality.

3. *Should education be for all or for the select few?* The conservatives, in contrast to the more liberal progressives, are inclined to the elitist view that only a small, capable minority can benefit from higher education. One important practical difference that persisted until the early seventies was their respective opposition and support of public subsidies to private schools, since these schools provide the majority of opportunities at the postcompulsory level.

This conflict between the conservatives and the progressives, which began during the Occupation period, has been relatively evenhanded, with both sides achieving important victories. Still, from the perspective of the reforms brought about by the Occupation, there have been a number of setbacks and counterreforms that have been realized against strong objections, especially from the teachers. The effort to establish numerous, local school boards by popular elections, for example, was eventually abandoned in favor of a single board for each prefecture or large urban area, with board members appointed by the respective governors and mayors. Moreover, due to the inadequacy of local revenues, or rather to the central government's persistence in collecting the lion's share of government revenues, the central government has maintained its role as the effective policymaker both with respect to the finance of public schools and the salary levels of teachers. Arguing that quality was slipping and paper was being wasted, the central government again reasserted its role as the coordinator of textbook selection.

POSTWAR CHANGE IN HIGHER EDUCATION

Along with school-system reforms, educational policymakers during the Occupation also attempted to promote fundamental changes in higher education. The aim was a broadening of goals, a leveling of the traditional hierarchy, an expansion of opportunities, and above all, the decentralization of control. Most of the structural reforms at this level were only partially realized, however, and adequate funds simply could not be mobilized to insure the intended outcomes.[14]

The fate of private higher education is a case in point. In the prewar period the central bureaucracy awarded charters to private colleges and universities on the basis of a careful examination of an institution's resources, and a large grant often accompanied the official charter. In 1949 a private school law was passed by the Diet which transferred the chartering responsibility to a quasi-autonomous Private School Council. At the same time, the government renounced responsibility for the financing of the private institutions, alleging "no control, no support." Many of these colleges and universities had lost most of their assets during the wartime bombings and the rampant inflation of the immediate postwar period and were facing a very difficult financial prospect. Their solution was to expand enrollments more rapidly than staff or facilities, thereby gaining in tuition income; by the mid-1960s several private schools had student-teacher ratios in excess of 100 to 1. Then, as the plethora of postwar babies began to seek university places, the schools increased tuition and fee levels.

In the case of national universities, there were efforts, initially, to increase their independence, and a plan was drafted for governing each by a board of trustees. This plan was never effected, in part because professors in the universities preferred to depend on a central government that unquestionably could provide financing, rather than on newly created boards of trustees with no established source of funds. What evolved instead was a split system of control, with the central government receiving university budget requests but responding in terms of its own existing sets of budgetary priorities. Because of the new constitutional guarantee of university autonomy, the universities also gained complete control over the selection of their academic officers and staff, as well as over the selection of students.

Unlike public school teachers, who were officially hired by the local government, professers were direct employees of the national government. To improve their position a group of them formed a university teachers union which established formal ties with the schoolteachers union, Nikkyoso. But a substantial number of professors preferred to think of their status as being above that of the teachers and many very prominent national university professors preferred to address the national government on questions of salaries and related matters through the vehicle of the new Japan Science Council. Thus, most professors eschewed both unionization and a formal link with the teachers union or the progressive camp. At both the bureaucratic level, then, and in terms of professional ties, higher education and the schools were essentially separate domains.

The University Shapes the Schools

In this historical review I have suggested that the universities have, by and large, enjoyed the upper hand in the school-university relationship. As a late developer, Japan looked to the universities to introduce the knowledge essential for progress. Employers assumed that university graduates would be most in command of the vital knowledge and hence offered them exceptional benefits. Thus, ambitious young people sought university degrees with great intensity. For young people, then, the decision whether to follow the academic course through the higher school to a university, or to choose some other educational-cum-career course, was the most fateful of their lives.

The concern with university entrance has become progressively more prevalent over the postwar period. In 1950 less than one-half of the high school cohort actually attended a high school, and less than one-half of these took the college preparatory course. Even at that time, however, the college preparatory course was the first choice for most young people. Since then, the secondary system has expanded so much that today there are places for virtually all high-school-age youth (see table 5.2). Much of the expansion has been the result of the proliferation of private schools, and reflecting the desires of young people, the vast majority of the new places have been in college preparatory tracks. For economic reasons most young people would prefer to attend a good public upper secondary school; however, many finally decide that their chances for success in the university competition are better served by the private sector.

The rapid expansion of secondary education has been paralleled by an impressive expansion at the tertiary level, enabling at least half the high school graduates who wish to, to enter some college or university. However, the best universities have only marginally altered their size. Thus, objectively, the chance for a secondary-level student to get accepted to a top university has decreased.

The reforms brought about by the Occupation caused a major transformation in the institutions regulating the examination competition, and, initially, this caused much confusion. The number of places in the major national universities was not significantly expanded, thus preserving the exclusiveness of the top prizes in the academic competition. Middle schools, which previously had been the original point of competitive selection, became compulsory. Thus, far more youth completed nine years of academic education and hence were in a position to compete for university entrance. Higher schools, which previously had been the main focus of "exam fever," were disbanded. In their place the three-year comprehensive high school was established. Both the academic and

TABLE 5.2

HISTORICAL TRENDS IN NUMBERS ENROLLED AT THE SECONDARY AND HIGHER EDUCATIONAL LEVEL, AND RELATED INDICATORS

Year	Number in upper secondary	Percentage of age cohort	Percentage of upper secondary students in university preparatory	Percentage of university preparatory in private school	Percentage of all high school graduates going to university	Percentage of university preparatory going to university	Number in universities and junior colleges
1900	121,171	2.9	4.7	0	3*	60*	1,620
1910	259,734	15.9	2.4	0	2*	80*	5,821
1920	974,223	25.0	1.0	0	1*	90*	9,696
1930	1,047,223	36.1	1.9	10.9	2*	90*	46,690
1940	1,118,136	46.0	1.8	11.5	2*	90*	81.999
1950	1,935,118	69.3	65.2	24.1	20*	30*	447,486
1955	2,592,001	78.0	59.8	33.2	18.4	30.8	589,904
1960	3,239,416	80.0	59.3	49.4	17.2	29.0	698,726
1965	5,074,059	83.8	59.4	55.3	25.4	42.8	1,069,377
1970	4,273,506	89.2	58.4	52.0	24.2	41.4	1,645,062
1975	4,333,079	90.0	62.9	48.0	34.2	54.3	2,020,135
1980	4,621,936	92.0	68.2	41.2	31.9	46.8	2,124,915

SOURCE: Ministry of Education. *Educational Statistics in Japan: Present, Past and Future*, 1971.

Mombus no. *Wagu Kuni no Kyoiku Suijun*, 1981.

Mombus no. Tokei Shosaka: *Kyoiku Teihyo no Kokugai Kikaku*, 1982.

*Estimate

general track of these high schools provided young people with the qualifications necessary for university entrance, and many more places were created in these universities than had been available in the higher schools of the older system. Thus, the new system was providing far greater numbers of youth with the paper qualifications to compete for university entrance. The large majority of the new wave of university aspirants hoped to earn the top prize, that is, passing the exams of one of the elite universities. These institutions, however, could accommodate only a small fraction.

Inevitably, many young people were disappointed by their failure, and, at least in the early years, large numbers tended to express this through drastic measures, including suicide. The youth suicide rate sharply accelerated through the mid-1950s and then began a steady decline that continues into the eighties, suggesting that youth gradually became more realistic about the competition.

A number of mechanisms have evolved to help young people and their parents understand their prospects in the exam competition:

1. Cumulative knowledge is conveyed through the media that many fail despite good school records and outstanding ability.
2. An abundance of magazines and books provide information about the system and "how to beat it." For example, there are books that detail past competition rates for every faculty of every university, average scores on standardized achievement tests for past entering classes, and the most frequent high school alma maters of these classes. Other books provide the questions used in past entrance exams for leading universities, along with suggested answers.
3. A series of tests have been developed to provide norm-referenced indicators of individual ability, often given as early as kindergarten. Most important, however, are the mock tests administered nationally by Obonsha and other private companies, which provide students with their scores compared with the average scores of the individuals who succeeded in entering top universities the previous year.
4. Youth can apply and take admission exams at a host of primary and secondary schools that are known to excel in placing students in the top universities. Those who are offered admission to these schools, whether they accept or not, gain confidence in their chances to get into a top university.

Of course, those who are encouraged in other respects will also benefit from attending the right secondary school. The alternatives here are complex and have constantly shifted in response to student choices.

CHOOSING THE RIGHT SCHOOL

It is important to recognize that all secondary schools operate under national school standards that require them to provide a common curriculum. The standards for the curriculum have been set by the Ministry of Education with the aim of developing a well-rounded young person, not simply a youth capable of passing exams. Thus, the high school curriculum includes mandatory physical education, music, and so on. Schools are not really able to skimp on these subjects, even though the student's performance in these areas will not affect his chances for university entrance.[15]

Given the realities of student demand and the uniform curriculum standards, schools have developed an interesting range of responses. Some schools have responded by rejecting the need to offer special preparation for the exams, arguing that the best preparation is that outlined in the official curriculum. Most schools, however, have bent in some way to the exam pressure; the exam oriented adaptations are probably the major theme in postwar Japanese educational innovation.

Public Upper Secondary Education. Schools in the public sector are somewhat under the jurisdiction of local boards, who are obliged to provide secondary opportunities within a reasonable distance of a child's home. Most boards have a number of upper secondary schools under their jurisdiction and can consider various options for assigning students. The American Occupation proposed the neighborhood-school principle whereby children would be sent to the upper secondary school nearest their home; they also proposed that some effort be made to insure that all secondary schools be fairly identical in quality. This has come to be called the small-district system. At the opposite extreme is the large district, which includes five or more schools that are explicitly recognized as varying in quality; students with the best lower secondary performance are given a first option to the best school, and so on down the line, so that the weaker lower secondary students tend to get grouped in a low-quality upper secondary institution. The top schools of the large-district systems have a function much like the "keypoint schools" in China, described by Stanley Rosen.[16]

In the first blush of postwar democratic idealism, most prefectures organized their upper secondary schools according to the small-district principle. However, it was soon perceived, or believed, that the democratic mode of organization would cause all students to sink to the lowest common denominator in academic terms. Many districts decided that the small system would deprive the best students of their rightful opportunity to be exposed to the stimulation of other bright students and exceptional teachers. Thus, over time, many prefectures abandoned the small district for medium and large districts. In the large-district system an academic hierarchy is established with a particular school designated as the recipient of top scorers in a combined average of middle school grades and an upper secondary entrance exam. Another school is designated as second best, and so on. Only the top school offers a college preparatory course, but there will be others that offer a combination of academic and vocational tracks and, possibly, some schools that are exclusively vocational. This arrangement tends to relegate weak students to the vocational tracks. These tracks thus acquire a stigma that makes them the last choice among most young people seeking upper secondary education. Many youth who end up with an assignment in a public-sector vocational school thus make an effort to move out into the private sector.

In the prefectures that have adopted the large system, typically, the school with the longest tradition was designated as the main academic preparatory school. These famous older schools were once known not only for their academic excellence but also for the prowess of their students in such national athletic competitions as the annual baseball match. Now their teams lose out, at an early stage, to teams from schools lower in the academic pecking order. Thus, the large-district system fails to serve the whole-man educational ideal.

Only those school districts run by progressive governments have maintained the small system; Kyoto, under Governor Ninagawa, was for many years a lone example. Schools in small-district systems strive to offer a full program of both curricular and extracurricular activities, but, increasingly, they find that third-year students are unwilling to participate in anything that competes with their studies. Moreover, a large segment of the public remains doubtful of the academic effectiveness of public schools that recruit from a small district and attempt to provide a comprehensive program with multiple tracks and a full program of extracurricular activities. The parents of high academic performers tend especially to send their children to outstanding private schools, rather than take a risk in the public sector.

National Schools. Distinct from the public schools are a small group of national schools that are the experimental schools for the teacher training faculties of national universities. Parents have always assumed that these schools ought to provide superior education, as they are supervised by educational experts and have the opportunity to select the most able teachers. The competition for entrance is thus quite severe. In general these attached schools have resisted parental pressure for special admissions or an exam oriented curriculum, and simply try to provide a stimulating and somewhat avant-garde education. But to the extent that the graduates of the national schools fail to do well in the university competition, the public may disparage their innovative educational ideas. As a result, several national schools bias their chances for good exam results by picking top applicants and offering exam oriented instruction within the framework of the official curriculum.

Private Schools. The notion of opening up a school to serve the public or realize some personal ideal or whim is firmly rooted in the Japanese educational tradition. The constraints on the scale and program of public upper secondary education, combined with increased demand, has provided abundant opportunity for the growth of the private sector. Private schools have succeeded to the extent that they can offer an interesting program, a safe ticket, or simply hope.

Most of the earliest private schools were established to realize a special educational goal cherished by their founders. The majority were founded by foreign missionary groups and benefited from the input of foreign funds and teachers.[17] A few were established by local figures who wished to create independent men (Keio and Waseda) or women (Tsuda), or individuals with a creative and free spirit (Tamagawa Gakuin). Over the years these schools acquired their loyal alumni who often sent their children in turn. In the postwar educational expansion their fame increased, in considerable part because they had been around for so long and offered an alternative to public education. The quality of their applicants improved, so they tended to become more selective, even to the point of passing over the children of alumni. As they became more selective, their graduates did even better on exams, thus further enhancing their reputation. The improved reputation enabled an increase in tuition, hence better buildings and facilities. In many cases it was questionable whether their apparent success was consistent with the special goals that led to their foundation.

Since they are managed by private bodies, these schools are more capable of introducing innovations. One that has proven especially popular is providing children with a guaranteed route to a university, thus relieving them from the uncertainty of the standard exam cycle. In the extreme case, the private school is actually a system from kindergarten through the university, such as the Doshisha of Kyoto or Aoyama Gakuin in Tokyo. The lower levels of these systems have fewer places than the higher ones. Thus, if a child enters the kindergarten of the system, so long as academic performance is acceptable, he or she can eventually find a place in the system's university. Parents are prepared to pay the extra price of private tuition in order to preserve their child's ticket to the university.

The provision of a ticket has some potentially promising educational advantages. When the school and its children know that they will not have to face a crucial entrance exam two years hence, students feel under less pressure to become full-time grinds, and the schools can feel free to offer a broadly based educational program consisting of both academics and extracurricular activities. Thus, the sports and music programs at certain of the private schools are impressive. Because the offering of a ticket may invite a total disregard of study, however, most private schools assert their option to fail a minority.

Nada High School of Kobe, one of the most famous private secondary schools, does not have an attached university and therefore cannot offer a complete ticket. However, by taking in exceptionally able students at the lower secondary level and giving them a rapidly paced academic course over an uninterrupted six-year stretch, it is able to provide a firm background for the university exams. Students are expected to participate in extracurricular activities and are discouraged from attending exam preparation schools at night. Indeed, the majority of Nada's graduates enter top universities. Competition to enter Nada is keen; annually, busloads of children come from as far as Hokkaido (over 1500 miles) to sit for Nada's entrance exams.

Apart from the exceptional private upper secondary schools are many others, usually somewhat lower priced and less adequately provided for, which offer lower secondary graduates of average potential an option to the vocational tracks that they are offered in the public system. These less prestigious schools offer their entrants hope: the schools do cover the academic curriculum, and if the students apply themselves, they may make up for their past weak performance and yet compete successfully for a top university. While most students from the lesser private schools end up in lesser universities, a few do fly high.

THE *RONIN* PHENOMENON

Along with selecting the right school, some students attend special nighttime exam-preparation schools and may obtain tutors to increase the effectiveness of their private study. Nevertheless, for a large number of them, these efforts prove insufficient. Every year a substantial group fail to pass the annual entrance exams of the university first on their list.

A failure of this kind in most contemporary educational systems implies that the individual is not up to standard and hence ought to pursue a lesser goal; moreover, the institution that rejects the applicant may keep a record so as to automatically pass over any who try a second time. In Japan, however, the thinking is different. A first-time failure is not considered an indication of the individual's inherent ability. Rather, it suggests that the individual was poorly prepared or did not try hard enough. Thus, the universities keep no formal record of who fails, and applicants are free to try as many times as they wish.

A large number of students who fail in the exams decide to devote a further year of special study to exam preparation instead of entering a lesser university or the labor force. The youth who take this direction are known as *ronin*, and the number steadily increased from 1950 into the late sixties, after which it leveled off. Some are content with studying by themselves, but the majority seek the aid of special *yobiko*, preparatory schools that provide a stiff regimen of exam oriented lectures, often taught by the very individuals who have written the exams to be taken by the students. The prevalence of the ronin year has led some to say that the exam pressure has converted the official 6-3-3-4 system into a 6-3-3-1-4 system.

ADOLESCENT CULTURE

Concern with choosing the right schools, and doing well once there, has profound effects on young people's values and their use of time. In recent years there have been a number of excellent studies that document these aspects in a comparative perspective.[18] Perhaps the most informative are the findings from a 1978 survey jointly conducted by the prime minister's office in Japan and the Department of Health, Education and Welfare in the United States. Over 1500 students from a variety of high schools in each country answered a number of questions concerning their lives and values. This excellent study clearly shows that the primary concern of Japanese youth is school and study, and that most of their associations and activities are school related. In contrast, American youth are more interested in extracurricular activities, and they have more social relationships outside of school, including considerable involvement with members of the opposite sex.

The extraordinary commitment of Japanese youth to their studies is a large part of the explanation for the exceptionally high levels of achievement demonstrated in several recent international evaluations of academic achievement.[19] But additional factors also need to be taken into account. The Japanese school year is longer than it is in most other societies, which thus enable Japanese youth more time to cover the material, and Japanese school texts move more rapidly through many subjects than do the texts used in other public educational systems, especially those found in the United States; the typical Japanese ninth grader attacks problems in mathematics that few American students encounter until their first year of college, if ever.

Japan's higher academic standard is not caused by the adolescent culture, but the culture has supported the academic emphasis in the past. An important development of the last several years, however, has been the emergence of new trends in youth values. The dominant new trend appears to be toward greater equality and individuation and a more muted emphasis on achievement. While this trend does not threaten the existing system, it does result in modest changes in style and emphasis. Young persons are more willing to settle for second and third choices in universities; they expect to be given more responsibility and voice in school and work relations, and they seek more time for their own private pursuits.[20]

Notwithstanding, there are increasing signs that a counterculture is emerging which simply rejects all that is involved in the search for academic success and turns instead toward hedonism and even hooliganism; the most obvious expression of the countercultural trend is seen in the *bosozoku* gangs of motorcyclists who terrorize the streets of the central cities and certain highways on weekend nights.

UNIVERSITIES AS THE INTELLECTUAL RESERVE FOR SCHOOLS

The Japanese university system confers the status of university professor on nearly 150,000 individuals. The professor's salary is modest, however, and most seek additional income from outside work. One major form of outside work is to provide intellectual materials for the schools; most of the texts, dictionaries, and encyclopedias used in schools, especially at the secondary level, are written by university teachers. They are either created anew or written according to a formula supplied by a publisher. These texts are subject to review by the Ministry of Education and local school boards before final adoption in the school, and this process sometimes results in controversy. The best-known example is the lengthy dispute over the revised edition of Saburo Ienaga's Japanese history textbook. This case has led to fundamental questioning of the central government's right to review the content of textbooks.

University professors, because they compose and grade the entrance exams, are naturally invited to write for the many publications intended to aid students in preparation. Some of these cover general topics, while others provide guidance for the exams of a specific university. Since more than 50,000 students may take the entrance exams for some of the larger private universities, it is easy to appreciate the significance of this service. Further outside work is done by some university professors who actually teach in examination preparatory schools as well as write materials for them. Moreover, a large minority of university students teach either in the courses of the examination preparatory schools, or, as tutors, in the homes of high school students.

UNIVERSITIES TRAIN THE TEACHERS

With the inauguration of the new system, all the former teachers colleges were joined to universities as faculties of education, and an alternative route of gaining teacher certification was established through a regular bachelor of arts degree supplemented by a few education courses. Since then, the universities have become the training places for teachers, with well over half of all new recruits to teaching coming from the alternate route.

During the immediate postwar period, impoverished and alienated teachers formed various unions that eventually merged in Nikkyoso. Several of the central committee members of this union were, and continue to be, university teachers. These individuals view their university classrooms as a proper setting for conveying the ideals of Nikkyoso, thus exposing teachers to leftist thinking even before they begin their work.

The location of teacher training in the universities has resulted in considerable autonomy from outside influence, including that of the central government. Relative to old-system teachers, those of today are inclined to view themselves more as intellectuals than as officials. Further, they are more inclined to look to their university professors for intellectual guidance. Doubtless, the broad education provided by new-system universities has created a more independent teacher who has the courage to join with others in fighting the battles of the educational struggle outlined earlier.

The School Shapes the Universities

Only about 10,000 students come to Japan's universities from overseas, and only a very small number return to the university after they enter the labor force. Thus, Japan's schools are virtually the exclusive suppliers of students to the universities. Schools do not have a direct channel for shaping the universities, yet through the quantity and quality of students they prepare, it is clear that the schools have exerted a profound influence.

Table 5.2 shows the increase in the number of students completing the high school academic track, that is, 68 percent of the age group in 1980. In the fifties, surveys suggested that about 40 percent of all high school youth sought a place in a university. Today, over 80 percent seek to enter a higher educational institution. The majority of those seeking a place persist until they get one. The growing demand for higher education has enabled massive expansion, so that now Japan has more higher education institutions than any nation except the United States. Possibly even a greater percentage of Japanese youth attend these institutions than do their counterparts in the United States.

The ruling conservative party, which traditionally viewed higher education as a vehicle for elite training and the development of professional manpower, has not allowed public higher education to satisfy the demand but limited expansion primarily to technical fields. Thus, private universities have been the major source of response to expansion. Whereas they provided only 55 percent of the places in 1950, today they account for over 80 percent of them.

Although high schools have graduated increasing numbers of students, and although the overall standard of high school education has certainly improved, not all higher education aspirants seek an academic experience or are capable of doing demanding academic work. Indeed, a large proportion of them say they are continuing simply because their friends are doing the same. Others enter because it will add to their chances for marriage. These varied motives have put pressure on the universities to diversify their programs. The most obvious response has been the proliferation of junior colleges, which have proved especially popular for young girls, who make up over 75 percent of the student body. Most of the junior colleges offer low-cost finishing courses in such subjects as literature or social studies, while a few specialize in nursing or in child psychology courses that might be suitable for kindergarten teaching.

Distinct from junior colleges are a group of postsecondary specialized schools (*kakushi gakko*) that aim at providing vocational skills in computer programming, English translation, tour guiding, electronics, and similar areas. These schools have become especially popular over the last decade. Clearly, the high school's expanding supply of graduates has transformed the former elitist character of higher education so that a variety of needs and abilities are now accommodated.

The rising aspiration for higher education has been accompanied by an exceptionally strong demand for certain opportunities, especially acceptance into the elite universities or into a medical faculty at any university. Consequently, there have been a few instances in which well-placed individuals exploited these situations for personal gain. Exorbitant entrance fees became commonplace at most of the private medical faculties, and an applicant's ability to pay became more important than his ability to study. In most cases the revenues from these fees were turned over to the universities for institutional development, but there were instances of individual profiteering as well.

Regardless of the amount an individual paid to get accepted to a private institution, there were no guarantees of the quality of education he would receive. Given the general laissez-faire attitude toward educational standards, many private institutions permitted their student-teacher ratios to rise to alarming levels, sometimes in excess of 100 to 1.

These conditions were partially responsible for the vigorous protests that rocked Japanese higher education after the late sixties. The outcome was a new law to establish the Private School Promotion Foundation. This foundation, established primarily with government revenues in 1971, has gradually devised policies to reward private universities that upgrade the quality of their educational programs. Evidently, the expansion that first invited opportunism has now stimulated a healthy counteraction.[21]

REFORM OF THE EXAMINATION SYSTEM

With the proliferation of higher education institutions and the traditional practice of allowing each university to offer its own examination, the options for students are overwhelming; in fact, students find their lives dominated by exam preparation.

Concern for the plight of students has led to the consideration of a number of changes borrowed mainly from American experience. A few universities, for example, have established special arrangements with well-known high schools, granting the latter the privilege of nominating outstanding students for admission; these students are exempted from the entrance exams. Other universities have created preentrance exams for second-year high school students, which, if passed, relieve these students from the burden of taking the exam during their third year. Yet another development is the extension of special concessions to Japanese children educated overseas who complete the international baccalaureate degree.

The most publicized reform is that launched by the national university system. After much discussion, the national universities agreed to divide the entrance process into two stages. As a first stage all aspirants to national universities sit for a common entrance exam collectively administered by all the national universities. Students who do reasonably well on this exam are then eligible, in the second stage, to apply to take the particular entrance exam of one, and only one, national university. One application per student is allowed at one of the universities belonging to a group designated as first class; the second application can be sent to any one of the remaining national universities. Although it is difficult to see how this clumsy arrangement has substantially improved the welfare of students, it is noteworthy as a first step toward coordination between the highly independent national universities. High school teachers are invited to sit on the team preparing the first-stage exam, thus also initiating a modest degree of high school-university coordination.

THE CHANGING CLIMATE OF UNIVERSITIES

The most obvious cultural influence of universities upon schools has been to intensify the exam culture, but other influences can also be noted. Relative to the old system, teachers, through their liberal education and through their association with the leftist teachers union, have acquired a more independent outlook. They especially have come to identify with the democratic values of equality, participation, and individualism and have conveyed these values to youth in numerous ways, resulting in a profound transformation of the approach young people bring to human relations.

The university is the first step, after school, for many of these young people; this is where they seek greater participation in decisions about university matters and also more respect from their professors. These concerns were a major theme in the university crisis and led to a democratization of faculty-student relations. That the universities have become increasingly populated by more fun-seeking and play oriented students, as well as by an increasing proportion of young women, are additional noticeable trends.

Many changes at particular universities have evoked interest or concern. In the softer faculties of the major national universities one can observe the gradual displacement of males by females. In 1982, 20 percent of the students in the University of Tokyo's faculty of letters were female; a few years earlier, there were virtually none. The movement of talented females to the prestigious national universities has resulted in a reported decline in the quality of students at some of the better-known women's colleges such as Tsuda and Ocha no Mizu.

Overall, the increase in university enrollments has been accompanied by a proportionate increase in the representation of youths from working-class and low-income families. However, the available evidence suggests an actual decline in the proportion of such youths admitted to national universities and to those most prestigious. In other words, lower-class youth tend to be concentrated in lower-class higher education.[22]

Finally, in view of the seemingly impossible competition for places in the elite universities, many of the more able youth seem to have reduced their sights. Taking into account both the stress of competition for elite national universities and the cost of attendance if admitted, increasing numbers seem to be settling for hometown institutions. The result has been a geographic parochialization of admissions, such that today over half of the new entrants to Japan's most prestigious national university, the University of Tokyo, come from the Tokyo metropolitan area.

Conclusion

Japanese culture is basically reluctant to condone interpersonal evaluation. Thus, in the premodern period, heredity was the basic principle behind social promotion. In the modern period the introduction of modern technology and the spread of large organizations led to a movement for a new system of evaluation based on competence and performance. Formal education came to play an important part in this new society. However, educational institutions were as reluctant to judge as the broader society, and it was partly for this reason that educational institutions instituted rigorous and impersonal entrance exams at their gates to determine who could enter. The first examples of such examinations were those required by the higher schools. Gradually, the principle was imitated by other educational institutions both at the higher educational and other levels; indeed, all Japanese educational institutions, including those that are desperate to admit every student who applies, today have some form of entrance examination. In general, once a student enters an institution, his exit is guaranteed.

The procedures used by schools and universities for examining prospective students were never questioned in the old system. In the new one, the entrance exams have come under sharper scrutiny, and it is recognized that this system of testing has many undesirable consequences. Nevertheless, the critics have not been quite able to come up with viable alternatives, given that universities with their constitutionally guaranteed autonomy are relatively impervious to outside forces. The universities therefore retain their established procedures for admitting students. It is this that sets the tone of the relationship between secondary and higher education.

Notes

1. For a discussion of the German concept of maturity, see Teichler, "The Federal Republic of Germany," chap. 2 of this volume.
2. A noted discussion of *ie* psychology is Nakane, *Japanese Society;* for its implications in employee selection, see Azumi, *Higher Education and Business Recruitment in Japan.*
3. The American reference is to *A Nation at Risk;* a useful analysis of Japan's exam hell is Shimahara, *Adaptation and Education.*
4. These claims for Japan's premodern educational attainment are made in Dore, *Education in Tokugawa Japan.*
5. As translated in Passin, *Society and Education in Japan,* pp. 209–211.
6. Aso, *Erito to Kyoiku* (Elites and Education), especially pp. 217–219.

7. An excellent discussion of the old high schools is Roden, *Schooldays in Imperial Japan.*

8. The statistical ratios are reported in Kinmouth, *Self-Made Man,* p. 74.

9. An authoritative analysis of Mori's thinking is Hall, *Mori Arinori.*

10. As noted in Anderson, *Education in Japan,* p. 61.

11. United States Education Mission to Japan, *Report,* p. 4.

12. Ibid., p. 18.

13. A useful review of the role of Nikkyoso is found in Cummings, *Education and Equality in Japan,* pp. 40–76.

14. One review is Cummings, "The Crisis of Japanese Higher Education."

15. Rohlen in *Japan's High Schools* provides an excellent summary and ethnographic descriptions of several Japanese high schools including Nada, mentioned below.

16. See Rosen, "The People's Republic of China," chap. 6 of this volume, for a useful discussion of keypoint schools.

17. See Burnstein, *Protestant Colleges for Men in Japan.*

18. Reported with an English summary in Nihon Seinen Kekyusho, *Nichibei Seinen Hikaku Chosa Hokokusho.*

19. The results of several international achievement tests are summarized in Cummings, *Education and Equality in Japan,* pp. 172–176.

20. This is the argument presented in Cummings, *Education and Equality.*

21. One discussion of the private sector is Cummings, "The Japanese Private University."

22. See Rohlen, "Is Japanese Education Becoming Less Egalitarian?" pp. 37–70.

Bibliography

ANDERSON, RONALD S. *Education in Japan: A Century of Modern Development.* Washington, D.C.: U.S. Government Printing Office, 1975.

ASO, MAKOTO. *Erito to Kyoiku* (Elites and Education). Tokyo: Fukumura Shuppan, 1967.

AZUMI, KOYA. *Higher Education and Business Recruitment in Japan.* New York: Teachers College Press, 1969.

BURNSTEIN, IRA J. *The American Movement to Develop Protestant Colleges for Men in Japan, 1868–1912.* University of Michigan, Comparative Education Series, no. 11. Ann Arbor, 1967.

CUMMINGS, WILLIAM K. "The Crisis of Japanese Higher Education." *Minerva* 10 (October 1972): 631–638.

———. *Education and Equality in Japan.* Princeton: Princeton University Press, 1981.

———. "The Japanese Private University." *Minerva* 1 (July 1973): 348–371.

DORE, RONALD. *Education in Tokugawa Japan.* Berkeley: University of California Press, 1964.

HALL, IVAN. *Mori Arinori.* Cambridge, Mass.: Harvard University Press, 1973.

KINMOUTH, EARL H. *The Self-Made Man in Meiji Japanese Thought: From Samurai to Salary Man.* Berkeley: University of California Press, 1973.

NAKANE, CHIE. *Japanese Society.* Berkeley: University of California Press, 1973.

National Committee on Excellence in Education. *A Nation at Risk.* Washington: U.S. Government Printing Office, 1983.

NIHON SEINEN KENKYUSHO. *Nichibei Seinen Hikaku Chosa Hokokusho.* Tokyo, 1979.

PASSIN, HERBERT. *Society and Education in Japan.* New York: Teachers College Press, Columbia University, 1965.

RODEN, DONALD T. *Schooldays in Imperial Japan: A Study of the Culture of a Student Elite.* Berkeley: University of California Press, 1980.

ROHLEN, THOMAS G. "Is Japanese Education Becoming Less Egalitarian? Notes on High School Stratification and Reform." *Journal of Japanese Studies* 3, no. 1 (1977): 37–70.

―――― . *Japan's High Schools.* Berkeley, Los Angeles, London: University of California Press, 1983.

SHIMAHARA, NOBUO. *Adaptation and Education in Japan.* New York: Praeger, 1981.

United States Education Mission to Japan. *Report.* Tokyo, March 30, 1946. Mimeo.

6

The People's Republic of China

STANLEY ROSEN

SEVEN YEARS AFTER THE CULTURAL REVOLUTION (1966–76), China's educational system remains in transition. Although the present leadership is now secure enough to make long-range plans, including projected university enrollment figures to 1990, the current educational structure still bears some of the scars of the reforms that took place during the Cultural Revolution. Just as Cultural Revolution radicals entirely reshaped the educational system in an onslaught against the perceived defects of the earlier one, the reforms have, in turn, been denounced totally by the moderate leaders currently in office.[1] In this twenty-year struggle over a suitable educational form and content, perhaps no issue has proved as contentious as the proper relationship between secondary and higher education. Not only have China's political leaders differed fundamentally on this question but the issue has also been of utmost importance to educators, parents, and students. To appreciate the passions aroused by educational questions in general, and by the secondary-higher education relationship in particular, it is helpful to begin with an examination of the role education has been expected to play in China.

Since the establishment of the People's Republic of China in 1949, the educational system has been asked to perform a variety of tasks, involving both ideopolitical and academic functions. The transformation from a social and political order in which both traditional Confucian values and modern bourgeois perspectives were present, to a social and political order committed to modernization and economic development along Marxist-Leninist lines, was a daunting task in 1949, and it remains so today. The official goals of the educational system are to emphasize the moral, intellectual, and physical development of students and to produce mental and manual laborers who possess a socialist consciousness and culture. Further, the educational system is expected to provide mass education, implying popularization of courses taught to large numbers of students, at the same time providing high-quality and specialized training. Expressed another way, both Red and expert values are to be stressed.

In actual practice, however, the past thirty years have revealed the difficulties of incorporating the ideopolitical (Red) values and the academic (expert) values within the same educational structure. Since education follows the political line, priority has been given at different times to one set of values over the other. Numerous policies have been associated with ideopolitical values: the expansion and redistribution of educational opportunities, particularly to students of worker-peasant class origin; the introduction of vocational courses and manual labor into the curriculum of academic schools; the elimination of tracking; the deemphasis on formal classroom schooling; the use of political over academic criteria for promotion to advanced schooling; the decentralization of educational control and financing; the simplification of teaching materials; and the use of a wide variety of teaching personnel, including many who are noncertified. These policies have fostered egalitarianism and mass education and were associated with the political ascendancy of the radical faction, including Mao himself.

In contrast, the stress on academic values, an integral component of the developmental strategy of China's moderates, has given educational quality pride of place. When academic values have been strongly emphasized, the educational system has featured tracking and even streaming; the use of examinations for promotion and to determine the quality of students and schools; a hierarchical structure in which scarce financial and pedagogical resources were concentrated in a relatively small number of *keypoint* schools at all levels, where China's most outstanding students could be trained; and a concern with the proper academic training of teaching personnel.

In spite of the different educational strategies represented by these two models, it would be incorrect to assume—as one might if one were to read the Cultural Revolution denunciations of the educational developments of 1949 to 1976 or the current attacks on the Cultural Revolution—that there was no common ground on which Chinese leaders could agree, that little progress was made in education after 1949, or even that each model completely ignored the concerns of the other. In fact, elements of both models have been present continuously since 1949, although during certain periods one has been strongly emphasized over the other. Thus, during the Great Leap Forward (1958–60), expanded educational opportunities enabled children of workers, peasants, and party officials to be accommodated in secondary schools and universities. During the early 1960s this trend was reversed and was replaced by the tightening of academic standards to restore quality. The Cultural Revolution once again launched the expansion of educational opportunity and the adoption of egalitarian norms; these were followed as before by a concern with quality and hierarchy. Still, despite some twists and turns, China's formal educational system has expanded widely. Primary education, which all disputants agree is basic, has gradually become universal; but although 93 percent of school-age children have actually entered school, this substantial figure masks a host of difficulties.[2]

More problematic, however, have been the developments in secondary and higher education. Secondary education includes both junior and senior high (called junior and senior middle in China) and commonly must serve several functions simultaneously: at this level the decision is made regarding which individuals will proceed to higher education, which will be shunted onto a technical or vocational track, and which will have to forego further schooling entirely. Perhaps even more than in most societies, such decisions are crucial in China, where routes to upward mobility have traditionally led through the educational system.[3] It is on this battleground that radical and moderate educational philosophies have clashed most openly.

Higher education has presented a different, but related, problem. If the crucial issues at the secondary level have involved questions of tracking and access, both radicals and moderates have recognized the necessity of expanding educational opportunities at this level. In fact, China's enrollment ratios for primary and secondary school compare favorably with those of other developing countries. In higher education, however, except for the brief and ephemeral expansion during the Great Leap Forward, China has consistently lagged behind most other developing countries. According to World Bank figures, the average enrollment ratio in formal higher education institutions of ninety-two developing nations is between 4 and 5 percent; China's enrollment ratio remains below 2 percent.[4]

Given the small number of openings in universities and colleges, China has not had the problem, common elsewhere, of finding jobs for its college graduates. On the contrary, university entrance has been considered an "iron rice bowl," because it guaranteed assignment, by the state, to the most desirable jobs. Because of such rewards, access to higher education has been the most hotly contested educational issue during the past twenty-five years, and it remains so today.

An important focus of this chapter will be an examination of educational access and how it has changed over time. Entrance to the university has been so important that it has dominated the secondary-higher education relationship. Other aspects of the relationship have remained subordinate to this primary aspect. For example, assessments of the quality of regular, that is, academic, secondary schools have been based almost entirely on their promotion rates to universities, with schools ranked according to this standard. Those chosen as keypoint secondary schools, therefore, have been schools with the highest university promotion rates. Being so designated, the keypoint schools are allocated the best graduates of teacher training institutes, more generous funding, and so forth. These advantages enable them to attract the most promising students, the majority of whom go on to the university, thus maintaining the reputation of their schools and justifying the keypoint ranking. The curriculum is also affected by the importance of the university examinations; those subjects not tested on the annual entrance exams have received minimal attention from students and educators. Moreover, as the exams draw near in the senior year, the regular coursework is typically subordinated to exam review and preparation.

Even moderates thoroughly committed to quality education and rapid economic development have criticized the negative side effects stemming from the examination system. Their criticisms have been cautious, however, out of concern that a thoroughgoing critique of the deviations produced by the academic model might lead to an overemphasis on Red values over expert.

It was only during the years of the Cultural Revolution, when the radicals gained effective control over educational affairs, that the academic model, including both its positive and negative aspects, was virtually abandoned. With the passing of the Cultural Revolution, there has been a continuing attempt to reinstitute the "rationality" of the pre-cultural revolutionary model. The present relationship between secondary and higher education is a transitional one, representing neither the radical nor the moderate ideal. The direction is clear, but the educational structure envisioned by China's current leaders as most congruent with their modernization plans has yet to appear. Ironically, because of the need to fully dismantle the cultural revolutionary model, to make up for lost time, and to train qualified students as rapidly as possible, the transitional structure that does exist has been made considerably more elitist than its pre–cultural revolutionary predecessor. Moreover, for a variety of reasons, the deviations that have always flowed from the academic (examination) model have been exacerbated under current circumstances. These points will be developed fully later in this chapter. It is difficult, however, to understand present conditions without some knowledge of the educational structure of the 1960s and its cultural revolutionary replacement.

The Secondary School Structure Before and After the Cultural Revolution

Before the Cultural Revolution, the Chinese system was similar to others in the variety of options it offered. The major selection decisions were made after primary, junior high, and senior high school graduation. In the larger cities, junior high school education was universalized by the mid-1960s, so a student's decision regarding a future career might be delayed until graduation. At that point a variety of options were available: regular high schools that prepared students for university entrance; specialist (technical) schools that trained middle-level professional personnel such as accountants and nurses; worker training schools that trained middle-level technical workers such as carpenters and welders; and vocational schools that trained skilled workers and those with special skills, such as chefs, tailors, and photographers. In the countryside there were also agricultural middle schools. Among these types of schools further distinctions could be found. Some schools had full-day schedules, and some offered programs geared toward half work, half study; some regular schools were keypoint schools and some were ordinary schools.

The number of students in senior high school was kept deliberately low to coordinate with the needs of higher education and the labor force. Nationally, in 1965 only 9.1 percent of all secondary school students were in regular senior highs. By 1965 the enrollment ratio of senior high graduates to university enrollees was about 46 percent.

The results of the decisions that permitted students to further their education during the 1960s were also carefully monitored. Advancement through the educational system depended on three criteria: academic achievement, class origin, and political manifestation. Though these criteria varied from year to year, academic achievement was generally accorded greater weight as one moved up the educational ladder. The system was clearly a compromise, incorporating the divergent views of both radicals and moderates, with the year-to-year changes reflecting the shifts in the balance of political forces. In 1964, for example, it was exceedingly difficult for students whose parents had been capitalists, landlords, or rich peasants to gain entrance to a university, even with outstanding examination results. In 1962 a student's class origin was hardly a factor in determining university enrollment.

The Cultural Revolution, with its purge of moderate elements in the leadership, enabled the radicals to reshape the complex educational structure of the 1960s. Far from acknowledging the benefits of such a varied system, the radicals objected that the prime beneficiaries of this kind of educational structure were the children of intellectuals. The wide variety of options available were not options at all but simply levels of an educational pyramid. In this hierarchy the best schools were the keypoint schools. These schools received the most funding, had the best teachers and facilities, and had their choice of the country's most desirable students. In effect, this meant that a disproportionate number of students at the best keypoints were children of intellectuals, recruited for their outstanding academic ability. Many of the students chosen by the country's best universities were products of these keypoint schools. Similarly, regular schools were considered superior to work-study, vocational, or worker training schools. From the perspective of the radical reformers, those with the fewest options were the children of workers and peasants, since they could not match the academic achievements of those from intellectual families. Nor did the advantages that accrued to children of "good" class origin necessarily favor those of worker-peasant background. Just as their academic achievements were often inferior to those from intellectual homes, their class origins, as calculated by educational decision makers, were considered a cut below those born into families of party or military officials.[5]

In June 1966 most of China's schools shut down as students divided themselves into antagonistic Red Guard factions. By 1968, when the schools began to reopen, a different secondary school structure emerged. Since objections to this new structure have frequently been described in the literature, some of the basic changes need be mentioned only briefly here.[6] The new system sought to eliminate the inequalities of the old. A major object of the reforms was to eliminate distinctions between schools and between students. Not only was the division between keypoint and ordinary schools abolished but divisions between work-study and full-day schools also disappeared. In fact, almost all academic distinctions that had divided one school from another and one student from another were eliminated. For example, entrance examinations for secondary school and the university were abolished, removing the most important advantage possessed by children from intellectual homes. Moreover, all students were expected to spend at least two years after graduation from secondary school performing manual labor before becoming eligible for the university. With this break between secondary school and the university, the raison d'être of the keypoint system evaporated. To insure equality between students and between schools in the urban areas, virtually all junior high schools and technical, vocational, and work-study schools were transformed into ordinary middle schools with junior and senior high sections. Enrollment in secondary schools went from about 14.4 million in 1965 to almost 69 million by early 1978. The length of secondary schooling was reduced from the original twelve years to nine or ten. Within the schools, teaching materials were revised to stress practical above theoretical learning. No students were to be held back or allowed to skip grades, nor was there to be division by ability (streaming) within each grade. Some teachers were transferred from the former keypoint schools to the newly established schools. The entire precultural revolutionary educational system and the "bourgeois academic authorities" who were alleged to have been in control of that system were incessantly vilified during this period.

The effects of these structural changes on university-secondary school relations were monumental. Prior to the Cultural Revolution, regular secondary schools competed with one another to send their graduates on to the university; a school's ranking depended on this competition, although an open ranking system was officially discouraged. The schools that had become keypoints were essentially those with the highest university promotion rates. Elimination of the entrance examinations for university and secondary school admission, and enactment of the minimum two-year work requirement, deprived middle school administrators of their basis for ranking. With students attending school in their neighborhoods and then going off to the countryside or to a factory job on graduation, there was no clear differentiation between the schools. Thus, the competition between the schools to recruit and train outstanding students disappeared. Cultural Revolution recruitment to the university was based more on recommendation from one's workmates and approval by political authorities than on examination results.[7]

Post-Mao China: A Slow Return to the 1960s

With the death of Mao Zedong and the political demise of the radicals (September–October 1976), China's leaders were given a relatively unencumbered opportunity to institute changes in a wide variety of policy fields. Perhaps their top priority was education, where radical control had been particularly pronounced. Most urgent was the restoration of educational quality, which they claimed the radicals had subordinated in an effort to expand educational benefits throughout the country. Various problems required solutions concurrently. Students, teachers, and administrators who saw little incentive in expending their efforts in cultural revolutionary schools had to be remotivated. Intellectuals, the stratum most disadvantaged by the radical reforms and most crucial to the realization of the new policies, had to be convinced that the "illegitimate" educational and social alterations of the previous ten years would be replaced by a rational program.

The first step was a dismantling of the cultural revolutionary structure and its replacement by an educational system roughly similar to the 1960s model. The current educational ladder, particularly in its reemphasis on academic and vocational tracking and the direct link between senior high schools and the university, is a close approximation of its precultural revolutionary counterpart. But this surface similarity masks a host of differences between the two models. Moreover, it does not accurately reflect the evolution of educational policy between 1977 and 1983. This period, still continuing, has been a transitional one, marked by a gradual strengthening of academic standards as part of a general commitment to educational quality.

The revival of the old ladder has meant the reappearance of old desires. Thus, the pursuit of university entrance has again become a legitimate aspiration. Indeed, under post-Mao conditions, the rewards of university entrance, and the punishments for failure, have become the strongest motivating factors for a variety of interested parties, including students and school administrators. Because of its importance in Chinese society, let us consider the beneficiaries, the victims, and the evolution of the entrance examination process from 1977 to 1983.

To understand the importance of the university entrance examination in Chinese society, and particularly its importance in post-Mao China, one must start with the structure of opportunity at the secondary level. Table 6.1 shows important differences between the 1960s and the 1980s. The great expansion in senior high schooling, which reached its peak in 1977, has been reversed. Since 1977 many of those schools have either been shut down, transformed into junior highs, or have had individual classrooms converted to accommodate vocational schooling. While school closures have been common, vocational expansion has been limited.

Earlier, in 1964 and 1965, the rapid expansion in vocational schooling was coupled with the first big push to send urban students to the countryside. In those days, vocational education, though less desirable than a regular senior high education that could lead to university entrance, brought with it a guarantee of urban employment. Least agreeable to most students was the likelihood of rustication that awaited many urban junior high graduates.[8] Today no youths are compelled to leave the cities, making the haven of vocational schooling less attractive. Moreover, unlike university or secondary specialist school graduates, vocational school graduates are not guaranteed jobs by the state, leaving most to fend for themselves upon graduation.

If students (and their parents) are less than enthusiastic about vocational schooling, educational administrators often view vocational school growth as a threat. For example, although virtually the only expansion presently scheduled at the secondary level is in vocational and agricultural middle school education, many provinces have explicitly forbidden new vocational school construction. New vocational classrooms are to be carved out of existing regular secondary schools. For an administrator, the gradual transformation of his school from regular to vocational is an indicator of failure. Those schools slated for such transformation have often been the least successful in producing students for the university. Calls for increased vocational education therefore are likely to cause administrators at regular schools to step up their competitive efforts to raise their school's promotion rate and thus avoid transformation. Nor is this problem likely to be solved quickly. The return to the 1960s is a long way from realization. In 1965, for example, of the 80,993 secondary schools, only 18,102 were regular schools. By

TABLE 6.1

STUDENTS IN VARIOUS FORMS OF SECONDARY SCHOOLING*

(EACH UNIT REPRESENTS 10,000 STUDENTS)

Year	Junior high students	Percent	Senior high students	Percent	Secondary specialist students	Percent	Agricultural, middle & vocational school students	Percent
1949	83.2	65.6	20.7	16.3	22.9	18.1		
1957	537.7	76.0	90.4	12.7	77.8	11.0	2.2	0.3
1960	858.46	58.0	167.49	11.3	221.59	15.0	230.2	15.6
1961	698.4	67.4	153.3	14.8	120.3	11.6	61.77	5.9
1962	618.83	74.3	133.9	16.1	53.49	6.4	26.66	3.2
1963	638.03	76.2	123.52	14.7	45.14	5.4	30.78	3.7
1964	729.28	71.5	124.67	12.2	53.16	5.2	112.34	11.0
1965	802.89	56.1	130.8	9.1	54.73	3.8	443.34	31.0
1976	4,352.9	73.7	1,483.6	25.1	69.0	1.1		
1977	4,979.9	72.7	1,800.0	26.3	68.9	1.0		
1979	4,613.0	76.3	1,292.0	21.3	119.9	1.9	23.5	0.39
1980	4,538.29	79.9	969.79	17.1	124.34	2.2	45.36	0.8
1981	4,144.58	82.6	714.98	14.2	106.9	2.1	48.09	0.99
1982	3,887.97	82.7	640.52	13.6	103.94	2.2	70.36	1.5
1983	3,768.75	81.1	628.98	13.5	114.78	2.5	122.01	2.6

SOURCES: For 1960–1965 see Gu Mingyuan, "Lun zhongdeng jiaoyu di renwu he jiegou," *Beijing shifan daxue xuebao*, No. 5, August 25, 1982, p. 7. For 1949, 1957, 1976, and 1979 see *Zhongguo baike nianjian 1980*, pp. 536, 544. For 1977 see *Zhongguo qingnian bao*, June 24, 1982, p. 1 and *Statistical Yearbook of China 1981* (English Edition), p. 451. For 1980 see *Zhongguo baike nianjian 1981*, p. 471. For 1981 see *Zhongguo jingji nianjian 1982*, p. V-389. For 1982 see *Zhongguo baike nianjian 1983*, p. 595. For 1983 see *Zhongguo jiaoyu bao*, May 15, 1984, p. 4.
*For a more complete picture of enrollment in secondary specialist and regular high schools from 1949–1982 which, however, does not break down the figures by junior and senior high levels, see *Statistical Yearbook of China 1982* (Chinese Edition), p. 511.

1976 fully 192,152 of the schools were regular schools. As late as 1983, of the 105,071 secondary schools, 96,500 were regular schools.[9]

The combination of demographic changes and the commitment to quality over the expansion of educational opportunity have jointly constricted educational opportunities beyond the junior high. There are proportionately fewer secondary school students at the senior high level than at any time since 1949. By 1981 over 82 percent of all secondary school students were in junior high school, the highest percentage since the founding of the People's Republic (table 6.1). The compression at the senior high level has raised the stakes both for junior high students and for administrators of senior high schools.

The emphasis on quality has also led to the resurrection of the keypoint school system of the 1960s. In 1977, when this decision was made, there was a bureaucratic consensus within the post-Mao leadership, shared by influential sectors of the populace, that a crisis in education existed. The closure of the universities from 1966 to 1970 deprived the country of valuable manpower, and the graduates of the reopened universities were of questionable quality. It was persuasively argued that extreme measures were required to guarantee the steady production of high-level and specialized technical personnel to compensate for losses due to previous policies as well as to meet the goals of the new and ambitious "Four Modernizations" program (modernization of industry, agriculture, science and technology, and national defense). By 1980–1981, however, the revived keypoint school system had become more hierarchical than its precultural revolutionary predecessor and had led to a new set of problems.

Whereas early opponents of the keypoint schools seem to have been concentrated among those who still felt that the cultural revolutionary model had something to offer, by 1983 widespread opposition had developed throughout Chinese society. Some of the nation's most prominent intellectuals were calling for the abolition of such schools at primary and secondary levels.[10] The dissatisfaction stems from the side effects associated with the keypoint school system. Keypoint secondary, and to a lesser extent, keypoint primary schools have become the main conduits to higher levels of schooling. Attendance at a keypoint senior high greatly enhances one's prospects for university enrollment. Students and their parents view entrance to a keypoint as essential for upward educational mobility.

Opposition to these elite institutions exists at each educational level, but the controversy is particularly acute at the secondary level. Most educators feel that the allocation of more money, better equipment, a stronger faculty, and the most outstanding students to the best universities is reasonable. The concentration of these scarce resources in the nation's 94 keypoint universities (out of 805 full-day colleges and universities) appears to many to be a good investment. The negative social consequences of the keypoint system at the secondary level, however, are much greater and highly visible.

Of the 112,000 regular high schools in 1980, 5,200 were designated keypoints. But this is misleading. These keypoints are further subdivided and ranked, placing the best schools under provincial administration, the next best under municipal administration, followed by those under district or county administration. Higher ranking leads to greater concentration of resources. A further move toward hierarchy came in the autumn of 1980 as the less efficient keypoints began to be weeded out, with priority investment given to 700 schools throughout the nation. Many of China's more than 2,000 counties have one keypoint school, which although accorded special attention by local authorities, is often of rather poor quality. The gap is large between the best urban keypoints in Beijing or Shanghai, which can get more than 90 percent of their graduates into college, and the keypoints of county towns, where the promotion rate may be well below 10 percent.

To compensate for their disadvantages, less well-endowed areas will often take extreme measures to prepare promising students for the university entrance exams. County authorities frequently interrupt schooling well before the term's end to bring together for extensive review sessions those with the greatest potential to succeed in the entrance exams. Participants include current-year as well as previous-year graduates. Published figures from some districts show these review classes to be almost double the normal class size (seventy students instead of forty).[11] Although provincial education bureaus have taken strong measures to stop this practice, the results have yet to be effective. Nor is this practice limited to suburban and rural counties. Individual schools in urban areas run their own tutorial classes to prepare prior graduates for the examinations. Under these conditions it is impossible for schools to adhere to the annual study outline. In particular, courses not tested on the exams are ignored.

In spite of the official criticism of the overemphasis on university preparation, China's leadership recognizes the need for more university graduates in the rural areas. Thus, *China Youth Daily* recently gave front-page coverage to a production brigade in Zhejiang province that offered a scholarship of 1,000 yuan ($555) to any child of a brigade member who was accepted by a college, 50 yuan a year for anybody who made it to senior high, and 20 yuan a year for those who went to junior high.[12]

If the gap between the schools within the keypoint system is wide, the chasm is unbridgeable between the large majority of ordinary high schools and the keypoints. Ordinary schools have tried to duplicate the conditions of keypoint schools by concentrating their best students in keypoint classrooms, with middling- and poor-quality students also streamed by ability. Although such streaming was considered absolutely necessary in the late 1970s, it has recently become much more controversial, with several provinces publicly announcing its elimination. The criticism of streaming, and of keypoint schools as well, reached a high tide in the autumn of 1981 after a series of investigations revealed that, although a small percentage of students were performing very well on the university entrance exams, the large majority, particularly those outside of keypoint schools or keypoint classrooms, had difficulty passing the graduation examination. Schools were devoting all their energies to those students more likely to advance through the educational ladder, while ignoring average and marginal ones.

Schools were judged primarily by their promotion rates. Students unable to test into keypoint schools or keypoint classrooms of ordinary schools quickly became demoralized through lack of attention. For schools concerned with maintaining a decent promotion rate, it was often necessary to persuade eager but mediocre students not to sit for the entrance examination for higher levels. A recent study in some districts in Beijing revealed that 52 percent of senior high students had already given up hope of entering a university.[13] The decline in opportunities at the senior high level had begun to push the overall promotion rate slowly back toward precultural revolutionary numbers. The "cooling out" mechanism has also been effective. Thus, from a promotion rate low of 4.03 percent in 1979 (275,000 university enrollees out of 6,827,000 senior high graduates), by 1983 the rate had reached 13.3 percent (360,000 enrollees and 2,700,000 graduates). This is still far from the 1965 promotion rate of 45.56 percent (164,000 enrollees and 360,000 graduates).[14] If only those students who actually sat for the exams were considered, the promotion rates would have been even higher (see table 6.2).

Critics have complained that the Chinese educational system is fostering a small elite, largely centered in urban areas and from families of intellectuals and party and state officials, who are best placed to ride the keypoint track from primary school to university. Further, they argue that no matter which individuals benefit from the keypoint system, the number of educated graduates produced will fall far short of manpower needs. For example, only 24 of the more than 1,000 middle schools in Beijing are key schools. Of the 211,000 middle school students recruited in the city in 1981, only 8,000 (3.8 percent) attended key schools. In addition, less than 30 percent of the 139,000 junior high graduates in the city reached the graduation standard. Among the 54,000 (38.7 percent) moving on to senior high, only 35.7 percent had a minimum passing score on the entrance exam.[15] The repudiation of cultural revolutionary quantity and its replacement by keypoint quality may be reassessed and adjusted.

In spite of the vocal opposition, equally strong voices and trends push toward further hierarchy. Senior high schooling, for example, which was reduced to two years during the Cultural Revolution, has reverted to a three-year system. Begun in 1980, this process should be completed by 1985. The extra year will be added to schools that have been chosen in sequence, beginning with the best keypoints in 1980 and finishing with the poorest of the ordinary schools in 1985. The large number of students who graduated from high school the previous year, and who registered for the university-exam review classes, consists partly of those still in two-year programs seeking to duplicate the conditions of the keypoint schools.

A more lasting contribution to hierarchy and elitism may result from the increasing autonomy universities, particularly the key universities, have been able to carve out for themselves. Although university reputations depend in no small part on the high-minimum passing scores on the national entrance exam, the universities have sought and received more flexibility and direct influence in recruiting students.

One method universities have used is the establishment of linkage (*guagou*) relationships with the best keypoint schools. In Shanghai, for example, virtually all the municipal keypoints and even some of the district keypoints have linkage relationships with a keypoint university. Jiaotong University by May 1980 had set up linkages with sixteen of the best keypoints in Shanghai. Fudan University, East China Normal University, and Shanghai Normal Institute had special ties to their own attached schools (*fuzhong*), all of which were municipal keypoints, in addition to linkages to other schools in the city. The best universities, such as Fudan and East China Normal, also ran primary schools on campus.

Under these linkage arrangements the university might, for example, invite teachers of the middle school to discuss and exchange experiences about their teaching outlines, might offer refresher courses for the teachers, or might provide library, laboratory, audio-visual, and other materials. Students from the middle school could visit the university to witness laboratory experiments and engage in scientific and technical activities of their own.[16] Somewhat less openly, the university encouraged the best students at the linked schools to list that particular university as a first preference on the university entrance application, with the understanding that such students would be given priority over those from less favored schools with roughly similar qualifications.

These linkages are advantageous for all participants. While enhancing the individual student's opportunity to attend the university and increasing the promotion rates of the linked high schools, this method offers the university a competitive advantage over nonlinked local schools and, equally important, over superior universities outside the locality. The nature of the university application process makes a student's first preference particularly important. To guarantee entrance to a good university, outstanding students who would normally apply to Beijing University or Qinghua University, the nation's best schools, might well opt for Fudan University, an excellent institution just a rung below the very top, because of the linkage relationship. Because the best secondary schools have links to more than one university, there is keen competition among universities to recruit outstanding high school seniors.

For the attached schools, the relationship was even closer, with the middle school's general party branch (*dangzongzhi*) under the supervision of the university's party committee (*dangwei*). Though vacations, term schedules, teaching materials, and teacher salaries came from the district education bureau, under the dual leadership principle, the university was in charge of personnel and external affairs of the middle school, including teacher allocation. The holding of concurrent positions was also important to the relationship. For example, the principal of Fudan Attached Middle School was also the deputy head of the Fudan University Education Office. The secretary of the attached school's general party branch was concurrently a member of the university's party committee. According to informants, this close relationship provides several advantages. The middle school is privy to developments in the university and, if changes are in the offing, can adjust quickly. The university can point out weaknesses in the middle school's educational program and may send teachers, on a temporary basis, to shore up weak areas. When administrators from an attached school go to district or municipal education bureau meetings, they have more clout because they also hold responsible positions at the university.

How much, then, are university entrance prospects enhanced by attendance at a keypoint senior high? On this sensitive issue national statistics are unavailable. Moreover, available aggregate statistics tend to obscure the great variance between the best provincial and municipal keypoints (over 90 percent promotion rate) and the poorest county-run keypoints. Further, just as keypoints are clearly distinguishable from each other, so are universities. Many of China's 805 universities are two- and three-year colleges of questionable quality. Ideally, one would like to obtain data that disaggregates the key universities from lesser institutions and differentiates keypoint secondary schools by level of administration. With these caveats in mind, some limited data can be examined. In Sichuan province in 1981 only 22 percent of the senior high graduates were in keypoint schools, but they formed 70 percent of the province's university recruits.[17] In Guangdong province in 1980, 50.89 percent of the students in the sixteen provincially run keypoints who took the university entrance exams passed (not everyone who passes makes it to the university, however).[18] In Liaoning province, the key-point promotion rate between 1979 and 1981 was about 33.3 percent; the rate for all senior highs in the province was 1.22 percent.[19] In Inner Mongolia the best keypoints had a promotion rate of 60–70 percent.[20] A visiting scholar was told by two key universities in 1980 that 60–70 percent of their freshman classes came from key schools.[21]

The Schools Serve the Universities: Candidates, Examinations, and Victors

When the Chinese decided to restore the university entrance examinations in 1977, they faced a basic question. Who should be permitted to sit for the exams?[22] In the 1960s the large majority of university candidates and entrants each year had been that year's senior high school graduates below the age of twenty. In the years immediately following the Cultural Revolution, educators felt that such restrictions were unwise. First, it was widely accepted that cultural revolutionary schools were weak academically, with current graduates demonstrably inferior to their counterparts during the 1960s. Second, many previous senior high graduates as far back as 1966 had used the intervening ten years to engage in self-study; academically, there was thus a wide range of untapped talent among them. Third, there were still some powerful leaders reluctant to depart from the two-year work requirement as a precondition for university entrance. The decision was thus made to cast the net as widely as possible. Although the age limit was set at twenty-five, a number of exceptions pushed the effective limit up to thirty. This opened the examinations to current-year graduates as well as to previous graduates as far back as 1966 and 1967. Although only 20–30 percent of university enrollees were expected to come from current-year graduates, it was implied that, in the future most university students would be thus chosen. In effect, the young victims of the Cultural Revolution, sometimes called the lost generation, were being offered, for a limited time, an opportunity to prove their worth. As table 6.2 shows, this open competition by examination has indeed receded, with each year's enrollment regulations introducing measures that further restrict the number of candidates.

By 1978 students already attending various types of technical schools were barred from the examinations, and half the candidates came directly from middle schools. Candidates under the age of twenty-five

TABLE 6.2

NATIONAL COLLEGE ENTRANCE EXAMINATION: CANDIDATES AND SUCCESSFUL ENTRANTS

Year	Candidates	Successful entrants	Percent Enrollment rate
1977	5,700,000[a]	278,000[a]	4.87
1978	6,000,000[b]	402,000[c]	6.70
1979	4,684,000[d]	275,000[d]	5.87
1980	3,600,000[e]	281,200[f]	7.81
1981	2,589,000[g]	278,777[h]	10.76
1982	1,860,000[i]	315,000[j]	16.93
1983	1,670,000[k]	360,000[k]	21.56
1984	1,643,000[l]	430,000[l]	26.17

SOURCE: (a) Peking Review No. 31, August 4, 1978, p. 5; (b) Ibid., p. 4; (c) Zhongguo baike nianjian 1981, p. 474; (d) Zhongguo baike nianjian 1980, p. 538; (e) Renmin jiaoyu No. 4, April 1981, p. 28; (f) Zhongguo baike nianjian 1981, p. 470; (g) Guangming ribao, August 4, 1981, p. 1; (h) Statistical Yearbook of China 1981, p. 455; (i) Guangming ribao, July 11, 1982, p. 1; (j) Beijing Review No. 19, May 9, 1983, p. X (Document Section); (k) Renmin ribao, July 7, 1983, p. 3; Renmin ribao, July 10, 1984, p. 1.

were preferred. By 1979, 60–70 percent of the candidates were current-year senior high graduates, with fewer exceptions made for candidates over the age of twenty-five. This trend continued in 1980; by that year only 1 percent of China's new university students were over the age of twenty-five.[23] In 1983 the age limit became fixed at twenty-five with no exceptions allowed.[24]

A more controversial restriction was introduced in 1980. Provinces with a large number of candidates began to require a preliminary examination to determine which students were permitted to sit for the actual entrance examination. By 1981 most provinces had adopted a preliminary examination, although the graduation examination from senior high often substituted for this. Before these screening exams were instituted, secondary school teachers and administrators had frequently sought—often unsuccessfully—to persuade those less academically qualified not to sit for the university exams. A school's reputation, after all, depended on its promotion rate. Children from worker and peasant families seem to have been the most upset at this additional hurdle because it came at the same time that examination levels were being raised and admission standards tightened.[25]

The post-Mao evolution of the examination requirements reflects a gradual return to greater selectivity and higher academic standards. Examination candidates in China are divided into two major groups: liberal arts, and science and engineering (including agriculture and medicine). For the first entrance examinations in 1977, each candidate took five equally weighted examinations in politics, Chinese language, and mathematics. Liberal arts candidates added history and geography to the list; science and engineering candidates added physics and chemistry. For those studying foreign languages, a language exam substituted for mathematics. As early as 1978 standards began to tighten. Unlike the 1977 exams, which had been written in the provinces and municipalities, beginning in 1978 the entire process was to be centralized, with unified exams written in Beijing and distributed nationally. A foreign language exam was added for liberal arts and science and engineering candidates, and a mathematics exam was included for foreign language students, although these scores were not to be used in the selection process. In 1979 the foreign language exam for liberal arts and science candidates was weighted at 10 percent of each of the other exams; since each exam was worth 100 points, the foreign language exam counted for 10 points out of a total 510. In 1980 the foreign language exam was worth 30 points, and for the first time the mathematics exam counted 10 points for foreign language candidates.

There were additional changes in 1981. A new examination in biology, worth 30 points, was added for students in science fields, bringing their examination total to 7. The weight of the foreign language examination was increased from a maximum of 30 to 50 points. The Ministry of Education further announced that all applicants, regardless of their overall scores, would need passing grades on the Chinese language examination, and that science and liberal arts candidates would need passing grades on the mathematics exam, or their chances would be greatly reduced. The trend continued in 1982, with biology now worth 50 and foreign language 70 points.[26] For 1983 the weights were as follows: Chinese language and mathematics, 120 points each; biology, 50 points; all the rest, 100 points. Foreign language students now have the same mathematics requirements as everyone else.[27] Table 6.3 provides information on the types of colleges and universities in China, together with recent enrollment and graduation figures. In recent years around 70 percent of college candidates have been in the sciences, with the remaining 30 percent in the liberal arts.

Given the importance of gaining university entrance, the small percentage of successful applicants, and the diverse and shifting criteria for choosing such students over the past twenty years, it is not surprising that the post-Mao standards have been heavily criticized. Perhaps the most persistent criticism has questioned the wisdom of basing an individual's entire future on performance on one set of examinations alone. Before the Cultural Revolution, academic achievement, based in large part on the entrance exam, was one of three explicit criteria for university

TABLE 6.3
INSTITUTIONS OF HIGHER LEARNING, 1981

	Number of institutions	Newly enrolled students	Enrolled students	Graduates	Full-time teachers	Total teachers
National total	704	278,777	1,279,472	139,640	249,876	666,339
Comprehensive universities	32	28,714	138,500	3,895	26,998	69,910
Colleges of sciences and engineering	207	95,194	484,658	11,498	101,776	286,063
Agricultural, forestry, and medical colleges	177	48,062	254,843	18,084	51,179	145,349
Teachers' colleges	186	87,222	316,785	103,121	49,317	113,519
Linguistic, literary, and arts colleges	37	3,787	19,234	1,028	7,641	18,519
Colleges of finance, economics, politics, and law	43	11,669	43,368	1,888	8,010	20,434
Physical culture and minority nationality institutes	22	4,129	22,084	126	4,955	12,545

SOURCE: *Statistical Yearbook of China 1981* (English Edition), p. 455.

entrance. The other two, class origin and political manifestation, were dismissed as part of the strong reaction against the superheated political atmosphere of the Cultural Revolution, and also to regain the support of the intellectuals. Although few were openly calling for a return to class origin as a factor, certainly by 1980 there was a stronger demand for more flexibility in the enrollment process; outstanding achievements—beyond exam scores—and model behavior could then be properly rewarded. The universities wanted greater independence in selecting their freshman classes as well. In 1981 such demands were beginning to be heeded and were reflected in the ensuing enrollment regulations, which stipulated that performance in middle school, including conduct, athletic ability, grades, and extracurricular activities, would be taken into consideration. There is strong evidence, however, that factors other than entrance examination scores were rarely used, and then only in borderline cases.[28]

By 1982 the enrollment regulations had become more specific, allowing outstanding student officers, "three-good students"—good academically, morally, and physically—who had been commended at the district level or above and athletes who had performed well in individual competition (top five places in district-level competition or above) or team competition (top three places) to be awarded extra points toward their total entrance examination score. To encourage students to become class officers—positions many had disdained because it detracted from study time—provincial and municipal enrollment committees were permitted to select such officers if they were within five points of the provincial minimum passing score on the entrance examinations.[29]

The enrollment process became even more flexible in 1983. First, colleges of agriculture, forestry, medicine, and teaching, which traditionally have difficulty recruiting students, lowered the standard admission examination grades for applicants in rural areas who agree to return upon graduation. Second, colleges were encouraged to sign personnel training contracts with employer units to provide more educated staff for small and collectively owned enterprises. Third, universities were given more autonomy in choosing enrollees. The published regulations are very cryptic on this point, referring to the need for universities to evaluate a candidate's character, political attitudes, health, and grades in middle school, in addition to the entrance exam score. The likely effect will be a strengthening of the bonds between the best universities and the foremost keypoint middle schools. Indeed, the vice-minister of education may have indicated this when he recently announced that students in middle schools with better conditions may be recruited by means of a formula giving weight to recommendations, as well as by exam results.[30]

With the increasing candor of the Chinese press and with information more readily provided to visiting scholars, we have more data than ever before on Chinese universities and university students. The data must be analyzed with some care, however. For example, selected information has recently been published on new university enrollees from 1979 to 1981. The data show that the percentage of female recruits to the university rose from 22.51 percent of all new students in 1979 to 25.12 percent in 1981. Over the same period, among new students, children of workers and of poor and lower-middle-class peasants climbed from 54.31 percent to 56.90 percent. Members of the Communist Youth League increased from 79.23 percent to 86.39 percent. Finally, recruitment of national minority students crept forward from 3.63 percent to 4.77 percent.[31] These figures require explanation.

China lags behind most socialist countries in the proportion of female university students. One reason for this is an attitude prevalent in China that girls develop more quickly than boys but begin to decline in ability by the last years of junior high school. One explanation given by Chinese educators to a visiting scholar attributed the decline to the smaller brain size of women. Partly as a result of this apparently widespread belief, women often have to score higher than men to gain entrance to the best senior high keypoints and universities. Although such discrimination has at times been criticized in the press, the practice has continued.[32] It should also be noted that the moderate increase in female enrollment from 1979 to 1981 may not have made up for a drop in their enrollment over the period from 1976 to 1979.[33]

The above figures on the children of workers and poor and lower middle-class peasants are a welcome improvement over recent statistics that claimed, for example, that 97.4 percent of the 1977 freshman class was from the families of workers, peasants, army men, cadres, and intellectuals and that over 99 percent of freshmen recruited in 1979 were from families of workers, peasants, and other laboring people.[34] One would still like to know how many children of peasants are able to enter the best urban universities, what percentage of successful peasant children are actually from well-off suburban areas or keypoint schools in county towns, and how many of those designated "peasant" are actually urban rusticated youths.[35]

The high percentage of Communist Youth League (CYL) members who gain entrance to the university is not surprising, nor should it be interpreted to mean that ideopolitical criteria for university entrance have once again become important. In fact, as I have argued elsewhere, it may be an indication of the reduced importance of such criteria in admissions decisions.[36] It apparently has become common for senior high schools to recruit virtually all students with the potential to pass the university entrance exams into the CYL. Entire classrooms of students in some keypoint schools have become league members.

Six percent of China's population consists of national minorities. There are ten institutes of higher learning considered *nationalities institutes*, at which minority cadres are trained. In 1981 these institutes enrolled 2,345 students, most of whom may very well be national minorities. Thus, perhaps 15 percent of China's national minority enrollees are likely to be at these nationalities institutes.

Using statistics provided by individual Chinese educational institutions, some scholars have argued that students from families of intellectuals and officials now predominate in many of the best tertiary institutions. For example, at Zhejiang University, a national keypoint, 25 percent of the students were reported to be from a peasant background, 15 percent from workers' families, 23 percent from the families of officials and other administrative employees, and 28 percent from intellectuals' families.[37]

The Universities Serve the Schools: Curriculum and Teacher Training

Given the importance middle school administrators, teachers, and students attach to university entrance, it is not surprising to find that the middle school curriculum has been arranged to coordinate with the requirements of the university entrance examination. Frequent injunctions in the educational press urge that the entrance examination questions not go beyond the middle school teaching plan. Although the teaching plan is unified nationally by the Ministry of Education, options are often provided for students in the second and third years of keypoint senior highs, separating those who plan to sit for the university exams in liberal arts from those who sit for science exams. (Students in keypoint or ordinary schools, and even in vocational programs, are all eligible to take the university entrance exams.) To provide some idea of variations among teaching plans table 6.4 compares proposed teaching plans for various types of senior high schools.

China, for a long period of time, has been emphasizing the training of scientists and engineers but has been neglecting liberal arts (including social sciences) training. With the majority of university places allocated to science students, middle schools have accordingly treated subjects in science as more crucial to the curriculum. For example, at the attached middle school of South China Normal Institute, long considered Guangzhou's best secondary school, students who fail in math, chemistry, physics, or Chinese language must repeat the class. Failure in other courses does not require a repeat.[38] As professors in the most prestigious science and engineering colleges have begun to discover, and complain, that some of their students have neither knowledge nor interest in such subjects as literature and history, and that they are unable to write logical and coherent graduation theses, some preliminary steps are being taken to introduce optional liberal arts courses into the university curriculum.[39]

This is part of a larger problem and reflects an improper fit between middle school training and the university curriculum. Still under the influence of the Soviet model imported during the 1950s, the university curriculum remains highly specialized. Before 1980 candidates for the university customarily listed their preferred field of study or specialty on the application form. Middle school graduates, upon the onset of their college careers, were often locking themselves into a rigid specialization about which they were largely uninformed. Owing perhaps to foreign criticism, more flexibility is now being built into China's higher education curriculum. In the last few years, for example, candidates for the universities have been encouraged to list only a preferred department on their application forms, with the selection of a specialty postponed until they have completed certain basic courses during their freshman year. As another recent innovation, authorities have been experimenting with a credit system similar to that of many Western countries. This should allow brighter students to graduate in less than four years, whereas weaker students may require five years to complete the coursework.[40] There is likely to be much experimentation and variety over the next few years as China pursues its policy of diversification in higher education. One Chinese observer has claimed that it would be wrong for China to move from the narrow Soviet model to the broad American model, suggesting that the Japanese model would be just right.[41]

Another important way the universities serve the schools is in the training of appropriate and qualified teaching personnel. Between 1949 and 1966 institutions of higher normal education trained and turned over to the state 414,000 qualified secondary school teachers.[42] As in other areas, however, the contradiction between mass education and specialized training, which came to a head in the Cultural Revolution, greatly influenced teacher training. Because of the rapid expansion of secondary schooling in the 1970s, it was no longer possible to employ certified normal school graduates in a majority of the schools. Quite often, primary school teachers were mobilized to teach in the junior high schools, while junior high teachers were moved to the senior high level. As replacements it was sometimes necessary to rely on junior high grad-

TABLE 6.4

TEACHING PLANS FOR VARIOUS KINDS OF SENIOR HIGH SCHOOLS*

(HOURS PER WEEK IN CLASS)

	Keypoint Schools								Ordinary Schools (Years)		Vocational and Agricultural High Schools (Years)		
	Classrooms not divided by coursework (Years)			Classrooms divided into Arts (A) and Science (B) students (Years)									
				1	2		3						
Course	1	2	3		A	B	A	B	1	2	1	2	3
Politics	2	2	2	2	2	2	2	2	2	2	2	2	2
Chinese language	5	4	4	5	7	4	8	4	4	4	5	4	4
Mathematics	5	5	5	5	3	6	3	6	6	6	5	5	5
Foreign language	5	5	4	5	5	5	5	4	3	3	2	2	2
Physics	4	3	4	4		4		5	4	4	4	4	
Chemistry	3	3	3	3	3	4		4	3	3	3	3	
History	3			3			3		2				
Geography		2			2		3			2			
Physical education	2	2	2	2	2	2	2	2	2	2	2	2	2
Biology			2		2	2		2					2

182

TABLE 6.4 (continued)

Course	Keypoint Schools								Ordinary Schools (Years)		Vocational and Agricultural High Schools (Years)		
	Classrooms not divided by coursework (Years)			Classrooms divided into Arts (A) and Science (B) students (Years)									
	1	2	3	1	2 A	2 B	3 A	3 B	1	2	1	2	3
Elective courses		4	4										
Vocational Classes									6	6			
Specialized technical courses											8	8	16
Labor training	4 weeks			4 weeks					2	2	2	2	2
Hours per week in class	29	30	30	29	26	29	26	29	34	34	33	32	33

NOTES: (a) Program A in Senior High 2 and 3 is for those who select a liberal arts specialty. (b) During the labor training period, there are 6 classes per day in Keypoint Schools; Ordinary and Vocational Schools can arrange labor training in accordance with their regular vocational or specialized courses. (c) The physics and chemistry textbooks for vocational schools are geared to a 2-year program, and are the less rigorous of the two levels of textbook available.

* Working Draft, January 1982-Guanzhou

I am grateful to Lau Wing Fong of the School of Education of the Chinese University of Hong Kong for providing me with various teaching plans.

183

TABLE 6.5

EDUCATIONAL LEVEL OF PRIMARY AND SECONDARY SCHOOL TEACHERS
(IN PERCENT)

Year	Primary school teachers with training at secondary-level normal schools or above	Junior high teachers with training in specialized courses at higher-level normal schools	Senior high teachers with training in their specialties at higher-level normal schools
1965	47.4	71.9	70.3
1973	28		
1977		14.3	33.2
1978		9.8	45.9
1979	47	10.6	50.8
1981*	51.8	17.6	36.0

SOURCE: For 1965, 1973, and 1977, see *Banhao Shifan jiaoyu, fazhan jiaoyu kexue [Conduct Teacher Training Well, Develop Educational Science]* (Beijing: People's Education Publishers, 1979), p. 32. For 1978, see *Zhengming* [China], no. 2, 1981, p. 19. For 1979, see *Jiaoyu yanjiu*, no. 4, 1980, p. 8. For 1981 see *Zhongguo jiaoyu nianjian 1949–1981* (Beijing: China Encyclopedia Publishers, 1984), p. 198.
*The 1981 (yearbook) figures are most accurate; earlier ones are based on estimates.

uates to teach in the junior high schools, and senior high graduates to teach in the senior high schools. In fact, in the general reduction of universities in that period, the number of higher normal schools dropped from sixty-one to forty-four.

With the new emphasis on quality and specialized training, there have been frequent articles in publications directed toward those engaged in education which lament the results of cultural revolutionary policies and call for a vast expansion in formal teacher training. As table 6.5 shows, China has begun to recover from the decline in the number of primary and high school teachers during the Cultural Revolution. However, as educators complain, teacher training in China continues to lag behind other countries. Although teacher training institutes in China and the Soviet Union constitute 23 to 24 percent of all colleges and universities, the Soviet Union, with only about 25 percent of China's population, has more than two and one-half times as many students in such institutes.[43] In recent years the number of students turned out by normal institutes and colleges has begun to increase dramatically. The major impetus came from a January 1979 decision that permitted provincial and municipal authorities to organize 153 new institutes and colleges. Seventy-seven of the new colleges were teachers colleges.[44] Table 6.6 shows the recent growth in higher-level normal colleges.

TABLE 6.6

TEACHER TRAINING FOR SECONDARY SCHOOLS

Year	Number of colleges and universities	Graduating students	Students in school
1949	12	1,890	12,039
1957	58	15,948	114,795
1965	59	28,966	94,268
1976	58	32,153	109,731
1978	157	35,430	249,940
1979	161	24,331	311,168
1980	172	61,942	338,197
1981	186	103,422	321,944
1982 (May)	194*	129,463	289,448

SOURCES: For 1949–1981 see *Zhongguo jiaoyu nianjian 1949–1981* (Beijing: China Encyclopedia Publishers, 1984), pp. 965, 966, 971. For 1982 see *Zhongguo tongji nianjian 1983* (Beijing: State Statistical Bureau, 1983).

*This includes sixty-nine regular, four-year institutions and 123 two- and three-year institutions. The four-year schools primarily train senior high teachers, while the two- and three-year schools train junior high teachers. Two institutions are key institutions.

Conclusion

The relationship between higher and secondary education in China has been conditioned most strongly by the university entrance examination. Unlike some other developing countries, China has consistently kept university enrollment low. University graduates have never had a problem finding acceptable employment; on the contrary, university entrance has provided an "iron rice bowl." The unemployed and underemployed were limited to those unable to reach the university. In the years immediately prior to the Cultural Revolution, such unsuccessful students were sent to the countryside, ostensibly to integrate themselves with the peasants. In the post–Cultural Revolution era, China has openly acknowledged the difficulties of finding employment for its high school graduates. With the removal of the ideological trappings of the 1960s and 1970s, under which the rustication of youths was considered glorious, and all work—whether collecting night soil or conducting experiments in theoretical physics—was considered equally important for the revolution, the quest for university entrance has become more "shameless." Secondary schools, like students, are in practice graded on their promotion rate.

The Chinese educational structure is still in transition. Enrollment estimates for the sixth five-year plan (1981–85) and some projections for 1987 and 1990 have been published. From these figures we may see what the current priorities are and attempt to make some predictions about the future secondary-higher education relationship. Generally speaking, the expansion and improvement of higher education is the first priority. The emphasis will be on "walking on two legs," or to use a current expression, "many levels, many standards, many forms." A recent report issued by the Ministry of Education and the State Planning Commission has urged various localities to develop whatever form of higher education is most feasible, given the economic conditions. This effort was already initiated by the late 1970s with the development of branch schools at some Chinese universities and included vocational universities as well. Essentially commuter schools, students are locally recruited, expected to live at home, must pay tuition fees amounting to twenty to twenty-five yuan per semester, and are not assigned jobs by the state following graduation.

The greatest expansion will be in nonformal education, such as in universities that offer coursework by television, correspondence universities, factory-run universities for staff and workers, county-run universities for peasants, and the like. Enrollments in these alternative forms is slated to increase from 290,000 recruited in 1982 to 1,100,000 in 1987; total enrollment will go from 640,000 to 2,370,000.[45] Clearly, the shortage of funds for education has dictated educational planning. Whereas it costs the state 8–10 thousand yuan for each regular resident student from admittance to graduation, the cost for a tuition-paying commuter student is only 400–800 yuan, and that for a correspondence student a mere 150 yuan.[46] The demand for university education has become so great that the government has supported the establishment of private colleges. For example, Yanjing Foreign Languages Institute in Beijing, established in April 1983, is training more than 200 students to be journalists. Unlike the tuition-free, state-run colleges, Yanjing charges a whopping (by Chinese standards) annual tuition of 250 yuan.[47] In the interest of providing some opportunity for everyone, any Chinese citizen regardless of age or education may apply to take a college equivalency examination. Designed to encourage self-study, this is an expansion of a program in effect since 1981 in three major cities and one province. Examinees are given a certificate after passing a test on one subject. Those who earn the required number of certificates are granted a diploma theoretically equivalent to that granted to regular two- or four-year college graduates.[48]

Enrollment in full-day universities is expected to go from the 315,000 recruited in 1982 to 400,000 in 1985, 550,000 in 1987, and 600,000 in 1990.

This would raise the number of full-time undergraduate students to about 2 million. Here the trend is toward shorter programs. Whereas the large majority of students in regular universities are currently in four-year programs, by 1985 two- and three-year students should account for over 30 percent of the annual enrollment figures. Overall, the number of regular college students will increase by 53 percent between 1983 and 1987, while the number of other college students will increase by 270 percent. Increases scheduled for graduate education are also impressive. In 1980, graduate schools enrolled 3,600 new students; in 1981, 11,000; in 1983, 15,000; and by 1985 the projected figure is 20,000.[49]

The rapid expansion and improvement of technical and vocational education is a second priority. Once again the basic inhibiting factor is likely to be cost. China is not prepared to invest the relatively large sums of money necessary to bring its technical/vocational schools up to international standards. Projected figures for secondary education show a steady decline in regular middle schools, particularly at the senior high level. By 1985 it is expected that regular senior high schools will admit 2.8 million students, 1 million less than in 1980. At the same time, 1.4 million students will be engaged in vocational and agricultural middle school programs, 1.16 million more than in 1980. Thus, vocational and agricultural middle school enrollment will have increased 6.5 and 7.1 times, respectively, from 1980 to 1985. Most of the new vocational school students will be enrolled in existing classrooms formerly devoted to regular senior high schooling. Specialized (technical) school enrollment, which students consider far more desirable than vocational education, will expand only modestly over the same period. In 1980 such schools recruited 433,200 students and had a total enrollment of 1,069,000. By 1985 the projected figures call for 500,000 recruits and a total enrollment of 1,250,000. The emphasis will be on training specialists in finance and economics, political science and law, management, light and other textile industries, and construction.[50]

Given these figures, several conclusions may be drawn. First, Chinese students will be compelled to scale down their aspirations. Because of demographic changes, the present and the next generation of youths clearly cannot expect a return to the opportunities of the mid-1950s, when there were more university openings each year than senior high graduates, or even of the mid-1960s, when employment and education opportunities had already started to decline. Educational expansion, particularly at the secondary level, will be in those forms of schooling which have been least popular with students. For example, in Beijing in 1982 the number of students who applied to secondary specialist schools (other than teacher training schools) as their first choice was 29.3 times more than could be recruited; the number who applied for vocational education as their first choice was only twice the number that could be recruited.[51] The expansion in university enrollment coupled with the decline in regular senior high enrollment will continue to raise the overall promotion rate. By 1985 this rate might reach 30–35 percent.

Second, the increasing diversity in higher education will open up many more places in universities, but the range in the quality of education, from the best of the keypoints down to the county-run schools, not to mention for those engaged in self-study, is enormous. Even among the key universities the quality gap is likely to expand. The World Bank has invested $300 million to assist the Chinese government in improving both undergraduate and graduate education in science and engineering in twenty-six key universities. Moreover, some of China's most prominent educators have urged the accelerated investment of resources in several dozen of the nation's best universities. Proposing that China emulate the "famous institutions of higher learning in the world," almost all of which are multisubject universities, they wholeheartedly support the trend toward comprehensive universities. If their plan is adopted, they estimate that, prior to 1990, these select universities "will be able to train, in all fields, several hundred thousand high-quality undergraduates, tens of thousands of Masters' candidates and several thousand Ph.D. candidates." In addition to providing personnel for the country's economic reconstruction, these elite universities would train the leading teachers for other higher institutions of learning.[52]

Third, public acceptance of the "many levels, many standards, many forms" philosophy in education will depend in part on the expansion of the job market. In particular, following the argument made almost twenty years ago by Philip Foster, clear links between vocational education and assured employment must be developed.[53] If students (and their parents) continue to perceive entrance to vocational and agricultural middle schools as second-class education, these schools will continue to attract only those who have failed the examination for regular middle schools.[54] Some movement in this direction has already occurred. Officials at Tianjin Middle School in Shanghai, unable to get more than 7 percent of their graduates into the university, realized that the school would never be able to match the quality of the keypoints. They began to establish links with the First Commerce Bureau of Shanghai. Even though employment was not guaranteed, the Commerce Bureau did agree to employ the best of the school's graduates. Partly because of this relationship, in 1982 more than 4,000 of the 6,200 graduating junior high students in the district applied for vocational coursework at this school, although only 170 could be recruited.[55]

Finally, although the post-Mao leadership appears secure and the great debates on the educational front which marked the Cultural Revolution are no longer heard, the current system does face formidable opposition. The old quality-versus-quantity debate continues in a different form in the controversy over keypoint schools. Even those Chinese who support this policy, including educational officials I have interviewed in Beijing, remain somewhat defensive, arguing that such a concentration of resources is necessary until the damage caused by the reforms of the Cultural Revolution is completely negated. In the interim, the educational system is perilously close to establishing two tiers, one for a small group of successful students who test into the best secondary schools and universities, and another for the vast majority unable to perform at an equivalent level. Such a situation would be potentially explosive for most societies; in China, with its Maoist legacy and continuing espousal of socialist norms, the risks of a backlash appear substantially greater.

Notes

1. I have dealt with the pre–Cultural Revolution educational system in much greater detail in *Red Guard Factionalism*, chap. 1 and 2, and in Chan, Rosen, and Unger, "Students and Class Warfare," pp. 397–446. Also see Shirk, *Competitive Comrades*, and Unger, *Education Under Mao*. The Cultural Revolution educational reforms have been discussed in Unger, *Education Under Mao*, pp. 139–206; Chen, *Chinese Education Since 1949*, pp. 63–152; Pepper, "Education and Revolution," pp. 847–890.

2. Although 93 percent may enter primary school, official figures show that only 65 percent finish; see *Beijing Review*, No. 4, January 24, 1983, p. 25. Moreover, only half who finish are up to standard. The situation is even worse in the countryside, as a recent traveller's report revealed. See Mauger, "Changing Policy and Practice in Chinese Rural Education," pp. 138–148.

3. Of course, during the Chinese Revolution the Chinese Communist Party and the military were the most important routes to upward mobility, but these means diminished after victory in 1949.

4. World Bank, *China*, p. 134.

5. In China, those of good class origin include the "five red categories," i.e., revolutionary cadre, revolutionary military, worker, poor and lower-middle-class peasant, and revolutionary martyr. Those of bad class origin include capitalist, "rightist," rich peasant, landlord, "bad element," and counterrevolutionary. Those of middle-class origin include both nonintelligentsia middle class (peddlers, store clerks, and so forth) and intelligentsia middle class (teachers, professionals, office workers, and so forth). These class designations, inheritable through the male line, were based on a man's employment three years prior to liberation. They have been an important factor in determining a student's

prospects for educational advancement. By 1979, in a series of policy changes, China's moderate leaders gave less importance to the role of class in Chinese life: the "rightist" label, which had given bad class status to 400,000 families, was expunged; the middle-class professionals were designated mental laborers, thus becoming part of the working class; the class designations of former exploiters "who had worked honestly and done no evil" were removed. In the countryside this meant that former landlords and rich peasants—and their children—were now classified as "commune members." The most detailed account of the evolving concept of class in Chinese life is given by Kraus in *Class Conflict in Chinese Socialism*.

6. Pepper, "Education and Revolution"; Pepper, "Chinese Education After Mao," pp. 2–4.

7. The costs and benefits of university admission based on an examination model or a recommendation model are discussed in Bratton, "University Admissions Policies in China, 1970–1978," pp. 1008–1022.

8. On this point, see Rosen, *The Role of Sent-Down Youth in the Chinese Cultural Revolution*.

9. A fuller discussion of this appears in Rosen, "New Directions in Secondary Schooling."

10. I have dealt with this debate in "Restoring Keypoint Secondary Schools in Post-Mao China." For the call for abolition, made by Fei Xiaotong, Qian Weichang, and ten other representatives at the fifth session of the fifth political consultative conference in Beijing in December 1982, see *Dagong Bao* [Impartial News] (Hong Kong), December 6, 1982, p. 2.

11. For examples of the problem, see *Renmin Jiaoyu* [People's Education] (Beijing), No. 3, March 1982, pp. 30–33 and *Guangming Ribao* [Glorious Daily] (Beijing), March 6, 1983, p. 2, for Hubei province; *Guangming Ribao*, October 7, 1982, p. 2 for Shandong province. The county report is from *Zhejiang Jiaoyu* [Zhejiang Education] (Hangzhou) (middle school edition), No. 6, June 1982, pp. 10–13.

12. *Zhongguo Qingnian Bao* [China Youth News] March 31, 1983, p. 1.

13. *Beijing Keji Bao* [Beijing Science and Technology News], February 22, 1982, p. 1.

14. See Rosen, "Restoring Keypoint Schools," for a table on promotion rates and university enrollments, 1950–1983.

15. Daily Report - China, November 20, 1981, pp. K7–8 (Renmin Ribao, [People's Daily] (Beijing), November 17); Daily Report, November 18, 1981, pp. K4–5 (Renmin Ribao, November 12).

16. *Jiefang Ribao* [Liberation Daily] (Shanghai) June 9, 1980, p. 1; *Shehui Kexue* [Social Sciences] (Shanghai) No. 5, October 1980, p. 37.

17. Interview with Y. J. H., April 2, 1983.

18. *Renmin Jiaoyu*, No. 3, March 1982, p. 34 and *Guangdong Jiaoyu*, [Guangdong Education] (Guangzhou), No. 2, February 1981, p. 3.

19. *Liaoning Jiaoyu* [Liaoning Education] (Shenyang) No. 1, January 1982,

p. 2 and No. 3, March 1982, p. 2; Lau, "Zhongguo Nongcun Jiaoyu Zhi Yanjiu," footnote 33, p. A16.

20. *Neimenggu Shehui Kexue* [Inner Mongolia Social Sciences] (Hohhot), No. 3, 1982, pp. 27–30.

21. Pepper, *China's Universities*, p. 109.

22. The discussion below is based primarily on the following issues of Daily Report (Foreign Broadcast Information Service, Washington): October 27, 1977, pp. E16–20 (New China News Agency [NCNA], October 21); December 27, 1977, pp. E15–16 (NCNA, December 25); April 27, 1978, p. E13 (Radio Peking, April 25); May 17, 1978, pp. E5–9 (NCNA, May 11); June 13, 1978, p. E7 (NCNA, June 11); June 15, 1978, pp. E5–6 (NCNA, June 13); June 26, 1978, pp. E3–6 (*Guangming Daily*, June 14); July 21, 1978, pp. E16–17 (NCNA, July 20); May 17, 1979, p. L17 (NCNA, May 16); July 11, 1979, pp. L19–20 (NCNA, July 7); May 13, 1980, pp. L2–9 (NCNA, May 9); March 16, 1981, pp. L23–24 (NCNA, March 15); March 17, 1981, pp. L20–21 (NCNA, March 16); April 12, 1982, pp. K11–13 (NCNA, April 11); March 18, 1983, pp. K9–10 (NCNA, March 16); March 21, 1983, pp. K1–4 (NCNA, March 16). The best secondary source is Sidel, "University Enrollment in the People's Republic of China, 1977–1981," pp. 257–270.

23. Rosen, "Obstacles to Educational Reform in China," p. 23.

24. The preferred age limit for foreign language institutions and specializations has been twenty-three.

25. Sidel, "University Enrollment," p. 262.

26. *Guangming Ribao*, April 12, 1982, p. 1. The weight of the foreign language exam for applicants to colleges for specialized professional training (*Zhuanke Xuexiao*) might be decided by provincial, municipal, or autonomous district officials.

27. *Guangming Ribao*, March 17, 1983, p. 1.

28. Sidel, "University Enrollment," p. 264, and Rosen, Interview at the Ministry of Education, August 1982.

29. *Guangming Ribao*, April 13, 1982, p. 1. The provincial minimum passing score is a statement of the relationship between the provincial quota of college freshmen and the top scores achieved. If the quota for a province is 10,000, the 10,000 candidates with the highest scores will be allowed to pass regardless of their absolute scores. The minimum score is therefore the lowest achieved by the top 10,000 candidates in the province. On this point see Pepper, *China's Universities*, chap. 3.

30. *Guangming Ribao*, January 22, 1983, p. 1.

31. *Zhongguo Baike Nianjian 1982* [China Encyclopedia Yearbook], p. 573.

32. This issue is discussed in Pepper, *China's Universities* (draft). For comments on this in the Chinese press, see *Guangming Ribao*, August 11, 1982, p. 2; *Guangzhou Ribao* [Guangzhou Daily], June 24, 1981, p. 4; *Zhongguo Qingnian Bao*, April 12, 1983, p. 1.

33. Pepper, *China's Universities*, table 20, p. 142.

34. *Peking Review,* No. 30, July 28, 1978, p. 18. It was admitted however, that the number of students from families of intellectuals "was greater in proportion to the total population than in previous years." *Zhongguo Baike Nianjian 1980,* p. 538.

35. For example, Fudan University in Shanghai, one of the country's top schools, took only "20-odd" of its 1,342 freshmen in 1980 from the countryside. See Pepper, *China's Universities,* p. 109. A recent report on new university students for 1982 shows that only 15.63 percent were current-year graduates from rural areas, 18.76 percent were current-year graduates from county towns, 20.93 percent were urban rusticated youths and returned village youths, 21.40 percent were current-year graduates of urban middle schools, with most of the remaining 23.28 percent former senior high graduates repeating the exams. See *Wenhui Bao* [Literary News] (Shanghai), November 3, 1982, p. 1.

36. Rosen, "Education and the Political Socialization of Chinese Youths."

37. The figures are for 1980. Interview, Naomi Woronov, cited in Sidel, "University Enrollment," p. 266. Also see Pepper, *China's Universities,* tables 13–19.

38. Interview at the school conducted by Irving Epstein, March 19, 1983.

39. *Beijing Review,* vol. 26, No. 3, January 17, 1983, p. 9.

40. Orleans, "The Training and Utilization of Scientific and Engineering Manpower," pp. 27–28; Pepper, *China's Universities,* p. 59.

41. Joint Publications Research Service (JPRS) No. 76237, August 15, 1980, from *Guangming Ribao,* July 10, 1980, as cited in Orleans, p. 28.

42. *Zhongguo Baike Nianjian 1980,* translated in *Chinese Education,* vol. 14, No. 4, Winter 1981–82, p. 69.

43. *Nanjing Shiyuan Xuebao* [Nanjing Normal Institute Journal], No. 2, May 20, 1982, p. 6.

44. Daily Report, January 11, 1979, p. E15 (NCNA, January 10).

45. Daily Report, May 19, 1983, pp. P4–5 (NCNA, May 18) and *Renmin Ribao,* March 5, 1983, p. 3.

46. *Beijing Review,* vol. 26, No. 4, January 24, 1983, pp. 29–30.

47. Daily Report, August 16, 1983, p. K18 (NCNA, August 15).

48. Daily Report, September 1, 1983, p. K19 (NCNA, August 30).

49. Daily Report, May 20, 1983, p. K7 (NCNA, May 19); *Beijing Review,* No. 6, February 7, 1983, pp. 21–23 and JPRS No. 82991, March 2, 1983, p. 126 (*Dazhong Ribao* [Masses Daily], December 4, 1982).

50. See the Sixth 5-Year Plan in *Beijing Review,* vol. 26, No. 22, May 30, 1983, supplement pp. X–XI, and Rosen, "New Directions in Secondary Schooling." For earlier and more detailed government projections for 1981–1990, see World Bank, *China,* p. 220–227.

51. *Beijing Ribao,* July 28, 1982, p. 1. Even teacher training schools attracted 17.9 times more applicants than could be accepted.

52. JPRS No. 84047, August 4, 1983, pp. 5–6 (*Renmin Ribao,* June 11).

53. Foster, "The Vocational School Fallacy in Development Planning," pp. 356–365.

54. This point is made in Mauger, "Changing Policy and Practice in Chinese Rural Education," pp. 138–148.

55. Shanghai *Wenhui Bao*, March 31, 1983, p. 1.

Bibliography

Beijing Shifan Daxue Xuebao [Beijing Normal University Journal] (bimonthly)

BRATTON, DALE. "University Admissions Policies in China, 1970–1978." *Asian Survey*, 19 (Oct. 1979): 1008–1022.

CHAN, ANITA, STANLEY ROSEN, and JONATHAN UNGER. "Students and Class Warfare: The Social Roots of the Red Guard Conflict in Canton." *The China Quarterly*, no. 83 (1980): 397–446.

CHEN, THEODORE HSI-EN. *Chinese Education Since 1949: Academic and Revolutionary Models*. Elmsford, New York: Pergamon, 1981.

FOSTER, PHILIP. "The Vocational School Fallacy in Development Planning." In *Power and Ideology in Education*, ed. Jerome Karabel and A. H. Halsey. New York: Oxford University Press, 1977. Pp. 356–365.

Guangdong Jiaoyu [Guangdong Education] (Guangzhou, monthly).

KRAUS, RICHARD CURT. *Class Conflict in Chinese Socialism*. New York: Columbia University Press, 1981.

LAU, WING FONG. "Zhongguo Nongcun Jiaoyu Zhi Yanjiu: Taishanxian Jiaoyu Fazhan zhi xiankuang." ["Research on Chinese Rural Education: The Current Situation of Educational Development in Taishan County (Guangdong)"]. M.A. thesis, School of Education, Chinese University of Hong Kong, 1982.

Liaoning Jiaoyu [Liaoning Education] (Shenyang, monthly).

LO, BILLIE L. C. *Research Guide to Education in China After Mao, 1977–1981*. Hong Kong: Centre for Asian Studies, University of Hong Kong, 1983.

MAUGER, PETER. "Changing Policy and Practice in Chinese Rural Education." *The China Quarterly*, no. 93 (Mar. 1983): 138–148.

Nanjing Shiyuan Xuebao [Nanjing Normal Institute Journal] (Nanjing, quarterly).

Neimenggu Shehui Kexue [Inner Mongolia Social Sciences] (Hohhot, bimonthly).

ORLEANS, LEO. "Communist China's Education: Policies, Problems and Prospects." In *An Economic Profile of Mainland China*. Joint Economic Committee of the U.S. Congress. New York: Praeger, 1968. Pp. 501–518.

––––––. "The Training and Utilization of Scientific and Engineering Manpower in the People's Republic of China." Committee on Science and Technology, U.S. House of Representatives, Ninety-Eighth Congress, October, 1983.

PEPPER, SUZANNE. "Education and Revolution: The 'Chinese Model' Revisited." *Asian Survey* 18, no. 9 (1978): 847–890.

––––––. "Chinese Education After Mao: Two Steps Forward Two Steps Back and Begin Again?" *The China Quarterly*, no. 81 (Mar. 1980): 1–65.

––––––. *China's Universities: Post-Mao Enrollment Policies and their Impact on the*

Structure of Secondary Education. Ann Arbor: Center for Chinese Studies, University of Michigan, 1984.

Renmin Jiaoyu [People's Education] (Beijing, monthly).

Renmin Shouce [People's Handbook] (Beijing, yearly to 1965).

ROSEN, STANLEY. *The Role of Sent-Down Youth in the Chinese Cultural Revolution: The Case of Guangzhou*. Berkeley: Center for Chinese Studies, University of California, Berkeley, 1981.

————. *Red Guard Factionalism and the Cultural Revolution in Guangzhou*. Boulder: Westview Press, 1982.

————. "Obstacles to Educational Reform in China." *Modern China* 8, no. 1 (1982): 3–40.

————. "Restoring Keypoint Secondary Schools in Post-Mao China: The Politics of Competition and Educational Quality, 1978–1983." Paper presented at the Social Science Research Council Conference on Policy Implementation in Post-Mao China, Ohio State University, June 20–24, 1983.

————. "New Directions in Secondary Schooling." In *Contemporary Chinese Education*, ed. Ruth Hayhoe. London: Croom Helm, 1984.

————. "Education and the Political Socialization of Chinese Youths." In *Education and Social Change in the People's Republic of China*, ed. John N. Hawkins. New York: Praeger, 1983.

Shehui Kexue [Social Sciences] (Shanghai, monthly since 1982).

SHIRK, SUSAN. *Competitive Comrades: Career Incentives and Student Strategies in China*. Berkeley: University of California Press, 1982.

SIDEL, MARK. "University Enrollment in the People's Republic of China, 1977–1981: The Examination Model Returns." *Comparative Education* 18, no. 3 (1982): 257–270.

Statistical Yearbook of China 1981. Hong Kong: Economic Information and Agency, 1982.

UNGER, JONATHAN. *Education Under Mao: Class and Competition in Canton Schools, 1960–1980*. New York: Columbia University Press, 1982.

World Bank. *China: Socialist Economic Development*. Vol. III. Washington, D.C., 1983.

Zhejiang Jiaoyu [Zhejiang Education] (Hangzhou, monthly).

Zhongguo Baike Nianjian [China Encyclopedia Yearbook] (Beijing and Shanghai, yearly since 1980).

Zhongguo Goadeng Xuexiao Jianjie [A Brief Introduction to Higher Education Institutions in China] (Beijing, 1982).

Zhongguo Jiaoyu Bao [China Education News] (Beijing, twice weekly).

Zhongguo Jiaoyu Nianjian 1949–1981 [China Education Yearbook] (Beijing, 1984).

Zhongguo Jingji Nianjian [China Economics Yearbook] (Beijing, yearly since 1981).

Zhongguo Tongji Nianjian 1983 [Statistical Yearbook of China] (Beijing, 1983).

7

Latin America

ERNESTO SCHIEFELBEIN

THROUGHOUT LATIN AMERICA ACCESS TO higher education is an extremely important matter. Those trained at universities can look forward to favorable prospects of employment and high lifetime earnings. An increasing number of secondary school graduates with middle-class backgrounds have therefore sought, in recent decades, to fill university places that once were reserved almost completely for the upper class. With social demand rising rapidly, including greater numbers of young women wishing a higher degree, the universities have undergone dramatic expansion. They have made some structural changes, reaching both downward and upward in their operations, as they have taken on some of the traditional functions of the schools while concurrently moving toward a "fourth level" of advanced education and research. At the same time, Latin American universities distinctively continue to be places where political careers are launched, a role that affects their academic effectiveness and also adds greatly to their direct impact on the political order. This societal linkage is one of the reasons some military regimes in Latin American countries seek to reshape, in a functional way, the higher education sector and the relationship between the school and the university.

Though these characteristics are fairly common throughout Latin America, there are also sharp differences. For example, whereas less than 15 percent of the corresponding age group are enrolled in secondary education in such countries as Haiti, Guatemala, and Honduras, over 40 percent are enrolled in that sector in ten other countries. In seven countries less than 30 percent of the teaching staff is certified, whereas in another eight over 60 percent of the teachers hold appropriate certificates. In this chapter I will treat the situation in large countries, such as Brazil, Colombia, and Mexico, as representative of Latin America. Statements with no reference to specific countries will correspond to the average situation of "middle-level" nations. Examples from other countries will be used occasionally as a complement to present a more realistic view of the region.[1]

The Educational Sector

Since the 1950s at all levels of education enrollments, which started from a low base, have increased considerably. Except for a few small countries such as Haiti and Guatemala, most children by the late 1970s were attending at least one year of primary school. The coverage of elementary education in the region as a whole rose from 57 to 78 percent between 1960 and 1975. Secondary school enrollment climbed to 35 percent of the age group. In those same years the number of university students increased over 300 percent in Central America and the Caribbean and 600 percent in South America. Private universities shared in this expansion, absorbing 70 percent of the total enrollment in recent years in Brazil, the largest country in the region, and exhibited a wide range in quality. Table 7.1 summarizes annual rates of growth of the different levels of education between 1960 and 1980, showing the phenomenal increases experienced in secondary, and especially higher, education.

In the last ten to fifteen years there has been a growing awareness of the social characteristics of students who advance as far as the university.[2] Half of the age group drop out before primary education ends, and half of the survivors graduate from the secondary level. The attrition is heavily related to socioeconomic background: the select group attending the university comes from families in higher income brackets. For example, children from families where the household head has a primary education have a lower than 5 percent probability of entering the university (and then mainly to a relatively low-prestige field of study); the figures also show that the probability is more than 50 percent for children whose parents have a university education. Free higher education, therefore, redistributes income toward the wealthier sectors of the population. Increasing awareness of this basic fact, as evident in public debate in Argentina, Colombia, Chile, and Brazil, has given support to the idea of charging tuition at the university level.

Educational activities are of course embedded in an educational system that is a subsystem of the whole society. These activities are shaped by such general features of the larger society as population growth and increase in per capita income, as well as by objectives defined by the state in regard to social justice, liberty, and general well-being. This chapter will not pursue these many external connections, but particular mention must be made of the spector of unemployment and how it

TABLE 7.1

ANNUAL RATES OF GROWTH IN LATIN AMERICAN EDUCATION, 1960–1980
(IN PERCENT)

Time period	Elementary education	Secondary education	Higher education	Enrollments in higher education at the end of each period
1960–65	5.6	10.4	9.8	914,000
1965–70	5.4	8.3	12.4	1,637,100
1970–75	3.9	9.3	16.1	3,451,400
1975–80	3.5	6.8	10.2	5,599,100

SOURCE: UNESCO-BIE, Conferencia Internacional de Educación, XXXVI Reunión, "Evolución de la matrícula escolar: tendencias y proyecciones estadísticas, regionales y mundiales 1960–2000," ED/BIE/CONFINTED 36/4/Rev. 2, Paris, 1977.

conditions student aspirations and intentions. If secondary school graduates find real job opportunities with reasonable salaries and good perspectives for promotion and upgrading, then they can look favorably upon plunging immediately into the labor market instead of attempting to continue their schooling. But in Latin America the job market has been, and remains, poor for such graduates, with 6 to 10 percent unemployment in times of prosperity and 15 to 30 percent in recessions and depressions. (The figures may be twice as large for youngsters seeking their first job.) Few are willing to start as unqualified workers unless forced by the need to survive.

The hope that more education might support a self-sustaining trend of economic development faded during the 1970s. Several countries, Costa Rica, Chile, and Ecuador, for example, are now trying to curtail further expansion of university enrollments and even, in the case of Chile, secondary education. However, the traditional autonomy claimed by Latin American universities has made it very difficult to design coordinated policies, even under military regimes. And universities have played an important political role in the last fifty years: political careers are often started in student associations,[3] and many political figures, defeated in the ballot box, have found a university chair from which to improve their strategies, find some rest before the next election, or plot the next revolt. Having such political clout, the universities are not readily marked for reduction. Nevertheless, the military regimes governing Argentina, Brazil, Chile, and Uruguay during the 1970s kept close control over political actions in the universities to the point of expelling professors and staff involved in active and sometimes even passive political opposition.[4]

The Basic Structure

A relatively common structure of education in Latin American countries as of the 1960s consisted of six years of elementary education, six years of secondary education—with the upper years, in particular, divided between academic and vocational tracks—and five or more years in the university. The structure has been rapidly changing.[5] The addition of two or more years to primary education (now eight years in many countries) and large increases in enrollment have tended to transform the primary and secondary sectors into a single block of basic education.[6] Postsecondary education is now offered by a vast array of institutions in addition to universities. The small amount of research carried out in many Latin American universities is usually done after regular professional training; research begins with students who have already obtained a professional degree as a physician, engineer, lawyer, or accountant. These graduate studies are creating a fourth level of advanced education in special institutions such as El Colegio de Mexico, the Fundaçao Getulio Vargas in Brazil, the Grupo de Bariloche and the Instituto Torcuato di Tella in Argentina, and the Institutos (INTEC or CIM) in Chile.[7] The traditional universities are therefore mainly transmitting accepted professional technology rather than training people in research or scholarship. Table 7.2 shows some of the shifts in enrollment among the disciplines within the universities during the 1960s, principally a major reduction, proportionately, in medicine and a large proportionate increase in teaching, humanities, and the arts. Science remained relatively small, with less than 5 percent of the enrollment.

At the same time, some countries (for example, Chile, Peru, and Venezuela) are trying to halt the demand for higher education by developing or strengthening vocational programs at the secondary level, where diplomas do not allow students to apply for entry into the university (laws specify which diplomas are required); or by diverting students to nonuniversity alternatives, such as the *technologicos* or *institutos technicos*.[8] But these institutions usually lobby the legislative or military regimes or other authorities until they receive university status. Most nonuniversity forms of higher education in Latin America are considered very second-rate, with their graduates tending to receive lower salaries in the labor market.[9] While certain countries have diversified higher education, other countries have offered devaluated quality in alternative institutions, such as the *scolas isoladas* in Brazil.

The tremendous increase in enrollments along with better social control are now supporting the operation of more objective admission systems.[10] There are entrance examination systems operating in several countries, including Brazil, Chile, Colombia, and Costa Rica. In the first

TABLE 7.2

DISTRIBUTION OF ENROLLMENTS IN LATIN AMERICAN
UNIVERSITIES, BY DISCIPLINE, 1960–1970
(IN PERCENT)

Discipline	1960	1965	1970
Law and Social Sciences	35.6	33.3	32.3
Teaching, Humanities, and Arts	19.8	24.8	25.9
Medicine	21.3	17.1	14.7
Engineering	15.2	14.9	15.2
Science	4.2	4.5	4.8
Agriculture	3.3	4.1	4.5
Other	0.6	1.8	2.6
Total	100.0	100.0	100.0
Total Enrollment	545,000	865,000	1,541,000

SOURCE: P. Latapí, "Trends in Latin American Universities: Selected Problems and Perspectives," UNESCO, Division of Higher Education, Paris, 1978.

two countries the same exams are used by several universities. In Chile there is a national unified system; in Brazil, regional systems. Some private (commercial) Brazilian universities are withdrawing from those systems because they receive the worst students and because they have realized that they can get large amounts of money from examination fees. Further coordination is also sought through national boards of university presidents operating in Colombia, Costa Rica, Chile, Mexico, and Peru.

It is important to recall a basic difference in the educational developments of Latin America and the developed countries. The latter enrolled most of their population in the elementary level, while university students were a small fraction of the corresponding population. In the last fifty years Latin America developed secondary and university enrollments of a similar relative size to that of the developed European countries in the late sixties; but universal elementary education was not achieved until recently, and even now there are pockets of population with no access to schools.[11]

In Latin America, then, large enrollment increments, including the massification of the university, are occurring, while at the same time the absolute number of illiterates is increasing. This paradox is associated with large increments in educational expense and bitter competition among the primary, secondary, and university levels for the available resources. In spite of its smaller number of students, the university takes about one-third (but in some cases has obtained up to 40 percent) of the available resources. Even if expenses for research or services (hospital or television stations) may somewhat distort the figures on educational expenditures, increasing the university share, the unit expenses per student are still relatively high in comparison with those in primary education (twenty to forty times higher). There is no doubt, however, that in a publicly financed, free-education system, the university leverage may be difficult to harness.

The Influence of Secondary Education on the University

Given that a large share—over 80 percent—of students graduating from high school hope to continue at the university,[12] the demand for places depends mainly on the size of enrollments in the last grade of the secondary level. Table 7.1 shows the rapid rate of increased enrollment in secondary education. Attempts to reduce the demand through terminal secondary education that might channel graduates into the labor market have been unsuccessful.[13] One clear example is agricultural secondary education: graduates do not want to return to the countryside; instead, they look for an urban job or seek to continue their education. The actual labor market structure does not offer interesting job opportunities for youngsters graduating from high school, and investment in further education is usually associated with positive rates of return.[14]

The expansion of secondary education implies including students with less ability or willingness to devote time to active study. While those students from academically oriented families were already attending secondary schools, the expansion of secondary education drew students from families with a lower educational or socioeconomic background. The less selective the high school, the less homogeneous its graduates in skills, aspirations, family support, and achievement levels. Thus, when the pressure of too many high school graduates forces an increase in university openings, the gap widens between aspirations and reality in terms of more repetition and higher dropout rates at the university level. Repetition or dropout rates of 20 to 30 percent in the first year are common in most countries. There are also substantial numbers of students switching from one university career to another, especially from low-prestige to high-prestige institutions, mainly because of better future employment and salaries.[15]

When a branch of secondary education does not offer opportunities for further education, its social prestige is reduced, and future applications will be among the lower half of the pool in quality. Terminal education is perceived as a social injustice. Where such a strategy was attempted, it failed. Sooner or later the number of students fulfilling the requirements for joining the university increased in all Latin American countries. Even though attempts to screen students through entrance examinations have been implemented, they have not offset the pressures. As shown in table 7.3 for the years 1965–1975, a larger percentage of the population of a given age group is now enrolled at the university, in spite of the rapid increase in population. For example, in those ten years alone, the participation rate increased in Argentina from 10 to 20 percent; in Brazil, from less than 2 to over 7 percent; in Chile, from 9 to nearly 11 percent.

In most Latin American countries (those not able to screen students not meeting certain objective standards), secondary education has determined the entry-level knowledge and the abilities of university students as well as the demand for places. University professors claim that students are no longer as good as they used to be. Some partial evidence suggests, for example, that Latin American students still have serious limitations in systematic thinking, in addition to problems in spelling and grammar. These problems may explain the existence of Mexican *preparatorias*, under the direction of selected universities, and why some universities have started preuniversity courses (for example, the Universidad Nacional in Costa Rica, or the Tecnológico in Ecuador) as an alternative for those failing to meet entrance standards or as a prerequisite for all students. Students in such courses in Ecuador are considered bona fide university students and are financed with government funds.[16] These developments can be considered as a "secondarization" of the university, where the university takes on more of the functions traditionally carried out by the secondary schools.[17]

Two additional mechanisms can be observed in the expansion of universities which also lead them to replicate certain characteristics of secondary education. First, enrollments and campuses have grown many times, leading to a massification that is associated somewhat with characteristics of secondary education; large classes in order to reduce costs; memorization of textbooks when laboratory or fieldwork is difficult to expand; summative rather than formative evaluation; lack of use of scientific and professional journals; and reduction of seminar work.[18] Second, in some cases these characteristics of secondarization are particularly prevalent in new universities that have evolved from private high schools of prominent standing in order to meet the demand for places at the higher education level. Even if new professors are hired and adequate equipment is acquired, some traditions of the *liceo* remain. It takes some time before authentic university traditions of inquiry and the search for systematic knowledge become part and parcel of such new institutions, if they ever do.

In any case, the quick expansion of universities generated by the increase of high school graduates (in some countries there have been annual growth rates of 20 percent in university enrollments) places heavy

TABLE 7.3

RATES OF SCHOOLING IN LATIN AMERICAN HIGHER EDUCATION
IN 1965 AND 1975, BY SELECTED COUNTRIES

	Total population	Population age 19–25	Higher education enrollment	Schooling rate (percent)
	1965			
Columbia	17,966	1,833,979	44,403	2.3
Brazil	82,541	9,923,491	155,781	1.6
Mexico	42,859	4,917,680	133,374	2.7
Argentina	22,179	2,441,965	246,680	10.1
Peru	11,440	1,403,315	79,259	5.6
Venezuela	9,105	1,009,867	46,825	4.6
Chile	8,701	1,030,015	43,608	4.2
Ecuador	5,095	605,290	15,395	2.5
Guatemala	4,583	540,589	7,782	1.4
Bolivia	4,246	516,511	16,912	3.3
Dominican Republic	3,703	434,958	7,359	1.7
El Salvador	2,954	342,895	3,438	1.0
Paraguay	1,973	233,253	5,890	2.5
Panama	1,261	147,416	7,247	4.9
	1975			
Columbia	23,577	2,944,750	176,098	6.0
Brazil	109,730	14,049,790	1,003,919	7.2
Mexico	59,204	7,378,946	520,194	7.0
Argentina	25,384	2,952,163	601,395	20.4
Peru	15,326	1,966,618	190,635	9.7
Venezuela	12,213	1,577,445	221,581	14.0
Chile	10,621	1,383,707	149,647	10.8
Ecuador	7,090	873,029	141,213	16.2
Guatemala	6,129	781,536	27,006	3.4
Bolivia	5,410	683,753	51,585	7.5
Dominican Republic	5,118	963,406	43,941	4.6
El Salvador	4,108	438,007	14,744	3.3
Paraguay	2,628	348,105	14,358	4.1
Panama	1,676	312,176	30,642	9.8

SOURCE: ICFES, "Historia estadística de la educación superior," ICFES, Bogotá, 1979.

demands on the quality of the academic staff. Vacancies are often filled with secondary teachers. This trend may also be another factor in the reduction of the ability to explore knowledge through research.

But admission to the university does not necessarily mean admission to the career the student most desires. Secondary grades and entrance examinations may channel students into quite different university careers. Selectivity thus depends to a large extent on the previous judgments of secondary teachers. Nevertheless, the available evidence suggests that only small differences exist between the predictive value of grades, on the one hand, and objective entrance exams, on the other. This is a relatively well-known aspect, and no further comments seem necessary.[19]

While secondary education affects student demand and training (or selection and certification) at the university level, the financing of education plays a major role in the centralized operation of the educational system. The ministries of education (or the ministries of finance) sometimes strike a bargain with the universities whereby larger enrollments or better quality is requested in return for additional funds. The bargaining process is complex because funds for education have relatively rigid constraints, and more money for the university usually means less for elementary, secondary, or other cultural or research activities. In fact, rate-of-return studies suggest that primary education provides a higher payoff than higher education as a whole.

In Chile, additional funds are obtained by enrolling the best high school graduates. For each student who has entrance scores in the upper two-thirds of the total number of students joining the university for the first time, the university receives a lump sum. This is an experimental policy that may not last, but the principle of allocating funds according to demand is being tried and deserves mention. As a result of this policy, university managers show great interest in pursuing students from that group. The system is being revised, however, given the distortions generated in the operation of the universities and the sudden expansion of careers demanded by students with good admission scores, demands incongruent with any reasonable forecast of the future labor market.

To pay for a child's private education is similar to buying insurance against failure. Attending private secondary schools usually raises the probability of acceptance to the university because the peer group, family support, and quality of education positively affect the student's chances.[20] In Brazil students from expensive private secondary schools go to excellent, free public universities, while poor students from free public secondary schools end up in the expensive, low-quality, private Brazilian universities. To change this pattern, certain countries or universities are now establishing minimum university fees equivalent to those paid at secondary schools. Thus, the interest in investing in private secondary education in order to obtain free university education is lessening. Generally, however, many consider payment for privileged secondary education reasonable, if it also helps the student gain admission to an almost free public higher education. In any case, the proportion of university students who have a private school background has been much larger than the proportion of the private school enrollment among all secondary students.[21]

The University Shapes the School

It is clear that the university influences school curricula; that it has a say in the selecting and training of school personnel; that it strongly influences the modeling of student political action; and that it shapes school reform and policies. But, overwhelmingly, the principal influence of the university in Latin America appears to be its effect on student (and family) aspirations. This comes about primarily because university students and graduates act as role models in society, but also because the university operates in a particular manner.

Latin American university students usually receive several fringe benefits. In addition to free public education, they occasionally have access to subsidized transportation, housing, and food, free health insurance, sports facilities (often likened to country clubs), equipment, free language courses, textbooks, and tickets to many cultural events.[22] Many university students live in a situation in which the constraints of everyday life are severely limited. The comparison of the golden life of these students with the life of youngsters of a similar age, who spend eight or more hours each day in jobs, is an important factor in explaining student interest in attending the university. This is true even though suitable job opportunities and positive rates of return to investment in higher education are lacking.

Graduates from the university are usually among the 10 or 15 percent of the population with the highest income. As viewed by those in a lower socioeconomic status, or by those with less education, graduates appear to have solved the problems of unemployment (they can always bump someone in the lower echelon). University graduates are also included in the most prestigious groups of society, even receiving special titles in everyday life, such as *doctor, licenciado, ingeniero,* and *abogado.* The aura surrounding graduates from the university also explains why high school students are interested in gaining entry to the university.

These effects deriving from perceived roles of students and graduates are sometimes reinforced by specific actions of those groups. For example, the traditional ability of university graduates to gather in guilds (*colegios*) or unions and to lobby the parliament or the dictator in power leads to laws that limit certain activities to those who have a specific university diploma. Opportunities for working in certain areas are closed to those having the expertise but not the legally required diploma. The power of the guilds may also restrict access to certain careers, reducing the annual number of entrants and limiting the creation of new universities or new careers in other universities. The existence of these pressure groups may also explain why it is impossible for students in one career to enroll in courses of another, even if they do not attempt to get a degree in that area and there is room for them and they only wish to get credit for that course. Only in a few universities are students allowed to take a few elective courses beyond the common core group.

Even in those countries where there is no restriction upon the number of university students in each career track, for example, Argentina, Peru, or Mexico, the guilds or the traditions have supported large differences in salaries benefiting university graduates. (The differences are now becoming smaller in countries such as Mexico, Chile, or Peru.) The awesome expansion of universities in the last twenty years may partially explain the persistence of these differences, because the shortage of *catedraticos* (professors) for the new universities created an additional demand for university graduates. This demand has disappeared in those countries where the university growth rate has been reduced; pressure now exists due to excess supply which may be part of the reason for decreasing differences in salaries of university faculty (with respect to other jobs) observed in such countries as Argentina, Chile, Mexico, or Uruguay.

Changes in aspirations also have an impact on curriculum and motivation or on the willingness to spend time learning tasks. If most high school students wish to continue in higher education, for example, the schools must train them in those subjects included in the university entrance exams (UEE). Although in a few countries the screening is carried out in secondary schools, with all graduates then continuing on to the university, the entrance examinations have become the key to access to higher education and the main factor shaping the high school curriculum. This examination linkage is especially important in Latin America because the high school has, as a large common core, an academic curriculum. Thus, it becomes a nightmare to approve as university acceptable all courses taken by the great mass of students. In many countries there are no alternative tracks for entering the universities. In fact, in most countries less able students may transfer into vocational schools, but the diploma from those schools is usually not valid for entering the university. University aspirants are so stimulated by the substantial payoff, however, that it even compensates for the low probability of success in the competition for university entrance (similar to the *ronin* effect in Japan). Therefore, high school students and their parents usually reject any attempt to design and implement a curriculum fitted for early entrance into the job market rather than into the university. Trying to succeed in high school and then to attend the university—or any postsecondary institution—is rational in a society with much-distorted salary scales.[23]

Nevertheless, aspirations are affected by traditional occupational expectations of men and women. For example, although there are no significant differences in achievement scores for boys and girls at the completion of elementary schooling,[24] on the university entrance examination, females graduating from high school average lower scores than males (see table 7.4). The only explanation for the change in achievement levels during the years of secondary education is that a large proportion of women elect to follow careers that have lower test-score requirements, such as teaching, nursing, and social work, while male students choose to enter engineering, medicine, economics, architecture, and other fields that have much higher entrance exam standards.[25] As table 7.4 shows, over 70 percent of female enrollment is in education, nursing, and the social sciences (except economics), fields of study that have relatively low entrance requirements. In short, university sorting requirements by fields of study seem to affect the amount of effort high school students are willing to devote to mastering learning tasks.

The political role of university student leaders is another example of modeling attitudes for secondary school students. There is a long and powerful tradition of political activity in the university.[26] Student leaders frequently receive wide exposure in the mass media, especially when rallies, sieges of buildings, and strikes are carried out. Student federations operate at the secondary level in several countries, with their leaders playing similar roles as the leaders of university student associations. These politically prepared students can then move up into positions in the university federation of student councils. Obviously, some of the political activities are closely controlled in many Latin American countries under military regimes.[27]

High school teachers (*profesores*) and an increasing fraction of elementary teachers (*maestros*) in Latin America are now being trained at the university. But there are still excellent normal schools where elementary teachers are trained at the secondary level or, in Venezuela, *pedagogicos*, where secondary teachers are trained at a postsecondary but nonuniversity level. Because of this availability, the university, through the selection process, ends up allocating less able secondary students to teach in the school system. Normal schools have been able to attract

TABLE 7.4

FEMALE ENROLLMENT AND MINIMUM ADMISSION SCORES
BY UNIVERSITY FIELD OF STUDY

Field of study (in order of percentage female)	Female enrollment* (in percent)	Percent of all enrolled		Lowest admitted test score**
		Males	Females*	
Engineering	6.3	18.3	2.0	616
Agronomy and veterinary medicine	14.6	5.0	1.4	560 589
Economics and finance	19.2	11.5	4.4	647
Natural science (except chemistry)	22.8	.9	.4	655 (biochemistry) 611 (biology)
Law	25.2	4.8	2.6	533
Medicine	27.1	4.4	2.6	713.5
Architecture	30.1	3.0	2.0	557
Chemistry	37.8	.8	.7	557
Dentistry	43.4	1.2	1.5	638
Pharmacy	45.6	.7	.9	599
Education	60.9	19.8	49.3	501 (pedagogy) 501 (preschool) 477 (primary)
Social sciences (except economics)	67.6	3.1	10.1	573 (political science) 568 (anthropology) 538 (sociology)
Nursing	90.2	1.0	13.3	502

SOURCE: Schiefelbein and Farrell, "Women, Schooling and Work in Chile," *Comparative Education Review* 24, no. 2, Part 2 (June 1980): S169.

*América en cifras, 1974: Situación social (Washington, D.C.: Organization of American States, 1975), table 501–77: data refer to 1970.

**E. Schiefelbein, "Selectividad del sistema universitario," in *Universidad contemporanea: Un intento de análises empirico*, ed. E. Schiefelbein and N. McGinn. Santiago: Ediciones CPU, 1974, p. 261. (Data refer to 1972.)

capable students mainly from families in the low socioeconomic groups. Also, most of the training is provided through the "preaching" of the university professor (*catedratico*). Better teaching techniques are used in medicine, architecture, and sometimes in engineering, where laboratories, libraries, and tutorial fieldwork are considered important elements. Tutorial work and research on the effects of alternative educational techniques are still scarce despite their impressive increase in the last ten years.[28] In the schools and faculties that train teachers there is social pressure upon the catedraticos to show their amazing amount of knowledge through lecturing, rather than to train students in specific capabilities. Little attention is paid to the actual ability of future teachers to cope with the challenge of motivating students to achieve their potential. Nevertheless, the prestige of the catedraticos is high, and many of them are excellent "preachers." Therefore, the preaching style is adopted by new teachers as the model for their own style in elementary or high school teaching.

Final examples of how the university influences the school system relate to financing and planning. Universities have been very effective in lobbying for more funding. The combined efforts of university political muscle and the guilds (congressmen and high-ranking government officials are usually university graduates) have enabled universities to raise the share of resources devoted to university education. In some extreme cases this may reach 40 percent, and frequently up to one-third of the total amount allocated to education.

University professors are also very influential in educational decision making. Both their research (usually limited) and their opinions may introduce change in actual practice. Research sponsored by ministries of education was started in the mid-1960s and is increasing, but the magnitude of university-sponsored research is decreasing, although it is still important. Many textbooks are prepared by university professors even if, as suggested by the poor children of Barbiana, many of them "know the children only by memory."[29] Experimental schools attached to the university may sometimes play a key role as demonstration centers and may be models for other institutions. Professors are also hired as consultants for the preparation of projects concerned with the evaluation of ongoing educational experiences.

In sum, the university has had an important role in shaping school policies. But the large number of so-called reforms in secondary and elementary education in Latin America, coupled with the apparently few effective changes, leave questions about the efficacy of university involvement, at least with respect to the impact of university schools of education. The university-school linkages are clear, but if the university model of teaching is not adequate, suitable results may seldom be produced in the schools.

Common Characteristics

Although certain characteristics are common to both the second and third levels of education in Latin America, the direction of causality cannot easily be established. For example, the university curriculum at each level of a given career path is usually the same for all students enrolled in such a program, as it is also fixed for those in a given high school grade. It is difficult to demonstrate that the university model is replicated in high school or vice versa. In fact, the fixed curriculum may be a result of previous European models applied to both levels at the same time.

Selectivity achieved through failing students is somewhat similar in both educational levels. However, little by little, universities have been able to introduce the university entrance examination to restrict entry, whereas entrance to secondary education has tended to become available for all who demand access after completing primary school. There are very few good studies on attrition at both levels, but the fragmentary evidence available suggests similar degrees of repetition and dropout.

Efforts to introduce new educational technologies are also occurring at both levels. The most systematic efforts seem to be those carried out by the open universities and the medical schools, with technical assistance from the Panamerican Health Organization (PAHO). Well-defined, ideally measurable objectives exist for many subjects in the medical curriculum, and standard modules (including evaluation tests) have been prepared for achieving many of them. The little progress made in schools of education, however, probably matches what has been done in high schools.

Conclusion

Conclusions are constrained by the large differences observed among Latin American countries. Even the massive expansion in university enrollment shows a wide range in rate of growth. Significant differences are found in such areas as the extent of differentiation in higher education, the role of the private sector, and earnings of university graduates.

High unemployment and substantial differences in salary levels between secondary and higher education graduates remain powerful external elements that strongly affect the aspirations and decisions of high school students, narrowing the potential for an internal reshaping of aspirations. Many educational administrators in Latin America seem poorly informed on this issue; wider dissemination of basic information about it may be useful. The limited tools available for effecting some marginal change include the diffusion of objective information to students by means of improved counseling, scholarships for students from lower-income families, and university fees. But the tradition of the free university is difficult to overcome, in spite of its negative impact on equity.

Even if pressure for further expansion of the universities cannot be reduced, there is a need for rational assessment of the desired size of university enrollments. The effects of small labor markets, reduced migration, career choice based on family ties, and other factors make it difficult to estimate a suitable distribution by careers or disciplines. But at least the appropriate range for the overall size of universities may be estimated from international comparisons, taking into account the size and age distribution of the general population and its per capita income. In addition, an open discussion of the "cooling out" processes[30] used in Latin America for dampening the flow of students may shed some light on the effective alternatives open to each country. Special note must also be taken of the ways the career interests of young women, in such fields as nursing, teaching, and social work, have caused them to reduce their efforts at the secondary level. The increasing participation of women in other fields should help to change this traditional pattern.

Follow-up studies of graduates from high school and from the tracks open to students in secondary education may help to improve decision making about available alternatives. For example, in some countries, expensive technical or vocational secondary schools, with costs per student twice as high as those in the academic track, are used as alternative ways by which students can reach the university. It may be more efficient in those cases to expand the less expensive academic facilities in secondary education.

Teacher training at the universities has adjusted to the traditional attitudes and needs of large masses of secondary school teachers; this has devalued quality. Traditional in-service upgrading seminars have not been very successful. Certain areas such as mathematics or writing may be worthy targets of a massive secondary education effort. The introduction of textbooks and their effective use may be another way to tackle achievement problems. The training of new teachers at the university may help break the vicious circle of tradition. While prospective teachers in actual training are only a small part of the total present teaching force, their limited numbers may permit the introduction of improvements more readily. Any significant change, however, will probably require the capacity to evaluate effectively, that is, to do research; this is yet scarce in Latin America.

Meanwhile, the university is taking over some of the functions that secondary education cannot fulfill. Hence, it is undergoing some secondarization. At the same time, a new fourth level of education is emerging in the more advanced countries in the form of centers of excellence established for graduate studies and advanced research. Both of these developments require further analysis and evaluation. For example, it could become more widely recognized that many professional schools in universities do not need low student-teacher ratios or expensive research; hence their unit costs could be substantially reduced, while a few small centers of excellence could produce top-quality research and outstanding graduates.

Many political careers begin at the university. Since this particular role of Latin American universities seems to detract from their academic effectiveness, more attention needs to be given to displacing this role to other settings. If popular elections were created at the local level, for example, the launching of political careers might be linked with community development. If the decision must be made to reduce the political aspects of the university, other suitable mechanisms for launching political careers will have to be found.

The relationship between secondary and higher education in Latin America is a function of formidable social problems. Solutions to these problems seem mutually exclusive, or at least they are not easily harmonized. There are no ready answers in Latin America; in fact, experience suggests there is little room for optimism. However, a clearer definition of the problems is a good starting point. More information is becoming available, even if little of it is presently used in actual decision making. Just to dispel the myths about the existence of simple solutions would be an important advance toward the evolution of a more efficient and equitable educational system.

Notes

1. Comments of Daniel Levy, Thomas LaBelle, and Burton R. Clark were especially valuable in preparing the final version of this paper; discussion of the paper during the UCLA Conference was also very helpful.

2. Klubitschko, "El Origen Social de los Estudiantes de la Universidad de Buenos Aires"; Solari and Franco, "Igualdad de Oportunidades y Elitismo en la Universidad Uruguaya," pp. 117–134; de Britto and de Carvalho, "Condicionantes Socioeconómicos dos Estudantes da Universidade de Bahia," p. 53; Schiefelbein and Farrell, "Eight Years of Their Lives."

3. Schiefelbein and Grossi, "Differences Among American and Latin American Premises About Education and Work," pp. 11–18.

4. Levy, "Higher Education Policy in Authoritarian Regimes," p. 60.

5. Detailed descriptions of the educational systems of nine countries may be found on microfiche in the REDUC system: Guerra, "La Universidad Boliviana en Crisis"; Briones, "Las Universidades Chilenas en el Modelo de Economía Neo-liberal"; Morales, "El Conflicto en las Universidades," pp. 85–97; Castro et al., "Imagen de la Universidad de Costa Rica"; Trujillo, "La Universidad en el Sistema Educacional Ecuatoriano," pp. 9–14; Arena and Pallan, "La Planeación en las Universidades Mexicanas"; Ulloa et al., "Educación no Formal para Universitarios y Campesinos en Nayarit (México)," pp. 9–44; Roggi, "Universidad

y Sociedad en América Latina y Especialmente en Panamá," pp. 63–68; Palau, "Algunos Aspectos Cuantitativos de la Educación Superior en el Paraguay"; Universidad Nacional Abierta, "Análisis y Perfiles Ocupacionales de las Carreras Que Ofrece la Universidad Abierta".

6. Gómez Millas, "El Problema del Ingreso a la Educación Superior Desde el Punto de Vista de la Responsabilidad Social," p. 53.

7. Schiefelbein, "Cambios en la Función Educativa de la Universidad."

8. For example, Colombia had 32 universities in 1960; from 1960–1977, 57 universities and 25 technological institutes were created. See ICFES, "Historia Estadística de la Educación Colombiana."

9. See, for example, the problems associated with technical courses in the Catholic University in Paraguay in Rivarola, "Los Cursos Técnicos de la Universidad Católica, Filial Villarrica," pp. 140–146.

10. Vianna, "A Selecao de Candidatos a Traves de Provas Objetivas," Folha de Sao Paulo, December 25, 1973 (see also Cadernos de Pesquisa No. 38, Agosto 1981). Díaz et al., "Análisis de los Resultados de las Pruebas," p. 84. Zunino and Rodríguez, "Sistemas Especiales de Ingreso a la Universidad de Chile," p. 72. Himmel and Maltes, "El Problema de la Admisión y Selección Universitarias 1967–1977," pp. 126–138.

11. Solari, "Estudios Sobre Educación y Empleo."

12. We have evidence for Chile, and it seems to be true for most of the countries. See, for example, Fisher, "Factors Associated with College Aspirations and Expectations of Chilean Secondary School Pupils."

13. PREALC, "Educación y Empleo en América Latina," pp. 14–15.

14. The rates tend to be smaller the higher the educational level, but they are always positive. See Psacharopoulos, Returns to Education.

15. For the detailed analysis in the Chilean case see Klubitschko, "El Cambio de Carrera Como Deserción Interna en la Universidad Católica de Chile." See also CPU, no. 29, 1974.

16. Pozo de Ruiz and Schiefelbein, "Los Problemas de la Expansión . . . del Sistema Educaciónal de Ecuador," pp. 35–52.

17. The state may battle against this secondarization but this battle may be unsuccessful, especially when public universities retain considerable autonomy over many policies. See Levy, University and Government in Mexico.

18. A good description of these problems is illustrated in Castro, "Algunos Problemas Fundamentales en la Orientación de la Universidad Panameña," pp. 69–76.

19. For example, see Grassau and Segure, "El Rango Ocupado por el Alumno Durante los Estudios Secundarios como Índice de Predicción para los Estudios Universitarios," pp. 18–31.

20. See note 2.

21. For an analysis of the effects caused by the growth of private higher education from a marginal status to one where it holds one-third of total enrollments, see Levy, "The State and Higher Education in Latin America."

22. Castro, "Growth, Misunderstanding, and Crisis in Latin American Universities," pp. 35–42.

23. See my comment in note 14.

24. There is evidence for Chile, but it may be representative of other countries. See Farrell and Schiefelbein, "Expanding the Scope of Educational Planning," pp. 18–29.

25. Schiefelbein and Farrell, "Women, Schooling and Work in Chile," pp. S160–S170. Similar results have been found in Costa Rica and will be reported in the near future.

26. For an analytical overview of student policies in Latin America with special emphasis on the 1970s, see Levy, "Student Politics in Contemporary Latin America," pp. 368–371. For examples of national studies see: Rodrígues, "Partidos Políticos y Autonomía Universitaria"; Brunner, "Universidad Católica y Cultura Nacional en los Años 60"; Garretón, "Universidad y Política en los Procesos de Transformación y Reversión en Chile 1967–1977"; Caravajal et al., "Los Conflictos de la Educación Superior Venezolana," pp. 87–132; Bronfenmajer and Casanova, "Proposiciónes sobre la Universidad Venezolana."

27. See, for example, comments by Puryear, in *Higher Education, Development Assistance, and Repressive Regimes.*

28. Schiefelbein and García-Huidobro, "La Investigación Educacional en América Latina," p. 551.

29. Schoolboys of Barbiana, *Letter to a Teacher.*

30. Clark, "The 'Cooling Out' Function Revisited," pp. 15–41. The discussion of this topic as it relates to Ecuador is presented in note 16.

Bibliography

For those interested in documents that may be difficult to find in American libraries, the number of "Resúmenes Analíticos en Educación (RAE)" is included at the end of each item; the abstract or original can be obtained from the associated centers.

ARENA, E., and C. PALLAN. "La Planeación en las Universidades Mexicanas." Mexico: Subsecretaría de Educación e Investigación Científica, 1979. RAE 1785.

BRIONES, G. "Las Universidades Chilenas en el Modelo de Economía Neo-liberal, 1973–1981." Santiago: PIIE, 1982. RAE 2310.

BRONFENMAJER, G., and R. CASANOVA. "Proposiciónes sobre la Universidad Venezolana: Radicalización Política, Diferención y Polarización Ideologica en un Contexto de Dominación Democrático Burguesa y Capitalismo Dependiente." Caracas: Universidade Venezuela, Escuela de Educacion, 1980. RAE 2043.

BRUNNER, J. J. "Universidad Católica y Cultura Nacional en los Años 60. Los Intelectuales Tradiciónals y Movimento Estudiantil." Santiago: FLASCO, 1981. RAE 2314.

CARAVAJAL, L., et al. "Los Conflictos de la Educación Superior Venezolana. Interpretaciónes y Otendencias (1976–1977)." *Cuadernos de Educacion*, no. 68–69 (1979): 87–132. RAE 1925.

CASTRO, C. MOURA. "Growth, Misunderstanding, and Crisis in Latin American Universities." In *Education and Work: a Symposium*, ed. D. Heyduk. New York, Institute of International Education, 1979. Pp. 35–42.

CASTRO, G., et al. "Imagen de la Universidad de Costa Rica." Universidades de Costa Rica, 1978. RAE 1741.

CASTRO, N. "Algunos Problemas Fundamentales en la Orientación de la Universidad Panameña." *Acción y Reflexión Educativa*, no. 4 (1979): 69–76. RAE 2165.

CLARK, BURTON R. "The 'Cooling Out' Function Revisited." In *Questioning the Community College Role. New Directions of Community Colleges*, 8, no. 4, 1980. San Francisco: Jossey-Bass. Pp. 15–41.

DE BRITTO, L. N., and M. M. DE CARVALHO. "Condicionantes Socioeconómicos dos Estudiantes de Universidade de Bahia." Salvador: UFBA, 1978. RAE 1874.

DÍAZ, E., et al. "Análisis de los Resultados de las Pruebas." Santiago: Servicio de Selección y Registro de Estudiantes, Universidad de Chile, 1979. RAE 1756.

FARRELL, JOE, and ERNESTO SCHIEFELBEIN. "Expanding the Scope of Educational Planning: The Experience of Chile." *Interchange* 5, no. 2 (1974): 18–29. RAE 1288.

FISHER, J. "Factors Associated with College Aspirations and Expectations of Chilean Secondary School Pupils." Ph.D. dissertation, University of California, March, 1972. RAE 54.

GARRETÓN, G. A. "Universidad y Política en los Procesos de Transformación y Reversión en Chile 1967–1977." Santiago: FLASCO, 1978. RAE 2322.

GOMEZ MILLAS, J. "El Problema del Ingreso a la Educación Superior desde el Punto de Vista de la Responsabilidad Social." CPU, Doc. de Trabajo, no. 27. Santiago, 1976. RAE 1874.

GRASSAU, E., and T. SEGURE. "El Rango Ocupado por el Alumno Durante los Estudios Secundarios como Indice de Predicción para los Estudios Universitarios." *Boletin Estadístico de la Universidad de Chile* 5, no. 2 (1969): 18–31.

GUERRA, J. "La Universidad Boliviana en Crisis." La Paz: Los Amigos Del Libro, 1975. RAE 2272.

HIMMEL, E., and S. MALTES. "El Problema de la Admisión y Selección Universitarias 1967–1977." *Anales de la Escuela de Educación*, no. 1. Santiago: Universidad Católica, 1979. Pp. 126–138. RAE 2954.

ICFES. "Historia Estadística de la Educación Colombiana." Bogotá, 1979. RAE 2707.

KLUBITSCHKO, D. El Origen Social de los Estudientes de la Universidad de Buenos Aires. DEALC, proyecto UNESCO/CEPAL/PNUD, 1980. RAE 1965.

_____. "El Cambio de Carrera como Deserción Interna en la Universidad Católica de Chile." Santiago: PIIE, October, 1974.

LEVY, DANIEL C. Higher Education Policy in Authoritarian Regimes: Comparative Perspectives on the Chilean Case. Higher Education Research Group Working Paper, no. 45. New Haven, Conn.: Yale University, May 1980.

_____. University and Government in Mexico: Autonomy in an Authoritarian System. New York: Praeger, 1980.

_____. "Student Politics in Contemporary Latin America." Canadian Journal of Political Science 14 (June 1981): 368–371.

_____. The State and Higher Education in Latin America: Comparing Private and Public Sectors. Chicago: University of Chicago Press, 1985.

MORALES, A. "El Conflicto en las Universidades." In Mundo Universitario, no. 10. Colombia: Boyaca, 1979. Pp. 85–97. RAE 1739.

PALAU, T. "Algunos Aspectos Cuantitativos de la Educación Superior en al Paraguay." Asuncion: CPES, 1978. RAE 1794.

POZO DE RUIZ, C., and ERNESTO SCHIEFELBEIN. "Los Problemas de la Expansión Acelerada el Caso del Desarrolo del Sistema Educaciónal de Ecuador." Estudios Sociales no. 26, Trimestre 4. Santiago: CPU, 1980. Pp. 35–52. RAE 2982.

PREALC. "Educación y Empleo en América Latina." Investigaciónes Sobre Empleo, no. 10. Santiago: ILO, 1978. Pp. 14–15.

PSACHAROPOULOS, GEORGE. Returns to Education: an International Comparison. Amsterdam: Elsevier, 1972.

PURYEAR, JEFFREY M. Higher Education, Development Assistance and Repressive Regimes. New York: Ford Foundation, February, 1983.

RIVAROLA, M. M. "Los Cursos Técnicos de la Universidad Católica, Filial Villarrica. Programa Paraguayo Aleman de Educación, 1979." Pp. 140–146. RAE 1976.

RODRÍGUES, F. "Partidos Políticos y Autonomía Universitaria." Series de Investigaciónes, no. 6, June 1979. Bogotá: Pontificia Universidad Javeriana. RAE 2292.

ROGGI, L. "Universidad y Sociedad en América Latina y Especialmente en Panamá." Acción y Reflexión Educativa, no. 4. Panama: ICASE, 1979. Pp. 63–68. RAE 2170.

SCHIEFELBEIN, ERNESTO. "Cambios en la Functión Educativa de la Universidad." Santiago: CPU, August, 1981.

SCHIEFELBEIN, ERNESTO, and JOE FARRELL. Eight years of Their Lives. Ottawa: International Development Research Center, 1982. RAE 2554.

_____. "Women, Schooling and Work in Chile." Comparative Education Review 24, no. 2, pt. 2 (June 1980): Pp. S160–S179.

SCHIEFELBEIN, ERNESTO, and J. E. GARCÍA-HUIDOBRO. "La Investigación Educacional en América Latina: Situación y Perspectivas." Doc. de Trabajo, no. 3. Santiago: CIDE, 1980.

SCHIEFELBEIN, ERNESTO, and M. C. GROSSI. "Differences Among American and Latin American Premises About Education and Work." In Education and Work: a Symposium, ed. D. Heyduk. New York: Institute of International Education, 1979. Pp. 11–18. (IIE-CHEAR).

Schoolboys of Barbiana. *Letter To a Teacher.* New York: Random House, 1970.

SOLARI, A. "Estudios Sobre Educación y Empleo." *Cuadernos de ILPES,* ser. 11, no. 18 (1973). RAE 223.

SOLARI, A., and R. FRANCO. "Igualidad de Opportunidades y Elitismo en la Universidad Uruguaya." *Revista Latino-Americana de Estudios Educativos* (México) 9, no. 4 (1979): 117–134.

TRUJILLO, J. C. "La Universidad en el Sistema Educacional Ecuatoriano." *Revista de la Universidad Catolica* (Quito) II, no. 2 (1974): 9–44. RAE 2343.

ULLOA, M., et al. "Educación no Formal para Universitarios y Campesinos en Nayarit (México)." In *Revista Latinoamericana de Estudios Educativos* (México) 12, no. 1 (1982): 9–44. RAE 2572.

Universidad Nacional Abierta. "Análisis y Perfiles Ocupaciónales de las Carreras que Offrece la Universidad Abierta." Programa de Investigaciones Unidad de Análisis Ocupaciónal, 1979. RAE 1929.

ZUNINO, L., and C. RODRÍguez. "Sistemas Especiales de Ingreso a la Universidad de Chile." Santiago: Servicio de Selección y Registro de Estudiante, 1981. RAE 2559.

8

Africa

PHILIP FOSTER

Most of the essays in this volume treat the school and the university from a national perspective. Even in Europe, however, it is misleading to assume that educational history is to be written solely in terms of the educational policies and initiatives of the nation-state. In Africa a national perspective is even less compelling, for it is a continent whose nation-states are largely the result of the fortuitous consequences of colonial overrule and whose educational policies are still influenced by colonial precedents that were often interregional in origin. In addition, the course of educational development in Africa has often been influenced less by the edicts of the colonial powers and their successors than by economic and social forces that have been exogenous to educational structures. Thus, one can often gain a greater understanding of the reasons for the rapid expansion of schooling in Africa by looking at the characteristics of the occupational structures of these new states than by perusing national educational and manpower plans.

The preceding chapter on Latin America rightly emphasized the dangers of generalizing about educational developments on that diverse continent; in the case of Africa these risks are even greater. In Latin America, at least, it can be argued that there exists a common thread resulting from the shared imposition of Hispanic educational structures and language. In sub-Saharan Africa (I will not consider the Maghrib in this discussion) no common colonial tradition exists; four major colonial powers have each left their mark on educational development. In very gross terms, however, sub-Saharan states can be distinguished from one another in three major ways.

The first is the level of development of formal educational systems. Even in the simplest quantitative terms, the range of variation is just as great as that in Latin America, although average levels of formal education are substantially lower than in the latter. Africa still remains, by far, the least educated of all the continents. Less commonly known is that intranational variations in educational enrollments are typically greater than international disparities. Indeed, vast inequalities in educational provision within nations have frequently generated serious internal political conflict during the postcolonial era.

Second, the earlier colonial regimes have left their imprint on the educational histories of the new African states. These are still manifest in differing educational structures and curricula described in a substantial descriptive literature. Less attention has been paid to the various strategies adopted by the colonial powers with respect to the finance and support of education. To be sure, all colonial regimes were parsimonious in educational expenditures, which normally stood at some 3 to 5 percent of national budgets (as opposed to 20 to 25 percent today). However, the British practice of allowing substantial mission initiatives in schooling, while providing "topping-up" grants-in-aid to voluntary agencies, produced, on the average, a greater quantitative diffusion of schooling than occurred in the francophonic territories, where mission activities were frequently regarded with some suspicion by government, and where the expansion of education depended more heavily on limited, direct state financing and the principle of free education.

Third, the reaction of African peoples themselves to the phenomenon of Western education has been extremely variable. With one major exception (Somalia), sub-Saharan nations are pluralistic aggregations of ethnic groups distinguished by language, culture, and social structure. It is therefore not surprising that various minorities have often reacted substantially differently to the intrusion and expansion of formal schooling.[1] With few notable exceptions, this aspect of African educational history has been rather neglected; most future work on this theme will very likely be conducted by a generation of African scholars more equipped to deal with the complexities of earlier cultural interaction.

For these reasons, anyone who tries to treat even such a limited theme as the relation between secondary and higher education in sub-Saharan Africa from a continental perspective cannot do justice to the nuances and complexities of educational development. This chapter will therefore focus on the anglophonic states, while not entirely ignoring some useful contrasts to be drawn between these and the francophonic nations.

Table 8.1 gives a general quantitative picture of educational development in anglophonic Africa, though the figures must be treated with substantial reservation; a 10 percent margin of error is a minimal cautionary estimate for the primary level. Moreover, owing to substantial rates of wastage throughout the system, data of this kind tend to underestimate the diffusion of primary schooling. Statistics may show a 50 percent enrollment rate for an age cohort at any one point in time even though some 80 or 90 percent of that cohort may have experienced some schooling at one time or other. Further, in a country such as Nigeria, national primary enrollments stand at a putative 62 percent, but these range from almost 100 percent in sections of the littoral to well below 20 percent in portions of the north.

More pertinent to our discussion are the data on secondary- and tertiary-level enrollments. The secondary estimates in table 8.1 are probably on the high side, and direct comparisons can be very misleading. Thus, although Ghana is outstanding in its provision of postprimary schooling, it must be recognized that the vast majority of students at this level are enrolled in nonselective middle schools that represent an upward extension of the basic primary school system. By contrast, the Tanzanian statistics record only the 4 percent of the age cohort who are enrolled in academically selective secondary schools. It is demonstrable that the relationship between primary and secondary enrollments is far from linear. To note the extreme cases, Gambia claims only 37 percent of the relevant age cohort at primary school, with 12 percent of the appropriate cohort in secondary institutions, whereas in Zimbabwe, with almost full primary enrollment, only 9 percent of the relevant age group are in secondary schools.

The materials on tertiary enrollments are striking. Only in tiny Swaziland do they reach 3 percent of the age cohort, while most territories still hover at or below the 1 percent level. Yet these statistics alone do little justice to the incredibly explosive growth in universities and secondary schools in sub-Saharan Africa, particularly the anglophonic areas, over the last two or three decades. Table 8.1 shows the substantial increase in secondary provision but understates the realities of university growth. From the perspective of the developed world, a cohort representation of approximately 1 or 2 percent may look derisory, but this represents a fifteenfold expansion in tertiary enrollments over the three decades 1950–1980. University education in all of sub-Saharan Africa is extremely high-cost education relative to gross domestic product per capita, and this rate of expansion testifies to the immense (if sometimes misguided) efforts of African states to increase their supply of high-level manpower expressed in terms of university outputs.

In short, educational growth in anglophonic Africa parallels but lags behind that of other less developed continents. An explosive period of primary school growth began directly after World War II, and although absolute enrollments continue to rise, the rate of expansion is now beginning to slacken. Rapid expansion at lower levels places immense pressures on the intermediate sector, resulting in substantial rates of expansion in secondary schooling, which still show little sign of tapering off. At present, expanding secondary outputs are making their presence

TABLE 8.1

EDUCATIONAL ENROLLMENTS IN ANGLOPHONIC AFRICA

Country*	Primary school enrollments as percentage of age group		Secondary school enrollments as percentage of age group		Number enrolled in higher education as percentage of population	
	1960	1978	1960	1978	1960	1978
Botswana	42	89	1	20		
Gambia	14	37	3	12		
Ghana	38	71	5	32	(.)**	1
Kenya	47	99	2	18	(.)	1
Lesotho	83	100	3	17	(.)	(.)
Malawi		59	1	4		(.)
Nigeria	36	62	4	13	(.)	1
Sierra Leone	23	37	2	12	(.)	1
Sudan	25	50	3	16	(.)	2
Swaziland	58	92	5	32		3
Tanzania	25	70	2	4		(.)
Uganda	49	50	3	5	(.)	1
Zambia	42	98	2	16		2
Zimbabwe	96	97	6	9	(.)	(.)

SOURCE: The World Bank, *Accelerated Development in Sub-Saharan Africa*, Washington, D.C., 1981, p. 181.

*The special situation prevailing in The Republic of South Africa excludes it from this discussion. Mauritius is conventionally included in sub-Saharan statistics for purposes of convenience rather than substance, and thus it is omitted. The Sudan was never formally a British colony nor protectorate; it has, however, been included for comparative purposes.
**(.) is equal to less than 1 percent.

felt at the doors of highly selective and, for the most part, academically very demanding universities.

As elsewhere, the problem of allocation of resources to educational systems as a whole and to sectors within them becomes an essentially political issue. Consequently, what we might term the threshold of political sensitivity tends to move upward through the educational system. Thus, in the earlier wave of post–World War II expansion, differential access to primary schooling between regions and ethnic groups became the focus of political conflict. Once demand at this level was partly met, however, the question of provision of postprimary schooling became salient. Although such schooling is still in short supply relative to demand, most African anglophonic states have undertaken substantial efforts to increase rates of access over the last two decades. Such efforts have, predictably, stimulated the demand for tertiary education. But, paradoxically, while university enrollments have risen dramatically in absolute terms, the proportion of students who complete secondary schooling and then proceed to other studies has actually dropped in some areas. The currently dominant issue in African educational politics therefore hinges increasingly on the articulation between postprimary systems, with their rapidly expanding output, and universities and other tertiary institutions. Conflict centers not only on rate of access to the tertiary sector but also on modes of selection and the character and content of higher education itself.

This pattern of explosive growth of educational demand in all of sub-Saharan Africa is essentially economic in origin. As a result of the character of the emerging occupational structures of African states and the massive levels of public subsidy of education, private rates of return to levels of schooling are remarkably high, both in relation to those found in the developed nations and to those in most other areas of the less developed world.[2] As long as this is true, demand can be expected to escalate. Yet a dilemma faces most African regimes because of the disparity between private and social rates of return to different levels of formal education. A gap exists between national policies designed to maximize rates of economic development and the aspirations of African consumers of education. Most governments attach great importance to the role of educational investment as a stimulant to economic development. From the perspective of social rates of return, it can be cogently argued that regimes would do well to continue to emphasize the expansion of primary schooling in view of its low cost and consequently substantial benefits. In view of its lower social rate of return, governments would be well advised to be cautious in expanding the provision of tertiary education. Such education is enormously expensive, and the ratio of university to primary school costs per capita is frequently about 90 to 1. At the same time, since governments have pledged themselves to the provision of free places at the tertiary level, resting upon substantial public subsidy, private rates of return to this level are artificially inflated. The consequence of such policies has been to enormously increase the volume of demand for higher education. The political conflict over access to higher education, resulting from its substantial income rewards, is thus exacerbated by the efforts of governments to provide uniformly free tertiary education in the pursuit of "social equity."

The preceding observations hold true for much of sub-Saharan Africa irrespective of colonial traditions and current level of educational development. Yet it is also apparent that general and common processes are manifested in varying structural and institutional arrangements in differing regions. Let us therefore turn to anglophonic Africa as a useful unit of analysis, a case study in which common educational issues can be seen in terms of a particular historical context.

The Development of Secondary and Higher Education in the Colonial Period

A salient characteristic of British colonial policy was its initial reluctance to accord the state a primary role in the provision of education. This did not necessarily reflect an opposition to schooling for Africans, except in such territories as Kenya and Rhodesia (now Zimbabwe), where the presence of a substantial and powerful white settler population retarded expansion; it was based on the nineteenth-century belief, also powerful with regard to the home country itself, that the development of schools was best left in the hands of voluntary agencies.

The history of formal education in British Africa is partly an account of how these earlier laissez-faire policies were slowly eroded and how colonial governments assumed greater responsibility for educational provision. Initially, this took the form of limited grants-in-aid to voluntary-agency schools able to meet certain minimal standards, but subsequently, the government took responsibility for the payment of teacher salaries, the extension of capital grants, the provision of teacher training facilities, and in some few cases, the creation of entirely state supported institutions at the primary and secondary level. By the end of the colonial period, the balance had swung from mission to state; and while the role of the voluntary agencies was still substantial, the pace and nature of educational expansion was increasingly dictated by colonial governments, which were increasingly obliged to respond to mounting African demand for schooling. Postcolonial educational history records how newly independent African governments have tried to meet this demand while incorporating voluntary-agency schools into a more comprehensive, national, publicly financed system of education.

Initially, British authorities were hardly concerned with postprimary schooling. Where education was in short supply, the provision of basic literacy and numeracy and a modicum of religious knowledge were the most that could be hoped for, although there was lively debate in some territories concerning the medium of instruction and the desirability of introducing agriculture and technical-vocational subjects into the primary school curriculum.

By default, then, the development of secondary education, such as it was, rested largely with mission initiatives—largely but not entirely, since recent historical research has shown the extent to which African pressure for education beyond the primary level was sometimes significant and decisive. This obviously was not the case in those areas where primary schooling was sparse and an articulate African opinion did not exist. Yet on the littoral of West Africa, particularly in Lagos and the then Gold Coast, schools had existed for a long enough time to produce, by the late nineteenth century, a highly articulate, if tiny, minority of Africans who had occasionally pursued further studies in England and had subsequently become men of substance in law and commerce. This minority was insistent in its demand for the development of postprimary schooling and, more daringly, urged the creation of a West African university.[3] Even in East and Central Africa with its far shorter history of Western schooling, ethnic minorities who had obtained an early lead in access to education, such as the Baganda of Uganda and the Gikuyu of Kenya, early perceived the significance of the economic advantage to be derived from postprimary schooling. In the latter case the Gikuyu had been able, through their own initiatives, to develop primary education in partial defiance of a colonial regime still influenced by the opposition of white settlers to schools for Africans.

Mission attitudes to secondary education were varied, although they were usually favorable. Clearly, the voluntary agencies saw that Africans needed to be educated beyond the level of the village catechist if proselytization was to proceed; but they also were not unsympathetic to African aspirations, which led them, in some instances, to confrontation with more reluctant colonial administrators.

Finally, governments themselves were persuaded to assist or directly provide secondary education as the result of growing pressure and self-interest. Colonial regimes increasingly required limited cohorts of educated Africans to man the intermediate and lower levels of local administrations, and for this purpose the primary school graduate was progressively less adequate. Moreover, in some cases, attempts to fuse colonial regimes with traditional authority structures resulted in the creation of special postprimary schools for the sons of chiefs or traditional notables; in this way it was hoped that the scions of "noble houses" could be trained to attachment to the British interest. Such efforts did not usually achieve their purpose, however, and these institutions either disappeared or began to enroll a wider spectrum of the African population.

Thus, very slowly, a tiny cluster of secondary schools emerged, superimposed upon an expanding primary school system of variable quality. Throughout the colonial period these institutions absorbed less than 1 percent of the relevant age cohort. Although most were grant-aided institutions, in nearly every territory there was one or more government school entirely financed from public sources. Entry to these schools was intensely selective, usually based on academic performance. Their geographical distribution was limited, and as they tended to be concentrated in zones of earlier mission enterprise, they recruited disproportionately from ethnic groups who had already attained a lead in Western schooling. The most outstanding institutions, however, recruited on a colony-wide basis; thus, the emerging educated elites of British Africa took on an interethnic character.

Most important, in their curriculum these institutions progressively took on the characteristics of the British grammar school. To be sure, throughout the colonial period there was much discussion about the need to adapt secondary schooling to the realities of the African environment. Such educational clichés, often revolving around the desirability of introducing agriculture into the curriculum, were inadequate, for they ignored two crucial issues. First, they failed to perceive that occupational opportunities in the emerging modern sector of colonial economies were largely clerical and administrative in nature, and an academic education was seen to be well suited for access to such jobs by British administrators and Africans alike. Second, in the virtual absence of university or other tertiary training in the colonies, the limited but growing number of Africans who aspired to such education were obliged to seek it in England. For this purpose qualifications acceptable to British universities were required. Thus, long before the great surge to independence in the 1960s, all secondary schools prepared pupils for one of the school-certificate examinations conducted by examining bodies set up by English universities (particularly the Oxford and Cambridge syndicate). A sufficiently good pass in such examinations also carried exemption from the matriculation examinations of British universities and for a while enabled access to those institutions.

The situation thus largely replicated that in England: the school-certificate examination not only demonstrated successful completion of a secondary school program but adequate performance also qualified a student for university access. This is not to suggest that African secondary curricula were carbon copies of those prevailing in Britain, for the university syndicates made efforts to modify examination content to perceived local needs, particularly in the area of social studies (more accurately, history and geography). Nevertheless, there can be no doubt that the character of secondary education in British colonial Africa was overwhelmingly influenced by the requirements of the English tertiary sector even though only a small number of Africans ever entered it. During this period, then, it was the university that progressively influenced the school, a situation that has continued largely throughout the postcolonial era.

From the mid-nineteenth century onward, a tiny trickle of West Africans obtained entry to British universities, and by the 1930s these were joined by a few other aspirants from British East and Central Africa. Although we have referred earlier to the virtual absence of higher education in British Africa before World War II, it is true that a limited provision of postsecondary education did exist. Since 1876, the students of tiny Fourah Bay College in Sierra Leone had been allowed to sit for degrees in theology and humanities in affiliation with Durham University. Postsecondary education was also available in limited form in, for example, the Gold Coast and Uganda, but no institutions could claim full university status. The real development of universities in British Africa was essentially a post–World War II phenomenon stemming from the recommendations of the *Report of the Commission on Higher Education in the Colonies* (the Asquith Report) of 1944–1945 and other commissions or reports that originated in Africa.[4] The formal history of the evolution of universities in British, and now anglophonic, Africa from that date until the late sixties has been fully documented elsewhere.[5] For our purposes, it is sufficient merely to indicate certain basic characteristics of these institutions as they were conceived by their original architects.

First, they were to be elite institutions. Obviously, they were so designated not in terms of the social or ethnic provenance of their students but in the sense that they were to remain small (with some few thousand students at most) and that access to them was to be based on academic merit as measured by outstanding performance on the General School Certificate Examination. The British, recognizing the imminence of self-government, were anxious that the colonial guardians be succeeded by Africans who would be their equals in quality. Although the estimation of manpower needs only subsequently became fashionable, it is fair to say that the British conceived that requirements in administration, agriculture, and medicine, for example, could be met by a relatively tiny number of highly trained Africans. Mass higher education was not only impossible but, in terms of British notions of quality, quite unthinkable.

The geographical corollary of such elitism was that tertiary institutions were to be planned on an interregional, rather than an individual colonial, basis. For example, it was conceived that one institution based in Nigeria (subsequently decided upon as Ibadan) would be generally sufficient to meet the needs of the four territories of Nigeria, the then Gold Coast, Sierra Leone, and The Gambia; and in East Africa, a University College at Makerere, Uganda, would meet the requirements not only of Uganda but also of Kenya and Tanganyika.

Second, and of crucial importance, was that these new universities were to enter into a special relationship with the University of London, and African graduates were to receive London degrees. A great deal of debate, some of it acrimonious, has subsequently centered upon the intent of this arrangement.[6] For some it has been seen as an attempt to reproduce British higher education in its entirety in Africa, with all the consequent charges of cultural imperialism and failure to develop truly indigenous universities. Actually, such statements are rather vacuous. What is evident is that the structure of London degrees was maintained, but substantial efforts were made, on the basis of joint consultation, to progressively adapt course content to perceived local needs and realities. Even during the earliest period, there were marked differences between London and African university curricula, and these were progressively increased as time went on. What was important, and in this informed British and educated African opinion were solidly united, was that the degrees had to be comparable in quality to those of Great Britain. The critics of this view have simply failed to recognize its immense symbolic importance to Africans at that time. Recommendations concerning the course that African universities might have taken misinterpret the nature of the colonial situation and the perceptivity of Africans themselves. Developments away from British precedents became possible only in the postcolonial era.

Finally, it was envisaged that the new institutions, while they remained in a particular relationship with the University of London, would be termed *university colleges*. Once soundly established as viable institutions, however, the umbilical cord would be severed, and they would emerge as entirely independent institutions with power to examine for and award their own degrees. The evolutionary policies thus envisaged constituted the higher education analog of classical British notions of the progressive move from political dependence to self-government and independence.

This represents an overview of the relationships that prevailed between secondary and higher education in British colonial Africa. Nevertheless, one element is lacking. Although teacher training institutions provided an ostensibly postprimary education, they were never formally regarded as part of the secondary system, since the term *secondary* was applied to institutions whose students prepared for the General School Certificate Examination. Teacher training colleges, however, provided courses of variable length and quality for graduates of African primary schools who, upon the award of a certificate, returned to those primary schools as teachers. To all intents and purposes, teacher training remained a closed cycle unarticulated with the world of secondary and higher education, substantially paralleling the situation that prevailed in Britain itself until the close of the nineteenth century. In contrast to francophonic Africa, teacher training was not seen as an integral part of a secondary cycle. To be sure, a few African teachers, often by dint of private effort, ultimately gained undergraduate status, and the new university colleges sometimes provided one-year associateship courses for the upgrading of experienced African primary school teachers. However, teacher training remained very much the stepchild of the postprimary sector. By contrast, secondary schools were manned almost entirely by expatriate university graduates supplemented by a small number of Africans who either held British university degrees or who had recently graduated from the new African university colleges.

Given the extremely constricted nature of the educational structure and the type of examination system that emerged, there was little likelihood that secondary schools would have any influence on universities in the colonial era. Rather, the opposite was the case. Long before Western-style universities existed on the continent, the status of African secondary schools was increasingly dependent on the success of their students in the General School Certificate examinations administered by syndicates based at British universities. The power of this certificate was immense since it provided not only evidence of successful completion of terminal secondary studies but also constituted a university entrance qualification. It was the gatekeeper to economic reward and occupational success. The creation of university colleges in situ did not alter this situation, since the examination system remained intact. Unquestionably, examination syndicates sometimes modified examination curricula in the light of local needs, but it was simply too much to expect the secondary school tail to wag the tertiary dog.

The Postcolonial Experience

Understandably, the elites of independent African nations have questioned the legitimacy of many institutional forms created during the colonial period. This is particularly evident in anglophonic Africa, where the legacy of multiparty parliamentary regimes has been largely replaced by the apparatus of the one-party state. This divergence, paradoxically, has not occurred in education. Despite much revolutionary rhetoric, the institutions and structures created by colonial regimes at the secondary and university levels have commanded a remarkable degree of legitimacy in the postcolonial period. The skeptic might observe that the cast of characters has changed but the play is essentially the same; in some respects postcolonial educational structures have become more like British ones since independence.

The real area of dissent between colonial regimes and their successors has focused on the question of quantitative provision and educational opportunity. We have seen that the earlier growth of schooling resulted in massive regional and ethnic inequalities in access and that even in the educationally most advanced areas popular demand far outstripped supply by the end of the colonial period. African governments have moved with great resolution to reduce such imparities, although they remain substantial. Indeed, a considerable body of empirical research demonstrates that very marked inequalities exist in access to secondary and higher education along regional, urban-rural, ethnic, and increasingly socioeconomic lines.[7] At intermediate levels of educational development, even massive increases in educational provision do not diminish such imparities very rapidly; currently in anglophonic Africa, less than 10 percent of the age cohort proceeds to postprimary schooling. More strikingly, total tertiary enrollments are less than 100,000 in a population that now exceeds 200 million. Given quantitative constraints and current methods of educational selection, parity of access in regional, ethnic, or social terms is quite impossible.

Methods of educational selection and the underlying institutional arrangements have not changed dramatically since colonial times, although university development has diverged, in some respects, from initial plans. The type of interregional provision envisaged by the Asquith Report foundered very early on the rocks of nationalism. In West Africa the "Ibadan plan" met with opposition within the then Gold Coast, and subsequently a separate university college was established there. Similarly, in East Africa, the "Makerere emphasis" was resisted in Kenya and Tanganyika, and ultimately interregional arrangements broke down with the establishment of separate higher institutions in each territory. Even the idea of one university per new nation was rapidly eroded in West Africa. In postindependence Ghana the original university college at Legon was supplemented by new ones in Kumasi and Cape Coast. In Nigeria the original monopoly of the older federal university college at Ibadan was broken by the establishment of institutions in the old constitutional regions of the east, west, and north. Indeed, local pressures in Nigeria, increased by the existence of substantial oil revenues, are now likely to lead to the creation of new universities in each of the nineteen new states of that nation. Such proliferation was not characteristic of the anglophonic states of East and Central Africa, where one national university remains substantially the rule, although enrollments have grown.

Expansion or proliferation has been everywhere accompanied by educational autonomy. Many of the newly created universities have never had the London connection envisaged by the Asquith Report; they have been independent institutions since their inception. The older Asquith university colleges have severed their former tutelary relationship with London University far more rapidly than was originally envisioned and have now emerged as full-fledged independent African universities with power to regulate their own intake patterns, degree structures, curricula, and examination procedures. Despite this, many universities have maintained the peculiarly British institution of the external examiner, whereby senior academics from Britain or, increasingly, from other African universities, are invited to scrutinize curricula, examination papers, and student performance in order to confirm that appropriate international academic standards are maintained. Such "neocolonialist" practices may draw a sneer in some quarters, but they testify to the intense pride of most African nations in their universities and to their desire to remain on the academic gold standard. Many American graduate schools can testify that this standard has been maintained in view of the high quality of students who have undertaken undergraduate training in African universities.

How do these few highly selective and academically demanding institutions articulate with lower levels of the system? To understand this let us describe a typical system while recognizing that local variations exist and that we do some injustice to national particularities.

Everywhere, expanding primary school systems are characterized by high rates of wastage and dropout. The typical 60 or 70 percent of students who complete the primary school course, which varies from six to eight grades, are faced by a terminal test usually designated the Primary School Leaving Examination (PLE). A pass in this examination not only signifies successful completion of the primary school program but also constitutes, for the small minority who perform exceedingly well, a ticket for entry to secondary school. Earlier, colonial schools often held their own entry examinations, but now access is governed by performance in these centrally administered, standardized examinations held on an annual basis. Secondary school entry is obtained through achievement in a national *concours* by means of which a variable percentage of top performers are selected to match the number of available places in the schools. Typically, these examinations test competence in English, mathematics, and general knowledge, and results are sometimes supplemented by school records and teacher assessment. Usually candidates are required to list three secondary schools of their choice; the most prestigious national institutions are therefore able to select the cream of the crop.

The vast majority of children, even if they pass the PLE, are not selected for secondary school. Most proceed directly to employment (or more accurately unemployment) in the modern sector of local economies, while others repeat the final grade of primary school to resit the examination in the hope of ultimate success. Some states have attempted to provide a form of nonselective postprimary schooling for students who wish to continue their education. Ghana has been the leader in this development, with a substantial provision of middle schools that offer up to four years of schooling for nonselected students. Other nations have followed suit. Usually such institutions attempt to provide some measure of vocational training for pupils. These schools are terminal in nature and are not linked to the universities. If a student does not obtain entry to conventional secondary school, the chances of university entry are virtually nil.

So great has been the frustration of parents and students that in some countries the demand for secondary education has been met by the development of private or proprietary secondary schools run by educational entrepreneurs. Fees, not academic ability, enable entry to such schools, and their standards generally are such that very few students are successful in the secondary school leaving examinations, which they are allowed to take along with their more academically able counterparts in the public secondary sector.

What then of the fortunate minority, perhaps only 5 percent of the total age cohort, who have entered the prestigious sector that alone leads to university education? Their experience will differ little from that of their predecessors in the colonial period. Even though curricular modifications have been made, structural changes, for the most part, have continued to parallel British developments.

The schools have made substantial strides in Africanizing the curriculum, particularly in such areas as history, geography, and literature; these developments have been important, although curricula in mathematics and the sciences show scant signs of change. In some nations, such as Tanzania, vocational tracks in science and technology, commerce, and agriculture have been created alongside the more conventional academic program; in practice this often amounts to no more than the curricular window dressing that has occurred in many developed countries in the last few decades. Most African secondary students recognize that their educational and occupational future will depend almost entirely on their performance in a set of higher academic examinations taken at the end of their basic secondary school program. Numerous surveys have shown that students, almost universally, hope to enter the university; a majority, perhaps unrealistically, expect to enter tertiary institutions. As long as this is the case, it will be the universities that call the tune.

African educators may deplore the so-called examination mania, but this is surely a misnomer. The term *mania* suggests that behavior rests upon some irrational perception of reality. African student behavior, however, reflects an all too realistic assessment of the situation. In societies where occupational opportunities are limited and largely confined to the public sector, educational credentials are of overwhelming importance, and subsidized university education commands access to enhanced social mobility. This situation has remained since colonial times; all that has occurred is minimal change in structure.

Recall that in the late colonial period access to university education could be gained through superior performance in one of the General School Certificate examinations administered by British university syndicates. Before the end of the colonial era, it was already recognized that these syndicates would not undertake this function indefinitely. Thus, the education authorities created regional, African based examination councils, which were to become progressively responsible for the administration of secondary school and other examinations with the cooperation of local universities. A West African Examination Council became responsible for the conduct of examinations in Nigeria, Ghana, Sierra Leone, and The Gambia, while a similar East African Council supervised examinations in Kenya, Uganda, and Tanzania. Consequently, autonomy in examination policies was achieved. These international organizations still remain, though not entirely along the lines first established by their founders. The British organizations have not entirely disappeared from the African scene; in Zambia and Zimbabwe, for example, the Secondary School Certificate Examination is still administered by the Cambridge syndicate.

The nature of the examination system did not change with this shift in responsibility; indeed, the structures took on a gradually more British cast. To explain this, some digression concerning postwar developments in England itself is necessary. In Great Britain, although matriculation or matriculation exemption theoretically held out the possibility of university entrance, this qualification became progressively inadequate in the eyes of the universities. Thus, in the immediate post–World War II years, the career of a university-bound student in the state secondary-grammar-school sector progressed along the following lines. A basic five-year secondary program was crowned by success (or not) in the General School Certificate Examination, at which point the vast majority of students proceeded into the labor market. The more talented among them, those who usually aspired to university entry, proceeded to two further years of intensive and specialized study in the sciences, humanities, or social sciences in that peculiarly English institution, the sixth form. This two-year program culminated in the Higher School Certificate Examination, which, once again, became not only a certificate of completion of higher secondary studies but was also acceptable as a qualification for university entry. It should be noted, however, that the relation between this level of education and university access has always differed dramatically from that prevailing in most of continental Europe. Until recently, at least, completion of the *baccalauréat* in France or the *Abitur* in Germany led to mandatory university entrance. In England greater autonomy enabled universities to set their own minimal requirements, with the result that success in the Higher School Certificate Examination did not guarantee university access.

This situation prevailed until the early 1950s, when a series of modifications in the examination system were effected which, in terms of university entrance, have been more cosmetic than real (as is the case with a good deal of so-called educational reform in England). In the older General School and Higher School Certificate examinations, a pass required satisfactory performance in a grouping of subjects. It was thus possible for a candidate to succeed in some papers but fail to gain a certificate by virtue of failure in one or more of the other subjects. This two-tiered, General School and Higher School Certificate system was now replaced by a General Certificate of Education, at the Ordinary and Advanced levels, GCE(O) and GCE(A). Candidates were no longer required to pass a group of subjects to obtain a certificate but were awarded one in those subjects in which they had passed, irrespective of number or curricular topic. Students could add subjects to their certificate as a result of subsequent examination. This certainly provided much more flexibility and a greater degree of student choice, but it must be remembered that the universities were still free to determine what level of success was acceptable to them.

The situation became critical in the 1950s when vastly increased numbers of candidates holding GCE(A) qualifications beat upon the doors of universities whose available places were increasing but slowly. In response, the universities proceeded to ratchet up the minimal GCE(A) requirements for entry in order to match enrollments with places. This pattern prevailed until the period of major university expansion in the 1960s, when excess demand was increasingly sopped up. Thus, while Continental universities wrestled with a similar problem of demand for university places and were obliged to consider unpopular higher *numerus clausus* provisions that undermined the whole logic of the baccalauréat and Abitur traditions, the English universities employed a very handy and flexible device for coping with precisely this very issue.

These developments have profoundly influenced relationships between the schools and the universities in independent anglophonic Africa. We have noted the similarities between African and British secondary schools in the colonial period, but one substantial difference existed: African schools did not possess sixth forms, nor did their pupils sit for a higher-school-certificate examination. These institutions merely provided a basic secondary school course leading to the General School Certificate, with the result that the newly created African universities were obliged to adapt their normal British-inspired, three-year, general- and honors-degree programs to take account of lower standards of entry.

This was usually effected by introducing a preparatory university year before the full three-year degree program, which somewhat resembled the French *année propédeutique*. Students with superior General School Certificate Examination results were recruited directly from secondary school but were required to successfully complete this preparatory year before they were admitted to degree programs. They were thus expected to pursue work, at this level, roughly comparable to that covered by the English sixth forms.

Predictably, this development was opposed by university faculty (expatriate and African alike), who did not envision their function to be conducting secondary school classes. African secondary schools were encouraged to develop sixth forms, and appropriate higher-level school certificates were developed to meet the needs of their students, and more important, those of the universities. Gradually, as the new sixth forms or their equivalents were established, the preparatory year was phased out in most universities, and the latter were once more free to concentrate upon three-year degree programs. Zambia remains one of the few nations that have not developed the sixth form; it continues with a four-year program at the University of Zambia, to which access is obtained by a high pass in a lower-school-certificate examination still administered by the Cambridge syndicate.

What are the lessons to be learned from this recitation of the changes that have occurred at secondary and higher levels of education in anglophonic Africa since the end of the colonial episode? Everywhere there has been massive expansion of education provision, but as absolute levels of enrollment in the secondary sector have risen, pressures upon the universities have increased. This has led to a proliferation of universities in Nigeria and elsewhere, and an increase in the size of intake into lower-status national institutions. Nevertheless, there has been no substantial attempt to restructure the relationships between school and university; the system of selective examinations bequeathed by the British has remained substantially intact.

Where change has occurred at all, it has been toward structural modification along British lines, as, for example, in the introduction of sixth forms and higher-level secondary examinations. When the universities were obliged to inaugurate four-year programs to meet the needs of General School Certificate holders, they were ultimately successful in pushing the preparatory function back into the secondary schools through the creation of sixth forms or upper secondary divisions.

Thus, educational autonomy has not been accomplished by any real degree of rearticulation. Although the selective examinations at all levels are the result of consultation between school authorities and the universities, and although the latter have not been entirely impervious to curricular modifications originating from lower levels, the universities still essentially control the selective system and their influence is exerted downward, even to the requirements of the Primary School Leaving Examination.

The casual observer might be inclined to view this situation as merely the result of educational inertia and slavish adherence to British norms. Nothing could be further from the truth. Existing arrangements persist not through inertia but because they are intimately linked to the economic and occupational realities of these new states. Where occupational opportunities are limited and access to them overwhelmingly determined by educational achievement, the current selective system will prevail. Since the universities command the gateway to the highest economic rewards (which are enhanced by government subsidization), they will continue to dominate lower levels of the educational system even though only a tiny fraction of students ever enter them. This situation is not likely to alter without changes in African economies. Thus far the system commands legitimacy among both the elites and the masses.

Some Comparative Observations

This volume has been largely concerned with the relationships between secondary and higher education in a cluster of northern hemispheric states characterized by differences in size and historic tradition but united in their command of a volume of resources that would be inconceivable in most less developed nations. The struggle for universal primary schooling in wealthy states has long since past, and since World War II, mass secondary schooling has been achieved. The resulting pressure on higher education has led to university expansion and to some rethinking of the pattern of structural articulation between schools and universities. In Africa the link between educational achievement and opportunities for social and occupational mobility has fueled public demand, and reform has been pursued in the interests of greater equality of educational opportunity and higher rates of economic development.

In continental Europe current preoccupations center upon the elaboration of secondary school structures in the effort to break the traditional hegemony of the *lycée* or *gymnasium* and to provide further opportunities for sizable cohorts who have not taken the traditional "royal road" to the university. This has led to overelaborate systems of curricular tracks and emphases, with crossover points between them. These tracks may be linked with the universities through a broader set of alternative entry requirements. Thus, not only the young but also mature adults who missed out on earlier opportunities can be accommodated. As one observer remarked, European educational systems begin to take on the characteristics of wiring diagrams in their complexity. Under these circumstances, secondary and higher educational systems have a degree of reciprocal interaction, and the universities accommodate themselves to pressures emanating from below.

This is certainly not the case in sub-Saharan Africa even though expanding secondary enrollments have put pressure on the universities. In anglophonic Africa, in particular, we are not looking at wiring diagrams but distillation plants. From the mass of raw material that enters the system, a tiny trickle emerges from the universities as a result of wastage or direct selection. This is a structurally very simple system with no opportunities for reentry or reprocessing, a system that is not going to change.

Universal primary education has not been achieved and is not likely to be in a number of states. Sub-Saharan Africa is now entering the period of maximal rates of population expansion from which Latin America is now emerging, and governments will be hard pressed to maintain percentage enrollment levels, let alone increase them substantially. At the same time, they have belatedly recognized the significance of primary education in processes of economic development—in contrast to their earlier preoccupation with the production of high-level manpower—and realize that they must focus their efforts on the provision and, more important, the qualitative improvement of primary schooling.

Under these circumstances it is unlikely that there will be any massive expansion in the proportion of the age cohort entering postprimary schooling, although absolute enrollments will continue to rise. Governments, as we have seen, have attempted to provide some form of postprimary schooling with a nominal vocational bias for those who wish to continue their education but who have not been successful in entering the secondary schools. These alternatives are essentially terminal in nature, however, and no linkage exists nor is likely to exist between them and tertiary institutions. The secondary sector will remain understandably small, and most countries will be doing well to maintain enrollments at a level of 10 percent of the age cohort. In terms of purely economic criteria, there is a case to be made for state provision to remain at this level and to be supplemented by the presence of a small private sector.

Within the secondary schools themselves, it is conceivable that a greater degree of curricular diversification will occur. Some nations are experimenting with the development of more vocationally oriented tracks that will align secondary school graduates more directly with the labor market. But most students, statistical probabilities to the contrary, see themselves as university bound, and higher examination performance remains the key to entry. Moreover, curricular diversification, however desirable in itself, requires expansion and upgrading of the secondary school teaching force, which will not be easy given resource constraints.

There is no compelling reason to suppose that the structural linkages between schools and universities will be modified. Unquestionably, the universities are, and will be, under pressure to increase their intake; this will involve quantitative expansion, not the qualitative transformation of school-university relationships. Even if the African universities adhere to the conventional criteria of access they now employ, there will be, for the foreseeable future, a massive increase in the absolute numbers of students who can meet these criteria. This was precisely the point made by the 1961 Robbins Commission in England when it argued for increased university provision on the grounds that expanded secondary schooling had so swollen the number of candidates eligible on the basis of GCE(A) results that places could be massively increased without any fall in standards or changes in the notion of what constituted a proper university education. Expansion then went ahead without any real transformation of the relationship between lower and higher levels.

The universities of anglophonic Africa are in much the same position. The pool of talent as measured by conventional examination success is still growing, and they are thus under pressure to increase their intake but are not under any corresponding obligation to change their selection procedures. The converse of this situation obtains increasingly in the United States, where the responsiveness of universities rests partly on the fact that many are experiencing stable or declining enrollments and are already recruiting students who cannot meet the standards of conventional university performance. The universities are thus influenced by the schools whether they like it or not, although their vulnerability is rationalized by educational pieties such as democratization.

The crisis of the African universities centers on how they can meet demand, since it is apparent that governments pressure them to do so. Nigeria is fortunate because the existence of oil revenues has made the proliferation of universities possible, but other countries have not been so lucky, and the options open to them are limited. First, following earlier British precedent, they can ratchet up minimal requirements to match qualified applicants to places; doubtless such tactics commend themselves to university faculty, and they can be more subtly implemented than an overt numerus clausus. However, relationships between the universities and many governments have deteriorated in recent years, and it is unlikely that the latter will accept this as the sole policy alternative.[8] Second, a decline in faculty-student ratios can occur, and there is certainly room for change in this direction. Until recently, staffing ratios in anglophonic Africa have been superior to those prevailing in most developed nations. Unquestionably, such economies of scale could lead to university expansion, although this would be more difficult in science and technology, fields that require substantial capital inputs. Even a doubling of enrollment still implies a tiny university sector catering to 1 or 2 percent of the age cohort.

For reasons suggested earlier, African governments cannot be expected to increase their absolute level of investment in university training. Frequently, a quarter of total educational expenditures goes toward funding universities whose student bodies constitute less than 5 percent of aggregate educational enrollments, and there is a limit to this kind of largesse. For political reasons, usually student opposition, other financial options, such as the introduction of student loans, the levying of graduate education taxes, or even the imposition of fees in some quarters, seem to be foreclosed to governments. Under such a crushing burden, it is hardly surprising that African educational planners are not disposed to discuss the niceties of the relationship between the secondary and tertiary sectors which currently preoccupy their counterparts in the developed nations. Their educational agenda is different but no less compelling.

Notes

1. For two excellent examples of comparative analysis along these lines, see Kay, "Early Educational Development in East Africa," and Asiwaju, "Formal Education in Western Yorubaland, 1889–1960." The first documents the reactions of two closely related African groups which were differentiated in terms of some aspects of their social structure and culture to similar mission influence. The second deals with the differential response of a culturally and structurally homogeneous people to two distinct colonial systems.

2. See Psacharopoulos, "Returns to Education," particularly pp. 326–329.

3. Notable in this effort were James A. B. Horton, Edward W. Blyden, and J. E. Casely Hayford.

4. For a complete list of official sources see Ashby, *Universities*, pp. 531–534.

5. Lord Ashby's major work remains the most completely documented account of the evolution of higher education in Africa at least until the mid-1960s. It must be noted, however, that the interpretation he places upon events remains controversial.

6. See, for example, the comments of Carr-Saunders in "Britain and Universities in Africa."

7. For a review and bibliography of this literature, see Foster, "Education and Social Inequality in Sub-Saharan Africa."

8. The changing relations between universities and government in sub-Saharan Africa and the controversy over funding are treated in Foster, "False and Real Problems of African Universities."

Bibliography

ASHBY, ERIC. *Universities: British, Indian, African*. Cambridge: Harvard University Press, 1966.

ASIWAJU, A. I. "Formal Education in Western Yorubaland, 1889–1960: A Comparison of the French and British Colonial Systems," *Comparative Education Review* 19 (1975): 434–450.

BLYDEN, EDWARD W. *The West African University: Correspondence Between Edward W. Blyden and His Excellency, J. Pope-Hennessy*. Freetown: Negro University Press, 1872.

CARR-SAUNDERS, A. M. "Britain and Universities in Africa," *Universities Quarterly* XIX (1965): 227–239.

CASELY HAYFORD, J. E. *Ethiopia Unbound: Studies in Race Emancipation*, London, 1911.

FOSTER, PHILIP. "False and Real Problems of African Universities," *Minerva* XIII (1975): 466–478.

———— . "Education and Social Inequality in Sub-Saharan Africa," *Journal of Modern African Studies* 18 (1980): 201–236.

Great Britain. *Report on Higher Education in the Colonies, 1944–45*. Cmd. 6647, London H.M.S.O., 1945. (The Asquith Report.)

———— . *Higher Education: Report of the Committee Appointed by the Prime Minister Under the Chairmanship of Lord Robbins 1961–63*. Cmd. 2154, London H.M.S.O., 1963.

KAY, STAFFORD. "Early Educational Development in East Africa: A Case Study," *Comparative Education Review* 23 (1979): 66–81.

PSACHAROPOULOS, GEORGE. "Returns to Education: An Updated International Comparison," *Comparative Education* 17 (1981): 321–341.

9

The United States

CAROL STOCKING

FOR MUCH OF ITS HISTORY, the American educational system has been a focus of public attention. Public pressure has vacillated over time between concern for equity and concern for excellence. Although these two values are often viewed as opposing pressures, whether they are necessarily so remains open to investigation. Clearly, as goals for education they have competed sharply for resources and for priority on the national agenda.

The decade of the sixties opened on a keynote of excellence, launched by Sputnik. High schools were closely examined, federal dollars were poured into mathematics, science, and foreign-language education, in part to regain purportedly lost international status. In the 1980s excellence is again the key word: high schools are being closely examined (a 1983 conference brought together representatives of two dozen national high school studies and projects then underway), federal dollars are being poured into mathematics and science education, international status is again supposedly at risk. Between these calls to excellence there has been, in the past two decades, a dramatic and quite sustained push for equity that has had an important, measurable impact on both secondary and higher education.

In this chapter these two levels of education will be examined with a view describing the effects upon them of emphasizing equity or excellence. I will also explore mediating factors between schools and colleges during this period, particularly the changing role of the federal government; look at some functions of indistinct areas between secondary schools and colleges which came about as an accommodation to pressures for equity and excellence; and examine the emerging boundary-defining role of standardized testing. Finally, I shall briefly review the traditional paths of influence between schools and colleges and try to bring the listing of relationships up to date.

The Secondary Education System

The secondary education system has both public and private sectors. In 1981 there were about 24,000 public secondary schools in 15,600 local school districts. The public sector is supported by funds from local, state, and federal sources. During the past two decades the contribution to the public schools of each of these levels of government has shifted significantly. In 1960 local sources provided 56 percent of public school funds; by 1980 the local contribution was reduced to 43 percent.[1] Concurrently, the notion of local control of the schools, long a magical concept, has been expanded to include state influence. The antonym of local control is now federal control.

There are also about 5,600 private secondary schools. The ratio of the number of private to public high schools has remained essentially unchanged over the past two decades. Since, on the average, private high schools are much smaller than public ones, about 90 percent of secondary students are in public schools. This proportion too has remained relatively constant for the last twenty years. Sporadic development of private (segregated) academies and of fundamentalist Christian schools have occurred in this period, and federal initiatives to provide tuition tax credits for parents of private school students also have been in evidence. This, and prayer in the schools, have been top education priorities of the current administration.

In the year in which the cabinet-level Department of Education was established in the United States (1979), the federal government did not have a complete listing of public and private secondary schools in the nation. State departments of education had public school lists of various kinds; these, depending on the state, were variously inclusive and variously available to the federal government.

The private school universe is far more diverse than the public one and is only partially unified by associations. For example, not all Catholic schools belong to the National Catholic Educational Association; only a subset of independent schools is included in the National Association of Independent Schools, and so on. Many private schools are ephemeral. Groups of private schools were founded by persons explicitly wishing to avoid involvement with the federal government. For these reasons, statements about the number of private secondary schools in the United States are always estimates. In 1980 serious sampling statisticians considered searching for unlisted private schools by hiring people in selected areas to drive around looking for them, so that a more accurate estimate could be made of the total number of such schools in the nation.

During the sixties and seventies, the post–World War II baby-boom generation entered elementary school, high school, and college. These large birth cohorts and the simultaneously increasing proportions of secondary and college attendance made this a period of remarkable institutional expansion. After the peak birth year (1961), births dropped sharply; enrollments declined in elementary schools in the seventies and began to decline in secondary schools after 1975.

Secondary education is usually defined as grades nine through twelve but sometimes as grades ten through twelve. Legal school-leaving age is also somewhat variously defined; it is usually sixteen, but the range is from thirteen, in one state, to eighteen.

There is a certain amount of curricular specialization among public high schools. Some are vocational, some are specialized magnet schools, some are schools of performing arts, and so on. However, about 90 percent of all high schools are comprehensive, that is, they provide more than one curriculum for students. In 1982 about 38 percent of all public school seniors were in academic, 24 percent in vocational, and 36 percent in general programs. Some students reported that they selected a program after consultation with teachers, counselors, family, or friends; others (about 40 percent) reported they were assigned to a program. Placement in a secondary school program has long-lasting implications; in 1980, 86 percent of first-time college entrants were from academic programs. Vocational students tend to have smooth transitions to post-high-school careers. Students in general programs usually do not get sufficient instruction to meet entrance requirements at four-year colleges, or at a program planned to provide an adequate terminal degree, nor do they receive any significant vocational training.

Beginning in the 1960s federal programs in secondary schools provided additional funds for the economically disadvantaged and for students with limited English, students in desegregating schools, students with handicaps, and so on.

In 1980, 74 percent of the age cohort (defined as students who entered fifth grade in 1972) graduated from high school. Virtually all students who entered the fifth grade continued to secondary school. In 1960, 62 percent of the age cohort that entered fifth grade in 1952 graduated from secondary school. Since about 90 percent of that group entered secondary school, the retention rate has increased from about 56 percent to 74 percent in the past two decades.[2]

Although a higher proportion of students complete secondary school, research done in 1975 indicated that about 12 percent of 17-year-old high school students were "grossly illiterate, unable to comprehend and respond to very simple instructions."[3] Some argue that state funding, which is based on the number of students enrolled in high school, and community pressure to prevent students from dropping out of high school to enter the already flooded youth labor market, have generated a situation in which a major subset of students is kept in school in undemanding programs and allowed to graduate without academic effort. Seventy-one percent of high school seniors in 1982 reported spending less than five hours a week on homework. Only a tiny proportion of students (7 percent) report getting poor marks in high school (Cs and Ds) or below. Although it is true that not all students have been successfully enlisted in the education enterprise, there are indications that among younger children from low socioeconomic backgrounds, federally funded preschool and elementary school programs have improved reading and other test scores; these students may arrive in high school prepared for it.

Recently, and dramatically, attention has been directed to a relatively long-term (twenty-year) decline at the top of the test-score distribution. In the view of some, too much effort has been based on notions of equity. They urge redirection of attention and resources to the search for excellence.

The Higher Education System

Public and private sectors also comprise the higher education system in the United States. Although more than half (54 percent) of the institutions of higher education are private, they enroll only about one-fifth of the students. The proportion of students enrolled in private colleges has declined from about 40 percent to 20 percent over the past two decades.[4]

The higher education system is diverse and complex. There are two-year colleges (junior or community colleges awarding associate degrees) offering the first two years of study toward the baccalaureate degree and, increasingly, a wide variety of vocational programs; four-year colleges (awarding the baccalaureate degree); and universities (usually awarding the baccalaureate and graduate and professional degrees).

Of 3,253 institutions of higher education in 1982, about 1,500 were publicly controlled (supported by tax funds). The terms *public* and *private* should not be taken completely literally. Private universities receive public research money, and students at those schools are eligible for public loans and grants. Public universities receive research grants from private industry and seek and obtain significant donations from the private sector. They get about 30 percent of all voluntary support for colleges, an increase from about 17 percent in 1960. For the past decade average costs to students at private colleges have been about four times those at public colleges.[5]

There were nearly 600 more institutions of higher education in 1978 than there were in 1966. The most dramatic increase was in the number of public two-year colleges (367), although there are also about 200 more private four-year colleges than there were at the beginning of this period of expansion. These increases understate the total number of new institutions, since they are not adjusted for the approximately 200 institutions that closed during the same period. It may be of interest to note that the number of institutions that close their doors is regularly reported in the education statistics published by the United States government.

Another way of describing the size of the higher education enterprise is to point out that over 900,000 students received bachelor's degrees in 1981; nearly 300,000 received master's degrees; and over 32,000 received doctorates. Three-quarters of the postdoctorates ever awarded in the United States have been granted since 1960.

Institutions of higher education are often ranked along various dimensions. Few would disagree that there are both elite private colleges and elite public and private research universities, and that individual schools and departments within colleges are of varying quality. A recent survey indicated that 10 percent of colleges are competitive (that is, the best students compete to attend, and the colleges compete for the most qualified), and 56 percent are selective (colleges that do not admit all of their applicants); the remaining 34 percent have open-access admissions policies.[6] Open access may mean that any high school graduate, or any applicant, including those without high school diplomas, will be accepted as a student. The largest amount of growth in the higher education system has been of two-year, open-access colleges. These colleges are now less often the first two years of a standard college program; they have become major providers of vocational certification. In fact a growing number of "reverse transfer" students are leaving four-year colleges for vocational training at two-year institutions.

Of the high school graduates in 1980, 46 percent entered college in the year after graduation, an increase from 33 percent twenty years earlier. It is expected that more than 60 percent of the 1980 graduates will take courses in colleges in the next few years. The enrollment trend is clear: a higher proportion of students are staying in high school, going on to college, and planning to go to graduate school. Since college attendance is often spread over more than four years, it is somewhat difficult to estimate college completion rates. For example, research on the high school class of 1972 indicates that about 15 percent of the class graduated from college by 1976 (on time) and an additional 8 percent finished college in the next few years.[7]

In 1960 Martin Trow suggested that the transformation of education in the United States might continue until higher education was nearly universal.[8] Some movement has been made in this direction. By 1979,

65 percent of the high school class of 1972 had some college education. However, even with improved access, students of high socioeconomic status (SES) were twice as likely to go to college as low SES students and, having gone, were four times as likely to earn a baccalaureate degree.

In 1960, 24 percent of white high school graduates and 18 percent of black high school graduates (between 18 and 24 years old) were enrolled in college, and in 1981, using a similar base, 32 percent of whites and 28 percent of blacks were enrolled.[9] Of the students who entered college in 1980, 20 percent reported receiving federal (Pell) grants, 19 percent had federally guaranteed loans, and 11 percent had other federal loans and grants. Institutions that receive federal research and other funds are responsible for meeting various federal guidelines. The racial, ethnic, and gender compositions of student and faculty populations received close scrutiny in the past two decades and were to some extent adjusted by colleges in the interests of campus tranquility, continued federal funding, and equity.

When students do persist and graduate from college, they now enter what the press describes as the bleakest job market in at least twenty years. One-third of the graduates leave campus without any job prospects or with jobs for which a degree has not been necessary in the past. Employers choose college graduates as the more desirable applicants, so their overall unemployment rate is well below the national average. This varies among population groups, however: a Bureau of Labor Statistics survey in March of 1982 (when the overall unemployment rate was 9 percent) indicated that the unemployment rate for white male college graduates was 2.6 percent; the rate for black male college graduates was 8.9 percent.[10] The rate for college-educated black males is better than that for their less educated peers, but it is clearly recognized that unemployment among black males at every educational level is at least two times that of white males.

Mediating between Schools and Colleges

Although it is possible to diagram the secondary and higher education systems in a way that seems to link them in an orderly fashion, the two levels are surprisingly separate. The gap between them has been mediated by special professions, private organizations, state departments of education, and recently, the federal government. Standardized tests, designed and controlled largely by private organizations, have had a critical role.

MEDIATING GROUPS AND ORGANIZATIONS

Mediating Professions. Counselors in high schools are one group who help to interpret the system for students. Another are college admissions officers; they scrutinize class standings, high school grades, recommendations, and—for the most selective, and all competitive, colleges—scores on standardized tests. Colleges themselves seek students in many ways: they send recruiters (who never have that title) to selected high schools; they send letters and brochures to students who take standardized tests; and they advertise in newspapers. The average cost of recruiting a student was $151 in 1981–82; selective liberal arts colleges spent an average of $709 per student.[11]

Persons in these mediating professions may belong to several professional organizations, including the National Association for College Admissions Counselors, the National Association for Student Financial Aid Administrators, the American Association of Collegiate Registrars, and the American School Counselors Association. Only the first of these has members from both high schools and colleges.

Mediation by Private Organizations. Relations between schools and colleges are also mediated by a number of private organizations, all doing well by doing good. The first of these, and still by far the most powerful, is the College Entrance Examination Board (CEEB). CEEB was originally founded in 1900 to give examinations to high school seniors, the results of which would be used by the private colleges to which the students had applied for admission. This was intended to extract some order from the changing high school curriculum and to allow colleges to know what their applicants actually learned in various courses in high school. The functions of CEEB have greatly diversified over time. For example, CEEB was a founding sponsor of the Educational Testing Service (ETS), the giant of the standardized testing industry. CEEB now sponsors a wide variety of examinations designed and processed by ETS and serves as one clearinghouse for financial-aid information. CEEB collects the Financial Assistance Form (FAF) from about 2.4 million students each year (at $6.50 each); the form is processed by ETS and sent to the colleges from which the student is seeking financial aid. The FAF is one method of application for federal financial aid. CEEB is also active in many other areas of school and college relations, for example, in a project that has been attempting, with the aid of over one thousand high school and college teachers, to devise a standardized high school curriculum articulated with college entrance requirements.

Mediation at the State Level. Within state departments of education there is sometimes a bureaucratic connection between those influencing the curriculum of secondary schools and those influencing admission policies for state colleges and universities. But this does not mean that there has been negotiation or consultation between the two levels, even within states. There are commissions of school and college relations in some states which provide a forum for the two levels. As one facet of recently initiated school-improvement programs, some state universities have set new admission standards. Although these were often unilateral decisions, there was a built-in delay before adoption to allow high schools time to prepare their students to meet the new requirements.

Mediation by the Federal Government. During the past two decades, the role of the federal government as mediator between high schools and colleges has greatly expanded. This has occurred in three main channels, which are unified by the notion of equity. First, because the federal government provided substantial assistance to strengthen the education of the most disadvantaged students, the potential pool of high school graduates and applicants for higher education was increased. Second, enforcing legislation prohibiting discrimination on the basis of race or gender has increased the plausibility of certain education or career paths for new sets of applicants. Third, the federal government has provided substantial financial assistance to large numbers of college students.

During this period the government acquired (and to some extent may now be relinquishing) effective influence over public secondary schools and over virtually all institutions of higher education. Although the proportion of financial support provided by the federal government to elementary and secondary schools doubled in that time, it still remains at less than 10 percent. The contribution to higher education in the form of student support and research funding amounted to more than $7 billion in 1980, as compared to a little over $1 billion in 1960. School districts and colleges not fulfilling civil rights and other federal guidelines were in danger of losing federal funding.

Most of the money provided to local education authorities was in the form of categorical aid to specified sets of students (the disadvantaged, the handicapped, those with limited ability in English, and so forth). These funds were often channeled through the state education department and required complex record keeping at both levels to show how students were selected for participation, exactly what services were provided, and evaluation results, among other things. Since there are numerous federal programs with legislation written at different times which often parallel similar state programs, schools, districts, and states complain about the burden of record keeping and added layers of bureaucracy that categorical federal funding requires. Research suggests, however, that such categorical aid is more likely to actually achieve its purpose than similar funding provided as a block grant. Block grants are more easily mixed with general education funds and may be used to substitute for, as opposed to supplement, local money.[12]

At the end of this period, a cabinet-level Department of Education was established; this was considered a triumph for the pressure techniques of the National Education Association. However, when Ronald Reagan was elected in 1980, he promised to disestablish the department. One aspect of Reagan's new federalism program was to provide funds to states and districts as block grants rather than categorical grants. With block grants the possibility of withholding federal funds from schools for noncompliance with civil rights or other federal guidelines is greatly reduced. Although equity remains the programmatic focus of federal education funds, funding-formula changes may affect the population such programs serve, and total federal expenditures for education have been reduced. Several bills have been introduced in Congress to disestablish the Department of Education, but education has become a highly visible political topic and the department may be safely entrenched.

In 1982 Secretary of Education Terrel H. Bell reported the administration's view of the proper federal role in education: first, protection of civil rights; second, leadership, advocacy, and constructive criticism; third, research and development; fourth, funding student financial aid and special programs for the disadvantaged (to build the capacity of districts to assume more responsibility); and fifth, strengthening the national research capability, particularly university based research.[13]

One of these functions, research, has not been recognized as an important influence of colleges and universities on schools. Universities conduct much of the research on teaching and learning (and certainly train all of the researchers). This will be discussed later in this chapter, but here we note that the function of funding research is seen as residing in the federal Department of Education. The education research agenda may thus be carried out by the universities and applied in the schools, but it is established by the federal government.

The federal role in education research is an extremely complex one. The amount of money required for large studies may only be available to the federal government. However, researchers carrying out projects paid for by federal funds cannot approach schools without approval from several organizations of state education officials, from district officials, and from the school principals involved. The only research instruments that do not require extensive state and federal review are standardized tests. Tests traditionally are imbued with mysterious authority.

Secretary Bell recently appointed a commission charged with the responsibility of examining the quality of American education; one early sign of a new federal focus was the name of this group, the National Commission on Excellence in Education. The commission studied the current educational scene and issued an alarmed report about a nation at risk of losing scientific and technological preeminence. Much of the evidence reviewed was of test results, compared over time (declining, including scores at the top) and internationally (disadvantageous to the United States). The commission's recommendations include a specified high school curriculum (four years of English, three years of math, one-half year of computer science, and so forth); adoption by schools and colleges of measurable standards; longer school days and more schoolwork; improvement in the preparation of teachers; and state and local leadership and fiscal support for school improvement.[14]

Two of these recommendations are particularly relevant. First, concern about teacher preparation (overwhelmingly the most important influence of the college on the school) was high on the commission's agenda. Second, the commission recommended a series of crucial standardized tests, to include (1) a nationwide "but not Federal" system of state and local standardized tests. In the early grades these would identify students needing remedial work and the gifted for accelerated programs; (2) standardized tests of achievement, "not to be confused with aptitude," which would be administered at major transition points, particularly from high school to college or the job market. They also recommended that colleges require prospective students to have specific levels of achievement on these tests in each of five basic subjects.

As in many other of its observations and recommendations, the commission was suggesting broader implementations of patterns already being established, for example, nationwide systems of tests.

MEDIATION BY STANDARDIZED TESTS

One way of evaluating education is by an overall national assessment in which age-group scores and trends over time can be identified. The National Assessment of Educational Progress (NAEP) is now an established program, one that tracks aggregates, not individuals. Assessment results were among those reviewed by the commission, particularly the decline in math and science among top students.

When the assessment was originally proposed, the specter of a national curriculum implied by national tests made implementation problematic. Plans were begun in 1964, however, and the project was funded by a private foundation; the first annual assessment, conducted by an organization of state education officials, was done in 1969. Funding was gradually assumed by the federal government during the planned period. The matrix-sampling system and complicated data-file structure limited the usefulness of the results to researchers. These limitations have been corrected to some degree over the course of the assessment's history.

Even with the conduct of the assessment in the hands of an organization of state education officials, concern persisted among states and local school districts that it might be used to diminish their authority. When hearings were held in Washington in 1978 about the possibility of another firm (not the organization of states) being awarded the grant to conduct the assessment, some of the testimony sounded threatening. "I was not going to say this, but there are four organizations that could . . . make things difficult. . . . If any, or if that group of folks decided that there was some question about the contractor, we could say, you cannot come into the schools."[15] These were four national organizations of education professionals informing the federal government that they would keep a research company selected by the government out of all of the public schools in the country. The grant was awarded to the state organization without competition that year. The assessment is structured by law so that it is governed by a policy committee of state and local educators that does not include a federal member. Power to make all major decisions is vested in that committee. In 1982 the same powerful education groups announced their continued support for the state organization but claimed willingness to work with whatever contractor the federal government might select. The contract was awarded to a private organization, the Educational Testing Service, and the states no longer directly control every aspect of the design and implementation of the National Assessment of Educational Progress.

A second system of tests, crucial to the transition from school to college, are college entrance tests, and the predominant one of these is the Scholastic Aptitude Test (SAT). These tests are designed, administered, and scored by the Educational Testing Service. SAT scores, nearly in isolation, can open or close college doors. In 1982, 13 percent of the high school seniors had taken SATs twice, once as juniors (the PSAT), once as seniors; 24 percent had taken them once. Thirty percent had taken the competing ACT test. Most students who take these tests consider themselves to be candidates for competitive or selective colleges.

In 1982 over a million students took the SAT (at $10.50 each). More than 150,000 took them three times.

The first set of students affected by the SATs is the two-thirds who do not take the tests. They have already selected themselves out of the elite higher education system. Second, the low-scoring students are selected out by their scores on the tests. The makers and scorers of standardized tests are so much a part of the education system that they are almost structural elements of it. Now that ETS also conducts the National Assessment of Educational Progress, it provides the two most visible indicators of the outcomes of the education system.

A third set of tests (not yet a system) is similar to those recommended by the commission to identify students needing remedial instruction, reveal the particularly talented, and after high school, certify the student's credentials. Many states (thirty-eight in 1983) have assessment, proficiency, or minimum-competency testing systems. Some states conduct assessments and provide group diagnostic information to schools. Some legislate assessment and set uniform standards for promotion and graduation; in others, passing grades are set by districts. In some states education departments have provided policy guidance, but implementation is left entirely to local districts.

Twenty states have an examination as a requirement for a high school diploma, either at local option or for the entire state. The week that the commission's report was released, the Florida supreme court upheld the constitutionality of a diploma test in Florida. This effectively removes certification from the high school and separates the functions of credentialing and certification.

Exactly how many students can be allowed to fail such an examination, that is, where to set the level of competence, is a political decision. In addition to students who complete the twelfth grade and then take (and fail) the examination, there may be others who leave school without attempting it. As Bourdieu and Passeron point out, passed-failed is a false perspective on any kind of test; there is also the category of not attempted. These are persons whose elimination by the test is concealed.[16]

The meaning of an uncertified credential is problematic. Eckland showed that refusal to grant a high school diploma to lower-achieving students could be expected to reduce black college attendance by 10 percent and have virtually no effect on white college attendance.[17] Another social fact is that disproportionate numbers of black students do not pass the diploma tests. Two-thirds of the students in Florida who did not get their high school diplomas were black.

The national commission also recommends that a student be required to achieve at a certain level in five subjects for admission to a four-year college. (This implies that two-year, open-access colleges have a role in the system clearly differentiated from that of four-year colleges.) At the top of the test-score distribution the gifted will be revealed; but those gifted students may have been discovered previously.

There is already a certain amount of private-sector support for the identification of excellence. In the Talent Search programs, seventh- and eighth-grade students shown by standardized tests to be in the top 5 percent of their age group may apply (at a cost of $8.00) to take the SAT test ($10.50). These students get information about their scores, become eligible for special summer programs, and are helped with future academic planning. In the midwestern region over 11,000 students participate each year.

The annual Merit Scholarship competition, held since 1955, is based partially on PSAT tests taken by juniors in high school. Last year about a million juniors took the PSAT test (at $4.25 each); 15,000 of them were honored as semifinalists, and 5,400 won scholarships (some provided by participating colleges and others donated by corporations, often for children of their personnel). Collectively, students pay $4,250,000 for the PSATs, and the semifinalists pay another $1,500,000 for the SATs that enable them to become eligible for the scholarships and for college entrance. These students get back about $9 million in scholarships, mainly from the private sector.

The national commission has urged the redirection of national attention from equity to excellence. A concern of many is that attention will be directed only to those students at the top of the achievement distribution after the distribution has been generated by a series of standardized tests.

The overall role of standardized tests (and mediation by private organizations) seems likely to increase in the coming period. And the role of the federal government may well decrease with the amount of money in the federal budget allocated to education. If federal funding is provided in block rather than categorical grants, opportunities for federal sanctions for noncompliance with civil-rights and other guidelines will decrease. If cuts in federal funds are taken from programs for the talented, there are indications that programs in the private sector could be used to identify and cultivate talent for economic and social purposes. But there seems to be no alternative source for funding programs for the disadvantaged.

UNNAMED TERRITORIES, UNMAPPED BOUNDARIES

Since relations between schools and colleges are not completely organized, there is some room for institutional development between the two. Schools and colleges must make some changes to adjust to demands for equity and for educational excellence. How do schools provide secondary education for nearly everyone and, at the same time, provide challenging experiences for the most talented students? How can access to higher education be facilitated? One way is by making changes at the margin between institutional spheres. We can look for evidence of such accommodation between secondary schools and colleges. Such changes blur the borders between the institutions and put students in ambiguous statuses that are tenuous and unnamed.

First, let us consider manifestations of these forces within high schools. Over 80 percent of American high schools offer remedial courses. Principals report that about one-fifth of their incoming students arrive needing remedial help, that is, enter high school requiring lower-level courses. About one-third of all high school seniors report taking remedial English in high school. Among the same group of high schools, slightly more than one-half report having special programs for gifted and talented students. One-fifth of the students report having been in an honors math course during high school. Thus, high schools provide remediation in the name of equity and programs for the gifted in search of excellence.

Remediation continues at the college level. It is estimated that about 35 percent of those who go to college require remediation.[18] Even competitive colleges provide noncredit remedial English composition and mathematics courses. Some two-year colleges specialize in such courses, which may be given for credit toward a college degree. Thus, definitions are blurred when college credit is given for courses taken in basic reading, writing, and arithmetic usually taught in elementary school.

We think of high school dropouts as persons who have terminated their formal education. But of the dropouts from the class of 1982, 14 percent have already earned their high school diploma by examination by the time their classmates graduated, and only 8 percent of the class of 1982 dropouts do not plan to earn a high school diploma in the future. The dropout rate is usually said to be about 25 percent but varies radically among population subgroups. This figure does not allow for the sometimes transitory nature of the dropout status.

Leaving high school before graduation has been considered to be economically disadvantageous, although it is not clear what social mechanism has made this the case; nor is it clear that the economic disadvantage still exists. Stinchcombe, Coleman, and others have suggested that age segregation and a lack of correspondence between high school experience and the adult world have led to disaffection, rebellion, and school-leaving by adolescents.[19] High school programs have been developed in response to such concerns. Two-thirds of public high schools provide off-campus credit programs, primarily in an effort to make staying in school more attractive for students who otherwise would be most vulnerable to dropping out. One-third of the 1982 seniors reported that they spent part of the school day in programs outside the school (in work or in community-service settings). Although involvement in these programs varies considerably, 17 percent of these students spend half of each school day outside of school. In 8 percent of high schools in the United States, students can even earn school credit by traveling.

Fifteen percent of high schools offer credit by examination, so that passing a test is the equivalent of taking a course. There is a higher-education equivalent, the College Level Examination Program (CLEP) sponsored by CEEB. The test, developed by the Educational Testing Service, can be used to evaluate nontraditional (usually nonschool) education. The general section is used to estimate overall level of education, and additional subject-specific examinations approximate the level of information a student would gain if the subject were taken in college. More than 2,000 institutions of higher education accept CLEP exams for credit. The examinations cost $22 each, and about 90,000 students took 144,000 CLEP exams in 1982. Students spent over $3 million on CLEP exams that year.

One strategy adopted to accelerate the progress of talented high school students has been to facilitate early graduation. This can be done by scheduling regular classes in a more concentrated pattern or by exit examination. Sometimes early graduation is possible through registering in and attending a college; in these cases college attendance is an equal alternative to high school attendance. Over half of high schools report that students are eligible to take courses at a nearby college, and a third offer college courses in the high school. In these circumstances high schools maintain the students on their rosters, and any college credit given for courses is limited to the specific college involved in the program.

CEEB advanced placement (AP) courses are given in school by high school teachers and are accepted for credit by a large number of colleges, including the most prestigious. CEEB provides a more or less detailed curriculum for the college-level course; a high school teacher prepares and presents it; and some (or all) of the students enrolled then take the ETS-designed test to determine their competence in the subject area. Sometimes these are ordinary advanced high school courses (for example, Vergil or calculus). Students who pass the exam get college credit for a course taken in high school. The advanced placement examination fee is a bargain for a college course ($42 in 1983). It is possible but very unusual to take three AP courses in high school and then finish college in three years. In 1982 about 150,000 students from more than 5,000 high schools took AP examinations in a wide variety of subjects; students spent nearly $8 million on AP examinations that year.

Some students take a high school course that, with an examination and $42 to CEEB, may be transformed to a college course. Others take an examination that, with a $22 fee to CEEB, will transform life experiences into college courses (CLEP). Still other students take examinations that are the equivalent of a high school diploma. Some earn high school credit at regular jobs, by community service work, or by traveling; some earn high school diplomas that are then certified by passing an examination or devalued by failing that examination. In these poorly understood border areas, the examination is needed to define the student's experience as successful or not and to locate it in school or in college. If passing an examination is a substitute for taking courses, or if a high school course taken by one student is a college course for the student at the next desk, the possibilities seem almost endless.

One of the most complex effects that schools exert on colleges is that of socializing students to believe that school is something you do while you are doing something else. Nearly two-thirds of seniors in 1982 had part-time jobs; most of them worked about twenty hours a week. Of those with jobs, about one-fifth reported their jobs to be more important than school.

Preliminary analysis of data from the high school class of 1972 has suggested that persons who take advantage of the optional delays possible before entering college, or who drift in and out and come back to finish, may be the stronger students; but this holds only among students with good high school grades and those from higher socioeconomic backgrounds, for whom going to college is almost automatic. They are on a college-competition trajectory, and the odd interruption or year off does not deflect them from their original goal.[20]

We can be either heartened or disturbed that 70 percent of high school dropouts report that they plan to complete a high school diploma in the future, and nearly one-fifth of them expect to complete college or an advanced degree. The more flexible, open, and accepting the system is or seems to be, the easier it is for all young people to imagine that they are going to enter it and complete some long-range plan.

The School Shapes the University

STUDENT SELECTION

We have seen that both the federal government and the testing agencies have major roles in channeling students from schools to universities. The federal role has mainly been a force for equity—in funding for compensatory education programs, in financial aid to college students, and in scrutiny of university admission and hiring policies. The role of the testing agencies is more ambiguous. One might imagine that tests provide a bold step toward meritocracy; they do have a strong aura of magic and have recently been prescribed as one part of the cure for the problems of secondary education.

High schools provide counseling of varying quality and quantity to students, who must make numerous important decisions with imperfect information. One-third of high school seniors report that they do not know what their high school guidance counselors thought they should do after high school.

Exactly which public high school a student attends is largely, but not entirely, dependent on residence. The dropout rate at high schools varies from near zero to about 50 percent. Less than 10 percent of graduates from some high schools attend any kind of college; at other schools more than 90 percent of the graduates go on to college. The quality of the local public high school is likely to be closely related to the socioeconomic status of the community.

Recent research suggests that students from lower socioeconomic backgrounds who attend Catholic and other private high schools learn more than their matched peers in public schools. Although the influence of self-selection (really parent selection) cannot ever be removed by statistical tricks, there is no reason to discredit such findings. Private schools have better attendance, better student behavior, greater attention to homework, and more academically oriented programs. It is reasonable to assume that students in such schools ought to achieve more. But there is also no reason to believe that all the students who could be motivated to achieve more have found their way to private schools. If one-half, or even one-third, of the students in the general tracks of public high schools could become engaged by a more academic program, they might enjoy school more and have a better chance of passing minimum-competency and other tests that inevitably lie ahead of them.

After a student has entered a public high school, he or she is assigned to (or selects) a program. This is usually done on the basis of tests, elementary school grades, and previous school record. This assignment or choice greatly affects the academic experience the student has in secondary school. It also affects the likelihood of completing high school or attending any college; and for those students not placed in the academic track, it eliminates the possibility of attending competitive, selective colleges.

College admission may depend simply on applying (open access) and on having a high school diploma, or it may depend on a combination of test scores, grades, and teacher recommendations, with various standards depending on the college. High school grades provide students only veiled information about how well they are doing in school. Only 7 percent of seniors report average grades below C, once the putative average grade. Original program assignment also tells students something about the school's expectations for them. Program assignment has far-reaching concomitants in terms of peer pressure, attitudes toward school, and attitudes toward self. Many students attend and graduate from high school without ever really being engaged by any schoolwork. For example, half of the seniors do less than three hours of homework a week. Nevertheless, in 1982, about 80 percent of the seniors imagined that they had the study skills and ability to complete college if they wished to attend.

STUDENT TRAINING

High school graduation requirements differ by program. The diversity of courses with similar names has caused difficulty since before the turn of the century. Some English courses involve no writing; literature courses may involve no reading, and so on. (A course called "Bachelor Living" has been a target of presidential humor.) Under the impetus for campus tranquillity in the late sixties, courses in search of relevance proliferated, and graduation requirements were reduced. In 1982, two-thirds of the high schools had no foreign-language requirement for graduation in the academic track.

Numerous states and some districts have, in the past few years, introduced school-improvement programs. These are called SIPS; educationists beget acronyms. Setting high school graduation requirements has been one aspect of these programs in some states. The National Commission on Excellence in Education recommended a set of high school graduation requirements "for all students seeking a diploma." Meanwhile the College Examination Entrance Board's project EQuality—almost always referred to in print as EQuality—after "countless meetings" with more than 1,400 high school and college teachers, produced a listing of what a high school education should achieve and provided a suggested set of requirements for the college bound.

But, as has been pointed out, in 1975 about 13 percent of high school seniors were found to be close to illiterate. A substantial group of Florida high school graduates did not pass the competency test required for graduation. What will happen to students at the bottom if curricular attention is riveted on students at the top?

STUDENT CERTIFICATION

The literal certification of students has been removed, in some areas, from the hands of the high schools and put into those of the test developers. Thus, although a much higher percentage of the age cohort is and has been completing high school, it is possible that the percentage actually receiving diplomas may decrease slightly. It would not be politically viable to allow a high proportion of students to fail, so it is assumed that competence standards will be set accordingly. We may be moving to a two-level high school diploma, one for general students (perhaps on the New York model, a local diploma) and one for academic students. These would involve different graduation requirements and passing the minimum-competency tests at different levels.

IDEOLOGY

Highly motivated students are carrying on in much the same way as they always have—studying hard, competing for the highest grades, seeking advanced courses, taking SAT exams two or three times, contending for the highest-status colleges. Like professional athletes they sometimes sell themselves to the highest bidder among schools to which they apply. The special aura of a school, formerly propounded as the major reason to attend it, is now sometimes replaced by the lure of getting money, important considerations being how much of it and under what conditions. This is probably a function of both the high costs at elite colleges and a reduction of the formerly powerful institutional charisma of such schools. Other students want training for particular careers, and they view college as vocational training.

Students want a good future life, and they want as much education as is needed to have a good life. But many of them have been uninvolved in their secondary education; they have taken the least demanding courses, have earned credit by working at jobs outside of the high school, have done little studying in or out of school. Courses can be taken and passed without doing any homework; there is little that can be called rigorous in the high school experiences of many students. Two-thirds of seniors are employed elsewhere during their last year of high school, and they report spending most of the money they earn on entertainment and car maintenance. The high school is implicated in the definition of going to school as something you do while you are doing something else.

The University Shapes the School

SELECTION AND TRAINING OF SCHOOL PERSONNEL

Overwhelmingly, the most important influence of the university on the school, the selection and training of school personnel, will be discussed in chapter ten.

DETERMINATION OF SCHOOL CURRICULUM

In 1906 a school principal in Michigan noted a direct correlation between the number of colleges in his state requiring Latin for entrance and the number of students studying Latin in high school.[21] The university still affects the school curriculum by setting the requirements for its entering students. One of the ways this is accomplished is through representation on the bodies that recommend new high school graduation requirements. The schools attempt, in their academic-track graduation requirements, to meet the requirements of university entrance. In the past there has been little consultation between schools and universities on these matters: the university simply changed requirements for its own purposes. This still happens, but within states at least, there has been systematic dissemination of information and an attempt to coordinate school-graduation and university-entrance requirements. In 1982 the Carnegie Foundation organized the first national meeting ever held between state school superintendents and college presidents. Requirements are becoming more specific; the number of courses students must take in particular subjects for college entrance is increasingly spelled out.

This is a reaction to an earlier trend away from such specificity in favor of reliance on recommendations, class standing, and SAT scores, conceived to be less rigid. Research has shown that half of one year's summa cum laude students at Harvard would not have been admitted had there been a three-year foreign-language entrance requirement.[22] There was of course no way to test whether those summas would have taken three years of language in high school had Harvard been known to require three years of language for entrance.

Universities also affect the high school curriculum by the gradual introduction of new knowledge generated at the universities. This is usually but not always watered down in textbooks, but it does slowly infiltrate the curriculum. Textbook content may be less responsive to new knowledge than to political trends. When a creationism law was passed in one state, many textbooks introduced evolutionism and creationism as alternative hypotheses and gave them equal space. Some colleges and the recent National Commission on Excellence in Education have suggested that high schools teach computer science. In 1982 about 15 percent of all high schools provided computer courses. Exactly how computer literacy will be defined when the field is developing so rapidly and so few schools are prepared with personnel and equipment to teach students about the computer, remains to be discovered.

There appears in the thinking of the national commission a kind of reasoning similar to that of Latinists early in the century. It was observed then that ambitious students liked to study Latin even when they did not plan to go to college because of the challenge of the topic. And there was a side effect: students were better behaved in schools where large percentages studied Latin (a language that seemed to restrain the boyish mind).[23] Whether they were taking Latin because they were upwardly mobile or whether they were upwardly mobile because they were taking Latin did not trouble the writer. The national commission also seems to imply that offering the possibility of academic rigor elicits commitment to academic goals. It does not take into account the fact that the rewards and punishments of schools are particularly enticing (or upsetting) to those students who are upwardly mobile and already likely to succeed. Students from the lowest social class are more likely to be indifferent to those same rewards and punishments.[24] It is not possible to evoke attachment simply by making apprenticeship rigorous. The apprentice must already be enlisted to undertake the challenge.

SHAPING OF SCHOOL IDEOLOGY AND POLICY

Higher education is diverse; there is probably no single ideological message relayed to the high schools. Open-access colleges seem to provide a set of opportunities for students who are not on the conventional academic path. As the size of the college-age cohort decreases, colleges are competing for students; the best colleges compete for the best students. Also, the college population has been aging. In 1980 about a fourth of the students were twenty-five or older. This is an entirely new market for colleges, one filled with potential students who can sometimes do without financial aid.

Everyone is still being covertly promised economic returns from a college education, despite recent research that suggests such returns are decreasing.[25] Some older students are promised career advancement; others are promised returns in spiritual money, personal enrichment. High school students are likely to infer two ideological messages: there is a college for everyone, and going to college will pay off economically.

RESEARCH ON TEACHING AND LEARNING

The university is the seat of most of the research on teaching, learning, test construction, test evaluation, and the outcomes of education policy. The university also trains the researchers who work in other settings and the federal bureaucrats who are involved in establishing the national research agenda.

We have seen that funding for education research is agreed to be a responsibility of the federal government. In a system as large and diverse as that of the United States, research done in one school or district is often said not to apply in general. (This is particularly true if the findings do not confirm previously held beliefs and practice.) For ethical and political reasons it is virtually impossible to conduct experimental research in schools if it means denying some resource to a control group. Larger studies of well-drawn samples of schools (or students or teachers) have quantitative credibility but are sometimes disavowed as ignoring ineffable qualities in the education process. Many of the large research projects on teaching, learning, the effects of schooling, and so forth, are funded by the federal government; members of the federal education bureaucracy often establish the research agenda by defining, in some detail, the kinds of research to be funded. The amount of funding for research is established by the federal budget, and the focus of research is strongly influenced by political trends. (The American Education Research Association maintains a full-time government and professional liaison in Washington to advance the interests of the education research establishment.) University researchers apply for grants and contracts to do research specified by the funding agencies; if they design their own research, they may be influenced by the availability of funds.

School teachers and administrators often complain that university based research is far removed from what actually goes on in the classroom. (The head of one of the largest school systems in the country was heard to tell one researcher that hiring only sensitive geniuses as teachers was not a practical option.) The research is also seen as focused on the wrong level of schooling or not helpful in the classroom or not useful in persuading legislative funding committees. But whatever the disinclination of the school establishment to making changes suggested by research, the focus of much research in the past two decades has been on students with the greatest need, and research results do gradually find their way into policy and practice. The research agenda of the federal government may change in the coming period from investigations on issues of equity, access, compensatory education, and programs for the disadvantaged and handicapped to the identification and fostering of scientific, mathematical, and other talent.

Conclusion

In the United States, the relationship between the school and the university is complex and ambiguous. The educational system is both decentralized and very large. The connections between these two levels of education vary from the public to the private sector, from one state to another, within states from one school district to another, and nationally from one type of college to another. It becomes a major enterprise to describe the variety that exists in student selection, training, certification, and ideology, the mechanisms through which the school is considered to shape the university. It is similarly difficult to describe the variety that exists in teacher training, curricular requirements, educational ideology, and educational research, through which the university shapes the school.

From the vantage point of cross-national comparisons, certain central tendencies may be noted in this confusing variety. The United States higher education segment is easy to enter. The secondary segment has open access and sponsors the great mass of students to high school graduation and hence to the possibility of entering higher education. Entry standards for higher education overall are minimal; standards of passage at the secondary level overall are all equally minimal. The modal secondary student works in an outside job as well as goes to school and, in or out of school, does relatively little schoolwork. The structure of arrangements and rewards diminishes student commitment.

Massive institutional complexes, the secondary and higher education systems seem to diverge, pulled apart by different agendas. Traditional direct links become strained, even broken. In response, we can observe an array of mediators that emerge to link the two levels. There are the mediating professionals also: counselors, recruiters, admissions personnel, and financial-aid experts. A major role is assumed by the major private testing organizations, whose tests have become powerful tools for allocating students to different types of universities and colleges. And increasingly prominent is the mediating influence of federal government as it has attempted to increase equity in American education and now, in the 1980s, as once before in the post-Sputnik years, seeks to emphasize excellence.

The array of mediating groups, institutional devices, and social statuses is the best indicator of the amount of disorder and confusion that has grown through the years in the relationship between the school and the university in America. We should expect such mediation to continue and to expand. The connection between the levels will not again be left primarily to teachers at one end and professors at the other.

Notes

1. Unless otherwise specified all numbers are from Grant and Eiden, *Digest of Education Statistics 1982*, or Jones et al., *High School and Beyond*.
2. *Statistical Abstract of the United States, 1982–1983*, p. 156.
3. Lerner, "American Education," pp. 59–82.
4. Ibid, p. 159.

5. Data from the Council for Financial Aid to Education and the College Scholarship Service, reported in *The Chronicle of Higher Education*, May 25, 1983, pp. 4, 5.

6. Survey reported in *The Chronicle of Higher Education*, January 19, 1982, p. 8.

7. Kolstad, "What College Dropout and Dropin Rates Tell Us," p. 32.

8. Trow, "The Second Transformation of American Secondary Education," pp. 144–166.

9. *Statistical Abstract of the United States, 1982–1983*, p. 159.

10. J. L. Burden, "Graduates Face Toughest Search in Years for Jobs," *New York Times*, May 30, 1983, p. 1.

11. *The Chronicle of Higher Education*, May 4, 1983, p. 7.

12. Shapiro, "Federal Grants and Local Expenditures."

13. Bell, "The Federal Role in Education," pp. 375–380.

14. National Commission on Excellence in Education, *A Nation At Risk*.

15. Proceedings of hearings before the Advisory Council on Education Statistics, Department of Health, Education and Welfare, February 9, 1978, p. 67.

16. Bourdieu and Passeron, *Reproduction in Education, Society and Culture*, p. 162.

17. Eckland, "Sociodemographic Implications of Minimum Competency Testing," pp. 124–135.

18. Michael O'Keefe, quoted in *The Chronicle of Higher Education*, November 3, 1982, p. 8.

19. Stinchcombe, *Rebellion in High School*, and Coleman et al., *Youth: Transition to Adulthood*.

20. Andrew J. Kolstad, personal communication.

21. Kelsey, *Latin and Greek in American Education*, p. 5.

22. Menacker, *From School to College*, p. 47.

23. Kelsey, *Latin and Greek in American Education*, p. 23.

24. Bourdieu and Passeron, *Reproduction in Education, Society, and Culture*, p. 28.

25. Stephen P. Dresh and Russell Rumberger statements at hearings of National Commission on Student Financial Assistance. Reported in *The Chronicle of Higher Education*, June 15, 1983.

Bibliography

BELL, TERREL H. "The Federal Role in Education." *Harvard Educational Review* 52 (1982): 375–380.

BOURDIEU, PIERRE, and JEAN-CLAUDE PASSERON. *Reproduction in Education, Society and Culture*, trans. Richard Nice. London: Sage Publications, 1977.

COLEMAN, JAMES S., ROBERT H. BREMNER, BURTON R. CLARK, JOHN B. DAVIS, DOROTHY

H. EICHORN, ZVI GRILICHES, JOSEPH F. KETT, NORMAN B. RYDER, ZAHAVA BLUM DOERING, and JOHN MAYS. *Youth: Transition to Adulthood*. Chicago: University of Chicago Press, 1974.

ECKLAND, BRUCE K. "Sociodemographic Implications of Minimum Competency Testing." In *Minimum Competency Achievement Testing*, ed. Richard M. Jaeger and Carol Kehr Tittle. Berkeley: McCutchan, 1980. Pp. 124–135.

GRANT, W. VANCE, and L. J. EIDEN. *Digest of Education Statistics, 1982*. Washington, D.C.: National Center for Education Statistics, 1982.

JONES, CALVIN, MIRIAM CLARK, GERALDINE MOONEY, HAROLD MCWILLIAMS, IOANNA CRAWFORD, BRUCE STEPHENSON, and ROGER TOURANGEAU. *High School and Beyond, First Follow-Up (1982) Data File User's Manual*. Washington, D.C.: National Center for Education Statistics, April 1983.

KELSEY, FRANCIS W. *Latin and Greek in American Education*. New York: Macmillan, 1911.

KOLSTAD, ANDREW J. "What College Dropout and Dropin Rates Tell Us." *American Education* 17 (1981): 31–33.

LERNER, BARBARA. "American Education: How Are We Doing?" *The Public Interest* 69 (Fall 1982): 59–82.

MENACKER, JULIUS. *From School to College: Articulation and Transfer*. Washington, D.C.: American Council on Education, 1975.

National Commission on Excellence in Education. *A Nation at Risk: The Imperative for Educational Reform*. Washington, D.C.: U.S. Department of Education, April, 1983.

SHAPIRO, ROBERT. "Federal Grants and Local Expenditures." Department of Political Science, University of Chicago, 1980. Mimeo.

STINCHCOMBE, ARTHUR. *Rebellion in High School*. Chicago: Quadrangle Books, 1964.

TROW, MARTIN. "The Second Transformation of American Secondary Education." *Comparative Sociology* 2 (1961): 144–166.

U.S. Department of Commerce. Bureau of the Census. *Statistical Abstract of the United States, 1982–83*. Washington, D.C.: U.S. Government Printing Office, 1982.

10

Teacher Education in the United States

GARY SYKES

T EACHER EDUCATION IS A SPECIAL case of the relationship between secondary and postsecondary education. Secondary schools provide students for the teacher preparation programs at colleges and universities, which in turn produce teachers for the secondary schools. Each segment of the system supplies a market for the other, and this economic exchange, like most others, thrives on growth. Increases in this circular flow of students mean prosperity for all, while decline in one market threatens the survival of institutions in the other. In this chapter the United States provides an example of the strains that may develop in this relationship when declining enrollments end a long period of expansion in secondary and postsecondary education.

There are some 3,250 higher education institutions in the United States today. The majority (1,978) are four-year colleges or universities, 1,200 of which prepare teachers.[1] Sixty-five percent of the teacher training institutions are private, but they turn out less than 25 percent of the new teachers. A small set of public master's- and doctoral-level institutions account, respectively, for 42 and 28 percent of the education graduates.[2] Until the mid-seventies, the education major accounted for one-fifth of all baccalaureate degrees (more than one-third of all degrees awarded to women), by far the largest undergraduate specialty. As demand for teachers disappeared in the seventies, however, both the absolute and relative numbers of new teachers declined substantially. Currently, less than 13 percent of undergraduates are majoring in education, with further losses projected.[3]

Professional training for teachers takes place within the four-year course leading to the baccalaureate and is divided into three parts. The great majority of coursework is in the liberal arts, with major emphasis on a single subject such as history, biology, or mathematics. The remaining coursework, typically about one-fifth of the total for secondary education majors, is in education. The education courses include both study of the education field and teaching methods. The third component, practice teaching, takes up less than 10 percent of the student's time near completion of the program and occurs in schools under the supervision of a cooperating teacher.[4]

In the twentieth century professional education in most fields has significantly expanded in the United States. The august professions of law and medicine have increased the number of years of training required for licensure, but this trend applies as well to pharmacology, and even to barbering. In education, however, no comparable extension has occurred. The tripartite allocation among theory, practice, and subject matter has remained fixed over the past half-century, squeezed uneasily into a four-year term.

Teacher education occupies an uncomfortable niche within the American multiversity. On one hand, it has been crucial to degree production, expanding along with the entire system of postsecondary institutions; on the other, it is starving fiscally in comparison with other departments and programs on campus. Most states allocate funds to university programs based on an index of complexity, which sets the relative training costs in various professional fields. With a base of 1.0, education ranks 1.04 on this scale and so receives a meager per capita allocation (by contrast, engineering ranks 2.07, and nursing 2.74).[5] One study in 1978 calculated an annual expenditure of only $927 per education student.[6] At the same time, the public schools spent an average of $1,400 per secondary student, revealing a marked discrepancy but a clear indication of education's low priority at state universities.

Resource poverty is but one symptom of the deeper problems afflicting teacher education. What follows is an account of these difficulties together with an assessment of the prospects of reform.

What Troubles Teacher Education

A paradox lies at the heart of teacher education in America. For nearly half a century critics of all persuasions have scolded, even reviled, teacher education as a benighted and ill-starred enterprise, the very heel of our schooling system. Yet over this period it has remained largely unchanged in important respects despite a variety of efforts at reform. True, teacher education shifted from the normal school to the teachers college to the university, and the general educational level of teachers has risen. In 1961 nearly 15 percent of the teacher work force still held less than a bachelor's degree; less than a quarter had earned a master's degree. By 1981 nearly one-half of all teachers held a master's degree, while the other half were college graduates.[7] This may be counted true progress (although it paralleled a more general rise in educational attainment in the United States over these two decades), but the debate over teacher education never slackened, nor did the sense of malaise, of something badly amiss, lift appreciably. What accounts for the persistence of the status quo in teacher education, for its low esteem, and for the failure to professionalize teaching?

Teacher education involves a smorgasbord of enduring, unresolved difficulties along which critics in each era pass, making selections to fit the mood and spirit of the times. The central conflict has always involved the proper balance and relationship among what nearly everyone regards as the four necessary and sufficient components of a program: a strong liberal arts education, solid grounding in at least one subject area (particularly for secondary teachers), an introduction to education as a subject of inquiry and to the emerging science of pedagogy, and the opportunity to practice and experience teaching in a real, yet controlled, setting. These components seem hardly to require elaborate justification. Yet no practical synthesis has established the nature of their interrelationship, and the politics of teacher education have remained a zero-sum game featuring imperialist forays from the contending faculties of arts and sciences and of education.

An ambiguity of competence[8] lies at the core of this territorial dispute. Teaching, like many undertakings, involves the employment of both special and ordinary knowledge, but it stands apart in its reliance on the extraordinary use of ordinary knowledge. Teaching style appears to depend largely on personality and on tacit, idiosyncratic approaches to human relations. To many, teaching, like parenting, is a natural, spontaneous, organic human activity. Knowing subject matter and caring about children are the primary ingredients for success, around which some technical embellishments can marginally matter. Given this basic view, the notions of a "scientific basis of the art of teaching"[9] or of "sources of a science of education"[10] seem dubious, mystifications of an essentially simple, universal activity.

By another view, however, teaching is an enormously complicated act whose full import has eluded the increasingly sophisticated methodological and conceptual tools of the social sciences. Some argue that in the last decade progress has been made and the rudiments of a paradigm have emerged, giving promise for the steady advance that characterizes the coming of age in a scientific field. The great hope, a scientifically validated knowledge base, an emergent science of pedagogy, seems less forlorn now, and the modest successes with applications suggest that stronger links between knowledge and practice are in the offing. But these steps are not widely known or credited, and the grounding of competence in science is a project still open to doubt and to counterclaims about the kinds of knowledge most useful to the aspiring teacher. Science is the preeminent legitimating force in our society, the source of the dream of reason, and occupations naturally seek its prestige in their service. Yet, absent a certainty about its utility, absent an obvious demonstration of its potency (such as a cure or a moon shot), skepticism will remain.

In teacher education, there is also an unhappy legacy to live down. Visitors to college campuses have come away too often with a low opinion about the actual quality of faculty, students, courses, and standards in schools and departments of education. The paint has long dried on this portrait of mediocrity, of insipid if not anti-intellectual fare, of pseudoscientific methods courses and a professional jargon that apes social science (Koerner labeled it "educanto").[11] Although the fraternity of teacher educators and researchers doggedly issue analyses proclaiming an imminent millennium if only the resources will be made available and the purposes properly fixed, this history of disconcerting reports from the nation's campuses has belied such optimism. Conservatives, perennialists, and devotees of the liberal arts have gleefully contributed to or seized on this literature to support their position. A close look, however, usually uncovers an indictment of higher education in general, with the faculties of arts and sciences coming in for their share of blame and criticism. Undergraduate liberal education at many universities lacks rigor and coherence, falling as short of any commune with the sublime portrayed by savants as teacher education fails to represent a true science of pedagogy. Yet teacher education's position at the bottom of the academic pecking order is undisputed, a terrible handicap for those whose project is to raise this enterprise via the fruits of science.

Still another difficulty stems from the institutionalization of teacher education in the university. Complicating the indignities of internecine strife is the tenuous relation to the schools, the future work settings of teacher education's clients. One dilemma here is common to professional education in all fields: whether to accept the conditions of practice, warts and all, preparing novices to fit a sadly imperfect status quo, or whether to take a critical stance toward current practice, imbuing the next generation with the need for change, the imperative to make, not take, the role assigned. The alternating currents of discourse on this point have largely overlooked the evidence suggesting that socialization plays a far stronger role than formal training in shaping a teaching style. Research on the subject divides formative influences into four sets of factors: the "apprenticeship of observation" that candidates undergo during their 15,000 hours of experience as students;[12] the bureaucratic aspects of schools and the ecology of the classroom;[13] supervisors' and colleagues' impress on teachers;[14] and the impact of students as unintended agents of socialization.[15] So, although the stance to be taken toward the schools is a genuine vexation to teacher educators, teacher education appears to be such a weak treatment as to make moot the argument.

As a practical matter, however, the schools of education must nurture relations with the schools, which after all serve as the training ground for beginners, provide a shadow extension of the faculty in the form of cooperating teachers, and supply the chief clientele for postbaccalaureate coursework and such consulting as supplements faculty incomes. This relationship is uneasy, at best, with little mutual coincidence of interests. Schoolmen complain about how out of touch university faculty are; students typically find only their practice teaching helpful; and the professors who know how it should be done express dismay at the gap between their ideal and the realities of life in classrooms. Each point of view is valid, but the means for reconciliation or accommodation have not emerged, and so these laments persist generation after generation.

The shifting tasks and protean agenda of the schools make the relationship between the universities and the schools as unstable as it is uneasy. The remarkable growth of the school system in terms of numbers and retention rates has created serious strains, as educators are now expected to serve the full spectrum of the social structure, whereas in decades past a de facto policy of exclusion and indifference considerably narrowed the student population to whom teachers actually had to attend. Likewise, the transformation of the secondary school into a multipurpose social-service agency has complicated the teacher's role and expanded the domain of responsibilities to this larger, more diverse clientele. Underlying these changes has been a deeper conflict over the priority of excellence, equity, or efficiency in the schools' mission. As the emphasis among these central cultural values has shifted from one era to the next, so too have the charges leveled against the schools.

Teacher education is coupled to the unstable mission of the schools, while being vulnerable in its own right to fluid social imperatives. So the training institutions must now prepare teachers for the real world of inner-city schools, for multicultural education (that is, teachers must daily arbitrate the bilingual controversies that have stymied policymakers at all levels), for educating the handicapped, for distinguishing the subtle bases for sexual and racial inequities in their own and others' behavior, for the computer revolution, and so on. They must also act affirmatively with respect to hiring and admissions, while maintaining high standards and producing a teaching elite capable of supplying the advanced manpower for mastery in world technology markets. Neither schools nor universities can serve up such a volatile brew; after a while both institutions may be permitted a modest dispensation for hunkering down and resisting change.

A final difficulty fixing teacher education to an orbit about the schools are the status, wages, and other valuables associated with teaching. Client status typically sets limits on professional aspirations for social and economic mobility. As amply depicted in the writing of Hofstadter, Elsbree, Waller, Lortie, and others, teaching has always suffered an equivocal status compounded of respect and disdain, reverence and mockery. Moreover, some evidence suggests that teaching's occupational status actually declined between 1963 and 1980; according to one survey, teaching lost more ground than any other occupation ranked.[16] One telling indication of this trend comes from a Gallup Poll item. When asked, Would you like to have a child of yours take up teaching in the public schools as a career? 75 percent responded yes in 1969, 67 percent in 1972, 48 percent in 1980, and only 45 percent in 1983.[17] To enhance the status and prospects of teacher education independently of teaching seems unlikely. Similarly, proposals to extend professional education for teachers run up against objections that few students would be willing to undergo a genuine training ordeal such as medicine requires, or bear the costs of further schooling, for the meager annual salaries and lifetime earnings teaching supplies.

That teaching is the closest thing to a mass profession may alone preclude a more elite status. Until the last decade, teaching regularly consumed one-fifth of the college labor market, and training institutions were hard pressed to supply the requisite numbers, never mind their quality. Indeed, easy access to teaching has historically served as both a potent recruitment incentive for individuals and a guarantee that supply would not lag too far behind demand in a tight labor market. The route to sovereignty in the true professions of law and medicine, restricted access under the protective mantle of a meritocratic ideology, was never available to an occupation whose single, overriding imperative was growth. Schools of law and medicine number several hundred; at 1200, schools of education number an order of magnitude greater, and likewise the number of doctors and lawyers versus teachers. It is little coincidence that the word *common* means both "plentiful" and "vulgar." The drive to raise the dignity of the common school and its staff suffers a conjunction captured in etymology; it is the fundamental condition that scarcity enhances value while availability detracts from it.

Teacher Education and the Rise of Professions

Here a comparative perspective is useful. Schools of law and medicine provide the models for the free-standing professional school. Educators for years have used these occupations as the reference point, but the development of a special school requires that an occupation gain professional status (the business school may be the exception). This status relies on two assets: a body of abstract, codified knowledge, and the ideal of service. The professional school embodies and transmits the knowledge whose possession distinguishes the expert from the layman. The profession's code of ethics and its claim to self-regulation follow from its service ideal and the technical expertise needed to assure competence in practice.

Sociologists have made careful study of the rise of the professions, and several features of their analysis are helpful. The drive to achieve professional standing is both an economic and a cultural project. To achieve sovereignty, occupations must create demand for services, then establish a monopoly over the supply. The commodity in this case is the service provider, the licensed professional. The training program standardizes production of professionals and restricts access to the occupation, thereby restricting the supply. Lest this economic project be too nakedly self-serving, the profession on the make must also establish its moral authority and gain the trust of clients. The service ideal is indispensable in securing this deed of public trust. But the balance is delicate. The ideology of professionalism involves a thin line between the service ideal and the drive to control a market, between protecting society and securing privileged status, between intrinsic and extrinsic values of work.

Professions also require solidarity among their members and therefore the resolution of various internal conflicts. All professions are internally stratified and increasingly specialized. Professionalization demands cohesiveness among practitioners despite differences in their class background and the prestige of the professional school they attended. Conflicts within a profession can also break out between those who practice, those who conduct research, and those who train practitioners. In medicine, licensed physicians carry out all three functions with few status differences among them. In law, bitter disputes between practitioners and educators were nearly fatal in the century's early decades, but the resolution established high standards and a uniform curriculum.

The growth of formal organizations may also constitute a threat to professional autonomy. Conflicting forms of bureaucratic and professional control over work have developed, and a range of new managerial occupations has arisen which themselves seek to professionalize, including hospital and school administrators, middle-level executives, various consultants, and others. So, while the dramatic expansion of the state service sector has generated jobs for such aspiring professionals as teachers, social workers, and public health officers, their subordination to other emergent professionals has created organizational strains.

Occupational control is at stake in the development of a university based professional school. The school is a crucial resource in the quest to professionalize. But internal divisions and questions about the knowledge base threaten the aspiring profession's position. Educators fervently desire the control gained by practitioners in law and medicine and explicitly model themselves on the so-called true professions. Against this sketch of the professions, then, we can look at the case of education, assessing the plight of teacher education in the university.

The Tyranny of Education's Market

At first glance the case of education is quite puzzling. While other occupations had first to guarantee a market for their services, then secure a monopoly within it, educators from the outset enjoyed freedom from competition in a large, publicly subsidized, expanding market. Why in the face of strong demand for increasingly valued services were teachers unable to secure high wages, status, and professional autonomy? And why were the teacher training institutions similarly unable to establish their value and legitimacy in the public eye?

Part of the answer lies in the dynamics of system growth. Demand for teachers is a volatile compound made up of demographic trends and social choices concerning years of mandatory schooling, attendance and retention rates, class sizes, and program differentiation requiring staff specialization.[18] Through the middle decades of this century, the system grew so rapidly that demand far outstripped supply. Two responses to this situation have been fateful to professionalism in teaching.

One was the turn to women as an untapped source of cheap, pliable labor. The feminization of teaching served to keep wages low, to undergird subordinate status, and to undercut long-term professional commitment by meshing teaching with family responsibilities. Teaching's truncated career meant that women became homemakers while men moved on to higher-level administrative positions or grander prospects. This pattern prevails today, and teaching is marked by high turnover in the first five to seven years.

The other development was the inability of the emerging profession to gain control over teacher supply in the face of runaway demand. The successful professions were able to establish standards and restrict access through professional schools sanctioned by the state and shaped by professional associations. Once established, the principle of professional standards served to limit access and allow the market to determine wages. Occupational control meant fixing standards and letting wages fluctuate to clear the market. In teaching, however, the claim to standards never took hold, and so control over supply was never gained. Instead, wages were fixed by political process and standards allowed to fluctuate to clear the market. In the absence of visible, painful consequences, this relationship between system growth and wage-setting persisted. Once established, the principle of "emergency" credentials and waivers seemed to give the lie to professional pretensions.

As schools sprang up in the fifties and early sixties—the boom years—and filled with underqualified teachers, kids still learned to read and write, more and more went on to college, and there appeared to be no compelling reason to do anything about teacher quality. Then, in 1966, James Coleman and colleagues issued their famous report widely interpreted as proving that schools don't make a difference compared to family background.[19] Subsequent methodological critiques of the Coleman report failed to dispel the initial impression, which Christopher Jencks and coworkers underscored with their study of inequality some years later.[20] At the same time, a half-century's worth of research on teaching failed to uncover any significant relationship between teacher characteristics and student outcomes. In short, social science looked, shrugged its shoulders, and pronounced teachers unimportant.

While the true professions successfully created and then captured a market for their services, in education a large, unruly market captured and made subservient to it an occupation. In this process, ironically, science served to delegitimate the claim to professional status in teaching. The application of input-output analysis to the "education production function" revealed no robust relationships between school factors and student outcomes. Social critics and fiscal conservatives eagerly seized on such findings, while those whose common sense told them otherwise occupied, temporarily at least, a weak position in the public debate. The upshot in a critical period of expansion was the loss of a vital ideological resource and the growth of public skepticism about the prerequisites for teaching.

Occupational Processes and the Nature of Teaching Work

Historically, then, external barriers to professionalization developed early and persisted as influences on occupational processes and ethos. Recruitment came to rely on easy access, a monopoly over the supply of college-educated women based on their restricted access to other professions, and a working day and year well suited to the demands of marriage and motherhood. The service ideal operated not to enhance status and income but to keep teachers in their place. The fusion of antithetical elements in the ideology of other professions (an orientation to the market and to occupational control versus serving the public interest) failed in education, so that efforts to improve the rewards of teaching produced collective frowns. Genteel poverty and the nurturant image of women's work came to be associated with teaching as a calling. The public's benign but patronizing regard for teachers surely served as some small comfort but ultimately helped produce the disgruntlement over depressed wages and working conditions which led to unionization.

As teaching failed to secure the cultural authority necessary to advancement, so did conditions of work, and a series of internal accommodations undercut professionalization. For example, in teaching, socialization is largely self-achieved. Teachers work in isolation, and the beginner struggles alone to survive the first year and master the craft. Patterns of interaction within schools fail to encourage collegial exchange on professional matters, and "shop talk" in the teachers' lounge or lunchroom is often taboo. Neither school principals nor central office staff spend much time in teachers' classrooms, nor do teachers observe one another. With little chance to observe and reflect on practice during training and almost no opportunities on the job, inquiry is a norm honored largely in the breach.

Furthermore, the rewards of teaching come primarily from students, so teachers concentrate their attention on life behind the classroom door. There, the daily experience of teaching has about it an unpredictable, fickle quality. Lessons succeed or fail for obscure reasons, and the relationship between teachers' planful efforts and the outcomes of instruction is often indeterminate. The "feel" of teaching may just not be hospitable to an analytic approach. From the standpoint of the professionalization, this is most significant. One student of teaching notes:

> Today we usually think of knowledge-building in terms of scientific methodologies. A scientific approach, however, normally begins with the assumption that there is an underlying order in the phenomena under study. It is not clear that all or most teachers make that assumption about their world. Some see teaching outcomes as capricious and describe short-term results in almost mysterious terms. If that viewpoint is widespread, it is not surprising that teachers do not invest in searching for general principles to inform their work. If they suspect that classroom events are beyond comprehension, inquiry is futile.[21]

The lack of a technical subculture in teaching, then, stems not only from the absence of a professional school, or a societal commitment of resources for research, but from the nature of the work itself as experienced by practitioners.

If teaching has failed to establish a scientific knowledge base, so, too, have threats to its service ideal proved damaging. Unionization (about which more in a moment) has significantly altered teaching's status in many communities. More fundamentally, the structure of teaching itself makes the service ideal difficult to sustain as a working reality for the practitioner. In common with other public service occupations where workers must confront clients in batches, the myth of altruism is hard to maintain.[22] The ideal calls for providing help and care to others in a personal way, treating persons fairly yet individually to account for their unique needs. But the resources to provide such care are always inadequate, and latent demand typically absorbs any increase in service levels; vague, ambiguous, and conflicting goals provide little guidance for daily practice; and clients who are often nonvoluntary fail to serve as an important reference group.

As a result of these basic features of work, public-service providers develop a common set of coping responses. These include the inequitable rationing of services, a client-processing mentality, lowered expectations to close the gap between accomplishments and objectives, and the use of lowest-common-denominator routines to reduce uncertainties. Such responses allow teachers and other "street-level bureaucrats" to cope with the strains of work but can lead to disillusionment. Indeed, the existential consequences of work in such occupations are often alienation or burn-out. Conditions in particular schools can ease or intensify these problems, but in general this contradiction between the expectation to serve and the need for rationing makes the service ideal difficult to sustain among practitioners and in the public's mind.

Unionization: The Proletarian Challenge to the Professional Project

Most fateful to professionalization in teaching has been the rise of unions and collective bargaining as an alternative means to gain occupational control. In 1962 when the first major collective bargaining agreement was signed between a teacher's union and a board of education in New York City, about 59 percent of those teaching belonged to a teacher's organization. Today over 90 percent of teachers are unionized, a growth paralleling other white collar, public-sector employees but counter to the trend in the private sector, where blue-collar unions have actually declined.

Why did this occur? Theorists speculate it had to do with teaching's location in the educational system. One student of professionalization writes, "The structural predisposition toward collective bargaining power will be greater whenever an aspiring professional is subordinated to a hierarchy of authority, which itself includes categories with 'superior' claims to expertise."[23] In education, school administrators have sought to professionalize and hold superior positions to teachers. Trapped in a subordinate, gender-linked position, teachers, and more recently nurses, adopted the more class-conscious and openly aggressive strategy of unionization.

The assertation of direct, collective control over teaching labor works counter to professionalism. Most obviously, labor unions have no claim to moral authority, to representing other than their own narrow interests. The service ideal ceases to be a credible ideological resource, and any concern with professional matters is suspect for ulterior motives. So the unions are not in a strong position to argue for standards and definitions of practice, for public policy regulating teaching, for qualifications to teach, or for the necessity of rigorous training. (They will of course continue to press hard on such matters and to have their way in some cases based on political muscle. But their cultural authority qua organization is largely bankrupt.) The scope of interest narrows to wages, job security, and working conditions. Negotiation and confrontation rather than persuasion become the chief means of advancement.

With the turn to unions, teaching's image and cultural authority have shifted markedly. "Unions," notes an observer, "are, in fact an instrument of power of the working class, and as such are symbolic of a loss in general social status."[24] Militant unionism results in forfeit of any claim to trust and community goodwill. As push comes to shove in the pursuit of economic interests, unions sunder the fiduciary relation to the public interest. Teaching's social standing has probably suffered as a result, although this varies community by community. Between isolated instances in the fifties and today, the number of teacher strikes has risen dramatically (leveling and dropping off somewhat from a peak in the late seventies), deeply influencing perceptions of teachers and of the teaching occupation.

The significance of this shift to union control lies in its impact on public policy. While parents and community leaders still encounter dedicated teachers who aspire to professional norms, their leaders and organizations can no longer credibly pursue such aspirations collectively. Instead, conflict based strategies relying on hard bargaining, job actions, and grievances provoke an adversarial, power-equalizing response among policymakers. The public machinery has always been available both to establish occupational self-control and to protect the public. Professionalization lays claim to the former under the guise of the latter. Unionization helps break this equivalence, encouraging others to regulate the occupation.

Unionism also undermined the solidarity necessary to the professional project. In other fields relying on science to create a knowledge base for practice, cohesiveness among elite practitioners, researchers, and professional educators was necessary. From their collaboration emerged the professional schools, which regulated entry and defined the technical basis for competence. When teachers organized to protect their interests, however, they no longer had a vital stake in creating a professional school. Collective bargaining superseded restricted access via training as the means to gain market power. Teachers' abandonment of training as a vital concern cast adrift university based teacher educators. With the loss of a powerful ally, they retained little capacity to pursue the professional project on their own. The creation of a knowledge base and a professional school became a secondary concern to organized teachers, while teacher educators, obeying the imperatives of university life and of their own search for status, have continued to insist on the centrality of pedagogical science.

The center had not held. Research, training, and practice, largely divorced from one another, meet here and there for brief periods as expediency dictates but lack a common project, a genuine mutuality of interest. Union and profession coexist uneasily, and unionization has isolated the schools of education, depriving them of an ally in their quest for standing. Given their already weak position within the university, this has been a crucial loss.

Students and Status:
Unhappy Pursuits in Higher Education's Dual Markets

The preparation of teachers evolved along with and as an accommodation to other aspects of teaching, but developed its own contradictions. Teacher education emerged as a modest, intellectually undemanding affair, coextensive with undergraduate education. Whereas prolonged intense professional education in other fields weeds out the faint of purpose and develops genuine commitment to profession and career, teacher education is a dilatory option for many, recommended chiefly because it forestalls occupational commitment. The education major serves as a temporizing choice, particularly for those who transfer in after discovering that other majors prove too demanding.

In past decades, with demand galloping ahead of supply in the teacher labor market, there were few restrictions on entry. All who came were welcomed, and the course was not strenuous. Access to teacher education expanded along with access to postsecondary education in general. Teaching served as a social escalator from blue to white collar, while the availability of a widely dispersed set of training institutions, and of public subsidization for college, eased geographical and financial access for millions. The lack of standards likewise eased academic access. Teacher education, then, provided social mobility for thousands in our society nicely gauged to the expanding demand for new teachers. The teachers college, and later the multipurpose public university, helped many realize one version of the American dream. But teaching itself never became more than a temporary resting point in the quest for status.

With teacher education struggling both to establish its place in higher education and to supply an occupation suffering growing pains, contradictions inevitably emerged. As the teaching occupation became captive to its service market, so, too, teacher education was captured by the growing higher education market. On public campuses teacher training attracted students and resources. State finance formulas came to reward enrollments but redistributed funds among programs based on relative training costs. Teaching, as we have seen, ranks near the bottom of these allocation indices, and is a blue chip investment for universities, generating but not consuming state funds. So while university administrators would happily assent to innovations in programs, they greeted either the assertion of higher entry standards or the move to eliminate teacher education with horror. Any form of quality control adversely affected the financial prospects of the university at large and so met with little enthusiasm among those charged with the care and feeding of academe.

The university enjoyed another benefit from this arrangement at the expense of teacher education. The lack of standards and the need to yield quantities of graduates meant that students preparing for teaching were generally the least able on campus. The arts and sciences faculty could embrace the most promising students while nudging lesser lights into teacher education. Such programs became safety valves and dumping grounds on too many campuses, serving to collect higher education's outcasts in one spot and, over time, stigmatizing the entire enterprise. Teaching's equivocal status is probably the root cause for teacher education's unenviable reputation on college campuses, but these specific institutional processes have surely exacerbated this problem.

Another curious pattern developed as well. Universities profit from simultaneously luring students into teaching then freeing them from such bondage. The route out of the classroom into a burgeoning education industry detours through a university credentialing process. Graduate programs in education serve two purposes: to augment teacher salaries and to facilitate escape from the classroom to more prestigious, lucrative jobs. Master's-degree students are often teachers taking individual courses on the margins of their workday to gain increments on the pay scale. Doctoral students may also be part-timers seeking administrative credentials or full-time students desiring research related careers. Master's students are a valuable commodity in that they supply tuition and maintain enrollments without requiring (or getting) much in return. No one has ever pretended that the master's degree in education is more than an economic convenience and a mutually beneficial medium of exchange in the traffic between the university and the schools. Doctoral students invite more serious attention, predicated, however, on the common desire to shun teaching in favor of higher matters. Individuals aim to put teaching behind them, while institutions similarly seek status through involvement either with research or with administration. At these advanced levels of the system, then, the universities are divorced from teaching and so fail to support professionalism in teaching.

Put differently, teacher education is trapped in a number of market games that must be played but cannot be won. In the market game to attract students and revenue, the enemy is standards. State university systems with multiple campuses are responsible for producing a sizable fraction of the nation's teachers. Within such states no individual campuses can afford to drop teacher education for fear of loss of revenue and of standing with the state legislature. Enrollment declines are similarly threatening and must be offset through a downward shift in standards. In the market game to enhance status, however, standards are a resource in themselves and a means to improve both student and faculty quality. Given the financial means, institutions can elevate their position, department by department, by attracting notables to the faculty and setting a higher cut-off point for students. Thus do college presidents and deans assiduously cultivate reputations.

System dynamics determine the linkage between students and status markets. In an expansionary period education programs can happily pursue both students and status. With an excess of students enrolling, selectivity is possible, and universities can support multiple incompatible purposes because slack resources allow their compartmentalized pursuit free of competition for scarce funds. So schools of education under conditions of growth can fly the twin banners of excellence and equity, claiming both high standards and equal, even affirmative, access. Likewise, elite universities may graciously extend their concern for public education to the training of teachers without contaminating their high status or compromising their primary focus on scholarship and new knowledge. With decline, however, the joint pursuit of students and status becomes impossible. Universities must either relinquish their market share of students to maintain standards and concentrate dwindling resources on the core mission or seek to maintain enrollments but risk loss of status through increasingly nonselective intake policies and feeble, diffuse initiatives.

Teacher education, in Harry Judge's phrase, "rests upon a deeply institutionalized error."[25] Trapped within the undergraduate liberal arts program, it has not emerged as a separate professional school nor melded comfortably with the liberal arts. The so-called all-university approach to teacher education is a lofty ideal concealing a sometimes cynical struggle for students. Education faculties utilizing accrediting bodies and state certification machinery seek to expand their domain via additional course requirements in education. Representatives of the arts and sciences on faculty oversight committees protect their interests by resisting decreases in liberal arts coursework. At stake in both cases are faculty positions, student enrollments, and work for graduate teaching assistants.

Strapped into a demographic roller coaster, the education schools play out their status anxieties either by emulating the scholarly pursuits of academic departments or by resolutely seeking to train practitioners in imitation of the free-standing professional schools. In the first case, education must shun its association with teaching's low status and with the schools in order to pursue the quest for knowledge. This is the pattern Judge so eloquently describes in his 1982 report on the elite graduate schools of education. In the second case, education turns to the practical problems of the schools but fails to maintain contact with new knowledge. In their study of knowledge production in education, for example, Clark and Guba found that less than 10 percent of the education faculty are located in schools or departments that can be characterized as research oriented, revealing a pattern of teacher training absent of much involvement with inquiry.[26]

Taken together these recent studies of teacher education reveal mixed patterns in resolving the dilemmas of competition for status and students. There is no institutional consensus on the proper mission of schools and departments of education, merely strategic scrambles for advancement and survival in the ebb and flow of enrollments and of soft money for new projects. The link between knowledge production and use has never been forged, nor has an enduring relation between the schools of education and the public schools. Finally, the elite universities in the nation are only minimally involved in the preparation of teachers and so fail to provide either practical guidance or moral authority to the training enterprise.

Over the past decade retrenchment has further complicated these woes. Between the early seventies and the early eighties, enrollments in teacher education dropped more than 50 percent, threatening the survival of many programs. The decline in education students was particularly steep among those in the upper quartile of the academic ability distribution, as capable women and blacks, previously excluded from many careers, began choosing business, law, medicine, and computer science over the traditional careers of teaching, nursing, and social work. Consequently, institutions with high entry standards were likely to lose disproportionately more students than open-enrollment schools.[27] The individual cream-skimming soon developed an institutional counterpart as elite universities abandoned teacher education. Other schools increased their share of low-scoring students to minimize their losses, but this further stigmatized the whole enterprise. The center of academic gravity has been sinking in education, a trend the schools of education are relatively powerless to affect but which affects them deeply.

The pieces fell apart, not together, for the professional project in education. In the country's middle decades a feminized work force failed to gain control of supply in the market for school teachers. This failure doomed efforts to legitimize standards and secure high wages. Rather than support professionalism, social science actually undercut it, contributing a view of teaching as largely ineffectual. Work structures and occupational processes evolved in ways antithetical both to the development of a technical subculture and to satisfaction of the service ideal. Not surprisingly, unionization eventually emerged in the early sixties as an alternative means to gain occupational control. Unions supplied a new form of solidarity and a new project of great initial appeal. But unionization also drove a wedge between teachers and other interests, tarnishing an image today in desperate need of furbishing. Teacher education grew in accommodation to these other trends but responded as well to conflicts within higher education's community. There, too, market forces and system dynamics held sway, shaping the pursuit of students and status.

Prospects for an Enlightened Future

Various efforts over the years to reform teacher education have achieved some limited and temporary success but not a thoroughgoing transformation. The enterprise as a whole seems fixed by a range of institutional, demographic, and economic forces at an unacceptable level of quality, incapable of setting and enforcing—or even of articulating and projecting—high standards. Invidious distinctions of status among the institutions of higher education, among departments and schools within the university, and between the universities and the schools, frustrate the search for a common cause. The mission is shortchanged. Teacher education is underfunded and lacks life space. It is a small, old outboard propelling a very large cabin cruiser through the water at an unsurprisingly imperceptible rate.

Proposals for reform abound. Some urge an advanced degree in teaching for the minority who wish a career in the classroom,[28] coupled with higher salary and expanded responsibilities. Others argue that teacher education as a whole must become a postbaccalaureate program and that through accreditation we must reduce the number of institutions that prepare teachers.[29] Still others favor a genuine school of pedagogy based on accumulating knowledge about teaching, using the most advanced techniques to impart such knowledge;[30] or they propose extended programs that integrate liberal arts, professional education, and practical experience over five or six years.[31] Most friendly critics also appreciate that reforms of teacher education stand little chance unless linked to changes in the schools, in the teaching occupation, and in the policy framework shaping the whole enterprise. They emphasize that teacher salaries must be higher, working conditions must better support teachers,[32] teaching must attract and hold more academically able recruits, and state policy, particularly allocation formulas to the universities, must supply more resources.[33]

If the past is prologue in teacher education, then widespread, comprehensive reform is unlikely. The prospect of converting teacher education to a post-baccalaureate program, whether integrated with the undergraduate curriculum or not, appears slim. In the past, moves to extend teacher training matched the state of the teacher labor market. Internships increased when there was a surplus of teachers (for example, during the Depression) but dropped off as shortages developed. Both the master of arts in teaching (MAT) program and the early Teacher Corps established postbaccalaureate programs but reached a minority of new teachers. To require an extended program of training for all new teachers without a corresponding increase in the rewards of teaching is not feasible: market pressures will continue to dominate standards. Likewise, no major reallocation or infusion of resources to teacher education is likely. The training venture has not gained sufficient warrant for this, in part because its rationale is derivative: teacher education exists to improve teaching. With ever-present arguments that both teaching and teacher education are underfunded, and absent an impressive demonstration of the latter's potency, policymakers will most often direct funds to teaching.

Other grand strategies promising a breakthrough are not imminent. Harvard's president James Conant, hailed as education's Samuel Flexner, had little impact on the field, and accreditation has not served over the years to legitimize institutional standards; weak programs have persisted. Proposals for structural reform have never materialized either: both Conant's suggestion for a new role,[34] the clinical professor, and B. O. Smith's idea for a new institution, the training complex,[35] came to nought, although each pointed up the difficulty in joining research to practice, the universities to the schools. Finally, social science knowledge is unlikely to rationalize a technical transformation of the professional curriculum. No paradigm orders inquiry in education, no "sciences of the artificial" or eclectic arts conjoin basic knowledge and design;[36] rather, in education the technical base grows fitfully and in small increments.

Short of ambitious reforms, though, teacher education has several modest prospects. Both the MAT strategy and the Teacher Corps demonstrated that special programs can enhance status, supply an esprit otherwise lacking, and recruit able college graduates despite teaching's low pay. For a limited number of prospective teachers a selective post-baccalaureate program highly regarded at the university and by the community will be attractive. The MAT approach never received much trial in the mainline institutions yet might well serve as an alternative on more campuses.

Efforts to extend training into the first year of teaching point to another promising trend. State-mandated induction or intern programs, such as Oklahoma's, join the university and the schools in providing support, supervision, and evaluation for first-year teachers, a step that is intermediate to and less costly than a full extended program but still lengthens training somewhat. Intern programs have several virtues: they are job related, they do not defer income for young teachers, they can involve experienced teachers in passing along their lore, and they provide a performance base for certification. The Teacher Corps experience underscored the importance of boundary spanners between universities and schools, and the new state mandates may help provide a framework within which such positions will develop; they appear crucial to effective collaboration.

Finally, a gradual accumulation of usable pedagogical knowledge provides a more spacious avenue for technical improvements in the professional curriculum. For some time, advocates have faulted the training programs for failing to stay abreast and to use the best available knowledge, arguing that the translation and use of knowledge, not its quality or quantity, is the fundamental problem. Progress in the coming decades, then, will take the form of better knowledge use in the training program and stronger connections between research and training.

The Neglected Dimension

Interpreted in light of the professional project, teacher education appears bereft, trapped in a force field admitting only small movements in any direction. Yet other histories and interpretations are available. This account omits a counterpart at the level of individual institutions, where stories of success and failure, triumph and tragedy, progress and stasis have played out over the decades. A whiff of determinism often accompanies history written as global sweep, denying the choices and maneuvering room actually open to individuals. A step down from the slow movements of history and the grant strategies of reformers to the prospects for renewal and excellence in particular institutions reveals other possibilities.

Worry over what is lacking in teacher education often centers on such things as funds, status, standards, life space, and knowledge, with corresponding attention to these resources in reform proposals. Yet this emphasis on the instrumental neglects an important dimension in the lives of individuals and institutions. What is more fundamentally missing in teacher education is both a conception and a conviction of its value. The enterprise of preparing teachers in our society is not esteemed, and the consequences are devastating. Absent sufficient caring, we have no appreciative framework for teacher education, no shared conception of quality, no capacity to recognize excellence, no vocabulary to describe nor occasions to celebrate it. Stated differently, the process of educating teachers is essentially invisible, a sure sign of what is valueless in a culture.

The outward manifestations of this problem should by now be clear, but there is a toll on the inner life as well. Every professional practice requires a discourse continuously enriched through reference to transcendent ideals. Central to human services is a sense of mission powerful enough to inspire and sustain, to give meaning and significance to the work. Without occasions for pride and a sense of connection to important values, the vicissitudes of human service work can be great. As any teacher will acknowledge, working with others has both a light and dark side, an inevitable feature in the pursuit of ideals that at once compel but admit of no easy realization. Teaching can provide joy and fulfillment but can be frustrating and enervating too. Visions of excellence nourish the light side, enabling buoyancy and resilience. Their absence leads to low morale, failure of nerve, loss of expectations.

Missing from the rhetoric of reform in teacher education is attention to this expressive side, to the inner life of the enterprise. Consider, by contrast, the emphasis in some recent writing on management which hails the creation of corporate cultures as a hallmark of excellence.[37] In these accounts of successful businesses and business leaders, it is not technological breakthroughs or rational management schemes that matter but attention to the human side of enterprise. The corporate exemplars stand for and communicate a set of values through rites and rituals, organizational sagas, and proud traditions filled with heroes and champions. The new language used to describe corporate life is remarkably primitive, smacking more of Margaret Mead on Samoa than of Harold Geneen on the International Telephone and Telegraph Company. It is an anthropological language redolent of mythology and symbolism, a language appropriate to the centrality of values.

"Companies succeed," claims one observer, "because their employees can identify, embrace, and act on the values of the organization."[38] So, too, do programs of teacher education, yet preoccupations there are unrelievedly literal, instrumental, and parochial. The rhetoric is too often plaintive, too seldom inspirational. Needed is not another six-point program of reform, complete with arguments pro and con and steps toward implementation, but eloquently rendered visions of excellence. To repeat: what the leadership has most sadly neglected in teacher education is not resource calculations or the mechanisms of reform but reasons and ways to care.

This concern for value, for meaning, is not mere froth on the bracing brew of hardheaded practice. Rather it is something more serious, more fundamental to the life of an institution. Although I have argued that the larger predicament of teacher education is in a sense tragic—the show must go on but with no promise of greatness on a grand scale— there is room for affirmation and progress at any institution that prepares teachers. But the starting point for those who are interested—the university president, the dean, the professors—must be the value of the enterprise itself, even asserted in the face of public indifference, narrow institutional confines, and resource poverty. Teacher education needs its heroes, its sagas, its proud traditions that embody and convey what is valuable in the undertaking.

The moral rearmament of teacher education has no single referent. Higher education in America is astonishingly diverse, and no set of blueprints would apply universally. Rather, each college or university that prepares teachers should plumb its special strengths, creating virtue from its own institutional necessities. The forms of excellence are many. One school might reaffirm its commitment to teacher education with a cross-disciplinary program of study based in the liberal arts. Under the vigorous leadership of the dean or the college president, faculty from the arts and sciences would fashion a demanding course of study based on the classic texts of Western civilization and seek applications to the problems of education. Faculty might model Socratic teaching in such a program, cultivating a reflective turn of mind in students while demonstrating at the same time a powerful teaching style.

A second university devoted to empirical research might create a curriculum based on the accumulation of usable knowledge on teaching. Critics have easily lampooned such efforts in the past as mere technical training unsuitable for the preparation of professionals who must learn to use judgment, not just employ skills. But an emerging, more sophisticated approach uses research results as the starting point for discussion with practitioners rather than as prescriptions for drill and practice. Such a program might pioneer in thoughtfully joining research to practice, demonstrating that research based teaching is not unfriendly to humanist conceptions of the role.

Another school might blaze a third compelling trail. In the tradition of many community colleges whose forte is service, this school might build strong connections to local schools. Such a program might feature regular experiences in the schools over the four-year course, heavy faculty involvement in school improvement projects, and adjunct professorships for master teachers at the college: in short, a thoroughly collaborative, status-equalizing partnership between the college and the surrounding schools, in which each makes substantial contributions to the other so that superintendents, principals, and teachers union leaders become the program's strongest advocates.

Leadership breathes life into such schematic depictions as these, a leadership projecting a vision of excellence in teaching, of excellence in the preparation of teachers, and of excellence in an institution that trains teachers. A second common element of such programs is the conviction to be uncommon. Timid reforms, patch-ups of the prevailing wisdom which emerge from committees, will not do. Teacher education needs more rogues, uncompromising fellows who make enemies but get things done, who stand against in their willingness to stand for, who trail excitement in their wake. With such forcefulness must come a passion for high standards, a tough-minded insistence on the best in individuals and programs. But standards, not standardization—*pace* the accreditation crowd—are necessary. These rise out of particular visions of excellence rather than residing in common program elements such as staff-student ratios or the size of the library. Standards speak for the unique merit in a program, guide participants in their work, supply the bedrock for pride in accomplishment, and proclaim to all what a program stands for. This is the key, then, a leadership willing to project uncommon initiatives, at whose heart is an adamant insistence on excellence.

There is an alternative perspective. Teacher education has suffered a complacent expansion, heedless of the need for standards. By one reckoning approximately 50 percent of the training institutions produce 90 percent of the teachers who score in the lower fifth of the academic ability distribution.[39] A handful of outstanding programs would barely leaven the general mediocrity, disturbing the status quo but little. Public policy must take on two purposes, then: to issue the summons to excellence and to thin the ranks. The renewal of teacher education will be a local drama, but state and federal funds can supply the stimulus. The systematic cultivation of idiosyncratic merit would require unencumbered grants-in-aid that demand evidence only of leadership, a vision eloquently rendered, and a commitment to high standards. The second purpose, undoubtedly more difficult to achieve, requires professional program evaluation tied to funding decisions. States must institute a careful process of program review, drawing on expert judgment and a wide range of qualitative evidence, to close down inferior programs. This quid pro quo is the starting point for a public agenda on teacher education.

Notes

1. National Center for Education Statistics, *The Condition of Education, 1983*, p. 92.

2. Cyr, "Demographics of Teacher Education," p. 33.

3. Astin et al., *The American Freshman*.

4. National Center for Education Statistics. *Fast Response Survey of Teacher Education*.

5. Kerr, "Teaching Competence and Teacher Education in the United States," p. 136.

6. Peaseau and Orr, "The Outrageous Underfunding of Teacher Education," pp. 100–102.

7. National Education Association. *Status of the American Public School Teacher, 1980–81*, p. 21.

8. For this phrase and the related ideas I am indebted to David Cohen. See his unpublished manuscript, "Commitment and Uncertainty."

9. Gage, *The Scientific Basis of the Art of Teaching*.

10. Dewey, *The Sources of a Science of Education*.

11. Koerner, *Miseducation of American Teachers*.

12. Lortie, *Schoolteacher*.

13. Research by Wayne Hoy and colleagues emphasizes how the bureaucratic aspects of school shape teachers' pupil-control ideology. See Hoy, "The Influence of Experience on the Beginning Teacher," pp. 312–323; Hoy, "Pupil Control Ideology and Organizational Socialization," pp. 257–265; and Hoy and Rees, "The Bureaucratic Socialization of Student Teachers," pp. 23–26. A variety of studies explore the structural characteristics of classrooms that affect teachers. See, for example, Jackson, *Life in Classrooms*; Dreeben, "The School as Workplace"; Sharp and Green, *Education and Social Control*; and Doyle, "Learning the Classroom Environment," pp. 51–55.

14. Edgar and Warren, "Power and Autonomy in Teacher Socialization," pp. 386–399.

15. See, for example, Copeland, "Student Teachers and Co-operating Teachers," pp. 194–199; and Klein, "Student Influence on Teacher Behavior."

16. Reinhart, "The Persistence of Occupational Prestige."

17. Gallup, "The 15th Annual Gallup Poll of the Public's Attitudes Toward the Public Schools."

18. Green, *Predicting the Behavior of the Educational System.*

19. Coleman et al., *Equality of Educational Opportunity.*

20. Jencks et al., *Inequality.*

21. Lortie, *Schoolteacher,* p. 211.

22. Lipsky, *Street-Level Bureaucracy,* chap. 6.

23. Larson, *The Rise of Professionalism,* p. 185.

24. Ibid., p. 236.

25. Judge, *American Graduate Schools of Education,* p. 34.

26. Clark and Guba, "A Study of Teacher Education Institutions as Innovators, Knowledge Producers, and Change Agencies."

27. Schlechty and Vance, "Institutional Responses to the Quality/Quantity Issue in Teacher Training," pp. 94–101.

28. Kerr, "Teaching Competence and Teacher Education in the United States," p. 142. Lawrence Cremin has recommended that all aspiring educators receive the doctorate. See his article, "The Education of the Educating Professions."

29. Judge, *American Graduate Schools of Education,* pp. 58–63.

30. Smith, *A Design for a School of Pedagogy.*

31. Scannell et al., "Task Force Report on Extended Programs."

32. See Kerr, pp. 143–144, and Gideonse, "The Necessary Revolution in Teacher Education," pp. 15–18.

33. Smith, "Pedagogical Education," pp. 87–90.

34. Conant, *The Education of American Teachers.*

35. Smith, *Teachers for the Real World.*

36. See Simon, *The Sciences of the Artificial;* and Joseph J. Schwab, "The Practical: A Language for Curriculum," pp. 1–20, and "The Practical: Arts of Eclectic," pp. 493–542.

37. See, for example, Deal and Kennedy, *Corporate Cultures,* and Peters and Waterman, *In Search of Excellence.*

38. Deal and Kennedy, *Corporate Cultures,* p. 21.

39. Personal communication from Phillip Schlechty, based on unpublished data.

Bibliography

ASTIN, ALEXANDER W., MARGO R. KING, and GERALD T. RICHARDSON. *The American Freshman: National Norms for Fall 1981.* Los Angeles: UCLA Graduate School of Education. Cooperative Institutional Research Program, December 1981.

CLARK, DAVID, and EGON GUBA. "A Study of Teacher Education Institutions as Innovators, Knowledge Producers, and Change Agencies." Washington, D.C.: National Institute of Education, April 1977.

COHEN, DAVID. "Commitment and Uncertainty." Cambridge: Harvard Graduate School of Education, May 1982. Unpublished manuscript.

COLEMAN, JAMES S., ERNEST Q. CAMPBELL, CAROL J. HOBSON, JAMES MCPARTLAND, ALEXANDER M. WOOD, FREDERICK D. WEINFELD, and ROBERT L. YORK. *Equality of Educational Opportunity.* Washington, D.C.: U.S. Government Printing Office, 1966.

CONANT, JAMES B. *The Education of American Teachers.* New York: McGraw-Hill, 1963.

COPELAND, W. D. "Student Teachers and Co-operating Teachers: An Ecological Relationship." *Theory Into Practice* 18, no. 3 (1981): 194–199.

CYR, RALPH. "Demographics of Teacher Education: Implications for Policymaking." In *Policy for the Education of Educators: Issues and Implications.* Washington, D.C.: American Association of Colleges for Teacher Education, 1981.

DEAL, TERENCE E., and ALLAN A. KENNEDY. *Corporate Cultures.* Reading, Mass.: Addison-Wesley, 1982.

DEWEY, JOHN. *The Sources of a Science of Education.* New York: Liveright, 1929.

DOYLE, W. "Learning the Classroom Environment: An Ecological Analysis." *Journal of Teacher Education* 28 (Nov. 1977): 51–55.

DREEBEN, ROBERT. "The School as Workplace." In *The Second Handbook of Research on Teaching,* ed. R. Travers. Chicago: Rand McNally, 1973. Pp. 450–473.

EDGAR, D., and R. WARREN. "Power and Autonomy in Teacher Socialization." *Sociology of Education* 42 (1969): 389–399.

ELSBREE, W. *The American Teacher.* New York: American Book, 1939.

GAGE, N. L. *The Scientific Basis of the Art of Teaching.* New York: Teachers College Press, 1978.

GALLUP, GEORGE H. "The 15th Annual Gallup Poll of the Public's Attitudes Toward the Public Schools." *Phi Delta Kappan* 65 (Sept. 1983): 33–47.

GREEN, TOM. *Predicting the Behavior of the Educational System.* New York: Syracuse University Press, 1980.

HOFSTADTER, RICHARD. *Anti-Intellectualism in American Life.* New York: Vintage Books, 1962.

HOY, WAYNE. "The Influence of Experience on the Beginning Teacher." *School Review* 76 (1968): 312–323.

———. "Pupil Control Ideology and Organizational Socialization: A Further Examination of the Influence of Experience on the Beginning Teacher." *School Review* 77 (1969): 257–265.

HOY, WAYNE, and REES, R. "The Bureaucratic Socialization of Student Teachers." *Journal of Teacher Education* 28 (Jan.-Feb. 1977): 23–26.

JACKSON, PHILIP. *Life in Classrooms.* New York: Holt, Rinehart and Winston, 1968.

JENCKS, CHRISTOPHER et al. *Inequality: A Reassessment of the Effect of Family and Schooling in America.* New York: Basic Books, 1972.

JUDGE, HARRY. *American Graduate Schools of Education.* New York: Ford Foundation, 1982.

KERR, DONNA H. "Teaching Competence and Teacher Education in the United States." In *Handbook of Teaching and Policy*, ed. L. Shulman and G. Sykes. New York: Longman, 1983.

KLEIN, S. S. "Student Influence on Teacher Behavior." *American Educational Research Journal* 8 (1971): 403–421.

KOERNER, JAMES D. *The Miseducation of American Teachers*. Boston: Houghton Mifflin, 1963.

LARSON, MAGALI SARFATI. *The Rise of Professionalism*. Berkeley: University of California Press, 1977.

LIPSKY, MICHAEL. *Street-Level Bureaucracy: Dilemmas of the Individual in Public Services*. New York: Russell Sage, 1980.

LORTIE, DAN. *Schoolteacher*. Chicago: University of Chicago Press, 1975.

National Center for Education Statistics. *Projections of Education Statistics to 1988–89*. Washington, D.C., 1980.

———. *The Condition of Education, 1983*. Washington, D.C., 1983a.

———. *Fast Response Survey of Teacher Education: Perceptions of Methods of Improvement*. Washington, D.C., 1983b.

National Education Association. *Status of the American Public School Teacher 1980–81*. Washington, D.C., 1982.

PEASEAU, B., and P. ORR. "The Outrageous Underfunding of Teacher Education." *Phi Delta Kappan* 62 (Oct. 1980): 100–102.

PETERS, THOMAS J., and ROBERT H. WATERMAN, JR. *In Search of Excellence. Lessons From America's Best-Run Corporations*. New York: Harper and Row, 1982.

REINHART, G. R. "The Persistence of Occupational Prestige." Paper presented at the Southern Sociological Society, Louisville, Kentucky, 1981.

SCHLECHTY, P. C., and V. S. VANCE. "Institutional Responses to the Quality/ Quantity Issue in Teacher Training." *Phi Delta Kappan* 65 (Oct. 1983): 94–101.

SCHWAB, JOSEPH J. "The Practical: A Language for Curriculum." *School Review* 58 (Nov. 1969): 1–20.

———. "The Practical: Arts of Eclectic." *School Review* 59 (Nov. 1970): 493–542.

SHARP, R., and GREEN, A. *Education and Social Control*. London: Routledge and Kegan Paul, 1975.

SIMON, HERBERT. *The Sciences of the Artificial*. Cambridge: The MIT Press, 1969.

SMITH, B. O. *Teachers for the Real World*. Washington, D.C.: American Association of Colleges for Teacher Education, 1969.

———. *A Design for a School of Pedagogy*. Washington, D.C.: U.S. Department of Education, 1980.

———. "Pedagogical Education: How About Reform?" *Phi Delta Kappan* 62 (Oct. 1980): 87–90.

WALLER, WILLARD. *The Sociology of Teaching*. New York: John Wiley and Sons, 1932.

11

Conclusions

BURTON R. CLARK

T HE PRECEDING CHAPTERS CLARIFY THE relationship between secondary and higher education—the school and the university—in seven individual countries and much of Latin America and Africa. Together, they stretch from the most advanced educational systems to the most retarded, ranging from northern Europe, Japan, and the United States to some of the poorest nations of tropical Africa. The authors have reported on systems in the East as well as the West, on education in a country of over a billion people and in another of less than eight million. Such extended coverage insures some dramatic differences in linkages and practices. When, in one case, less than 1 percent of the age group moves between the school and the university, as in China, and in another case 50 percent or more do so, as in the United States, the first level will condition the second in sharply different ways. And despite much imitating and borrowing across national lines, each country retains unique educational characteristics that connect to the special nature of its own economy, polity, and cultural traditions. This variety inescapably commands our attention.

But striking similarities also become evident, first between neighboring countries, where they might be expected, and then even between societies that are geographically and culturally separated. Beyond the unique inner logic of each educational system, we soon note basic characteristics that are shared among a number of countries. There may even be a few common imperatives. Using the metaphor of a two-way street, there is always the upward flow of students to connect the school and the university to each other, with student selection and training a crucial matter. From this connection it follows everywhere that as the secondary school system becomes more accessible it pressures higher education to expand and diversify. In return there is always the downward flow of teachers, with their selection and training central to how the university shapes the school. There is an inescapable relationship of exchange:

290

when the school sends only top-flight students to the university, the university in turn sends top-flight teachers to the school; when the school sends everyman, the university is likely to send every-person in return.

Moving between variety and similarity, this final chapter will offer three sets of conclusions. The first section sorts some basic differences and similarities in the school-university relationship and in mediation by third-party institutions. As we sort through secondary curricular tracks and school examinations, for example, we can point to patterns that vary across national systems with fateful effects. The second section centers on the American system, exploring through international lenses the sources of the problems and weaknesses of the American high school. Is the repetitive crisis of the American school largely an artifact of swings in public attention, as it clearly is in part, or is it a result of errors in policy that can be readily remedied? Is something fundamentally out of sorts? Cross-national comparisons, particularly with Japan as a mirror, point to long-established American structures and practices that together contribute to weaknesses at the secondary level. There is a distinctive American problem. But a cross-national perspective also points to the likelihood that other societies will edge into a similar problem as they simultaneously absorb more of the young into upper secondary edu-cation, widen access to postsecondary institutions, and seek greater equality of educational opportunity.

The final section specifies a trend that affects all modern and mod-ernizing educational systems. With every passing decade the school and the university face a greater volume of tasks as they incorporate more people, connect to more occupations and affect more life chances, and seek to structure themselves around more—and more rapidly chang-ing—bodies of knowledge. At each level the expanding load of tasks leads to persistent problems of how to modify structures and alter pro-cedures in order to effectively do all that should be done. That burden tears at the relationship between the two tiers. The growing body of commitments strengthens centrifugal forces at each of the two levels. It multiplies their connections and promotes confusion about who is doing what to whom. Perhaps most important, this underlying trend of in-creasing complexity leads to diverging agendas for these two major sectors of education.

International Comparisons

We seek tentative generalizations within the main categories used in organizing the earlier chapters: how the school shapes the university, the reverse influence of the university upon the school, and the role played by mediating institutions.

HOW THE SCHOOL SHAPES THE UNIVERSITY

As emphasized in all the preceding chapters, secondary education determines higher education principally by shaping the upward flow of students. In this determination the main instruments of influence are curricular tracks and exit examinations.

A cross-national view of curricular tracks reveals a simple general point: the greater the degree of tracking at the secondary level, the clearer and more direct are the connections between the school and the university. As tracking is reduced, the linkages become blurred and often indirect. The empirical evidence is clear. At one pole is the strong streaming of the French system. There we find clear tracking by type of secondary school, with the upper secondary years serving as a major point of selection. A minority of students enter those preparatory schools and special programs that, in the first instance, lead to the *grandes écoles*. The best of these schools skim the cream of the cream. Everyone knows that this sharp selection occurs, conditioning and segmenting parental hopes and student aspirations while the young are in the elementary and lower secondary schools. Then, as a second decisive step, the system divides the upward-bound minority of students into more specific streams by tracking carefully by subject within the secondary preparatory schools. Majoring in certain subjects sharply affects destinations beyond the secondary level. As Guy Neave highlighted in chapter one, mathematics is the single subject in the French secondary system that opens all doors to higher education. Other subjects open only some doors while closing others.

At the extreme of intense tracking, therefore, we may speak of well-defined and highly structured lines of study that forge precise connections between the school and the university. A clear distinction is drawn between terminal lines and those that permit passage to higher education, and, more precisely, to designated parts of it.[1] Specialized schools make a first cut, subjects within schools effect a second.

Even after all the reforms of the post–World War II era and the steady expansion of access and participation, the separation of students into different types of secondary schools remains the modal pattern around the world. To a significant degree we find streaming-by-school in Germany and the United Kingdom, as well as in France, in Japan and China, and throughout Latin America and Africa. The highly selective keypoint school is a remarkable phenomenon in China, a central institution of the educational system and the nation in the forming of elites. The move toward comprehensive schools, which eliminates such separation, has made serious headway, but changes generally stop short of the upper secondary years. The United Kingdom retains the sixth form as a special upper tier within the secondary system which tailors a clientele for higher education. The Japanese system distinguishes sharply between lower and upper secondary education, treating the upper level as a place for streaming and selection.

The second form of heavy tracking, by subjects within schools, appears also as a worldwide modal pattern, although we know somewhat less about it. It is buried within the internal operations of schools and therefore not as immediately apparent as the separation of students among different types of schools. But the preceding chapters report such subject tracking in Germany, Britain, and France, the three major European models that have influenced secondary and higher education internationally. And in the much-reformed Swedish system, there were still, in the early 1980s, over twenty precise curricular streams within "integrated" schools. France is simply an extreme case among Western democracies of subject streaming, one that highlights a form of tracking that remains widespread.

At the other pole we find the school structure of the American system. Here the public comprehensive school dominates. Students are not streamed into different types of secondary schools only some of which lead to higher education. Under democratic ideals that envisioned all young people attending a common school, the secondary system has sought to be singular in institutional structure. Since the comprehensive school includes all curricula, it reduces the first major form of tracking to virtually zero. And, in sharp contrast to France, neither is tracking by subject carried out precisely. A student in the American high school does not need to major in mathematics or in any other particular subject to be favored for entry to higher education, including into its most prestigious institutions. Instead, students flow typically into and through three broad curricular tracks, academic, vocational, and general—the last being neither fish nor fowl. Among these broad groupings, which can overlap and among which transferring is possible, the academic track leads to the more selective sectors of higher education. Who enters that track is largely a matter of student choice, as shaped by social background and family expectations, and sometimes by the guidance of school counselors. Then, critically, students from all these tracks may enter the less selective components of the tertiary system, particularly the two-year community college. Hence, by cross-national comparison, tracking is relatively weak, blurring the connections between the school and the university.

In short, whereas the specialized secondary school, European style, advances selection to the time of entry into secondary education, and especially into its upper years, the comprehensive school, United States style, postpones selection, often to a point beyond the secondary level. Thus, the greater the degree of formal differentiation of schools in secondary education, the more selection is lodged in the transition between primary and secondary education or, now more generally in advanced systems, between compulsory and postcompulsory education. The less the differentiation, the more selection is shifted upward, to the transition between school and university and beyond. Worldwide, there is a tendency to postpone selection. But that postponement typically only goes as far as the upper secondary level, leaving selection largely lodged in the secondary system.

The other major device by which the school shapes student flow is the exit examination, simultaneously certifying completion of secondary schooling and guaranteeing admission to higher education. This form of examination has been part of the inner logic of most European systems. It became institutionalized in past decades, when only a small proportion of the age group attempted to pass through the academic school on their way to the university. Since that track offered prestige to teachers as well as to students, it was able to recruit competent subject specialists who became the professors of the secondary level. To American eyes, but not to French, it is surprising that leading French professor-intellectuals, such as Raymond Aron, taught in secondary schools during their careers. With comparable scholarly hands controlling a firm curricular track, the university could depend on the school for an output that would be, without further question, acceptable as its input. Thus grew the practice of the exit examination that guaranteed admission to higher education, an examination traditionally followed, in the German model in particular, by free student choice of both the university in which to enroll and the field in which to study. In this classic elite pattern, the school could be trusted, since a high level of competence was taken for granted.

That trust has continued into the present period. Even after the expansions, troubles, and reforms of the 1960s and 1970s, as Ulrich Teichler pointed out in the case of Germany, "the university cannot determine its own intake." (An important side effect of this lack of university control over admission is that students have little attachment to the university they attend.) Generally, the secondary exit examination, in contradiction to the university entrance examination, is part of the inner logic in which basic selection takes place at entry into secondary—now upper secondary—education, and in which those who enter the academic track—

Gymnasium (Germany), *lycée* (France), classical or scientific *liceo* (Italy)—are taken to be an already purified thin stream of excellence. The exit examination is a final touch of legitimation.

Exit examinations do not have this force in Japan and the United States. In the United States the 1500 private colleges and universities admit individually; the public institutions generally operate within broad categories of student qualifications for those students applying from within the home state, and then individually for out-of-state students. Private institutions generally use a mix of criteria, primarily school marks and broad aptitude test scores from examinations administered by voluntary associations, that is, the Educational Testing Service (ETS) and the Iowa organization that operates the counterpart American College Testing Program. The state universities and state colleges generally depend heavily on the student achievement record in the secondary school, supplemented by some use of scores from the nationally administered examinations. In any case, there are no guarantees of admission to the private institutions by virtue of high school passage, and any guarantees in the public sector are bounded by state citizenship. Most students attend public institutions in their home states, and hence their general certificate of school completion, backed by a transcript of courses and grades, is the nearest thing to a passport to the selective sectors of American higher education.

Japan, similarly, works more with university entrance exams than with secondary exit ones, and this is done much more sharply than in America. Public and private, the many hundreds of Japanese colleges and universities traditionally have each tested individually, on their own, without benefit of national services. As described by William Cummings in chapter five, a recent modification has introduced a double entrance screening in which a nationally available test constructed by a voluntary association is used as a first cut, followed by the university's own exam as a second. And, the Japanese system is enormously university-driven: control by examination at the institutional level has been a central mechanism of that dominance, radiating downward to decisively shape the school and the student at lower levels.

The brutal fact is that between systems that emphasize selection at entry into the university and those that are dependent on selection at the point of exit from the school there is a great difference in the degree of student access. Who is deemed qualified to enter higher education? Eighty-six and 75 percent of the age group, respectively, in Japan and the United States; 26, 21, 20, and 19 percent in France, Sweden, the United Kingdom, and the Federal Republic of Germany.[2] Such ratios are crude and may err considerably, but they suggest that the secondary exit examination is a crucial mechanism for sharply limiting the number of young people judged to be qualified to pass into postsecondary education.

Beyond selection, what else does the school do that might significantly shape the university? The school also socializes young people into attitudes and habits, notably toward, or away from, vigorous academic work. We know relatively little about such socialization, particularly in comparative terms. From a small number of case studies, some evidence has accumulated that highly selective secondary schools socialize their students intensively, instilling in them the values of high culture and national leadership, as was done in Eton and other leading grammar schools in Britain and in the higher school, which flourished in Japan from the late nineteenth century through World War II.[3] In contrast, American research literature has portrayed the comprehensive school, American style, as a place dominated by the values of a semiautonomous youth culture in which athletic prowess and an active social life are more important than academic achievement.[4] Student attitudes are diffused, with much effort deflected from academic work. We may suspect that, generally, selective academic schools socialize appropriately for the transition to higher education. That mission dominates. Nonselective comprehensive schools have a more difficult time in doing so unless they rigorously segregate an internal academic track; they accept everyone and have agendas that include the preparation of those going directly to work. The universal school must grapple with the needs and interests of students from lower social origins that, in many cases, did not provide them with the cultural equipment for climbing the educational ladder. Adolescent subcultures, antieducation in their general temper, become major barriers to academic socialization, even spreading among upper-middle-class youth, as Margaret Maden noted in the case of London.

Over the long term, secondary systems have shaped higher education in another structural but highly indirect way: certain types of schools have shifted into postsecondary systems, bringing with them their past traditions and practices. Most commonly, technical schools have made this transition, having raised their status by being redesignated as part of education beyond the secondary level. As reported by Ulrich Teichler, the German *Fachhochschulen* have been a noteworthy instance of such institutional upward mobility, becoming a major segment of German higher education. William Cummings also pointed to this phenomenon in Japan, and Ernesto Schiefelbein in Latin American countries, each noting that some traditions of the secondary school were thereby imported into higher education. Then, too, the massive community college component of the American system originated more in secondary than in higher education, developing conceptually as an upward extension of the secondary school and administratively as a part of unified school districts or segments of local junior college districts that were modeled on the local-school-district form of governance.

The upward migration of such units is part of the elaboration of schooling that seems to take place as lower levels more universally include the age group and more uniformly cover programs. Some specialized schools and programs are then pushed up a notch, to take hold after common schooling. There is also a pull upward, as well as a push from below, as technical and technological training becomes more complicated—for example, shifting from carpentry to computer programming—and semiprofessional levels of work and employment develop in many fields. The development of the American system is clear on all these points: the comprehensive high school became universal and general; selection was pushed upward; short-cycle higher education in the form of the community college then became the place for vocational, technical, and technological one- and two-year programs as well as for further selection into academic streams.

We note finally that the secondary level can be a political force that affects higher education. Considerably expanded in number, secondary school teachers and administrators have become increasingly organized to represent their own interests. Their voluntary associations are nearly always separate from those of higher education personnel. If they include members of another level, it is commonly from elementary education. They are represented in their own branches of central ministries; they are well-distributed geographically to become effective political lobbies and pressure groups; they get their own members or close supporters elected to public office; and they sit on national education commissions. Little is known systematically about this form of influence at the present time, but with its growing importance, some incisive research would be revealing.

HOW THE UNIVERSITY SHAPES THE SCHOOL

Higher education shapes the secondary level principally by means of its influence on the stream of teachers and administrators who pass through it on their way to staffing the schools. In this first line of determination, the crucial operational step is the assignment of potential school personnel to different curricular pathways, in part because of what they will learn in any one institution or field of study in comparison to another, but more because of the orientations and statuses they thereby acquire.

Our working knowledge of this highly important matter is primitive, since scholars and officials have provided little serious analysis of teacher access to secondary education,[5] in contrast to the growing body of thought and research, reflected in the previous chapters, on student access to higher education. The issue has been placed low on reform agendas, and even off them entirely when seen as settled and nonproblematic. But we can begin to gauge some fundamental national differences in teacher education which appear to have powerful effects. To simplify immensely, we can imagine a continuum of teacher training that ranges from strong to weak influence by the university sector, especially by the top universities. The continuum may be seen as ranging from university centered to school centered. Four modes of organization predominate along this continuum.

1. Closest to the pole of university domination is the mode in which teacher training is located primarily, even exclusively, in the major universities and is there given over to the subject-field departments, for example, physics, political science, history, literature. In this mode, potential future teachers pursue the same pathways through higher education as those majoring in the individual disciplines. They come under the tutelage of professors and peers who respond to the incentives of the disciplines—their commitment to research and to certain styles thereof and their definition of what knowledge is best and how best to go about acquiring and diffusing it. This is the mode in which the future teacher is likely to acquire the identity of a disciplinarian and to be rewarded with the relatively high academic status of being one, an identity and a status that are then carried into the secondary system and, over time, made a part of it.

Teacher education in France, the Federal Republic of Germany, and Sweden are cases of this mode. To take only Germany as an example, there Gymnasium teachers have always been trained in the universities. Teachers for the nonacademic schools traditionally were not; they normally attended teacher training institutions. In the 1960s and 1970s, however, their preparation also shifted toward the universities. Inside the German university today, those who are considering a career in teaching simply participate in the programs of the subject-matter specialties and take their degrees in those fields. To be certified to teach, they then can sit for national examinations. Only a minority of applicants pass, and only then do they go on to receive some practical training as probationary teachers.

Throughout Europe schoolteaching remains a popular field: it has prestige. Its status is raised by the elevated standing of those who staff the selective academic stream, much as the prestige of professors in higher education is enhanced by the public's perception of those who occupy top positions in research universities. Prestige is further enhanced by the location of teacher education within universities rather than in a separate segment that inherently has lower status. And status is enhanced still further by location within the subject-matter departments of the universities. Competitive examinations also help, particularly when only a few candidates pass.

When teaching in the academic part of upper secondary education remains dignified work for professors, or near-professors, a virtuous circle of status maintenance is likely to continue in the relationship between school and university. The preparation of teachers seems important to the universities, a worthy task for their agenda. As teachers flow out of prestigious faculties and departments in the universities, their preparation borrows that status and feeds it to the occupation of schoolteaching. Thus, it is clear that whatever the more general sources of the status of schoolteaching in a society, higher education is centrally involved in operationally upholding or diminishing that status.

2. The second mode of organization occurs when teacher training is embedded in the university sector but is there handled somewhat autonomously in a faculty of pedagogy or a school of education. This internal differentiation pulls teacher education away from the grasp of the specific fields of knowledge. But it also leaves it in the university setting, there to be shaped by the discipline-centeredness of the university structure and culture, its high valuation of research and intense specialization. The Italian system handles teacher training in this fashion;[6] the American system has a small part of its teacher training in this mode. In both cases the faculties of education are under steady normative pressure to adopt the research interests and commitment to specialization that are central to the basic disciplines.

3. In the third mode the education of secondary teachers is located in nonuniversity institutions, generally a separate set of teachers colleges that come under strong university influence. Here the field of education itself becomes the center of gravity in the training institution. More attention is paid to pedagogy and to adjusting teacher preparation to the character of secondary schoolwork as defined by school personnel themselves and by professors whose applied interests—such as supervising interns, visiting the schools frequently, and so on—put them close to the schools. The staff of the college is structurally separated from the disciplinary and research imperatives of the university. In this third mode, however, the separate teacher training institutions remain under heavy normative influence from systemwide standards that are set and policed primarily by university professors. The location is non-"U" structurally, but "U" norms dominate. The United Kingdom is an excellent case in point, where much teacher education has been located in teachers colleges but where the university-rooted commitment to high standards

includes careful control of access and close attention to curricula and student performance across all sectors.

4. In the fourth mode, teacher training appears in a nonuniversity sector that also possesses considerable normative autonomy from the universities. The teachers colleges come from a background of close connection to the schools; the genetic imprint is of the normal school. In the beginning their professors were schoolmarms. These colleges are likely to have evolved under the tutelage of state departments of education that supervised elementary and secondary, but not higher, education. They grew up from below, rather than down from the university. Their norms and practices have been much influenced by the operational imperatives of elementary as well as secondary schooling, and the status of lower levels of education has rubbed off on them. Colleges in this mode do little or no research; no one confuses their character with that of full-bodied universities.

The United States is our strong instance. Over a century ago the American universities let the preparation of teachers slide off into normal schools, which, in their own evolutionary way, became teachers colleges and then state colleges. For a long time, as Gary Sykes emphasized in chapter ten, the elite universities have been only minimally involved. Many of them turned their backs, beginning at the top with such distinguished private universities as Harvard, Yale, and Princeton. Teacher education was not an elite operation; the disciplinarians found future teachers to be uninteresting as students; and teacher education, first elementary and then secondary, became someone else's business. For example, neither Yale nor Princeton has, at present, a school of education, and neither prepares more than a handful of students to enter secondary schools each year. The public universities are more involved, but still far less so than the state college sector. And even in the realm of the state universities, the general rule is that the higher the status of the university, the more pressured it is to lessen its involvement in teacher preparation. The state colleges, joined by the less prestigious public and private universities, are where the work is done in a national system that is without the type of systemwide normative controls found in the third mode.

Thus, teacher training—internationally the principal way higher education shapes the school—appears in different nations in forms that are quite dissimilar. There is an elemental continuum along which teacher training varies from university dominance to university avoidance; from normative control by university disciplines to control by school personnel; and from precise to diffuse and hard to soft in the nature of this influence.

Higher education affects secondary education in a second major way by means of the requirements it sets for student entry and successful performance. An outstanding 1983 analysis of selection methods for access to higher education by the Organisation for Economic Co-operation and Development noted that "practically everywhere, academic secondary streams continue to be organized as pre-university courses . . . schools and teachers tend to stress the academic orientation of programmes in accordance with university requirements in order to increase the chances of their students in the competition for entry." And we return to the central role of prestige: "this [orientation] is also a means of preserving or increasing the prestige of schools and their staff whose status depends to a large extent on the number or proportion of their pupils who succeed in entering the more prestigious options of higher education."[7] In short, the "best" of the secondary level is intrinsically "pre-university"; university requirements weigh heavily, even decisively, in determining the courses and curricula of the leading schools and the choices and motivations of their teachers and students.

There are many variations of this theme as we move across countries. The university, as a center of intense specialization, may prefer that the school stress general education as a broad preparation and trust the school, as in Germany, to certify certain school graduates as ready and able. Or the university may look for competence in specific subjects, as in France, and trust the marks given by the school in those subjects. Or, less trusting, the university may use special entrance examinations to test students independently of the school. The examinations may be organized at the national level, by voluntary associations or by public authorities, or by each institution, and used in conjunction with school marks. As noted earlier, the Japanese have moved into a double examination system in which a national examination makes the first cut, and institutional examinations follow up with a second selection. The American system has something of everything: selective private universities and colleges use school marks, national examinations, letters of recommendation, and personal interviews; selective public universities and colleges rely heavily on school marks; community colleges make little use of any academic criteria. The pressure on the school to be preuniversity is thereby differentiated: very heavy in some schools and in some school segments; moderate in most, by international standards; and weak in schools and school segments that feed mainly to nearby two-year colleges.

Where do we know that university requirements set the heaviest pressure? Where cramming schools and individual tutoring emerge exclusively devoted to preparing students to meet those requirements.

Japan appears as an extreme case. There, students compete fiercely to enter a few elite universities that write their own exams, and teachers work very hard to prepare their students for them. But that is not enough; to help students further, private cramming schools have become widespread. When they have not been chosen by the institutions they prefer, students make additional repeated attempts in following years. In the late 1970s these *ronin* students were a fourth of the applicants to higher education. As Ulrich Teichler has remarked elsewhere about Japan, "there can be no other industrialized country in the world where the success in life of an individual hinges so dramatically on the results of such a short performance."[8]

University entrance examinations allow comparisons among schools. They are particularly useful in large countries such as the United States and Japan in enabling institutions to compare students flowing to them from a large number of schools. Where the school system is decentralized, and thereby additionally diversified, as in the United States, the general examinations become important markers for those institutions that draw students from throughout the country or from a sizable segment of it. Such tests also typically help legitimate the processes of selection, despite skepticism about their efficacy. Test scores and rankings based on examinations seem fairer to the general public than the local variations associated with school marks and the intangible preferences elicited in personal recommendations. The push for fairness in educational systems favors the formal over the informal, the objective over the subjective, and the bureaucratic over the collegial.

Of growing importance virtually everywhere is the variation in entrance requirements among major sectors of a national system, and among major groups of subjects within some of those sectors. The main cut among sectors has been the binary distinction between university and nonuniversity. In most continental European countries, the universities, until recently, maintained relatively open access, depending on the school to have made the decisive selection, whereas the nonuniversity sectors, ironically, were more selective. This was most clearly the case in France, where the small, elite grandes écoles sector was highly selective; but it also occurred more widely in France, and elsewhere, in less prestigious, and even short-cycle, technical institutions that sought qualified applicants from technical schools. Outside the Continent, however, universities have usually been more selective and nonuniversity institutions less so, shading down to the almost complete openness to all comers shown by community colleges in the United States and Canada.

Clearly, when they have different entrance requirements, the major sectors within higher education will exert different influences on the secondary level. In addition, the increasing complexity of tasks performed by the postsecondary level will dictate a greater number of parts, which will send more conflicting messages to the secondary system. Confusion is bound to increase, particularly in those countries that eliminate specialized schools and move all students into comprehensive ones. The extreme occurs in the American system, with its vast differentiation of types of higher education institutions. The comprehensive school must necessarily prepare students for a wide range of educational destinies. This becomes part of the overload of expectations under which the American school operates.

Variation in entrance requirements by major groups of subjects is also important. Such variation is formally introduced at a systemwide level when, as in Europe during the 1970s, some university components are given the right to have a numerus clausus, while other fields of study remain open. Under the weight of increased numbers, open access to the European university by qualified school graduates has gradually narrowed. Selection commonly began in medicine, then spread to such related fields as dentistry, pharmacy, and biology. It grew in science and technological faculties, where student places are costly and knowledge is heavily structured and specifically sequential. Openness commonly remained in the social sciences, the humanities, and in such professional fields as law and education, where expansion could be more quickly and cheaply managed.

The principle has spread in Europe that when demand exceeds formally defined capacity, selection can be enforced. In the 1970s the working out of this principle was high on European agendas of educational policy, with opinion and policy swinging back and forth in the play of national politics. The idea of closing some university doors to qualified school graduates, for example, has been accepted with difficulty in social democratic Sweden. But at the end of the 1970s, the Swedish parliament adopted the general principle "that numerus clausus could be introduced in all sectors and programmes of higher education when demand exceeded the number of places available."[9]

At the institutional level, variation in entrance requirements by academic field has long existed in a quiet, unpublic form simply on grounds of comparative difficulty.[10] Highly structured disciplines such as mathematics have been relatively difficult to enter and to remain in. Mathematicians everywhere arrange their courses in closely linked sequences and can distinguish clearly between beginning, intermediate, and advanced students. They establish precise barriers all along the way, guarding the doors of classrooms with prerequisites. The barriers form a narrow funnel. Even if they so desire, the majority of students entering a university cannot gain access to the higher levels of mathematical training. And since students perceive and weigh such difficulties, they self-select away from such fields. Similar elaborate course sequences are found in medicine, engineering, and throughout most of the physical and biological sciences.

In contrast, in many of the humanities, in the more qualitative of the social sciences, and in such semiprofessions as education, social work, and business, students find it not only easier to enter but also easier to persist, negotiating the ambiguities of the field as best they can, toward at least the first major degree. Most important, the advent of mass higher education has widened these selection differentials, as some knowledge units take all comers while others protect and enhance their standards and prestige by selecting more carefully from a much wider pool of applicants. Occurring quietly, student by student, classroom by classroom, course by course, specialty by specialty, such selection by fields of knowledge is widely accepted. Although little studied to date, it significantly influences the behavior of students in the school and in the transition from school to university.

This concluding point about the influence of university requirements leads directly to a recognition that disciplinary organization weighs heavily in the structuring of higher education. Mentioned particularly by Ernesto Schiefelbein in his coverage of the many countries of Latin America, the disciplinary imperative in the organization of advanced knowledge must be seen as a basic worldwide phenomenon, one easy to overlook because it is so obvious. In most countries, school personnel come under increasingly heavy pressure from disciplinary specialization: the more a school is preuniversity in nature, the more it is likely to be shaped by that thrust. And the rapidly changing bodies of knowledge in the disciplines that are most based on scientific research presents the schools with problems of keeping up, first in the competence of their teachers—do they understand "the new mathematics?"—and then in the revision of those courses that are expected to articulate with the knowledge fields in the university. There is always some linearity of subjects, in which the school and the university remain interdependent, downward as well as upward, and in increasingly complex ways. The secondary school subjects are considerably defined by how the disciplines within higher education define themselves. The subjects of both levels change as knowledge in the disciplines moves ahead.

There are undoubtedly other important ways in which higher and secondary education mutually shape each other. There is, for example, a pattern of interaction in which the university actually pushes talent away from itself toward employment in the school; in a contrary pattern, higher education pulls talent to itself and the school pushes it away. The first pattern appeared in many traditional European systems. Hans Bethe, a Nobel Prize winning physicist who emigrated to the United States, has described the situation in the German system in the 1920s, when he passed his doctoral examination.[11]

> The structure of the German university was hierarchical. Most departments consisted of one professor and in some cases an associate professor, called an "extraordinary" professor, and then there were some assistants—equivalent to our [American] instructors. There were few of these positions, and the salaries were low—enough for a bachelor but not enough for a family. It seemed quite uncertain whether I could get a job. Many people went into high-school teaching, because the high schools were eager for well-qualified people. In fact, I remember that in my high school practically every teacher had a doctor's degree. This was quite customary, and often necessary for advancement in the German high-school system.

Bethe did manage to get a teaching offer from a German university, but barely, while other talented academics flowed into the Gymnasium, to stay or to wait for a university appointment. Later, after his many years in the United States as a professor at Cornell, he described clearly the American difference in this regard: "One feature of our present situation here is worse—the high schools are generally not willing to take Ph.D.s in physics, or mathematics or English or anything else. They say that these people are overqualified. What a pity, both for the high-school students and for the young people looking for a job!"

The situation in Germany at the end of the 1920s was typical of Europe; that tradition has had lasting influence on the distribution of talent between the school and the university. There was a push-and-pull that caused bright academics to take up work in high schools: the narrow university structure, having little room for them, pushed them away; the more plentiful Gymnasiums, eager for well-qualified people, pulled them in, offering a job and security. The American situation, in the 1920s, the 1980s, and all years in between, has been a world apart. The push-and-pull works in the other direction: the comprehensive school, defining talented college graduates as overeducated, pushes them away; the broad university structure of employment, supplemented by diverse public and private colleges, pulls them into higher education.

There are basic structural reasons why the upper secondary level obtains a sizable allotment of scholarly talent in most societies and why the reverse has been true, and remains true, in the United States.

THE EMERGENCE OF MEDIATING INSTITUTIONS

Initially, highly selective schools and equally selective universities ex-change students and teachers directly. As long as the exchanges are few and the traffic each way is light, this overall relationship can be kept quite simple. The school can be trusted, as in Germany traditionally, or the individual university can do its own examining, as in Japan tradi-tionally, without the assistance of bureaucrats and cadres of autonomous professional testers. But the increase in type and number of transactions, which so many countries have witnessed in the last half of the twentieth century, encourages the flowering of mediation. As revealed in preced-ing chapters, this institutional mediation has two primary forms: gov-ernmental and nongovernmental. Although the data are still scanty, we can discern the differing inner logics of these two forms.

The governmental form is most clearly exemplified in state admin-istration of admissions tests to control the student flow to higher edu-cation and in state certification to control teacher access to the secondary school. Mediation by government officials in each of these two flows is strongly present, as Ulrich Teichler and Guy Neave have shown, in Germany and France. Indeed, such mediation has existed for a long time in those countries, reflecting the strong interest of the state, as histori-cally defined, in influencing the relationship. This form of mediation is driven by governmental definitions, needs, and styles of operation that push toward standardization. Bureaucracy and democracy converge in official rules, applied across the system, designed to promote universal, objective standards. Access up and access down must each be fair; ad-ministrative regulation is the tool for implementing this ideal. A set of official connections are made, beyond those the schools and the uni-versities themselves elaborate. A dramatic instance of this trend toward governmental regulation occurred in the Federal Republic of Germany during the 1970s, when judicial and executive action at the national level transformed admission to the more popular fields in the universities from a decentralized state-by-state process to one centered in a computer in a national admissions office, with numerical scores assigned to ap-plicants in elaborate national formulas.

The nongovernmental form of mediation has its most powerful expression in private associations that test students for entry to higher education, for example, in the United States the apparatus of the College Entrance Examination Board, the Educational Testing Service, and the Iowa based American College Testing Program. This form of mediation is driven by nongovernmental definitions, needs, and interests; indeed, it often emerges explicitly as a private-sector solution that keeps media-tion out of the hands of governmental officials. The compelling interests are those of the institutions themselves, especially the interests of universities and colleges in bringing order into the ever more complicated business of sorting among applicants and legitimating choices once they have been made. The style of operation serves limited uniformity and standardization; rules are adjusted by universities and colleges to their individual pools of applicants and their own definitions of appropriate students. The institutions may weigh the examination scores, heavily or lightly as they please, against such other criteria as the record of school achievement, letters of recommendation, and impressions gained in personal interviews. Institutions may even decide not to use the examinations at all. In short, the private form of mediation consists of direct assistance to the institutions of higher education which promotes their autonomy.

There are thus fundamentally important options in the emergence of a third element in the relationship of the school to the university. The governmental form institutionalizes a bias toward systemwide fairness and state protection of standards. The nongovernmental form expresses a bias toward institutional control and choice. These forms are an increasingly important part of what is now meant by *centralization* and *decentralization* in the control of higher education.

The Distinctive American Problem

In cross-national comparisons the American system of higher education shows to some advantage. It rates high in access; its research universities are twentieth-century pacesetters with an unqualified depth and breadth of productive activity in one field after another; and, overall, this mammoth array of three thousand universities and colleges seems capable of doing many things on many fronts reasonably well. But the American secondary system has been a different story. At home it has been seen as a weak link, a segment of education that performs poorly. At times, as in the late 1950s and the early 1980s, criticism has mounted to the point where the high school is depicted as a national scandal. International comparisons, including those based on quantitative assessment of student achievement, have confirmed some of the harshest domestic evaluations. In the last half of the twentieth century, the development of the American secondary system seems to have gone astray to the point where we can speak appropriately of a distinctive American problem, one that appears increasingly difficult to solve.

What has caused the American school to become so problematic that a 1982–1983 presidential commission could claim it put the nation at risk? The commission clearly exaggerated; but its report was followed by an impressive number of major studies that were somewhat more carefully reasoned, some even based on serious inquiry, sharing a concern that the school is full of serious deficiencies that require concerted reform.[12] The diagnoses and recommendations of the studies varied widely—from relatively simple claims that schools have strayed from the primary subjects and all would be well if they returned to "the basics," to long lists of weaknesses in school organization and in the profession of schoolteaching, whose remedies would necessitate extended, piece-by-piece reform.

At the same time, considerable doubt has been expressed that much of anything can be done in a major way from the top down. Schooling in America is a massive, highly decentralized complex, deeply embedded in the structures and cultures of the fifty states and thousands of separate cities and towns. It seems to roll on under the impetus of its own dynamics and possess its own way of responding to external pressures. Many recommendations voiced in the early 1980s repeat ones made in the post-Sputnik era of the late 1950s and early 1960s, which we now know led to little or no lasting improvement. Public attention soon turned to other issues; the focus of educational reform moved from achieving excellence to compensating for cultural deprivation, and then to racial integration and affirmative action. We can see, in retrospect, that the American high school has long been a deeply troubled institution, one whose difficulties simply deepened during the 1960s and the 1970s. In the eyes of critics from all parts of the political spectrum, and increasingly in the view of the general public, it has gone from bad to worse.

By the early 1980s, there is thus ample reason to judge that the weaknesses of the American secondary structure are deeply rooted, necessitating inquiries that dig deeply into how schools work and how teaching is shaped as an occupation. Classic research, not yet fully exploited, is found as far back as 1932 in Willard Waller's *The Sociology of Teaching* and as recently as 1975 in Dan C. Lortie's *Schoolteacher*.[13] An exacting formulation of how school districts shape schools, schools in turn shape grades and classes, and those levels of organization shape the interaction of teachers and students has been offered by Rebecca Barr and Robert Dreeben.[14] Domestic scholarly analysis holds much promise. Cross-national comparisons, in addition, offer rewarding angles of vision. To see the American system against a backdrop of the German, the French, the Swedish, the British, the Japanese, and even the economically less developed nations of the Third World, is to highlight standard conditions and rooted beliefs in the American system which may otherwise be only dimly perceived or even entirely overlooked as they are submerged in a thousand details.

From the preceding chapters and the comparisons offered earlier in this chapter, we can assemble a set of connected primary features of American education which are implicated in the problematic nature of American secondary schooling.

1. *Universal secondary education.* The first source of the problem of the American secondary school is the extent to which it has sought and achieved universal participation. The American secondary system moved into mass involvement a long time ago, as far back as the first two decades of this century.[15] European systems were then extremely elite in access and participation; they continued, throughout the century, to lag seriously behind the American evolution, moving toward universal coverage in lower secondary education only as late as the 1960s and the 1970s. We have seen that even after major reforms upper secondary education has not been made all-inclusive. The American system, in contrast, has pressed hard for all youth to remain in secondary school all the way through to graduation. As Carol Stocking pointed out in chapter nine, that pressure is not merely ideological. School administrators are under community pressure not to have dropouts; and since school funding is based on the number of students enrolled, they are rewarded financially by the state for keeping young people in the system. In an extremely heterogeneous society, the secondary system has therefore had to cope with a vast variety of cultural and racial backgrounds; it has been compelled to accommodate the deprived and disaffected as well as the advantaged and the motivated.

The excess of hope central to the American problem begins with the strong expectation inside and outside the system that the schools have failed if all of the age group do not persist for twelve years and graduate with a high school diploma. This institutionalization of American optimism stands out starkly in cross-national perspective.

2. *Comprehensive school organization.* The second structural source of the American problem is the extent to which the individual secondary school is asked to replicate the coverage of subjects and types of students found in the system at large. Again, the basic commitments were laid down a long time ago. In the decades between 1900 and World War II, the comprehensive high school swept the field, triumphing over the more specialized forms. Out went the academic school, the vocational school, and the arts school. Other than in a few instances in several major cities, it was replaced by the school that was to cover the full range of subjects and options and to include all the youth located in the assigned catchment area of a town or neighborhood.

Leaving Japan aside for now, the contrast with other major systems could hardly be sharper, since in one way or another they have retained elite streams, generally in the form of a secondary sector that is intensely academic, as portrayed in the chapters on France, Germany, and England. Even much-reformed Sweden, deeply intent on changes aimed at comprehensivization, still retained in 1980 over twenty curricular streams within its upper secondary schools. It is the American structure that became qualitatively different, thoroughly committed to the all-inclusive school throughout the secondary system, with just three major internal tracks—the academic, the vocational, and the general—serving as foci of differentiation. This type of school must operate on a wide variety of fronts, virtually attempting to please all the people all the time.

The huge hope of the system at large is thereby recapitulated in each of thousands of little worlds. Within the doors of the individual school, a substantial overload of expectations, responsibilities, and tasks becomes a critical organizational problem. The advantages of specialization, and especially of distinctiveness, are lost. Purpose is dulled, communities of common interest dispersed. As educational tasks multiply, the school that is asked to do them all finds it virtually impossible to maintain a sense of unifying mission. School unity is turned over to the football team.

3. *Downward Coupling*. The third feature of the basic structure of secondary schooling in America which undergirds the troubled nature of its general performance and especially its relationship to higher education is its close connection with primary education. In Europe and elsewhere in the world, the main break in the educational structure was located between the elementary and secondary levels. The elementary level was for all; the big break occurred when the great mass of students ended their education and only the few went on to secondary schools that were preuniversity in orientation and program. The German Gymnasium, the French lycée, and the British sixth form were of this type, and they operated as prestigious centers of selection and learning, on a different plane from the lower common school.

In contrast, the early move of the American system toward universal secondary education and the replacing of specialized schools with comprehensive schools put the secondary and elementary schools on a similar plane. One was as common as the other. They were intimately linked administratively, put together within unified school districts that operated under one school board, one superintendent, and a common set of central district officials. As teachers unions developed, they further united elementary and secondary teachers. The orientations and rules of the unions, as much as those of school management, coupled the combined teaching force. At the same time, higher education developed quite differently, away from the school districts and under private as well as state-level sponsorship. Only the community colleges in some states became parts of school districts, and the evolution of this sector has been away from such local coupling and toward independent districts and location in a state system.

With the secondary school linked philosophically and organizationally to the primary school, it has a built-in tendency toward primarization. There is little difference between the work conditions and status of a person teaching sixth grade in a six-year elementary school and one teaching seventh grade in a two- or three-year junior high school, or between teaching in the eighth grade of an eight-year school and the ninth grade of a four-year high school. Various school districts cut their grades as 6-3-3, 6-2-4, 8-4, or even 6-6, since it does not make much difference educationally; a structure can be picked that best utilizes the available physical space. In any case, teachers remain within a common administrative framework and even on common salary scales. And the lay boards and administrators whose responsibilities encompass the two levels inevitably have frames of reference that, for the secondary level, look downward rather than upward; for example, secondary school teachers who have twenty-five hours of classroom contact each week are seen as teaching less than elementary teachers who have thirty hours, rather than as teaching significantly more than instructors in higher education, who are off in a different world where teaching loads vary from a few hours to perhaps fifteen.

The coercive comparisons that operate strongly when different personnel strata are grouped within common administrative frameworks thereby pull the secondary level toward the primary school rather than toward the university. This is so natural in the American system as to be rarely thought about or questioned. It is cross-national comparison that reveals clearly the historical and continuing tendency for other systems to couple secondary and higher education and for the American system to couple the secondary and elementary schools.

4. *Local Control.* Most educational systems of the world operate without the benefit of local school boards. Instead, they group public schools in national or regional frameworks that place much school administration in far-off headquarters. Such national or regional systems become considerably bureaucratic over time; but at the operating level they generally leave teachers freer of the immediate constraints of lay supervisors, even walling them off considerably from parents. Professional autonomy then develops within the large administrative system, since teachers, like other major professional groups located in bureaucracies, learn to use their inside positions of power to influence the central bureaucrats into

accommodating their interests. Indeed, they occupy many of the bureaucratic positions. The first enemy of the professional group is the laity, not the bureaucratic staff.[16]

Operating as the most decentralized educational system in the world, American education puts the secondary and elementary staffs under the watchful eye of nearby lay chiefs and cadres of local administrators, as well as of parents who expect their voices to be heard and have regular avenues for intervention. District consolidation and the growth of old unified school districts in the cities has also caused the local administrative frameworks to become large and intensely bureaucratic. Administrative hierarchies are prominent, even notorious, with the rewards of administration raised considerably above the rewards of teaching. On an array of grounds, the autonomy of teachers as a professional group, and especially their sense of self-control, is thus adversely affected. The malaise of powerlessness becomes widespread. Among the major effects of local control over the secondary school is that of contributing to a deprofessionalization of school teaching.

5. *Local Monopoly.* Based on geographic zoning, the American common secondary school typically has a monopoly of clientele. School districts are themselves large geographic divisions of the overall secondary system, and each district in turn defines specific zones for individual schools. Within those assigned territories, monopolistic controls have gradually increased. As specialized public schools declined in number in various cities, they no longer drew many students from the catchments of the comprehensive schools. And since private secondary schools play only a minor role in most states and sections of the country, they, too, have been only a minor threat. Parents and students, as a result, have relatively little choice of schools; and schools have little reason to compete for students. The structuring of the system around thousands of small monopolies thus reduces choice, virtually eliminates academic competition among schools, and renders scholastic comparisons among schools operationally harmless. Geographic monopolization also means that the student composition of schools is decided by the social composition of neighborhoods within towns and cities, thereby grouping students by school according to the class, ethnic, religious, and racial makeup of those neighborhoods. Residence becomes the key; where you live determines what you get. And the common school is no longer very common.

Cross-national comparisons confirm what we already know from observation of the pockets in the American system which are less monopolistic in nature. Where specialized schools are available, students break out of neighborhoods: art students travel off in one direction, those seeking particular types of vocational training in another, and those who are academically clever in still another. The distribution of students among schools then becomes based in part on student interest, aptitude, and prior individual achievement. And as some schools concentrate on different arrays of tasks and group students accordingly, they become places that are common on grounds of interest, aptitude, or achievement, even as they become less inclusive of curricula. There is considerable irony in the simple fact that at home and abroad a set of schools that segregate students in special clusters are likely to offer more educational choice than an array of comprehensive schools that possess territorial monopolies.

Again, the comparison with American higher education could hardly be sharper. At the higher level, there is little monopolization: the many universities and colleges are enormously differentiated, most of them draw students out of a variety of neighborhoods, and they create individual mixtures of programs and clienteles. Private institutions compete sharply with one another as well as with public colleges and universities; the public ones compete among themselves, often aggressively so, as well as with the private enterprises. Compared to the secondary level, there is an abundance of student choice. This type of higher education system is inordinately dynamic and capable of much self-adjustment. The secondary system, in contrast, remains equipped mainly with the single institutional tool of the comprehensive school that need not attract and need not compete.

Universal upper secondary education, comprehensive school organization, downward coupling, local control, local monopoly—these five basic features of the secondary system undergird the problem of how to make that level of American education work effectively as measured by emerging international standards of academic achievement and by the expectations of higher education. These commitments and structures are deeply embedded and interlocked; they cannot easily be altered. They may change incrementally, a bit here and a bit there, as states and school districts experiment anew with specialized schools in such forms as magnet schools and theme schools, or as they raise the requirements for entry into and graduation from the comprehensive schools. Universities and colleges may tighten the upward coupling of the schools, pulling them more toward the norms of higher education. Disappointed parents may turn to private schools, thereby weakening local public school monopolies and stimulating some competition. But the existing structures of work and authority will be strongly resistant to major change, especially since they are intertwined with basic ideologies. Two broad beliefs play a special role in determining the nature of the American problem: one defines student access to secondary and higher education; the other defines student passage through the elementary and secondary years of schooling.

Everywhere, the ideal of social justice has become translated into the idea of equal opportunity in education, but that idea can be formulated and practiced in quite different ways.[17] Outside the United States, it commonly means equal chances to enter secondary and higher education "for those who are qualified." This important modifier juts out whenever we compare European and American rhetoric about this basic aspect of educational democracy. Americans leave out the qualifier, instead offering a populist interpretation in which equal means all. Everyone has a right to a secondary education; indeed, everyone has a right to enter higher education.

Running on a parallel course has been the norm of social promotion within the elementary and secondary schools, under which all students are passed along from one grade to the next without regard to academic qualification. Then, with the spread of the open-door community college, automatic promotion moves students into higher education, again without regard to any proven ability or achievement. Simply growing older is enough. Alternatively, the holding-back of students, making them repeat grades, has remained a stubborn feature of most other systems. In Europe the sentiment has remained that it is better to have the large fourteen-year-old boy who cannot do his numbers sit among small children in lower grades, with all that that means for his identity and possible accomplishment, than to see him promoted automatically and handed a graduation certificate while still functioning at a much lower academic level. American sentiment has not been willing to pay the first price, instead opting for the second. Hence the American embarrassment of having hundreds of thousands of young people graduate from the twelfth grade, the last year of secondary education, while still reading at the eighth-grade level or doing mathematics at the sixth-grade level or with some other serious academic deficiency. For school administrators that embarrassment has been the lesser of two evils; as Carol Stocking emphasized, it is not politically viable for them to allow a high proportion of students to fail. Standards are set accordingly. A large subset of students are kept in the comprehensive high school in undemanding programs and allowed to graduate without academic effort. The comprehensive school then truly becomes an educational parking lot, one that additionally performs the function of keeping young people away from an already flooded youth labor market.

The coupling of automatic promotion within each level and movement from one level to the next on a universal basis automatically creates the problem of remedial education. The secondary school must spend much time and effort doing work traditionally that of the elementary school. This is another source of primarization: instructional materials and daily teaching are pulled downward toward the instruction designed for the education of five-to-twelve-year olds. In turn, certain sectors of higher education must spend much time and effort doing work traditionally that of the secondary school. This is clearest in the case of the community college, which in the early 1980s has become largely an institution of thirteenth-year instruction, carrying a heavy load of remedial work for half or more of students entering directly from the secondary school. Other types of postsecondary institutions, notably the public four- and five-year colleges but also many private ones, are significantly loaded down with unwanted remedial effort. The overall effect is toward a secondarization of the undergraduate level, with subcollege courses made part of the normal scheme of affairs.

With community colleges guaranteeing entry without regard to qualification, and with many four-year colleges and universities, public and private, also generous in whom they admit, especially when applicants are in short supply, students coming out of secondary schools have second, third, and fourth chances in a fashion unimaginable in most other systems of higher education. Those students who want to go directly to the best colleges or universities have to do things right while in secondary school. But others do not have to get it right, and they know it. They can do it badly and still go on to higher education, within which they can later move from one institution to another, since at both the undergraduate and graduate levels such transfer is possible, expected, and well institutionalized. The large amount of opportunity and choice has many beneficial effects; preeminent is the chance for talent to rise. But looming large among the baleful effects are the disincentives to do well in secondary school. It seems that one's life chances can always be improved upon later, after graduation and even long after entry into the collegiate years.

There is a price paid for extremely high expectations. The dream of universal education in the form of the popular comprehensive school that includes all students and all curricula, with no individual failures, is indeed a huge burden upon the schools. This form of democratic idealism has sustained much hard work, supporting schooling for all in an extremely heterogeneous population and thereby contributing significantly to the integration of community and society even as conflicts raged over racial discrimination and structured inequalities. But the perceived failure of the American school is in part a shortfall of outcomes against expectations that the comprehensive school, operating as a local monopoly, can be helpful to all students from all different types of backgrounds, creatively catering to their individual abilities while minimizing invidious distinctions. The shortfall becomes much greater whenever international comparisons raise the academic part of the expectations, as in the perception, after Sputnik, that the Russians were setting a higher standard in science education. In the early 1980s it is the perception, now reasonably well grounded in fact, that the Japanese school sets a much higher standard of academic achievement. The overload of expectations is thereby increased. It is expected that the American school should meet this new standard while still doing all the many other things it tries to do, from inculcating a democratic spirit, to making all the young happy with their immediate lives, to fielding a first-rate football team—the latter a mission given high priority in thousands of communities.

THE JAPANESE MIRROR

Japanese education is also universal at the secondary level; its graduation rate exceeds that of the United States, in notable contrast to the European systems. It has also moved deeply into mass higher education, with a number of different types of institutions, including community colleges, which vary greatly in selectivity. The private sector of Japanese higher education, like the American counterpart, even shades off into degree mills and fraudulent practices. And post–World War II, following the dictates of the American Occupation, the Japanese also moved secondary schooling within a comprehensive school framework. What then are the crucial differences?

The differences center on the Japanese willingness to differentiate students sharply, even harshly, at entry to the secondary level and again at the point of entry to higher education. Schooling is uniform only until ninth grade. Up to that point, as in the American school, students are enrolled in schools strictly according to area of residence, providing "a solid base of relatively equal opportunity."[18] But as William Cummings noted in chapter five, the Japanese feared that if the democratic mode of similar comprehensiveness was carried further up the line, it would cause all students to sink toward the lowest common denominator. The old system that had been in place since the Meiji Restoration was premised on a selective secondary system, with some schools modeled after the severely academic German Gymnasium and others furnishing several vocational tracks. As early as 1900 special tutors and schools emerged to help students qualify for the academic tracks. Differentiation at the secondary level thus became deeply engrained in thought and practice, so much so that when the comprehensive secondary school was forced upon the system during the Occupation, it became something quite different from the schools the Americans intended to promote—schools similar in program and quality, each with its own monopoly of clientele. Instead, the Japanese deliberately differentiated their comprehensive schools, placing them within large districts that, according to Cummings, would include "five or more schools which are explicitly recognized as varying in quality."

Comprehensiveness was thereby married to selectivity; to borrow the Chinese term, the top schools became keypoint schools. Students had to compete for entry; the better students got first option. The contrast to the American arrangement could not be sharper. There are few keypoints in the American structure, students do not have to compete as they move into upper secondary, and the best students do not have first choice within a multischool, large-district framework. Thus, in Japan, the top comprehensive schools are not comprehensive in the American sense. Possessing a cohort of top-flight students, they need offer only a college-preparatory course of study, thereby becoming an academic specialized school. And the bite of examinations at the first critical level of selection is sharp. The high school entrance exams "sort each age cohort into what amounts to an eight- to ten-tier high school ranking system."[19]

Hard selection is then repeated at the transfer point between secondary and higher education, with students from the better schools in a superior position to do well. Hence, the system's downward influence, from higher to secondary to elementary levels, is extremely strong, to the degree that we can speak of the university as dominating the secondary school and the secondary school as dominating the level below it. Entrance exams are the central device for this dominance. And personnel are shaped accordingly. Much more than in the United States, Japanese professors write curricular material for the schools *and* compose and mark entrance exams *and*, through employment in special schools or as private tutors, help students prepare for those exams. The secondary and postsecondary levels are stitched together in a multiplicity of ways, with the desires and standards of university personnel driving student achievement in the schools.

An upward ratcheting of standards and achievement, accomplished first through tough selection between the major levels of education, is similarly promoted by institutional competition at the secondary level. The public schools compete among themselves, scrambling to be perceived as better in order to attract better students and guarding elite images and niches once they have been obtained. And, much more than the American, the Japanese secondary level is loaded with private school options. Over 40 percent of enrollment for university preparation is in the private sector, and many private schools develop their own special routes to particular universities.

In his excellent study of the Japanese high school, which draws comparisons between the United States and Japan, Thomas P. Rohlen offers two telling observations that can help inform American thinking about broad directions of school reform: (1) "The merit principle and hierarchical differentiation are inseparable in public education."[20] Efforts to equate public schools are a permanent drag on achieving greater degrees of excellence. (2) "Progress toward social equality that cannot be integrated with the pursuit of general excellence has no long-term viability."[21] Viability will be increasingly determined cross-nationally, with national systems having to compete in achievement in schooling and work.

As revealed by the Japanese mirror, the core of the American shortfall in secondary schooling is thus a lack of differentiation, a minimization of hierarchy, and an intolerance of competition. The pivotal question then is, does headway in solving the problem of secondary schooling in America require fundamental, even if gradual and tentative, structural change?[22] There may be no satisfactory solutions consistent with existing institutions. On the basis of comparative structure and orientation, we may say that the American system of unselective comprehensive schools puts equity first, social integration second, and excellence a distant third. But with the long-term imperatives of competence in mind, efforts to achieve educational justice and to use the schools for social integration may well have to be worked out *within* a willingness to differentiate students and to arrange schools in hierarchies. This means that within school districts and the secondary system at large, the appropriate direction of reform may well be more rather than less streaming of students, more rather than less comparative ranking of schools, and more rather than less competition among them.

Secondary education in America needs more special schools, centers of excellence in each city and state which concentrate different types of talent and interest. Such specialized schools provide visions of excellence, serving as models of competency for the comprehensive schools as they carry out more focused tasks. They sharpen purpose: indeed, the clarification of purpose and mission that virtually every national study has called for can only be realized by dividing functions among different types of upper secondary schools. Differentiation rather than unification is the nearest thing to a single key in reform. Centers of excellence also restore prestige to schoolteaching, providing jobs and students for teachers whose disciplinary expertise, in many cases, orients them toward colleagues in higher education. As elsewhere in the world, some secondary schools and teachers are thus uncommon, doing work that merits respect among those in higher education, top government circles, and the general public. By virtue of this enhanced prestige they exert a positive influence on the attitudes and motivations of other schools and teachers who are not so blessed.

There are many negative effects of the differentiation of secondary systems into elite and nonelite, noble and less noble, with the majority of schools, teachers, and students laboring on the dark side of the invidious comparison. The lowest of the low become dumping grounds. But the benefits of retaining high prestige for a leading segment of the secondary system stand out in stark relief when we contemplate the long, engrained decline in the prestige of schoolteaching in that system (the American) in which specialized academic schools have been eliminated most completely. High prestige recruits talent; it aids professionalization. Its loss is a major blow to the entire secondary system.

Specialized schools have the great advantage over comprehensive schools of being more coherent. By means of stronger symbolic and expressive components of organization, they are able to reap the benefits of distinctive character, much as distinctive colleges do in American higher education.[23] They are one answer to the need expressed eloquently by Gary Sykes for new "reasons and ways to care" that would help bolster teaching and teacher education. Comprehensive schools risk becoming emotionally flat; specialized schools are better positioned to enrich the lives of their participants with tangible and creditable meaning.

In short, the American system needs to evolve new combinations of comprehensive and specialized secondary schools, along lines already apparent here and there throughout the country (including, for example, a fascinating mode in which artistically motivated students attend a comprehensive school in the morning and a school for the performing arts in the afternoon). Such combinations can readily claim to be more rather than less democratic than the comprehensive school that does not allow for a robust form of grouping along lines of interest and motivation.

American higher education, like the Japanese secondary system, demonstrates that public educational institutions can compete sharply with one another in ways that enhance the viability of the whole. These two examples indicate that institutional hierarchies are benefited by assigning recognition to perceived excellence and thereby motivating thousands of semiautonomous professionals to levels of effort and achievement that bureaucratic controls cannot induce. While reformers tinker with such changes as requiring four years of English instead of three, a course or two in the mastery of computers, and a test of functional literacy for high school graduation, Americans need to consider whether noncompetitive and nonranked comprehensive high schools should be pushed toward competition, ranking, and specialization.

The lessons of examples from abroad are clearly different from what Americans say to one another when they repeat the conventional wisdom. Luckily, we only need to look to the American postsecondary level to understand that specialization, hierarchy, and competition can fit the American educational scene. How much this should, and can, be characteristic of the secondary level remains to be explored. But if the existing institutional order were challenged in a fundamental way, some of the dynamic qualities of the higher level might be transferred to the secondary system.

The Basic Trend

Underlying the many similarities and differences among national systems in the two-way flow of influence between the school and the university lurks a basic phenomenon, the trend toward increasing complexity. From Sweden to Latin America, China to the United States, we have seen that initially simple systems become complex. For both the secondary sphere and the higher education realm, tasks multiply, beliefs diversify, and controls elaborate. Each level becomes more segmented as more students enter, more subjects emerge, and more job connections develop. What were once direct links become mediated. What was once relatively clear becomes ambiguous and more problematic. The relationship between the school and the university becomes relationships. We may speak of the uncoupling of two levels, but it is more accurate to say that couplings multiply and change in character. Some remain tight and clear but others become loose and difficult to grasp.

In the simplest scenario the secondary institutions select and prepare a few students for a few universities that in turn send back a few teachers. But in the complex scenario toward which educational systems move, the secondary schools do many things, the postsecondary institutions do many things, and only some of the things connect. Secondary terminal tracks do not connect to higher education; indeed, their seeming irrelevance caused the authors of some of the preceding chapters to leave them out entirely. And advanced research and teaching in universities do not connect directly to the schools. The trend toward complexity therefore brings in its wake the compelling tendency for each of these two major educational segments to develop quasi-independent dynamics. Each develops some momentum of its own, some problems of its own. Each develops imperatives that flow from its own vested interests and from its own new groups seeking to become vested. Each develops traditions of its own which shape behavior; each has its own specific set of outside forces with which to contend. And each develops its own translation of external demands into internal actions.

We may conceive of the trend toward complexity as a process of maturation. Modern educational systems had origins and early immature stages of development. In time they moved into more mature phases. In such systems, as in individuals, mature character is more complex, with the capacity to perform a wide range of tasks, hold many thoughts, implement contradictory values, and function under various types of social controls that are simultaneously brought to bear. With all the emphasis on problems and potential decline in our perceptions of education in the last half of the twentieth century, we continually underestimate what a mature educational system does, how complexly it relates to ever more finely honed differences in carrying out thousands of tasks for millions of people. Perhaps the day will come when social science will give us the wit and imagination to appreciate the beauty of systems of education within which thousands upon thousands of specific enterprises, programs, and classrooms compose a virtually endless galaxy of operations—more so in secondary education than in primary schooling, and much more so in the higher tiers of postsecondary education.

Complexity is greatly affected by size. The sheer scale of systems, typically overlooked in studies of single countries, leaps out in crossnational comparisons. Sweden is a country of 8 million, with an advanced educational system of commensurate small size; on a scale of operations the country and the system could be tucked inside the state of Florida or the county of Los Angeles. The large nations of Western Europe—France, the Federal Republic of Germany, Italy, and the United Kingdom—are approximately six times larger; Japan, at over 100 million, is twelve times larger; the United States, over twenty-five times; and the People's Republic of China, with a population in the range of 1 billion, over one hundred times. As educational systems modernize, incorporating larger shares of the young population, their relative magnitude corresponds broadly to the relative size of their national populations. Sheerly on the basis of size, there is reason to perceive the complexity of the educational system of France as many times that of Sweden, and the complexity of such systems and their subsystems in Japan, the United States, and China as of a different magnitude entirely. The educational order of the large society cannot follow the order of the small one. It will be different in kind.

Huge scale, then, extends and deepens the problems of consciously shaping the school and the university and the relations between them. The understructure of the system increases in weight, through sheer numbers of work sites, students, and staff. Even such heavy-handed attempts at top-down controls as those witnessed in China during the last two decades cannot sustain the control necessary for a major re-shaping, even leaving aside the swings in ideology that push policy in opposite directions. There is a great tenacity in a gigantic educational understructure: the local school is embedded in local traditions, hopes, and controls; the university is composed of esoteric disciplines that are internally controlled, in part by international linkages, and affected by age-old academic traditions. Even in Sweden it becomes difficult to implement a central will as complexity increases. In the large countries the difficulties are enormous.

What we witness increasingly in the ordering of systems of education is a relatively inadequate institutional apparatus. Within the general population and especially among intellectual and political elites, ambitions for the system may grow at a rapid rate, much faster than coping machinery can be created, put in place, and stabilized. The gap between intention and reality thus becomes acute; of the countries and continents we have covered, this is most notable in China and Africa. The attitude that nothing will solve the problem then becomes relevant, in the sense that no centrally devised plan can put in place the complex of efficient administrative structures and competent teachers which might meet the expectations. Expectations may go through revolutions, but implementation is more constrained, generally having to evolve out of what has been and what is.

Systems of secondary and higher education have been through some troublesome and unsettling times during the 1960s and 1970s. Many have seen exceedingly rapid expansion, followed by the threat of contraction. New interest groups within and without have pushed their concerns onto the political agendas of education and made themselves part of the struggle for control and influence. Student discontent, for a time, heightened governmental and popular concern; the greatly increased cost of expanded secondary and higher education insures that such interest will remain high. Everywhere, those who people the school and the university are under increasingly critical scrutiny from many points of the compass.

In some countries there are now, and there will be in the future, some relatively quiet periods of consolidation and stability. Yet the basic trend toward complexity will continue to unsettle the school and the university and relations between them. Nostalgia for the simpler days will not help, since traditional images rely on simple scenarios that will not again obtain. A definite lack of clarity in the ordering of educational affairs, now a part of modern society, will require an adjustment in our conceptions that amounts to greater tolerance for ambiguity. We shall have to be modest in our desire to wrap things in global plans, a temptation that is virtually irresistible in nationalized systems where officials in central offices are held responsible for doing just that. To maintain that posture would be simply to stifle the creativity of educational systems and thereby fall behind. We shall have to devise, incrementally, the managerial capabilities and especially the institutional structures that best permit us to cope with bewildering complexity.

Useful ideas that push official and popular thinking in this direction are evolving. They include the ideal of dispersed power, particularly as found in the federalist principle in political thought; the logics of muddling-through and of mutual coordination by means of the interaction of officials, clarified in organizational analysis during the last twenty years; the long-standing grasp of the value of marketlike interactions found in economic thought; the positive value now placed on redundancy—overlap and duplication—in the new literature in public administration; the metaphors of loose coupling and organized anarchy that arose out of the study of schools and universities as organizations; and the idea that so-called decisions are often the result of an accretion of actions and constraints rather than of clear, decisive judgment.[24]

By means of a zig here and a zag there, social thought has moved toward ideological support for unclear variety, even the legitimation of disorder in formal systems. For good reason. We shall have to learn to praise ambiguity and enjoy its virtues, because we are more uncertain now than in the past that we fully understand the business of education and can consciously steer its affairs. The trend toward complexity insures that we will be even more uncertain in the future about the global relations of schools and universities.

Notes

1. See the discussion of streaming in upper secondary education in all Western European countries in Organisation for Economic Co-operation and Development, *Policies for Higher Education*, pp. 76–79.

2. Ibid., pp. 110–111.

3. Roden, *Schooldays in Imperial Japan*.

4. Coleman, *The Adolescent Society*; Stinchcombe, *Rebellion in the High School*; Coleman et al., *From Youth to Adulthood*.

5. One comparative start on this topic is Taylor, "Changing Priorities in Teacher Education."

6. See Clark, *Academic Power in Italy*, pp. 27–32.

7. Organisation for Economic Co-operation and Development, *Policies for Higher Education*, p. 144.

8. Teichler, "Some Aspects of Higher Education in Japan," p. 9.

9. Organisation for Economic Co-operation and Development, *Policies for Higher Education*, p. 128.

10. The following two paragraphs have been drawn from Clark, *The Higher*

Education System, pp. 38–41, that discusses at greater length how "knowledge contents" enter into the division of academic work.

11. Bernstein, *Hans Bethe*, pp. 21–22.

12. National Commission on Excellence in Education, *A Nation at Risk;* The Task Force on Education for Economic Growth, *Action for Excellence;* College Entrance Examination Board, *Academic Preparation for College;* The Twentieth Century Fund, *Making the Grade;* Boyer, *High School;* Goodlad, *A Place Called School;* Ravitch, *The Troubled Crusade;* Sizer, *Horace's Compromise.*

13. Waller, *The Sociology of Teaching;* Lortie, *Schoolteacher.*

14. Barr and Dreeben, *How Schools Work.*

15. See Cremin, *The Transformation of the School;* Trow, "The Second Transformation of American Secondary Education."

16. See Rhoades, *The Profession and the Laity* (tentative title, unpublished manuscript).

17. See Clark, *The Higher Education System,* chap. 7, "Values."

18. Rohlen, *Japan's High Schools,* p. 307; see also Cummings, *Education and Equality in Japan.*

19. Rohlen, *Japan's High Schools,* p. 308.

20. Ibid., p. 313.

21. Ibid., p. 326.

22. Charles E. Lindblom has raised the issue for policy analysis more generally of whether intentions to effect drastic institutional reform can be coupled with incremental implementation. See Lindblom, "Who Needs What Social Research for Policy Making?"

23. See Clark, *The Distinctive College;* and Clark, "Belief and Loyalty in College Organization."

24. For fuller discussion of these conceptions see Clark, *The Higher Education System,* pp. 273–275.

Bibliography

BARR, REBECCA, and ROBERT DREEBEN. *How Schools Work.* Chicago and London: University of Chicago Press, 1983.

BOYER, ERNEST L. *High School: A Report on Secondary Education in America.* New York: Harper and Row, 1983.

BERNSTEIN, JEREMY. *Hans Bethe: Prophet of Energy.* New York: Basic Books, 1979.

CLARK, BURTON R. *The Distinctive College: Antioch, Reed, and Swarthmore.* Chicago: Aldine, 1970.

————. "Belief and Loyalty in College Organization." *Journal of Higher Education* 42 (June 1971): 499–515.

————. *Academic Power in Italy: Bureaucracy and Oligarchy in a National University.* Chicago: University of Chicago Press, 1977.

————. *The Higher Education System: Academic Organization in Cross-National Perspective.* Berkeley, Los Angeles, London: University of California Press, 1983.

COLEMAN, JAMES S. *The Adolescent Society.* New York: The Free Press of Glencoe, 1961.

COLEMAN, JAMES S., ROBERT H. BREMNER, BURTON R. CLARK, and others. *Youth: Transition to Adulthood.* Chicago: University of Chicago Press, 1974.

The College Entrance Examination Board. *Academic Preparation for College: What Students Need to Know and Be Able To Do.* New York: CEEB, 1983.

CREMIN, LAURENCE A. *The Transformation of the School: Progressivism in American Education, 1876–1957.* New York: Alfred A. Knopf, 1961.

GOODLAD, JOHN I. *A Place Called School.* New York: McGraw-Hill, 1983.

GREEN, THOMAS F. *Predicting the Behavior of the Educational System.* Syracuse, NY: Syracuse University Press, 1980.

LINDBLOM, CHARLES E. "Who Needs What Social Research for Policy Making?" Rockefeller Lecture, State University of New York, Albany, October 1983.

LORTIE, DAN C. *Schoolteacher.* Chicago: University of Chicago Press, 1975.

The National Commission on Excellence in Education. *A Nation at Risk: The Imperative for Educational Reform.* Washington, D.C.: U.S. Government Printing Office, 1983.

Organisation for Economic Co-operation and Development. *Policies for Higher Education.* Paris, 1983.

RAVITCH, DIANE. *The Troubled Crusade: American Education, 1945–1980.* New York: Basic Books, 1983.

RHOADES, GARY. *The Profession and the Laity* (tentative title). Unpublished manuscript.

RODEN, DONALD T. *Schooldays in Imperial Japan.* Berkeley, Los Angeles, London: University of California Press, 1980.

ROHLEN, THOMAS P. *Japan's High Schools.* Berkeley, Los Angeles, London: University of California Press, 1983.

SIZER, THEODORE R. *Horace's Compromise: The Dilemma of the American High School.* Boston: Houghton Mifflin, 1984.

STINCHCOMBE, ARTHUR L. *Rebellion in High School.* Chicago: Quadrangle, 1964.

The Task Force on Education for Economic Growth. *Action for Excellence: A Comprehensive Plan to Improve our Nation's Schools.* Denver: Education Commission of the States, 1983.

TAYLOR, WILLIAM. "Changing Priorities in Teacher Education." In *Changing Priorities in Teacher Education.* London and Canberra: Croom Helm, 1982. Pp. 16–30.

TEICHLER, ULRICH. "Some Aspects of Higher Education in Japan." *KBS Bulletin on Japanese Culture* (June–July 1972): 9.

TROW, MARTIN A. "The Second Transformation of American Secondary Education." *The International Journal of Comparative Sociology* 11 (Sept. 1961): 144–166.

The Twentieth Century Fund. *Making the Grade: Report of the Twentieth Century Fund Task Force on Federal Elementary and Secondary Policy.* New York, 1983.

WALLER, WILLARD. *The Sociology of Teaching.* New York: Russell and Russell, 1961.

Conference Participants

Conference on "The School and the University:
An International Perspective"
University of California, Los Angeles
July 25–28, 1983

Professor Alexander W. Astin, Director
Higher Education Research Institute
Graduate School of Education
University of California, Los Angeles

Professor Tony Becher, Chairman
Education Area
University of Sussex, England

Dr. Barbara Burn, Director
International Programs
University of Massachusetts, Amherst

Dr. Ladislav Cerych, Director
European Institute of Education and Social Policy
European Cultural Foundation
Université de Paris IX - Dauphine

Professor Burton R. Clark, Chairman
Comparative Higher Education Research Group
Graduate School of Education
University of California, Los Angeles

Dr. William Cummings, Centerwide Fellow
East-West Center
Honolulu

Professor Jean Claude Eicher
Director, IREPU
Faculty of Science "Mirande"
University of Dijon, France

Dr. Lars Ekholm
Director of Higher Education
Ministry of Education and Cultural Affairs
Stockholm

Professor Philip Foster
School of Education
State University of New York, Albany

Dr. Dorotea Furth, Program Officer
Organisation for Economic Co-operation and Development
Paris

Professor John Hawkins, Chairman
Department of Education
University of California, Los Angeles

Professor Maurice Kogan, Head
Department of Government
Brunel University, England

Professor Thomas LaBelle
Graduate School of Education
University of California, Los Angeles

Professor Daniel Levy
School of Education
State University of New York, Albany

Margaret Maden, Director
Islington Sixth Form Centre
London

Dr. Guy Neave, Director of Research
European Institute of Education and Social Policy
European Cultural Foundation
Brussels

Dr. Gary Rhoades, Research Associate
Comparative Higher Education Research Group
Graduate School of Education
University of California, Los Angeles

Professor Stanley Rosen
Department of Political Science
University of Southern California, Los Angeles

Professor Sheldon Rothblatt, Chairman
Department of History
University of California, Berkeley

Dr. Ernesto F. Schiefelbein, Coordinator
AID-REDUC Research Diffusión Project
Santiago, Chile

Dr. Carol Stocking, Study Director
National Opinion Research Center
Center for the Study of Social Policy
University of Chicago, Chicago

Dr. Frank Sutton, Vice President
International Affairs
The Ford Foundation
New York City

Gary Sykes, Team Leader
Teaching-Policy Studies Team
National Institute of Education
Washington, D.C.

Professor Ulrich Teichler, Director
Wissenschaftliches Zentrum für Berufs-und Hochschulforschung
Gesamthochschule Kassel

Professor Martin A. Trow, Director
Center for Studies in Higher Education
University of California, Berkeley

Professor Morikazu Ushiogi
Faculty of Education
Nagoya University

Dr. Bjorn Wittrock, Associate Professor
Department of Political Science
University of Stockholm

Index

Designer: Robert S. Tinnon
Compositor: Publisher's Typography

Text: 10/12 Palatino
Display Palatino

CPSIA information can be obtained
at www.ICGtesting.com
Printed in the USA
BVHW042210160822
644778BV00002B/21